Praise for the first edition

'An admirably clear exposition of the main protagonists in the liberalism – communitarianism debate. Mulhall and Swift provide a valuable service by identifying the various issues in the debate, and by separating out the substance from the rhetoric on both sides.'

Will Kymlicka, author of *Liberalism, Community and Culture*

'Much of the debate about liberal political philosophy in the last decade has focused on the "communitarian" critique of liberalism, or, more broadly, on the challenge to the priority of the right over the good. The best overall account of this debate is Stephen Mulhall and Adam Swift, *Liberals and Communitarians*.'

Michael Sandel, author of *Liberalism and the Limits of Justice*

LIBERALS AND COMMUNITARIANS

Stephen Mulhall and Adam Swift

Second Edition

Copyright © Stephen Mulhall and Adam Swift, 1992, 1996

The right of Stephen Mulhall and Adam Swift to be identified as authors of this work has been asserted in accordance with the Copyright, Designs and Patents Act 1988.

First published 1992
Reprinted 1993 (twice), 1994, 1995
Second edition published 1996

Blackwell Publishers Ltd
108 Cowley Road
Oxford OX4 1JF
UK

Blackwell Publishers Inc.
238 Main Street
Cambridge, Massachusetts 02142
USA

British Library Cataloguing in Publication Data

A CIP catalogue record for this book is available from the British Library.

Library of Congress Cataloging-in-Publication Data
Mulhall, Stephen, 1962–
Liberals and communitarians / Stephen Mulhall and Adam Swift. – 2nd ed.
p. cm. –
Includes bibliographical references and index.
ISBN 0–631–19819–9 (pbk. : acid-free paper)
1. Rawls, John, 1921– Theory of justice. 2. Justice. 3. Liberalism. 4. Libertarianism. I. Swift, Adam. II. Title.
JC875.M78 1996
320'.01'1–dc20
95–404781
CIP

Typeset in 10 on 12 point Palatino
by Words & Graphics Ltd., Leicester
Printed in Great Britain by Hartnolls Limited, Bodmin, Cornwall

This book is printed on acid-free paper

Contents

Preface to the second edition

The publication of Rawls's *Political Liberalism* in 1993 meant that even if everything he said there were identical to that in the articles to which we referred in the previous edition, and even if we continued to interpret what he said in the same way, it would be necessary to update the references simply in order not to look out of date. Since Rawls assures his readers that he only came to his current understanding of his own position after the last of those articles, we feel no shame in acknowledging that our interpretation has changed also (though we do not pretend that all our previous misunderstandings can be put down to his). In terms of form, it now seems to us better to present the core idea of Rawls's political liberalism, to assess the relation between his position and the communitarian critique, and to examine whether his position can be sustained, in three separate chapters. In terms of content, we make more of an attempt to distinguish those responses to communitarian objections that depend upon his shift to the political from those that do not.

We are not sure why Dworkin did not warrant a chapter in the first edition. Now that we have written it, and accommodated the ripples it sends throughout Part III, we can think of many reasons not to have had him in, for his inclusion considerably complicates matters, requiring us explicitly to raise issues and introduce distinctions that remained only implicit last time. Unfortunately, we consider the variations sufficiently important as to justify this greater level of difficulty, and hope that we now present a fuller sense of the range of contemporary liberal theory, providing the reader with a better sense of the different issues at stake not only between liberals and communitarians but also within the liberal camp.

As well as rewriting the conclusion to accommodate the issues and distinctions just mentioned, we have made other minor improvements throughout; as a result, roughly forty per cent of the original text has been changed.

Simon Caney, Rainer Forst, Yota Spyropoulos, Steven Wall and Andrew Williams have made a difference to what we have written, in Andrew's case via conversations that took place before, but the force of which we came to appreciate only after, the first edition. The Philosophy Department at Essex has proved a congenial environment for one of us to go on talking and thinking about these issues, while Balliol continues to provide the other with more than could reasonably be expected in the way of stimulating colleagues and students.

Preface

It is our aim in this book to provide an introduction to a set of debates in political theory that have come to be grouped together under the label of the communitarian critique of liberalism. These debates became central to the discipline during the 1980s and continue, in one way or another, to inform a great deal of contemporary theory. By now, however, the dust is beginning to settle, and we feel that the time is right for a survey of the battleground intended to render it more accessible to the uninitiated, whether undergraduate or graduate.

The contents pages convey the shape of the book. After a first chapter outlining what we regard as the paradigm statement of contemporary liberal theory, the theory of justice as fairness articulated by John Rawls in his book *A Theory of Justice* (*TJ*), and establishing an agenda of issues to recur throughout the book, we present, in turn, the ideas of four thinkers generally regarded as communitarian critics of liberalism: Michael Sandel, Alasdair MacIntyre, Charles Taylor and Michael Walzer. Having identified the themes that these theorists have in common, the ways in which they differ, and their relation to the agenda already established, we go on to examine Rawls's more recent restatements of his position, what is commonly called 'the new Rawls'. Arguing that, on some readings at least, the new Rawls can be understood as attempting to formulate a liberal position that is sensitive to aspects of the communitarian critique, we then turn to three other theorists who can also be read as communitarian liberals, Richard Rorty, Ronald Dworkin and Joseph Raz, before concluding.

Such an account of what is to come, however, begs a number of questions that need to be dealt with, or at least acknowledged, at this early stage. Given our theme it would seem important to start by identifying what liberalism and communitarianism are. Unfortunately this is not as easy as it sounds for, as we shall see, there is a great deal of disagreement about what exactly one has to believe in order to qualify either as a liberal or as a communitarian. While it may be possible to recognize as constitutive of liberalism a commitment to a vague and general value such as the freedom or autonomy of the individual, and to relate this to the substantive political concern that individuals should have freedom of conscience, of expression and of association, this does not really get us very far. Similarly, our preliminary characterization of the communitarian critique as one that questions the liberal understanding of the relation between the individual and her society or community, and argues that the emphasis on individual freedom and rights that follows from that understanding is misplaced, leaves a deal of room for further specification. In both cases it is hard to be more precise without begging questions that can only properly arise later, and by the end of this book we shall of course have filled out these characterizations in much greater detail.

The problem is that both 'liberalism' and 'communitarianism' mean different things to different people. Even in the language of everyday politics the term 'liberal' means different things in the United States and in the United Kingdom, and it may be that our deliberately loose formulation in terms of individual freedom or autonomy already fails to capture that connotation particularly apparent in the North American usage which associates liberalism with support for a fairly generous redistributive welfare state. The point here is that in ordinary usage the term 'liberalism' tends to refer to a *package* of beliefs or policies which can be analytically separated from one another, and, as we shall see shortly below, our initial characterization undoubtedly reflects the fact that the communitarian critique, and hence this book, is primarily concerned with some of these and not others. As might be expected, things are even more complicated at the level of self-consciously theoretical debate, for here we find that, even with respect to those liberal beliefs or policies to which we do devote our attention, different liberals endorse them for different reasons. Thus one theorist's reasons for his belief in the right to freedom of expression may be quite different from another's, or two theorists both regarding themselves as liberals may have quite different conceptions of, for example, something apparently so central as autonomy or the proper relation between the state and the individual. This point is particularly important because a standard move by liberals in the face of the communitarian critique has been to deny that they assert, or need to assert, what it is that communitarians deny. Communitarians are thus accused of attributing to liberals, and then attacking, claims that liberals do not in fact make and which are not required for their conclusions. If this is right, if liberals do not commit the theoretical sins with which communitarians charge them, then this would seem to raise the possibility of a liberalism which does not conflict with, and perhaps can even take on board, the arguments which communitarians have to offer.

Not that 'communitarianism' is any more straightforward; if anything the reverse is true. Here, again, one problem concerns the relation between the essentially philosophical positions put forward by the academic theorists discussed in this book and the more popular appropriation of the term by what claims to be a political movement, and one that has commanded some attention in the media, and from political parties, on both sides of the Atlantic. The leader of this movement, Amitai Etzioni, whose book *The Spirit of Community* contains a communitarian platform to which individuals are invited to subscribe, occasionally draws upon the ideas of what we may think of as philosophical communitarians; but it is difficult to find anything more than very vague and general connections between the kind of programme he has in mind and the ideas that we will look at here. While of course we think that advocates of popular communtarianism would do well to read our book, in order to clarify their thoughts on the philosophical foundations that might or might not underlie their policy positions, we do not pretend to engage directly with the debate about community as that is carried out among politicians and journalists. So far as we are aware, none of our four communitarian theorists has signed up to Etzioni's programme, and our book might help to explain why.[1]

In addition to this mismatch between philosophical and popular senses of the term, two issues arise within the academic debate. The first concerns the extent to which it makes sense to talk about *the* communitarian critique at all. The label 'communitarian', although often used to characterize the four theorists whose ideas we examine in the second part of this book, is not one which they themselves employ to any great extent, and it is certainly not part of their self-understanding in the same way as the term 'liberal' is for liberals. As we shall see, the four theorists whose ideas we discuss address apparently different issues and certainly disagree in their substantive political conclusions. So one of the aims of our examination of their ideas is precisely to see exactly what, if anything, they share that would justify their being grouped together under a common label.

The second concerns the question of how we are to distinguish the communitarian critique of liberalism from the various other critiques that may be found in political-theoretical debate. For we should be clear that we focus quite specifically on this particular strand of criticism, all but ignoring the challenge to liberalism from conservatism, from Marxism, from feminism and from libertarianism.[2] Given this, it would seem important that we should be able clearly to identify the differences between the communitarian and these other critiques, but here again things are very complex. For example, we ourselves raise the issue of whether communitarianism is necessarily conservative in its implications, and, despite the claim of one communitarian that his position leads to demands for quite radical social and political change, there are clear affinities between these two strands of thought. Similarly, the etymological links between 'communitarianism' and 'communism' should suggest ways in which our area of concern might overlap with the Marxist critique of liberalism. Even more confusingly, it may be that what communitarians dislike about liberalism is something that liberalism shares with libertarianism. Indeed in many ways it makes sense to regard libertarianism as a strand of liberalism rather than its outright rejection.

This last point is worthy of attention at this preliminary stage, for one way of explaining how we understand the communitarian critique of liberalism is precisely to contrast it with the libertarian critique forcefully presented by Robert Nozick in his *Anarchy, State and Utopia* (1974). Such a contrast will also enable us to identify more clearly that particular aspect of liberalism that shall be our especial concern. We have said that we regard Rawls's theory of justice as fairness as the paradigmatic statement of contemporary liberalism and, while there are various defences of that claim that we might offer, the most immediately relevant is that which observes that Rawls's theory contains both of the two components which standardly go together as the liberal package: the commitment to the freedom of the individual embodied in the standard liberal support for civil liberties, and that belief in equality of opportunity and a more egalitarian distribution of resources than would result from the market alone which leads to support for a redistributive welfare state. The simple (and simplifying) point that we wish to make here is that the libertarian and the communitarian critiques focus on the different components of this package.

The essence of Nozick's objection to Rawls's theory is that its redistributive aspects involve a violation of the individual's rights to property and to self-ownership. In Nozick's view, Rawls, and all who support a redistributive welfare state, fails to take the individual seriously enough, since he is prepared to envisage a taxation system, analogous to forced labour, that involves using the talents that belong to some individuals as means to the ends of those other individuals who lack them. Nozick's libertarianism, then, involves a demand for more respect for individual liberty than Rawls acknowledges, and presents itself primarily as a rejection of those distributive and quasi-egalitarian aspects of Rawls's theory that correspond to the welfare state component of the liberal package. In contrast to this, the communitarian critique queries that priority accorded to the individual over the community upon which Nozick insists, and presents itself primarily as a rejection of the liberal emphasis on the freedom of the individual that corresponds to the civil liberties' component of the package. In a sense, then, the libertarian and the communitarian critiques are at once coming from different directions and concerned with different implications of contemporary liberal theory. Very crudely, for libertarians the distributive aspect of Rawls's theory shows that he does not take individuals and their freedoms seriously enough, while for communitarians the importance he gives to individual liberties reveals a mistaken prioritization of individuals over their communities.

Such a schematic opposition, though useful for introductory purposes, requires immediate qualification. First, as has already been suggested, in many ways Nozick's libertarianism is best understood as a version of liberalism rather than a rejection of it. Indeed, insofar as the essence of that classical liberalism of which

Locke is the best-known example is a claim about self-ownership, then it may plausibly be argued that Nozick is the true liberal, Rawls the revisionist. This would fit well with that reading of the communitarian critique that sees it as equally cogent, if not more so, when aimed at Nozick's libertarianism as at Rawls's liberalism. Second, we should be clear that the distributive aspects of Rawls's liberalism can also be put in terms of a claim about the relation between the individual and the community. But here Rawls, in taking people's talents to be in some sense common property, is the communitarian. Thus it may be that Rawls can best be understood as communitarian on distributional questions but liberal on questions concerning the freedom of the individual in relation to his or her community.

Usually, however, as we shall see, the communitarian critique has concerned itself rather with these freedom-related aspects of liberalism than with its equality-related or distributive aspects. In terms of substantive political issues, what this means is that where the debate between redistributive liberals and libertarians centres on the justifiability of the welfare state and the taxation required to pay for it, that between the liberal and the communitarian concerns itself rather with the importance of the individual's right to choose her own way of life and to express herself freely, even where this conflicts with the values and commitments of the community or society of which she is a member. It is this latter debate which is our concern in this book.

Two concluding prefatory points both arise out of the discussion above. First, mention of Locke and 'classical' liberalism raises the question of the relations between contemporary liberalism and communitarianism and the intellectual traditions from which they emanate. When we think of the liberal tradition we think of such theorists as Locke, Kant and Mill, each of whom made a distinct contribution to the heritage of modern liberalism. On the communitarian side our minds may perhaps turn to Aristotle, to Hegel, and even to Gramsci, although here, as the very heterogeneity of the list suggests, there is less of a self-conscious tradition, a point that corresponds to our earlier observation about how our four communitarians have tended not to define themselves as such. Nonetheless, there is no doubt that each of the theorists whose ideas we consider in this book owes a great deal to figures such as these, and it is very interesting to see the way in which the different theories that they come up with reflect the various strands of thought available to them from the traditions which they are continuing. Interesting, but not our concern in this book. While occasionally we shall make reference to such seminal thinkers, usually where the present-day theorists make much of the connection or where it is helpful for exegetical purposes, we shall not give much time and space to the intellectual-historical task of tracing the links. The arguments that our liberals and communitarians have to offer will be primarily assessed in their own terms and without very much reference to those who might very properly be regarded as their progenitors.[3]

We do not, however, and this is our second and final point, go so far down the analytical route that we consider the various ideas and arguments that we discuss altogether without reference to the wider systems of thought of which they form a part. What this means is that, rather than directly organizing our discussion around particular issues and themes, we adopt, as our title itself indicates, an author-based approach. The basic reason for this has already been given: the importance of identifying the different kinds of argument put forward by different theorists tells strongly in favour of an expository strategy which allows such differences to stand out. But there are other reasons too. First, it may be useful for students, who necessarily approach primary material in the author-based form in which it is written, to be able to go directly from a particular contribution to the debate to our attempt to identify, and present in accessible form, its key points. Second, we believe that the best way to understand what the various theorists are saying is to consider their positions as a whole. The attempt to isolate and address specific propositions in a theory without reference to their context can be misleading, if only because one may be neglecting the theoretical background necessary if one is to appreciate the reason for asserting, and thus a large part of the meaning of, the propositions in the first place. It may of course turn out that the propositions are false or unhelpful but at least one will have understood why the theorist was led to assert them, and they are thus far less likely to look absurd.

As this last observation suggests, this author-based approach to exegesis is intended only as a first step towards understanding, and it by no means precludes the possibility of stepping outside a thinker's presentation of his own arguments so as to be able to compare and contrast them with those of others. Clearly, our aim of identifying the differences between different theories involves just such a process of comparison, and this requires us to develop a theme- or issue-based approach to complement our primary mode of presentation. Indeed, as we have said, in our first chapter we seek precisely to formulate an agenda or map of issues to which we shall make frequent subsequent reference. In a sense, then, we seek to combine the exegetical advantages of an author-based approach with the analytical clarity to be had from an issue-oriented presentation. That we are able to do this is partly due to our decision to restrict our attention in the way already indicated. By concentrating exclusively on the communitarian critique of liberalism we are able to do that critique justice, to give ourselves the opportunity of a proper and careful examination of communitarian and liberal ideas that is not possible for those who seek in a single book to compass a greater variety of themes.

Notes

1 Daniel Bell's *Communitarianism and its Critics* – entertainingly written as a dialogue between two friends in a Paris cafe – has gone furthest in seeking to draw policy implications from philosophically communitarian positions of the kind that we discuss here.

2 As good places to start on these other critiques we suggest the following: Roger Scruton's *The Meaning of Conservatism*, Alan Buchanan's *Marx and Justice*, Alison Jaggar's *Feminist Politics and Human Nature*, and Robert Nozick's *Anarchy, State and Utopia*, the last of which we discuss very briefly below. Elizabeth Frazer and Nicola Lacey's *The Politics of Community* criticizes both liberalism and communitarianism from a feminist perspective.

3 Two books which attempt this intellectual-historical task alongside their own analytical discussions are, sketchily, John Gray's *Liberalism* and, at rather greater length, Anthony Arblaster's *The Rise and Decline of Western Liberalism*. Stephen Holmes's *The Anatomy of Antiliberalism* polemically discusses what he (somewhat controversially) regards as the ancestry of communitarian thinking.

Acknowledgements

We first indulged our interest in these issues in two classes held in Balliol College, Oxford, in the springs of 1990 and 1991. Andrew Williams was the third member of the teaching team, and we owe him a great deal of thanks for his efforts in helping us to appreciate – in those classes, in private discussions, and in helpful written comments – the complexity of many of the issues we discuss, we hope in not too simplistic a manner, in this book. The chapters on the new Rawls and Raz in particular have benefited from his untiring assistance. We are grateful also to those students whose contributions and questions in those classes forced us to get our thoughts straighter than they would otherwise be. Joseph Raz managed to combine personal and moral concerns by reading a draft of the chapter devoted to his work and indicating passages where it might be improved, and Will Kymlicka's constructive suggestions were also much appreciated. And we owe a great debt of thanks to Deborah McGovern, the Fellows' Secretary at All Souls, for her cheerful and efficient help in the preparation of the manuscript: there were no technical difficulties she could not resolve, and no deadlines she could not meet.

We are pleased to have the opportunity to acknowledge also the support of a number of institutions. Stephen Mulhall is grateful to All Souls for the luxury of a Prize Research Fellowship, and Adam Swift to the Kennedy Memorial Trust, the Economic and Social Research Council, Nuffield College, and Balliol College, each of whom kept him for a period while he worked on matters discussed in these pages.

While it is impossible clearly to identify the individual origins and authorship of particular chapters, especially in the context of a collaboration that goes back, in one form or another, to our arrival at Balliol as undergraduates in October 1980, this is a book about a debate, and the reader will not go too far wrong if she takes Stephen Mulhall to be the communitarian and Adam Swift to be the liberal in the argument. That we detect elements of compatibility between the two approaches perhaps reflects the fact that each cannot believe the other completely misguided.

One co-author dedicates this book to Danny Swift, who was born halfway through chapter 5, and to Lucy Butterwick, who makes all the difference; for the other, that difference is made by Alison Baker, to whom the book is also dedicated.

The authors and publisher wish to thank the following for permission to quote from material in copyright: Joseph Raz and Oxford University Press for extracts from J. Raz, *The Morality of Freedom* (1986); Basic Books for extracts from M. Walzer, *Spheres of Justice* (1983); Ronald Dworkin for extracts from *Equal Freedom*; and Harvard University Press for extracts from J. Rawls, *A Theory of Justice* (1971).

Abbreviations

INTRODUCTION:
Rawls's original position

We emphasized in the Preface that there are different kinds of both liberalism and communitarianism, and it follows from this that any particular liberal thinker with whose theory we might begin must be regarded as no more than a starting-point. This is especially true because we seek in this chapter only to identify some of the key themes and issues that we can think of as forming an agenda for the rest of the book. Since, however, we must begin somewhere, John Rawls's theory of justice as fairness is the obvious choice. The commonplace observation that the publication of Rawls's *A Theory of Justice* was the single most important stimulus to the renaissance of political theory during the 1970s and 1980s is not our particular concern, although the extent to which his theory established the terrain upon which subsequent political-theoretical battles were to be fought is clearly to the point. Both communitarian critics and defenders of versions of liberalism other than that offered by Rawls have formulated their positions in terms that make explicit reference to his theory, so that in many ways Rawls simply *did* define the agenda and continues to do so. It thus makes a lot of sense for us to begin with a basic exposition of his theory.

That our exposition be basic is demanded not only by the introductory role in which we are casting it but also by the fact that the theory of justice as fairness is subject to different interpretations. Most significantly, Rawls himself has published a second book – *Political Liberalism* – that changes the way in which he would have us understand his position. Since we do not wish to address the complications this raises until later on, we must, if we are to avoid begging questions, present the theory in its barest outline, giving only that level of detail that is required for us to be able to relate it to the agenda of themes that it is our primary purpose to present. Doubtless our presentation will be both selective and simplistic, and the reader already familiar with the variety of theoretical issues at stake will be uncomfortable at our glossing over difficult matters of interpretation. We can only remind the reader of our intended audience and hope that our awareness of the complexities around is apparent by the end of the book.

It is equally important that we present the theory in a way that will allow us to understand what it was about it that communitarians regarded as problematic. This is because we believe that the changes in Rawls's position can in part be understood as providing him with responses precisely to the sorts of criticism which communitarians brought against the theory as originally formulated. As well as providing another very good reason to start with Rawls, this belief necessarily affects the way that we present his theory; we want to see what it was that communitarians took him to be saying, for this is the best way of understanding both their arguments and his responses. Our exposition of justice as fairness, then, aims on the one hand to be minimal, so as not to beg questions of interpretation, and, on the other, to bring out those aspects of the theory which communitarians read as objectionable. Regarding *A Theory of Justice* as an agenda-setter, we leave open for the present the questions both of whether Rawls was indeed arguing what it was to which they objected and whether, if he was, their objections were cogent.

The chapter consists of two sections. In the first we present an elementary exposition of the theory of justice as fairness, and in the second we draw out from this exposition a list of those themes or issues on which communitarian attention has focused and to which we shall make frequent reference in the course of our subsequent discussion. We expect our readers already to be familiar with Rawls's theory to some extent, and accordingly do not regard ourselves as required to give an account of it that could serve as a useful introduction for those to whom it is completely new. Those who are in this position should probably begin elsewhere, either with Rawls's own presentation in *A Theory of Justice* or with a secondary source that gives a more systematic exegesis than is provided here.[1] We aim only to remind readers of the bare outline of the theory so as to be able quickly to turn to the agenda which is our central concern.

The basics of justice as fairness

The twin ideas at the heart of justice as fairness are that of the original position and the veil of ignorance. For Rawls, the way to think about what would be a just or fair organization of society is to imagine what principles would be agreed to by people who were denied knowledge of certain particular facts about themselves. Principles of justice, which are 'to govern the assignment of rights and duties and to regulate the distribution of social and economic advantages' (*TJ*, p. 61), should be understood as what would emerge as a hypothetical contract or agreement that would be arrived at by people ignorant of particular aspects of their own beliefs and circumstances. The intuition being captured here is that which links fairness to ignorance. If I don't know which of the five pieces of cake that I am cutting I am going to end up with, then it makes sense for me to cut the pieces fairly. Similarly, if people don't know who they are going to be, then it will make sense for them to choose fair or just principles to regulate their society.

Since the content of the principles of justice that emerge is clearly a function of the characterization of the original position, it makes sense for our attention to focus initially on that characterization. And here our vague attempt to identify the essence of the theory in terms of the cake-cutting analogy only of course immediately raises two crucial and related questions. First, what exactly is it of which people are ignorant in the original position? What information, that is, does the veil exclude? Second, why should we consider it appropriate to regard them as ignorant in such ways for the purposes of thinking about justice? What substantive theoretical claims about justice does the veil of ignorance embody? The answer to this more foundational second question is that the original position aims to model the sense in which it is appropriate, when thinking about justice, that people should be regarded as free and equal. Since this can most easily be understood in more concrete terms, let us immediately tie this in with the answer to the first question by noting that, in very crude terms, there are two kinds of thing, roughly corresponding to freedom and equality, that the people in the original position do not know about themselves. We indicated in our Preface that we shall be more concerned with the freedom- than with the equality-related aspects of the theory, but it is nonetheless useful to say something about both of these now, and we shall begin with the equality-based strand in the theory.

In the first place, then, they do not know what position in society they will occupy, whether they will be at the top or the bottom of the social ladder; nor do they know what their own talents or natural endowments will be. In real life, of course, people are born into particular families which are unequally placed in the distribution of advantage and, by a combination of natural and environmental factors, they have different abilities or disabilities which also lead to inequalities. The original position is intended to capture the idea that, when we think about justice, these differences are or should be irrelevant and that people should be regarded as equal. Now this has a great deal of intuitive appeal. There is a sense in which we think that, since people are not responsible for the fact that they were born into one family rather than another, or for the fact that they are talented or untalented, it should be the aim of a theory of justice to take no account of such differences. If I cannot be said to deserve my talents, how can I deserve the advantage that they can bring me? As Rawls puts it, the distribution of these attributes is 'arbitrary from a moral point of view' (*TJ*, p. 15).

In denying the people in the original position knowledge about their social location and their natural endowments, then, Rawls is trying to ensure that the principles to which they agree are not distorted by those chance inequalities that in the real world might be thought to bias distributive outcomes. One way of thinking about what happens in the original position is as a kind of bargaining process, in which each person, acting rationally in her own self-interest, seeks to get as good a deal as possible for herself. If, in that situation, people were allowed to know their own position in the distribution of these chance attributes, then the agreement reached would reflect the unequal bargaining power of the people involved and not justice or fairness. While this may well be what happens in real world negotiations, as between, say, employers and workers, the moral recognition that for the purposes of thinking about justice we are all equal despite our chance differences means that people in the original position should be denied knowledge of those inequalities likely to distort the outcome in favour of the lucky. Justice requires a bargain made under fair conditions, and this is why knowledge of inequalities is ruled out.

If their ignorance of circumstances is intended to capture the sense in which we are all equal, the people in the original position's ignorance of their own conceptions of the good is intended to model the sense in which, for the purposes of thinking about justice, it is appropriate to regard ourselves as free. What does it mean to say that they do not know their conception of the good? And how does this relate to an understanding of people as free?

To take the first question first, a person's conception of the good is her set of beliefs about how she should lead her life, about what makes her life worthwhile. Catholics have different conceptions of the good from atheists, those who devote all their leisure to the pursuit of excellence in, or perhaps just watching, a particular sport have a different conception of the good from those who prefer to spend their free time visiting art galleries. When we say that the people in Rawls's original position do not know their conceptions of the good, what this means is that they do not know what their beliefs are about how they should lead their lives. Considering this alongside the previous couple of paragraphs, we should be able to see how this will feed into the principles of justice that get chosen. Just as justice requires that no attention be paid to the different talents of different members of society, so, it would seem, it requires that no attention be paid to the particular conceptions of the good held by those members.

But, in contrast to the previous, here surely the argument seems rather mysterious. One way of thinking about the veil of ignorance is that it models the substantive moral claim that certain reasons should not be considered relevant to our thinking about justice. Now, as we argued above, it makes some intuitive sense to think that the social position into which a person happens to be born, or the talents or disabilities with which she happens naturally to be endowed, should be ruled out of such thinking. But in the case of conceptions of the good, things are more problematic. If one believes that some ways of life are better, worthier or more valuable, than others, why should one hold that it makes sense to ignore those beliefs when it comes to thinking about justice? The idea that we should arrange our society so that it be fair as between the talented and the untalented has a certain plausibility, but the idea that it should be organized so as to be fair as between someone who believes in the value of a life spent pursuing beauty and truth and someone who prefers alcohol, heavy metal rock music and counting blades of grass may seem less attractive. And in any case, we still have the question of what this has got to do with the point that it is their ignorance of conceptions of the good that constitutes the sense in which the original position models people as free.

The link between ignorance of conceptions of the good and freedom is as follows. Rather than being attributed particular conceptions of the good, and seeking to reach an agreement as favourable as possible to those particular conceptions, the people in the original position are taken to be motivated above all by an interest in protecting their capacity, as Rawls puts it, to 'frame, revise, and rationally to pursue' such conceptions. Of fundamental importance on the Rawlsian scheme are not the conceptions of the good that people have but something that lies behind such conceptions, their freedom to decide upon their own conceptions of the good, to act upon, and to change those decisions. In denying people in the original position knowledge of their beliefs about what makes a life worthy or valuable and attributing to them rather a 'highest-order interest' of this kind, Rawls is modelling the substantive moral claim that, when thinking about justice, what matters is people's freedom to make their own choices, and to change their minds, not whatever it is that they choose.

And the reason to exclude from our thinking about justice beliefs about which ways of life are better than others may now seem less bizarre than it did at first. If one thinks that what matters from the perspective of justice is not so much that people make good choices as that they are free to make their own choices, then the idea that the articulation of a conception of justice should ignore those reasons that lead us to hold some ways of life more valuable than others makes some sense. The connection between freedom, the value of our capacity to choose and change our minds about how we live our lives, and the exclusion of certain considerations about which ways of life are better than others, may still, perhaps, be less immediately intuitively appealing than the link between equality, chance, and the arbitrariness of talents that underlies the distributional aspect of Rawls's theory. The fact that someone occupies a particular social position is fairly straightforwardly not a good reason for them to support a way of arranging society that favours that position. But the fact that someone believes some ways of life to be more valuable than others may well seem a good reason for them to support a way of arranging society that favours those conceptions of the good. Indeed, a large part of this book will be devoted to thinkers who regard the exclusion of reasons of this second kind as deeply problematic (and one of them, Raz, is a liberal). But at least we now have a rough idea of the ground on which the debate will take place.

In Rawls's view, people in the original position, denied knowledge of their talents and endowments, motivated not by a particular conception of the good but by their interest in their capacity to frame, revise and rationally to pursue such conceptions, would agree that their society should be regulated by the following principles of justice. First:

> Each person is to have an equal right to the most extensive total system of equal basic liberties compatible with a similar system of liberty for all.

Second:

> Social and economic inequalities are to be arranged so that they are both (a) to the greatest benefit of the least advantaged, and (b) attached to offices and positions open to all under conditions of fair equality of opportunity. (*TJ*, p. 302)

They would agree, moreover, to a clear system of priorities among these principles: the first principle, that of equal basic liberties, has lexical priority over the second, which means that there can be no trade-offs between those liberties and the other forms of advantage that come under the second principle; and, within the second, (b) the principle of fair equality of opportunity has priority over (a) the part that says that inequalities must benefit the least advantaged, which latter is the difference principle.

It should be clear how these principles derive from the characterization of the original position. In terms of our previous simplifying distinction between the distributive or equality-related and the liberty-related aspects of the theory we can see how each of the principles concerns itself with a different aspect. The principle of equal basic liberties derives directly from the people in the original position's ignorance of, and concern to protect their freedom to choose, change and pursue their own conceptions of the good, while the second principle, and especially the difference principle, derives from their ignorance of their own likely position in the distribution of social and economic advantage. Given that ignorance, according to Rawls, it is rational for them to maximin, to ensure that the worst position is as good as it can be, and this leads them to support equality unless inequality will actually help that worst-off position. In fact, and this is one way of seeing how our distinction between the distributional and the liberty-related aspects of the theory is somewhat artificial, Rawls regards the liberties that are given priority in the first principle as among the goods (primary goods) that are to be distributed in accordance with the agreement reached in the original position, and their priority similarly follows from the application of maximin thinking. They are prior because the capacities that they protect are of such fundamental importance that the people in the original position will not envisage their being compromised for the sake of any of the other primary goods.

We have talked about the principles of justice being 'derived' from the original position, but the reader may suspect that this gives a rather misleading picture of the relation between these two components of the theory. The question of how to understand the original position and the nature of the agreement reached there is one that has occupied interpreters of Rawls for a long time, and our brief and selective account has attempted to steer clear of such matters as far as is possible. At various points our exegesis has suggested that one way of thinking about it is to see the principles of justice as what would be agreed to by individuals acting rationally in pursuit of their interests but ignorant of certain aspects of their situation. This strand, which relates the concept of justice to that branch of economic theory concerned with what it is rational for people to do in conditions of uncertainty, is clearly central in Rawls's own presentation, but it is obviously combined with a separate, more substantive strand, which is what leads to the original position being set up in the particular way that it is in the first place. Thus, even if it were rational for people characterized in a certain way to choose the principles of justice that Rawls says that they would choose, this would still leave the question of why we should characterize them in that way to begin with.

Clearly the original position embodies substantive normative claims. We recognized as much when we said that it is intended to model the sense in which it is appropriate to regard people as free and equal when thinking about justice. And since the principles that emerge as 'conclusions' are to some extent built into the very construction of the thought-experiment from which they are then 'derived' – it is hardly surprising, for example, that we end up with rights to equal basic liberties if the people making the agreement are attributed a highest-order interest in their capacity to choose, act on and change their minds about their own conceptions of the good – it is clear that we should see the weight of the theory as residing in that construction. The issues upon which critical attention has focused concern the substantive claims that are embodied in Rawls's characterization of the original position, and it is to an agenda of such issues that we now turn.

The agenda: claims modelled by the original position

There is a variety of questions that we might ask about the original position. We have already given a summary sketch of the sense in which the original position tries to model the idea that principles of justice should be understood as those which would be agreed to by people who are free and equal, and showed how this involves the claim that certain sorts of reasons are inappropriate when thinking about justice, but this leaves open a host of problems. In the rest of this introductory chapter we identify five themes upon which the debate between communitarians and liberals, and between different kinds of liberal, has focused. Because the aim here is to establish an agenda for the book as a whole, and because Rawls's position, however understood, by no means exhausts the theoretical resources available to liberalism, some of these issues are only indirectly raised by Rawls's theory, especially by that bare outline of his position which we have offered above. Nevertheless, while we aim here to introduce themes that go beyond both Rawls's own arguments and those that have been presented explicitly as objections to them, we hope to be able to show how the various issues relate to the idea of the original position, thereby justifying our claim that it was Rawls's theory that set the agenda for the debates that followed.

The conception of the person

A great deal of communitarian thought has presented itself in terms that make explicit reference to, and involve the explicit rejection of, the conception of the person that they regard as underlying liberal political theory. We shall see that Sandel and MacIntyre both formulate their objections to liberalism in these terms, and it is important to think about how these critiques might or might not relate to Rawls's original position. The general shape of the communitarian claim is that liberal political theory takes people to be distinct from their ends (or values, or conceptions of the good) in a way that simply fails to correspond to the way in which they actually do relate to those ends. For the communitarian, the liberal picture of the person as someone separate from her conception of the good ignores the extent to which people are constituted as the people that they are precisely by those conceptions themselves. Who, the communitarian asks, is the shadowy 'person' that exists independently of, and able freely to choose, the ends that give her life meaning and value?

Whatever we end up concluding about this issue – whether we decide that Rawls's theory does not actually involve such a conception of the person, or that even if it does other versions of liberalism need not, or that it does and, contrary to the communitarian critique, this can be justified – we should at least be able to see how the original position puts the question of conceptions of the person at the centre of political theoretical debate. While one might seek to downplay the metaphor of the original position insofar as that seems to involve us in imagining an actual process of negotiation between people characterized in terms quite unlike how people really are, and without any of that particularity that might serve to differentiate them, it is clear, and Rawls does not seek to deny, that the theory is built around a conception of the person. We can emphasize that reading of the original position that sees it merely as a device of representation for the idea that certain reasons should be deemed irrelevant to questions of justice, but this still leaves us with the question of why those reasons should be ruled out, and the answer to this surely leaves a claim about what is important about, or in the interests of, people at the centre of the theory. Even if the oddly disembodied selves who populate the original position are not intended as metaphorical portrayals of our essence as people, they explicitly stand for the claim that, when it comes to thinking about justice, people should be regarded as distinct from their particularity, both their particular natural endowments and social position and their particular conceptions of the good, and, of especial importance to us, possessed of a highest-order interest in their capacity to frame, revise, and rationally pursue conceptions of the good. We can address not the particular dramatic model but the substantive claims that it represents and still be left with a debate that properly focuses on the issue of the conception of the person, where this involves claims about what is important about people, what is in their interests, what constitutes their well-being, and so on.

Given that the conception of the person embodied in the original position is indeed central to Rawls's theory, the issues that arise concern, in an intricately interconnected web, the validity or coherence, the scope and status, the source or origin, and the desirability of that conception. On the first, the question is whether we can sensibly think of ourselves as relating to our conceptions of the good in the way that Rawls seems to suppose. The identification of our highest-order interest seems to presuppose that we are indeed individuals capable freely of forming, and changing, our own views about how we should live our lives. It is this capacity that the rights that are prioritized in the first principle are there to protect. But is this true to our moral experience? Can we really step back from the particular values that we have and change them for new ones, or are we rather made the very people that we are by the values that we endorse, so that such detachment is impossible?

The second set of issues concerns the precise scope of the conception of the person. Is it intended to be a conception pertinent when thinking about all aspects of our moral lives or might we think of it as restricted in its scope of application? We have consistently talked about the characterization of the original position as attempting to represent the way in which it is appropriate to conceive people *when thinking about justice*, and, if we contrast this more limited understanding with a fuller or more comprehensive one which involved claims about people *per se*, we see that this is one way in which we might construe the conception as deliberately narrow, as appropriate to some issues, specifically those concerned with justice, and not others. Another concerns not the areas of moral and political theory in which the conception might be thought appropriate but the range of cultures to which it might be thought applicable. However we read the claim about people being conceived as free and equal, is it a claim that is supposed to hold across cultures? Do those who have a highest-order interest in their freedom to frame, revise and rationally pursue their own conceptions of the good have it even if they have never heard of it, do not think that they have it, and would not want it if it were explained to them? Or is its being their highest-order interest rather in some way conditional on the sort of culture in which they live?

Clearly these questions about the scope of the conception of the person tie in closely with those relating to its status. Is it a conception of the person that, whatever its scope of application, attempts to capture our metaphysical essence? Is it even to be regarded as 'true' in any sense, or is the point rather just that it is a way of thinking about themselves to which people can agree? These in turn are intimately connected to the issue of its source or origin. Where does this conception come from? By what route does it come to play such a central role in the theory? If it is a conception that enters Rawls's liberalism because he takes it to be valid or correct in its own terms then its source would seem to be some independent moral justification. But if, on the other hand, the point, for Rawls, is not so much that it is true as that people believe it, that it is something to which people can agree despite their other differences, then the conception of the person enters the theory not as a substantive moral claim about what is important about people (whether restricted in scope or not) but as an empirical sociological claim about the beliefs of the citizenry of certain societies.

The fifth and final set of issues raised by the conception of the person is rather different in kind, and in a sense rather more straightforward. If the previous four questions were methodological in nature, the fifth, the question of desirability, is substantive. Whatever our conclusions about its validity, scope, status and source, however we end up specifying the precise claims modelled by its representation in the original position, there will still remain the question of whether the conception of the person at the heart of Rawls's theory is desirable. Even if, suitably delimited and understood, it can be reckoned valid or coherent, this does not mean that we must regard it as attractive, as capturing aspects of our self-understandings that we would wish to see developed into a theory of justice that is to regulate the social and political structures in which we live. Perhaps, that is, Rawls's, and liberalism's, prioritization of individual freedom is coherent but undesirable, unwarrantedly emphasizing one aspect of moral life at the cost of neglecting others.

Some of these remarks may be obscure at this stage. Perhaps all of them are. Such obscurities are unavoidable in any attempt to introduce a wide range of difficult theoretical issues in reasonably concise fashion, and the reader should be assured that we return, at much greater length, to all of the points identified above. That, indeed, is the reason why we identify them here. Our hope is that, as we present communitarian criticisms and liberal responses, at least the reader will have a rough idea of what to look out for.

Asocial individualism

A second theme in the communitarian critique of liberalism concerns the claim that the latter misunderstands the relation between the individual and her society or community, and, more specifically, ignores the extent to which it is the societies in which people live that shape who they are and the values that they have. Obviously this strand of argument overlaps considerably with some of the points that we considered under the previous heading, for it can readily be put in terms that make it a complaint about Rawls's conception of the person, but the precise angle identified here is sufficiently distinct and important to warrant a separate introduction. The charge is not the general one that the original position misrepresents the way that people relate to their conceptions of the good, regarding ends as chosen by a self that is defined prior to such conceptions, but the more specific one that the contractual approach to political theory, of which it is a modern example, embodies the mistaken view that people's ends are formed independently of or prior to society, which is regarded as the outcome of negotiation between individuals whose ends are already given. For the communitarian, this conception overlooks the way in which it is the kind of society in which people live that affects their understandings both of themselves and of how they should lead their lives.

The idea that society, and particularly its political arrangements, can be understood as the outcome of a contract between individuals has been a major theme in the history of liberal thought, and Rawls's theory clearly continues this contract tradition in many important ways. It would be foolish to deny that liberalism regards the individual as of ultimate importance, and the way in which justice as fairness involves the idea of people agreeing to a contract certainly reflects this strand. Part of the point, for Rawls, of conceiving justice as the outcome of an agreement reached between individuals characterized as free and equal is that such a conception rules out the possibility that some people, even a large majority in a particular community, will use others as means to their ends. In contrast to utilitarianism, Rawls's theory aims to take seriously the separateness of persons, and this is one way of thinking about the kind of individualism that is captured by the original position. Whether, however, his version of the contract is vulnerable to the kinds of criticism that some other accounts have attracted must remain an open question. If it is the idea that individuals in a pre-social state of nature come together in pursuit of their individual interests to form society that is considered objectionable, then we may think that Rawls's theory, which has no obvious place for such an understanding, is straightforwardly immune to such criticism, and Nozick's attempt to derive the legitimacy of a minimal state from strongly individualistic premises may seem a more appropriate target.

The fact that Rawls's liberalism has a significant place for the idea of society as contract makes it important for us to distinguish between two points that the contractual metaphor encourages us to run together. While both are aspects of the communitarian charge that liberalism is guilty of an inappropriately asocial individualism, it will be helpful to be clear at this early stage that they are indeed different. On the one hand, then, there is the sociological-cum-philosophical point that people necessarily derive their self-understandings and conceptions of the good from the social matrix. Whether this is put as a quasi-empirical claim about socialization processes, or as a conceptual claim about the impossibility of language, thought, or moral life outside a social setting – and it is these philosophical themes that communitarian theorists have given particular attention – the emphasis here is on liberalism's neglect of the way in which the individual is parasitic on society for the very way that she thinks, including the way that she thinks of herself as an individual. With this first point, the communitarian is insisting on recognition of the necessarily social or communal *origins* of the individual's self-understanding and conception of how she should lead her life, and it is a point that applies to *any* such understanding and conception.

The second strand of communitarian criticism that arises under this heading of asocial individualism is quite separate and concerns not the *source* of people's conceptions of themselves and of what makes their life worthwhile, but the particular kinds of *content* which, on the communitarian account, liberalism ignores and encourages. In contrast to the philosophical-cum-sociological point, the quite general applicability of which indicates that it is essentially methodological, this second point is straightforwardly substantive: the charge here is that liberalism builds upon, fosters, and promotes a particular understanding of the individual's relation to her community, and in so doing neglects, undermines, and even rules out, alternative ways of thinking about that relation. According to this communitarian objection, the liberal sees society as nothing more than a cooperative venture for the pursuit of individual advantage, as an essentially private association formed by individuals whose essential interests are defined independently of, and in a sense prior to, the community of which they are members. Conceptions of the good that are more strongly communal in content, that have as part of their very nature an insistence that social bonds are valuable in themselves, over and above their value as means to the attainment of other, merely individual, goods, are thereby downgraded. It is here, as we shall see in our discussion of Sandel, that it becomes impossible to separate the question of asocial individualism from that of liberalism's conception of the person, for one way of putting this communitarian point is to talk about the liberal's neglect of constitutive attachments, of the sense in which the individual may understand her own identity and interests to be constituted by her relations with others in ways that relate her more closely to the communities of which she is a member than this merely associational model can allow.

That the communities of which people are members are indeed plural is an important point, if only because it raises the possibility that different ways of conceiving the relation between those communities and the individuals who compose them may be appropriate in different cases, and it may be that the liberal can respond by asserting the significance of these differences. As

members of families, for example, or of religious faiths, we may well
have conceptions of the good that are indeed strongly communal in
content; we may believe that what makes a life valuable or
worthwhile is that it be lived in and for community with others in
a way that precludes an understanding of that community as a mere
scheme of cooperation. But perhaps the liberal can acknowledge
this, and grant the propriety of such conceptions, whilst at the same
time insisting that this is not a legitimate or proper way to
understand political community. While there are substantive
conceptions of human flourishing that regard the good life for
human beings as that devoted to participation in political life, so that
the content of individual well-being is inherently communal – and
communal at the level of political society – the liberal may defend
her individualism at least to the extent of denying that it is
appropriate to conceive the relation between the individual and the
state in this way.

These last remarks will make more sense when the reader has
reached the end of the second part of the book, but the distinction
between the two strands of the charge of asocial individualism
should at least be clear. It is easy to see why these two points will
tend to be run together, for the understanding of society as the
outcome of a contract or a process of negotiation between people
concerned to protect and promote their individual interests seems to
presuppose that those interests are themselves pre-social, given to
the individual prior to her membership of society. Indeed, it may
seem that the two stand or fall together, that recognition that we
derive our self-understandings and our goals from the social matrix
precludes any understanding of society as a mere association. We
cannot pursue the matter here, but it is worth holding onto our
initial suggestion that the two points are actually quite different in
kind, for this may lead one to regard this move as too quick. While
we may wish to reject any form of liberalism that takes the state of
nature or contract picture of society seriously as a historical account,
or even as a model of the relation of priority between the individual
and society, it is not clear that this is fatal to *any* contractual
component to liberal theory. The liberal, perhaps, can accept the
sociological-cum-philosophical point that her ends and self-understandings are derived by the individual from the social matrix but
argue that their content is such as to make certain aspects of the
contractual approach appropriate when thinking about justice.

It is in any case by no means clear that the liberal emphasis on the importance of individual freedoms neglects the significance of the social matrix which communitarians stress. While it is true that one way of getting to the importance of individual liberties might be by taking people's ends as fixed or given prior to society, so that people can be thought of as agreeing to cooperate in society only if they can continue to live their own lives without interference from others, this is not the only way. Indeed, it might be thought that if people's ends were fixed pre-socially, there would be no reason to care about guaranteeing them the social conditions necessary for them to be able to change their minds.[2] Some theorists argue for the standard individual rights and freedoms precisely because they recognize the importance of the kind of society in which they live to the capacities that people develop and the choices that they make. Rather than grounding those rights in the pre-social individual, they defend them by pointing to the value of a community that permits individuals to question not only the conceptions of the good that are dominant but also their own previous commitments. A liberal society is justified precisely because it fosters certain capacities, and perhaps even certain choices.

Recognition of the extent to which it is the kind of society in which we live that shapes our self-understandings, our capacities, and our conceptions of the good, would only be a problem for the liberal if it could be argued that a society with a liberal framework, such as one governed by Rawls's principles of justice, in some way undermined either those very capacities and self-understandings upon which liberals place so much importance or the value of the ways of life which are available to be chosen. In the first case, the claim would be that liberal theory is in some sense incoherent, since liberal conclusions guaranteeing the freedom of the individual would be said to lead to a society that did not foster the capacities and self-understandings that liberals take to be of such value and that themselves generate those conclusions. In the second, the claim would be rather that the capacity to make one's own choices is only as valuable as the choices that one can make, and that a liberal framework leads to a society in which valuable options, or at least some of them, are likely to wither away. While the second is less immediately problematic, since, as we shall see, the liberal does not have to agree that it is appropriate to worry about the value of the choices available to those choosing them, both lines of argument might be thought to tell against liberalism's apparent disattention to the social conditions necessary for the sustenance of those individual-level features in which it *is* interested. Of course, the onus is very much on the critic of liberalism to indicate the precise ways in which the liberal framework does undermine itself or lead to unpalatable consequences. It is hard *prima facie* to see how the guarantee of individual freedoms could lead to the withering away of individual capacities or valuable ways of life (indeed in the previous paragraph we suggested that the liberal might argue exactly the opposite), but we shall see that some do seek to argue something like this.

For now, our aim is just to point out why liberalism's emphasis on the individual might be thought to involve a neglect of the extent to which it is the society she lives in that makes her the individual that she is and makes available to her the kinds of life that she might live. While the contractual metaphor can lead us to confuse the two, we have made explicit the distinction between a claim about the *origins* of people's self-understandings and conceptions of the good (with the communitarian insisting on the extent to which these are necessarily derived from the social matrix) and a claim about its *content* (where the communitarian charge is that the liberal neglects or discriminates against those that are strongly communal in nature). In terms of Rawls's theory, both of these might seem to be suggested by the idea that principles of justice are understood as what would be contracted to by mutually disinterested individuals motivated to protect and promote their own interests, though we have suggested that to emphasize this aspect of theory may be to read Rawls as closer to the state of nature strand in the liberal tradition than a careful reading of his argument, and the role of the original position in it, would justify.

Universalism

The third theme we identify here is one that has already been mentioned under our heading of the conception of the person, and it is clearly closely interrelated with questions to do with the source, status, and scope of that conception. The specific issue here concerns whether liberalism claims that its conclusions apply universally and cross-culturally, or whether it might rather have room for the idea that different ways of organizing society are appropriate, and morally justified, in different sorts of culture, so that a liberal political framework is only argued for in societies of a certain kind. A significant strand of communitarian thinking has been directed at liberalism's alleged failure to attend to cultural particularity, to the ways in which different cultures embody different values and different social forms and institutions, and to the consequences that these differences might have for political theory.

It should be easy to see why Rawls's theory might be thought to involve pretensions to universality. We have already stressed the sense in which the original position involves abstraction from particularity, for the people behind the veil of ignorance are denied knowledge not only of their own social position but also of what their society is like and of their own particular beliefs about how they should lead their lives. There is a clear attempt to identify the respects in which we are all the same underneath, to characterize people in a way that detaches them from what it is that makes actual people different from each other, so it is not at all surprising that Rawls has been taken to neglect the variety, and the moral importance, of the different cultures in which people live and in whose terms they conceive themselves and the meaning of their lives. The emphasis on rationality in the original presentation of the theory suggests that Rawls is seeking to identify some conception of the rational essence of human beings, and his description of the original position as representing an 'Archimedean point' (TJ, pp. 260, 584) supports the suspicion that we are being offered a theory that is meant to apply cross-culturally. Certainly communitarian critics, and most obviously Walzer, who insists that an appreciation of cultural particularity is central to a proper understanding of how a community should arrange itself politically, have taken Rawls to be claiming, and have objected to, pretensions to universality.

If, as we have argued, the original position embodies claims about people's highest-order interests, then the question is really how universal those interests are taken to be. Do all people, whatever their cultural background and self-understandings, have an interest in their capacity to make their own choices about how they lead their lives, or is this an interest only of those living in certain sorts of society? If the latter, does that mean that liberalism is not the answer for those societies that do not have the appropriate institutions and practices already in place? Clearly difficult issues of moral and cultural relativism are raised by such questions, with communitarians, because of their emphasis on the senses in which it is the community and its traditions and practices that should be regarded as the locus of moral value, tending to be more relativistic than liberals. A major strand in the liberal tradition since the Enlightenment has been the idea that social arrangements and conventions should be subjected to rational and critical examination, not simply conformed to and respected, and contemporary liberals have tended very much to pursue this line.

It is especially interesting, therefore, to note that in his more recent writings Rawls himself seems to be denying that his theory makes any universalistic claims. We shall explore the various different ways of understanding the new Rawls in a later chapter, but on any interpretation it is clear that he is now endorsing a brand of cultural particularism of his own. If the conception of the person, and the identification of people's interests that it stands for, at the heart of Rawls's theory is taken itself to be a culture-specific understanding, and to derive its place in the theory because of its status as such, then it would seem that the liberal theory of justice as fairness that results is similarly culture-specific. To anticipate points that will be spelled out more fully later, we have said that it is the abstraction in Rawls's theory that seems to involve it in claims to universality and a neglect of cultural context, but it may be useful to distinguish between two senses in which that concept might be applied. On the one hand there is abstraction from people's particular social positions and particular conceptions of the good, and this Rawls's theory certainly does involve. But this does not necessarily imply a second kind of abstraction, that which separates people from their particular cultural traditions or social practices. It may be not only that Rawls's theory does not involve this second kind of abstraction, but also that this is precisely the reason why it does involve the first kind. If it is our particular cultural understandings that identify people's highest-order interests in a way that requires us to abstract from their particular conceptions of the good, then Rawls's liberalism can hardly be accused of disattending to cultural particularity.

Some liberals do not like what they would characterize as this retreat from universalism, and they seek to argue that liberalism's claims about the importance of people's interests do indeed capture something which is true of all people, whatever their cultural self-understandings and values. There thus occurs the slightly strange situation whereby other theorists seek to defend Rawls's theory in versions apparently stronger than those to which he himself is happy to subscribe. What matters at this stage is just that we should be prepared for this question of liberalism's pretensions to universality to come up at various places later on in the book.

Subjectivism or objectivism

If the original position and the conception of the person represented there models the claim that people's highest-order interest is in their capacity to frame, revise and rationally pursue their own conception of the good, attention must at some point turn to the theoretical assumptions that underlie that claim. What other sorts of beliefs about moral values must one hold in order to think that this is what is particularly important about people? More specifically, does their emphasis on the individual's choosing her own way of life mean that liberals must believe that such choices are arbitrary expressions of preference, that value is in the eye of the beholder, that moral judgements are completely subjective? Or is it possible, and perhaps even more coherent, to prioritize the individual's freedom to make her own choices while at the same time maintaining that some choices are very definitely better than others and that reason can help people discriminate between worthy and unworthy ways of life? Can one, that is, be a liberal and believe that judgements about value are objective? This is the fourth theme in the debate between liberalism and communitarianism that will recur in the rest of this book.

The reasons why one might take liberalism and moral subjectivism or scepticism to go together are reasonably straightforward. If no way of living is better than any other, if people's choices are simply expressions of preference, with no rational grounds available to justify claims about their value, like choices between flavours of ice cream, then it would seem crazy for the state to do anything other then let people make their own choices. In the absence of any right answers, or even rational criteria for thinking about how to come to right answers, about how people should lead their lives, the state would seem to have no justification for encouraging some ways of life and not others. If a life devoted to the pursuit of beauty and truth is no better than one spent playing video games, then it seems that we would be committed to a political framework that leaves people free to make an unbiased choice between the two.

We believe that a lot of people's commonsense intuitions supportive of liberalism derive from a vague sceptical belief that one choice is as good as any other, or more likely, and in effect just a variant on the sceptical theme, that even if some are better than others we cannot know which are which. The fact that people disagree in their conceptions of the good, in their views about what makes a life worthy or valuable, and are unable to provide each other with conclusive arguments for their own point of view, is often taken as evidence for the claim that there is no rational way of judging who is right, and the inference drawn is that people should make up their own minds. The reason to stress this pervasiveness of moral subjectivism at the level of commonsense intuitions relates to our earlier observation that communitarian critics of liberalism do not necessarily regard academic political theorists as their primary targets. Sometimes, and we are thinking here particularly of MacIntyre's worries about emotivism, their focus is rather on aspects of contemporary liberal culture more generally understood, with political theorists invoked merely as specific symptomatic illustrations of the more general disease afflicting that culture. This is important because, even if we were to decide both that liberalism need not be grounded in a sceptical claim and that particular liberals charged with so grounding it do not in fact do so, still we might think that the communitarian critique was pointing to something central to our contemporary self-understandings and conceptions of moral and political life that warranted criticism.

Since we regard subjectivism or scepticism as widespread, it is important to be clear about the *scope* of the moral scepticism that might seem to fit neatly with liberal politics. We are imagining a liberal who thinks that the fact that moral judgements are merely subjective expressions of preference means that the state ought to be liberal, ought to leave people free to make their own choices. But what is the status of this claim that the state ought to be liberal? It is surely a moral judgement. Does that mean that it is itself no more than a subjective expression of preference? Surely this would be incoherent and self-defeating, for if she allows this, then the liberal has to say that there is no rational basis for her endorsing a liberal state rather than a totalitarian one; that it is just a matter of taste, like the ice creams, which kind of political regime is better. When this is pointed out to her, the subjectivist liberal will tend to retreat from this self-defeating global scepticism to a more restricted version, arguing that there is a difference between judgements about how people should live their lives, which are indeed merely subjective, and judgements about how people ought to be treated by one another and by the state, which are objective. The claim now is that the fact that judgements of the first kind are subjective gives one an objective reason to leave people free to make such judgements for themselves. The liberal can stand up for the objective judgement that liberalism is right, but ground that judgement in the belief that judgements about how people should lead their lives are merely subjective.

We shall not pursue this matter here. Clearly a great deal of the subjectivist liberal's position depends upon the validity of the distinction between these two kinds of judgement, and, in our final chapter on Raz, we shall look at a liberal who rejects outright this attempt to divide moral judgements into two qualitatively different categories. For our purposes it is important just to be clear that when we discuss, in what follows, the relation between liberalism and subjectivism, it is not the (self-defeating, incoherent) global brand of subjectivism that we are talking about, but the more plausible view that judgements as to how people should lead their lives lack rational justification.

The important theoretical question is whether one has to endorse even this more limited form of subjectivism if one is to reach liberal conclusions, for it is clear that some liberals argue for those conclusions as consistent with, and perhaps even as implied by, the claim that judgements as to how one should live one's life are objective. A weak version, claiming only consistency, might hold that even though some ways of life are, and can be known to be, better than others, it is so important that people make their own choices that we should ignore that knowledge when thinking about how to organize our society politically. A stronger idea, arguing for a connection between liberalism and objectivism, might be that some ways of life are indeed better than others and that a framework of liberal rights is needed precisely to provide the conditions under which people can make informed and rational judgements about which are which. Here the argument merges with what we were saying earlier about how some liberals recognize the importance of social conditions in fostering certain self-understandings and conceptions of the good, for the claim is that liberal conditions – freedom of expression, of association, and so on – are required if people are to be able to find out what is valuable in life. Indeed, liberalism's insistence on the freedom to revise one's commitments, to change one's mind, only make sense, it might be argued, if we can be wrong about our goals and can come to see that they can be changed for the better.[3] If they really are arbitrary, why should the liberal accord such importance to our capacity to change them?

It is important to be clear about what this argument for the compatibility of liberalism with the claim that some ways of life are objectively better than others does or need *not* entail. Clearly, it does not commit one to the view that there is a single way of life that is uniformly right for everybody, but, perhaps more interestingly, it need not even maintain that for each individual there is a single conception of the good that is objectively superior to all others, as if reason could guide the individual to see exactly how she ought to live her life. The point here is that the claim that reason can tell us that some lives are worthier than others does not contradict the claim that there is, even for each individual, a plurality of conflicting and incompatible worthy ways of life. As we shall see in our chapter on Raz, it is perfectly coherent to argue that we can judge the life of an artist to be objectively more valuable than that of a gambler, without being able to judge whether the life of an artist is more valuable than that of a farmer.

There is, finally, another point which naturally arises under this heading, although the fact that it does so can be rather misleading since it concerns not so much the higher-order issue of the status of moral judgements as the substantive question of what makes a life good. The point here is that the claim that some choices are better than others most certainly does not mean that one can make someone live a better life by getting them to live a life that they have not themselves chosen or do not themselves endorse. This, of course, is the liberal bit of the objectivist liberal position, the idea that what matters is that people are free to choose for themselves. It does not follow from the claim that I can be mistaken in my beliefs about what makes my life valuable or worthwhile that someone else, or an institution such as the state, can improve my life by making me do things other than those in which I currently believe. But nor, for the objectivist, is it the case that whatever I choose is *ipso facto* valuable, as if all there was to a life's being valuable was that it had been willingly endorsed. People can freely choose a way of life, can believe it to be worthwhile and valuable, and be mistaken. While one cannot make a person's life go well by forcing them to live a life they have not in some sense chosen, one does not, for the objectivist, guarantee that their life goes well just by letting them choose it for themselves.

The connection between liberalism and subjectivism is an important item on our agenda because a significant strand in the communitarian critique of liberalism takes the form of a rejection of the moral subjectivism that is thought to underpin it. Even with the distinction between global and restricted subjectivism taken into account, however, we have suggested that the two need not necessarily go together, and that it is possible to support liberal politics despite a belief that some ways of life are objectively better than others. That said, we should at least be able to see that there is an affinity between the two, and why it might look as if the doctrine that (some) values are only subjective underwrites the claim, embodied in Rawls's original position, that our highest-order interest is in making our own choices.

Anti-perfectionism and neutrality

The fifth and last theme to recur in the book concerns the question of whether it makes sense to exclude, when thinking about politics and political morality, considerations that might be thought pertinent to individual private conduct. By now we have enough of our agenda in place to enable us to make connections between this and previous themes, and this, combined with the fact that the matters that fall under this heading are particularly complicated, requires us to treat this issue at slightly greater length. The central idea here is that rather than seeking to act on those ideals that guide people when they live their individual lives and pursue their own conceptions of the good, the state should deliberately ignore some or all of such ideals. At the extreme, if it excluded all such considerations, the state could be thought of as committing itself to being neutral between the different conceptions of the good held by its citizens. Rather than making its own judgements about how people should lead their lives, the argument might go, the state should deliberately eschew such judgements, and seek only to provide a neutral framework within which people can make their own choices.

We should be clear that this is an issue of direct concrete political relevance. At present, in the United Kingdom, the state uses money that it has raised through general taxation to subsidize a variety of activities that are believed to be worthy, and it taxes others that are believed to be unworthy. For example, those people whose conception of the good is a life spent gambling are penalized, in the form of duty levied on bets, to support, through state subsidy, those whose conception of the good is a life spent watching the Royal Shakespeare Company. If we were to decide that it was illegitimate for the state to act in accordance with judgements of this kind as to the relative merits of different ways of life, it would seem to follow that decisions about which forms of life thrived and which withered away should be left to the free market, the great virtue of which, it might seem, is precisely that it is the way of allocating resources that reflects only the judgements of individuals. Rather than deciding politically that some ways of life deserve encouragement and others discouragement, it might seem plausible to argue that we should just see what it is that people are willing to pay for. If opera lovers are not prepared to pay the real cost of a night at Covent Garden, then why should others be forced, in the form of taxation, to give resources to help them out? Of course it might be argued that the free market reflects the judgements of the wealthy rather more clearly than it reflects those of the poor, but this will hardly help the case for state subsidy of opera, where it is the lifestyle of a cultured and relatively well-off elite that requires assistance. More generally, the way to identify one's intuitions on this precise issue of state neutrality is to think about whether one would reject the free market, and support subsidy, if everybody had equal shares of resources to begin with. For in that case, the market really would reflect people's different choices equally.

While the above example concerns the ways in which the state might or might not be justified in distributing society's resources, thereby indicating the artificiality of our earlier distinction between the equality-related and the liberty-related aspects of contemporary liberalism, we should be clear that state anti-perfectionism also has implications of other kinds. The current British state recognizes only one form of marriage – a monogamous union between a man and woman – and this, as well as having great symbolic effects, feeds through into many aspects of its legislation: tax policy, inheritance rights, and so on. Since this is favouring one form of life over others, over, for example, that valued by homosexuals, it is clearly not anti-perfectionist. The state is making the judgement that some forms of life, and not others, are worthy and warrant state support and encouragement. Here again, any conclusion that the state should be anti-perfectionist, and hence thoroughgoingly agnostic on such questions, would have substantial concrete implications.

In our initial presentation of Rawls's theory we noted that one way of thinking about the veil of ignorance was that it excluded certain sorts of reason from thinking about justice, and we should now be able to see how it is the exclusion of beliefs about particular conceptions of the good that represents the sense in which his theory is anti-perfectionist. The force of denying people in the original position knowledge of their perfectionist commitments is that it models the claim that political morality should take no account of the reasons people might have for such commitments. The idea that justice is derived by thinking about what people would choose who did not know their conceptions of the good is a way of presenting the claim that those conceptions are somehow inappropriate to questions of justice.

Now it is important to see how this claim might relate to *political* morality specifically, and this because of the way in which Rawls has attempted to defend his theory from communitarian objections. The reader will recall that one of the communitarian criticisms of the conception of the person at the heart of Rawls's theory was that it misrepresented the way in which people relate to their ends or values, that in fact we do not think of ourselves as independent from, and able freely to choose, those commitments which give our lives meaning and value. We suggested in our earlier discussion that one way in which Rawls might try to deal with this objection would be to deny that his conception of the person is intended to capture something about our moral experience in general, but rather seeks to model the way in which it is appropriate to think of ourselves *when thinking about justice*, and we can now tie this point in with the emphasis on the specifically political focus of the theory. The claim of those advocating a neutral state is not at all that we should exclude perfectionist ideals from our thinking about how we should lead our lives as individual private citizens. That would be crazy. Rather it is that those moral considerations that quite properly guide us in our private lives are not appropriate to questions of political morality, to questions of how we should organize the political arrangements of our community in the form of the state. Thus, it might be argued, the communitarian criticism of the conception of the person as failing to be true to the phenomenology of our actual moral lives, to our moral experience, misses the point that the conception is not intended to be true to that experience we have as private individuals, but is intended to model the way in which it is appropriate to think of ourselves specifically when it comes to politics and justice.

Whatever the strengths or weakness of this move, and we may have doubts about the schizophrenia that would seem to be involved in this idea that people can bracket or suspend, when it comes to politics, those values to which they are committed as private individuals, the central issue is clearly that of *why* we should exclude reasons from political morality in this way. Here it may be helpful to think about how the question of anti-perfectionism relates to our previous discussion of objectivism and subjectivism. It seems that (restricted) subjectivism quite readily yields the conclusion that the state should not make, or embody in its political arrangements, judgements about which conceptions of the good are better than others, for the simple reason that subjectivism precisely denies that such judgements can be objective or rational. If one citizen's opinion about how to live her life is as good as any other's, or if there is no way of knowing who is right, then it would seem to make sense for the state simply to treat those opinions as equally valid. If there is no objective ground by which to judge a life with theatre more valuable than one with video games, then state subsidy for the Royal Shakespeare Company would seem to have no justification. Here anti-perfectionism follows from the denial that personal ideals are anything more than subjective expressions of preference. Things get more interesting, perhaps, if one believes in the objectivity of judgements about which ways of life are better than others. Given that belief, can it be coherent to hold that reasons that guide people as individuals should not guide the political community in which they live?

Various possible moves might be made by the objectivist anti-perfectionist. One would be to insist upon the point that a life must be freely chosen if it is to be valuable, and to point to the ways in which state perfectionism undermines that freedom. Taxation ultimately rests on the coercive power of the state (those who don't pay get locked up), so that every time I, who value video games, am taxed to pay for somebody else's theatre, my freedom is being infringed. Perhaps it might be argued that state promotion of some, and discouragement of other, ways of life distorts the choices that I make, so that I am denied the information about the actual costs of my choices that I would need to consider my choices genuinely free. Another would be to say that what matters is that we live in a society to whose political arrangements we can all agree and, since we clearly disagree about conceptions of the good, the only way to achieve this is to leave them out of the picture. If we think of this as a moral response to disagreement, in that it is the value of a society to which we can agree that drives the anti-perfectionism, there might alternatively be a practical response to that disagreement, which would take the form of saying that unless we regard our differing conceptions of the good as irrelevant to our political life, there will be continual trouble in the form of conflict and perhaps even civil war. Yet another move might be to insist that while there is nothing wrong in principle with the state embodying decisions about how people should lead their lives, there is little reason to think that it will embody the right decisions, or that it is dangerous to give it power of this kind. We do not seek here to assess the relative merits of these various arguments. Our aim remains that of giving an introductory overview of the issues to come up in the body of the book. In our chapters on the new Rawls, Dworkin and Raz we consider the ideas of three kinds of liberal, two anti-perfectionist and the other perfectionist, and there we shall go into these issues in greater depth.

We have talked about the idea of a neutral state, and since this is a dangerous concept, full of ambiguity, it may be helpful to end our discussion by saying something about the sense of 'neutrality' that is involved here. In the first place, it is clear that the liberal does not seek a political system that is neutral in all matters. The neutral state, which protects the rights of its citizens to pursue their own conceptions of the good, obviously is not neutral between the religious fundamentalist and the secular liberal, for it supports the belief of the latter in a strict separation between church and state. Nor, clearly, is it equally accommodating to the mass murderer and the law-abiding citizen. The point here is that the anti-perfectionist liberal does not argue that the state should be neutral on questions of justice or the right. On the contrary, her view is that the state is justified precisely in acting to protect people's rights, to ensure that justice is done, and this is what permits and requires it to uphold freedom of religion and to protect people from murderers. The kind of neutrality for which she will argue, is neutrality not with respect to questions of the right or of justice, but with respect to questions of the good, with respect to judgements about what makes a life good or valuable. Indeed, it is in order to ensure that all citizens are treated justly and accorded their proper rights that the state is required to be neutral with respect to such judgements. Were the state to get into the business of acting in favour of some ways of life and against others, the anti-perfectionist might argue, it would be failing to treat its citizens justly, failing to protect their right to make their own choices.

Now our examples already make clear that even in the case of those matters with respect to which the liberal state might seek neutrality, conceptions of the good, the neutrality sought is not neutrality of *effects*. A state which acts to protect people's rights will have the effect of favouring some ways of life and not others even if the *justification* of its action is neutral in the sense that it does not involve reference to judgements about the relative merits of those different ways of life. While it is true that the state can prevent someone from committing murder on the right-based grounds that the intended victim has a right to life, and not on the good-based grounds that a life with murder is worse than one without, the effect is the same: neutrality of justification will not be neutral in its effects. If the case of murder seems too stark, consider also the point that the decision of a state to eschew judgements about which ways of life are valuable or worthless will have the effect of favouring inexpensive ways of life over expensive ones. If the anti-perfectionist state is not permitted to subsidize opera, for example, and if opera is relatively expensive, then those whose conceptions of the good include opera will be disadvantaged, at least in comparison to the current situation in which state subsidy does go on. For the anti-perfectionist, this non-neutrality of effects is not a problem: the right is prior to the good in the sense that the rights which people have, and which it is the job of the state to protect, come first and stand as constraints on the conceptions of the good which people can choose to pursue.[4] If some ways of life cannot survive in a society in which everybody has what justice demands, and without perfectionist political action on their behalf, then that is unfortunate for those who favour such ways of life but no reason for the state to help them. Rather, they will have to revise their conception of the good to fit the constraints imposed by the priority of the right.

The anti-perfectionist liberal, then, argues for a state that is neutral in a specific and restricted sense: it is neutral between conceptions of the good and not on matters concerning justice or the right, and even with respect to the former it is not neutral in its effects, only in its justifications for action. We conclude by indicating two distinct kinds of objection that the perfectionist, whether liberal or communitarian, may raise against the demand for this particular kind of state neutrality: a worry that valuable ways of life will not survive without state support, and a more deep-rooted rejection of the very distinction between the right and the good upon which the claim that the liberal state is neutral in *any* sense seems to depend.

On the first, the reader will recall our initial characterization of communitarianism as concerned to assert the importance of the community in which the individual lives, in contrast to liberalism's apparent prioritization of the individual and her freedom to choose her own conception of the good, and we have seen, under the heading of asocial individualism, that one aspect of this counter-emphasis focuses on the extent to which it is the community in which people live that provides the cultural resources in terms of which individuals come to understand both themselves and the value of different ways of life. The implication of this in the context of a discussion of anti-perfectionism is that communitarians suspect that some valuable ways of life simply would not survive unless they were promoted by the state. On the one hand, as in the opera example, the free choices of individuals to spend their resources as they prefer might aggregate so as to leave valuable and worthy components of our culture to wither away. On the other, the argument might be that unless a particular valuable form of life, such as monogamous marriage, is given symbolic recognition by the state and embodiment in its public institutions, then it will gradually perish. If, and it is a big if, one thought both that a withering away thesis of this kind was plausible, and that the state was likely to judge correctly about which ways of life are worthy and which not, then considerations of this kind might lead one to argue for some form of state perfectionism.

The second objection is rather more fundamental, for it calls into question the very idea that we can distinguish between the right and the good in the way that the anti-perfectionist supposes. If this objection can be sustained, then the claim that the former is prior to, and requires that the state be neutral with respect to, the latter, will look problematic. Liberalism's pretensions to neutrality, its self-understanding as somehow above the substantive battle about how people should lead their lives may then seem highly misleading. Rather than acting as a neutral arbiter, it might be argued, the liberal state actually smuggles in, under the cover of its category of 'the right', its own particular understanding of how people should live, its own ideal of what makes a life a good one. Instead of eschewing judgements about what makes a life valuable, liberalism consists essentially of the claim that a good life is one which has been freely or autonomously chosen by the person living it. It is in accordance with this claim that the political community supports some ways of life and rules out or discourages others, such as those that require state perfectionism. Far from remaining above the fray, liberalism is built on a particular substantive view about what constitutes people's good, about what are people's essential interests, and talk about the priority of the right over the good only serves to conceal this crucial point.

Since we identified as the very core of Rawls's liberalism the identification of people's highest-order interest in their capacity to frame, revise, and rationally pursue their own conceptions of the good, it is obvious that his theory is substantive to some degree, and our discussion above indicates that pretensions to complete neutrality must be misguided. The question that remains concerns the precise extent to which liberalism can sustain its pretensions to neutrality. If talk about the priority of the right over the good, and claims to neutrality with respect to the latter, make it look as if the liberal can be completely agnostic with respect to the question of what makes people's lives valuable, then attention to the problems inherent in that distinction may reveal that such agnosticism is unavailable. And if it is liberalism's purporting to remain above the substantive battle about how people should live their lives that attracts people to that doctrine, then coming to see the senses in which, its presentation and self-understanding notwithstanding, it requires engagement in that battle may force them to think again. They may, of course, remain liberals, but their liberalism will involve claims that they had thought it able to avoid.

The questions raised by this issue of anti-perfectionism and neutrality are many and complex, partly because we are dealing here with the relatively concrete political implications of the various more abstract strands of argument that have gone before, and these strands can come together in a number of different combinations. As with the previous themes that we have identified, we aim to have done no more than provide a cursory overview of the arguments that are to be presented in greater detail in the bulk of the book. If the reader has a rough idea of what to expect, and of how Rawls's theory can be seen to raise the theoretical issues at stake, she is sufficiently prepared for the next part of the book, in which we consider in turn the ideas of four communitarian theorists.

Notes

1 Kukathas and Pettit, *Rawls*, is a recent book that devotes a few chapters to basic exegesis.
2 This is one of the many helpful points made by Kymlicka, *Liberalism, Community and Culture*, pp. 16–17.
3 Again, this thought is to be found in Kymlicka, ibid., p. 19.
4 Kymlicka, ibid., pp. 21–40, points out that Rawls uses the distinction between the right and the good in several different ways, and here we discuss only the sense that illustrates the specific communitarian objection under discussion. For Rawls's most recent observations on this distinction, see Lecture V of his *Political Liberalism*; which we discuss in chapter 6 below.

PART I

COMMUNITARIAN CRITIQUES

Introduction to Part I

Now that we have an agenda of issues in place, we can begin to explore the dense and confusing terrain for which it is intended to provide some preliminary orientation. Our next four chapters will each be devoted to a detailed examination of the work of one of the four thinkers we have grouped together as communitarian critics of liberalism – Sandel, MacIntyre, Taylor and Walzer. In each chapter, we will be attempting to provide answers to three fundamental questions – answers without which it will not be possible to go on and adjudicate between the opposing sides in this dispute.

First, and most importantly, we will try to summarize the most fundamental and distinctive claims of the thinker under examination, insofar as those claims seem to relate, and to stand in opposition, to the main tenets of liberalism in general and to Rawlsian liberalism in particular. However, it is vital to see that this must involve a great deal more than simply offering a list of theses. For such a list would detach each thesis from the surrounding framework of thought from which it emerges, and so would leave the reader with little idea of why the relevant theorist should want to propound it in the first place; and – as with most human utterances – if we do not know why a given speaker has said something, we are to that degree in the dark about what she actually means by what she has said. For similar reasons, we cannot always assume that two people who say roughly the same thing are committed thereby to exactly the same set of presuppositions or implications. For example,

MacIntyre and Sandel both accuse liberals of deploying a conception of the person that detaches the individual from her ends; but their reasons for making this accusation, and their sense of its consequences for liberalism, are significantly different – and as a result any critique of their positions may have to take a different form in each case. So, if we want to get clear on the plausibility of each communitarian's claims, the ways in which each might be vulnerable to criticism and the degree to which the four communitarians form a group, we must first get clear on *why* they say what they do as well as upon precisely *what* they say. This means that each chapter will involve a great deal of exposition; and it will sometimes embroil us in issues that do not seem immediately or obviously related to the central topic of this book, issues that may seem more philosophical than political. All that we can do is affirm that, in our view, what may look like detours are in fact integral to the thought of the theorist concerned, and that this will become clear by the end of the chapter even if it is less than clear halfway through it.

The two other questions that each chapter is intended to address are in a way implicit in what has already been said. For, of course, the topic as well as the title of this part of the book is 'communitarian critiques'; and this means that we need to demonstrate the sense in which the pertinent claims of each particular theorist appear to be both communitarian in nature and critical of Rawlsian liberalism (since, like many of the communitarians themselves, we are taking Rawls as our representative of the liberal tradition). With respect to both questions, the agenda of issues established in our first chapter will prove invaluable. For, amongst other things, that agenda specifies several concrete ways in which it might be thought that one's understanding of the concept of a community (and of the relation of the individual to the community) must play a central role in any political theory; and it also specifies several concrete ways in which Rawlsian liberalism might be thought to embody an inadequate understanding of these matters. Our attempts to answer these two questions with respect to each communitarian critic will therefore involve explicit reference to our agenda.

Establishing answers to those three questions is an essential preliminary to two further matters which must also be addressed, namely the question of whether the communitarians form a coherent group with shared views and aims, and the question of whether their criticisms of liberalism succeed in hitting and damaging their target. The issue of whether the communitarians form a group will be dealt with in the conclusion to this part of the book; and it will of course draw upon the work of the preceding chapters, since it is only after establishing the sense(s) in which each individual thinker can be called a communitarian that we can establish whether the four thinkers are communitarian in the same (or at least in a similar) sense. The issue of the cogency and power of their individual criticisms of Rawlsian liberalism will be dealt with in the chapter immediately following that conclusion, the one that deals with what we have been calling the new Rawls; and this, too, will presuppose the work of the preceding chapters, since it will amount to an assessment of the degree to which the appearance of anti-liberalism established in those chapters matches the reality – of the degree to which Rawls is really committed to views of which the communitarians are critical.

To summarize: the four chapters and conclusion that go to make up this part of the book form a self-contained whole because they are designed to advance the general argument of the book through a clearly defined set of stages. The four chapters will attempt to provide the reader with answers to the following three questions:

1 What are the central claims of each communitarian thinker insofar as they bear upon the topic of this book, how do they emerge from the more general frameworks of thought in which they are embedded, and what degree of independent plausibility do they possess?
2 In what sense does each thinker count as a communitarian?
3 Why might it seem that each thinker is a critic of liberalism?

The conclusion will attempt to provide an analytical surview of this material, primarily in order to address the following question:

4 To what degree do the four communitarians form a coherent group?

Armed with answers to these questions, the reader should then be prepared for the next stage of the debate, namely an assessment of the degree to which these putative criticisms of liberalism hit their target. That, however, will be the business of chapters 5 and 6, on the new Rawls.

1
SANDEL:
the limits of liberalism

It seems clear that any attempt to understand the communitarian critique of liberalism as a whole must begin with an assessment of the work of Michael Sandel. In the first place, it was the publication of his book *Liberalism and the Limits of Justice* in 1982 that initiated the debate with which we are concerned: even though Alisdair MacIntyre published *After Virtue* the previous year, it was Sandel's book that first elicited the label 'communitarian' and brought about the retrospective recruitment of other writers to that flag. Moreover, Sandel's book is explicitly structured as a critique of John Rawls's work: our decision to use Rawls as our representative liberal is thus no more than a reflection of the choice of the original communitarian thinker. And since Sandel accordingly offers a detailed reading of the text of *A Theory of Justice*, presenting an exegetical summary of Sandel's position will simultaneously make evident the ways in which Sandel sees himself as a critic of Rawlsian liberalism; no inferential leaps or speculative extrapolations will be needed to get from an understanding of the former to an understanding of the latter. We can therefore dispose of two of our three key questions at one and the same time. What may be less evident is the answer to the third of those questions – the sense in which Sandel's position is a communitarian one; but this too will become clearer if we begin with a brief summary of the ways in which Sandel's position relates to our agenda of issues.

Sandel's critique of Rawls clearly involves some version or other of most of the themes on that agenda. First, he argues that Rawls is committed to a conception of the person that is metaphysically rather than substantively flawed. That is, he takes Rawls's substantive political theory to presuppose a certain conception of the essential nature of personhood, a conception that rules out the possibility of a person's being constitutively attached to her ends; and he argues that this conception is invalid and incoherent rather than undesirable – a misrepresentation of the nature of moral experience rather than the advocacy of an unattractive form of moral life. Second, Sandel accuses Rawls of asocial individualism, in that, for Rawls, a sense of community can at best describe a possible aim of antecedently individuated selves rather than a possible ingredient of their identity; in particular, the good of political community is at best participation in a well-ordered system of cooperation for mutual advantage, a system to which the individuals that populate it are in some way logically prior. Third, Sandel claims that Rawls reduces moral choices to arbitrary expressions of preferences, thus committing himself to the subjectivist rather than the objectivist view of morality. Fourth, and as the above points – if true – help to demonstrate, Sandel suggests that Rawls's claim to be neutral between competing conceptions of the good is in reality much less plausible than it may seem. But Sandel also adds a fifth and final line of attack, one not listed on our agenda; he accuses Rawls of implicitly relying upon an intersubjective notion of the self in certain parts of his work, a conception that is inconsistent with the antecedently individuated conception of the self to which he is committed in other areas of that work.

It is the first two of these five elements of Sandel's critique that reveal the sense in which he is a communitarian, since they imply a belief on his part that Rawls has no room in his theory for the idea that individuals might be or become constitutively attached to their community and thereby gain access to a type of human good that they could not achieve on their own. But a full comprehension of any of the elements of Sandel's critique cannot, as we warned earlier, be derived from a summary of the sort offered above, even if that summary provides a useful guide for the reader as she follows the details of our presentation. Such comprehension will rather depend upon coming to see just what Sandel's notions of antecedently individuated selves, intersubjective selves and of constitutive attachments to the community might mean; and that is the task to which this chapter is primarily devoted. Since, however, Sandel's critique is ultimately based upon a claim that Rawls's theory of justice is a contemporary example of deontological liberalism, we must begin by coming to grips with what Sandel means by 'deontology'.

Liberalism and deontology

For Sandel, deontological liberalism is a theory about the primacy of justice amongst other political and moral ideals, one which Rawls himself summarizes in the slogan that the right is prior to the good. As we saw earlier, this slogan is meant to encapsulate the following thesis. Society, being composed of a plurality of persons each with her own aims, interests and conceptions of the good, is best arranged when it is governed by principles that do not themselves presuppose any particular conception of the good; what justifies those principles is not that they contribute to maximizing social welfare or otherwise promote the good, but rather that they conform to the concept of right – a moral category which is given prior to that of the good and which is independent of it.

When formulated in this way, the way favoured by Sandel, we can see that deontological liberalism gives justice primacy in two different but related senses. First, it assigns a moral primacy to justice, asserting that the demands of other political and social values can never be allowed to trump those of justice, that the rights of individual citizens cannot be sacrificed for the sake of other goods or goals. Second, it regards the value of justice as having a privileged justification; the right is prior to the good not only in the sense that its claims take precedence, but also in that its principles are independently derived.

It is this second claim, a claim about the foundation of morals or the derivation of moral principles, that (according to Sandel) distinguishes deontological liberalism from other varieties of that political and moral doctrine. Like many other forms of liberalism, the deontological variety – understood as a substantive or first-order ethical doctrine – stands opposed to consequentialism in that it assigns categorical priority to certain duties and prohibitions. But deontological liberalism is distinctive in also standing opposed to teleology on a foundational or meta-ethical level, in that it derives those unqualified duties and prohibitions in a way that does not presuppose any final human purposes or ends, or any determinate conception of the good life for human beings.

The attractions of combining an assignment of moral primacy to justice with an assignment of foundational primacy are twofold. First, the foundational primacy of justice would justify or account for its unqualified moral primacy: the liberal would be able to claim that justice stands as categorically privileged with respect to particular aims, interests and conceptions of the good precisely because its ground or justification is independent of and qualitatively different from such values. For example, if we regard the ultimate ground of justice as its contribution to social welfare, then we would be forced to admit that the priority of justice was contingent or qualified, since in any circumstances in which unjust rather than just action would make the greatest contribution to social welfare, we would be obliged to act unjustly. Second, if the derivation of the principles of justice did make reference to particular conceptions of the good, then the primacy assigned to them would in effect constitute the coercive imposition of one conception of the good upon persons who might hold differing conceptions of the good. So, in order to establish that the moral primacy of justice is both secure and non-coercive, it would seem that we need to provide a derivation of the principles of justice that grounds them in something other than the multiplicity of competing and circumstance-dependent aims, interests and ends adopted by human beings.

Kant, the greatest of classical deontological liberals, provides that ground in his account of the nature of the human subject; it is his theory of the person or conception of the self that explains the categorical priority of the right over the good. For Kant, human beings are possessed of a will and are capable of exercising it freely; they are capable of autonomous action. It is this capacity, rather than the results of exercising it, that is most fundamental to the dignity and worth of human beings because it distinguishes humans from other animals and elevates them above the realm of causally determined nature. What makes them a human subject at all is not the particular aims, interests and conceptions of the good that they decide to adopt and follow, but rather the capacity to think and act autonomously which is made manifest in such decisions. In other words, on the deontological view Kant exemplifies, what matters above all for human beings is not the ends we choose but the capacity to choose that is thereby presupposed; and if that capacity must be given prior to any particular end it is employed to affirm, then what really matters about the human subject is given prior to its ends. In short, just as the right is prior to the good, so the subject is prior to its ends; the deontological assignment of absolute priority to justice is paralleled by its assignment of absolute priority to the subject.

With this brief account of the nature of deontological liberalism in place, we can see the intended force of Sandel's claim that Rawls is a deontological liberal. In the first place, this characterization highlights Rawl's attribution of absolute *moral* primacy to justice:

> Justice is the first virtue of social institutions, as truth is of certain systems of thought. A theory however elegant and economical must be rejected or revised if it is untrue; likewise laws and institutions no matter how efficient and well-arranged must be reformed or abolished if they are unjust . . . Being first virtues of human activities, truth and justice are uncompromising. (*TJ*, pp. 3–4)

Second, it also highlights his attribution of foundational primacy to justice:

> We should . . . reverse the relation between the right and the good proposed by teleological doctrines and view the right as prior. (*TJ*, p. 560)

And third, it highlights the fact that Rawls assigns this twofold priority to justice because of his conception of what is fundamental to human personhood. Rawls's commitment to the regulation of society by principles of justice that do not depend upon any particular conception of the good is the direct result of his view that what really matters about human beings is their capacity to set, pursue and revise their own conceptions of the good; it reflects his explicit claim that people have a 'highest-order interest' in protecting that capacity. A state which, when regulating the lives of its citizens, encouraged or discriminated against particular conceptions of the good life for human beings (beyond the exclusion of those whose pursuit would violate the rights of other citizens) would fail to permit the full and equal exercise by all citizens of their capacity freely to determine how they should live. In short, human beings

understood as moral personalities are most fundamentally autonomous choosers of ends, and society must be organized in such a way
as to respect this feature of personhood above any other.

Rawls's theory of the person

As it stands, Rawls's conception of the subject is a claim about what
is most worthy of respect in our treatment of human beings; it is a
substantive moral position, and one which (as we saw earlier) Rawls
explicitly acknowledges as central to his theory. According to
Sandel, however, this first-order ethical view of the locus of human
worth presupposes in turn a particular second-order theory of the
self and its constitution to which Rawls has not acknowledged his
commitment; it presupposes a foundational account of the person, a
philosophical anthropology. Such a second-order account might
most generally be called metaphysical; it has to do with claims
concerning the essential nature of human subjectivity rather than
with claims about how people should be treated – its focus is upon
what selfhood consists in and how it is formed, fixed or bounded. In
the case of Kant, the metaphysical view of the self, which grounded
his moral claim that human beings had an absolute right to be
treated as ends rather than means, involved him in claims about a
noumenal realm beyond space and time in which all human beings
participated insofar as they were rational; human beings were dual-
aspect beings, a part of nature and yet simultaneously possessed of
faculties that transcended nature. Rawls wants to avoid this highly
controversial and seemingly unintelligible metaphysical framework.
According to Sandel, however, he is nonetheless committed to a
very specific set of views concerning the nature of the human subject
and its possible forms of identity – views which are most evident in
the way he pictures the relation between the self and its ends.

As we have already seen, the Rawlsian emphasis upon the human
being as an autonomous chooser of ends leads him to assign an
absolute moral priority to the subject over its ends. What most
fundamentally deserves respect in human beings is their capacity to
choose their aims and ends rather than the specific choices they
make; and since that capacity must be given prior to its exercise, the
locus of moral worth in a human being must be seen as given prior
to its ends. According to Sandel, however, this assignment of moral

priority is both matched and explained by his assignment of a metaphysical priority. Sandel claims that, for Rawls, the essential unity or identity of the self is also something given prior to the ends that it chooses; and it is the absoluteness of this metaphysical priority that accounts for the absoluteness of the moral priority. What is this metaphysical priority, and why does Sandel think that Rawls is committed to it?

Sandel bases his claim on certain passages from *A Theory of Justice* that seem to have a metaphysical rather than a moral ring to them. For example, at one point, Rawls says that '. . . the self is prior to the ends which are affirmed by it; even a dominant end must be chosen from among numerous possibilities . . .' (*TJ*, p. 560). In other words, the subject's ends are hers because she chooses them, and so presumably there must be a self already around to do the choosing. It seems to follow that the constitution of the self (its shape or identity) cannot be the result of the ends it chooses, for its unity is established prior to its making any given choice during the course of its experience. And this is a consequence which Rawls seems happy to embrace: 'The main idea is that given the priority of right, the choice of our conception of the good is framed within definite limits . . . The essential unity of the self is already provided by the conception of right' (*TJ*, p. 563). According to Sandel, this antecedant unity of the self means that, no matter how heavily an individual is conditioned by her surroundings, she is always and irreducibly prior to her values and ends; her sovereign agency is not dependent upon such circumstance but guaranteed in advance. Thus, to go against the Rawlsian assignment of absolute priority to the right over the good is not simply to commit an error in moral reasoning – to go wrong on the substantive level. It is to go wrong on the metaphysical level, to contradict our essential nature as persons.

> What we cannot do is express our nature by following a plan that views the sense of justice as but one desire to be weighed against others. For this sentiment reveals what the person is, and to compromise it is not to achieve for the self free reign, but to give way to the contingencies and accidents of the world. (*TJ*, p. 575)

In other words, Rawls sometimes seems to claim that a human being's capacity autonomously to choose its ends is not just one amongst many equally valuable capacities or features but rather forms the essence of her identity. It therefore follows that respect for human autonomy is not just one value amongst many in human life, but an absolutely fundamental one which must always trump any other; for to fail to respect that capacity is to fail to respect a metaphysically fundamental feature of personhood. In short: a subject for whom justice is the first virtue is not just an autonomous chooser of ends but an antecedently individuated subject; a self for whom justice has absolute priority over all other values is a self whose bounds are fixed absolutely prior to its choice of ends.

The original position

Sandel's view is that this metaphysical picture of the self as antecedently individuated is not only required to account for the absoluteness of the priority that Rawls assigns to autonomy; its centrality also becomes manifest in the details of his theory of justice. In particular, it is a vital component of the original position, which is of course the fulcrum of Rawls's project of justifying his theory of justice; every argument in his book passes through that imaginative construct. If his metaphysical picture of the self is indeed embedded within the original position, then it is undeniably at the foundation of his thought.

Sandel claims that Rawls makes certain significant assumptions about how the parties to the original position view themselves and their society when they deliberate – assumptions other than the imposition of constraints upon their knowledge which is dramatized in the veil of ignorance. According to Sandel, such further assumptions are essential: for in order to determine what the parties will decide when considering how the basic institutions of their society ought to be constructed, we must attribute to them some conception of the nature of society and of what they want from it, and so some conception of how they stand in relation to it and to its other members.

These assumptions are held to emerge when, for example, Rawls summarizes the conditions that engage the virtue of justice (the circumstances of justice): 'One can say, in brief, that the circumstances of justice obtain whenever mutually disinterested persons put forward conflicting claims to the division of social advantages under conditions of moderate scarcity' (*TJ*, p. 128).

According to Sandel, such a way of formulating the form and nature of the conflict that engenders the need for principles of justice makes sense only if Rawls is assuming that the parties to the original position will think of society as a cooperative venture for mutual advantage. For Rawls's talk of 'social advantages' seems to give exclusive weight to a conception of social membership as a source of personal advantage; it seems to imply that the sole (or at least the primary) reason people engage in social relations is to derive personal benefit from advantages that could not be accrued other than by such cooperation. Further, Rawls describes the parties as 'mutually disinterested', that is as concerned to advance their own conception of the good and no one else's, and as not bound to each other by prior moral ties when advancing those ends.

Again, as with the constraints of the veil of ignorance, Sandel is aware that Rawls is not claiming that the mutual disinterest and lack of prior moral ties attributed to parties to the original position hold for persons in real life. They are assumptions built into a device of representation, not sociological generalizations, and it is perfectly possible that when the veil of ignorance is lifted the parties may find that they are tied by sentiment and affection to others and want to advance their interests. According to Rawls, his assumptions simply have the merit of clarity, simplicity and weakness; assuming benevolence rather than mutual disinterest 'would defeat the purpose of grounding the theory of justice on weak stipulations' (*TJ*, p. 149). But Sandel finds such a justification of these assumptions insufficient. An assumption of benevolence would not be conceptually more problematic or contentious than one of mutual disinterest; and if Rawls means that assuming mutual disinterest is weaker in the sense of being more realistic, then he is embedding a controversial empirical generalization into a device of representation that is supposed to test our convictions about moral and political values. In reality, Sandel claims, Rawls builds these assumptions into the motivation of the parties because they flow from his conception of the subject and its relations to its ends.

Sandel attempts to justify this claim as follows. He points out that Rawls's picture of society as a system of cooperation between people each of whom possesses her own conception of the good is one way in which he stresses the fundamental plurality and separateness of individuals: '. . . the plurality of distinct persons with separate systems of ends is an essential feature of human societies' (*TJ*, p. 28).

Of course, on this picture it is perfectly possible for one person's systems of ends to overlap or coincide with another; if it were not there could be no basis for cooperation. But such an identity of interests is not itself an essential or fundamental feature of human society; on the contrary, according to Rawls's formulation, it is the separateness of each person's system of ends which is essential, whereas the possible overlap of any of those systems is a happy accident that is sometimes actualized and sometimes not.

In short, according to Sandel, Rawls assigns a different degree of metaphysical importance to two obvious facts about human beings – the fact that each person is one distinct being amongst a multiplicity of other such beings, and the fact that the interests and goals of any given person can overlap or coincide with those of any other. He regards the plurality and separateness of persons as an aspect of the fundamental nature of human subjectivity (treating such separateness from others as just a part of what it is to be a person); but he regards any actual coincidence of their chosen ends as at best a happy fact about their circumstances. Metaphysically speaking, we are distinct individuals first and only later do we form relationships with others and engage in cooperative activity; so those relationships cannot be integral to our constitution as selves. On Sandel's view, regarding society as primarily a system of cooperation involves viewing its members as already constituted individuals when they enter into it for their mutual advantage; they need not be selfishly motivated when they do so, but they are essentially constituted as selves in advance of any such engagement with others. In this sense, the plurality of persons is prior to their unity.

Sandel argues that the assumption of mutual disinterest has similar metaphysical underpinnings. It is of course not an assumption that human subjects are motivated only by self-interest or selfishness; but it is, he claims, an assumption about the form of the relationship between a human subject and its motivations in general (whether selfish or selfless): 'Although the interests advanced by [their] plans are not assumed to be interests in the self, they are interests of a self that regards its conception of the good as worthy of recognition' (*TJ*, p. 127). All interests must be the interests of some individual subject; more specifically, they must be the interests of an antecedently individuated subject. They are the interests of a self in the sense that they are merely possessed by that self; the identity of that self is not constituted by any of those ends –

my ends are always mine, never me. According to Sandel, Rawls assumes not just that all human beings are individuals, but that they are individuated (their identity is fixed) prior to the ends, desires or interests that they may possess; the self is prior to its ends: 'It is not our ends that primarily reveal our nature' (*TJ*, p. 560).

The flaws in Rawls's theory of the person

Let us suppose that Sandel has correctly identified the philosophical anthropology that underlies Rawls's theory of justice and his emphasis upon the moral personality of human beings as residing in their capacity to be autonomous choosers of ends. What objections does he make against this conception of the person as antecedently individuated? After all, it places no restriction upon the content of individual's desires and ends; Rawlsian selves are as likely to be benevolent as to be selfish when the veil of ignorance is lifted, and the fact that all interests must be interests of a self does not entail that they must be self-interested.

According to Sandel, there are three main reasons for concern. The first is that Rawls's conception of the person entails that a person's goals, aims and ends are always things that she chooses to attach herself to; they are related to her (and therefore presumably detachable from her) by an exercise of her will. This voluntaristic picture is not the only available way of characterizing our relation to our ends. For example, one might suggest that in many cases human beings relate to their ends through acts of cognition rather than acts of will; they come to commit themselves to a certain goal or life-project as the result of a process of self-scrutiny, and regard that commitment as a manifestation of a deeper self-understanding. On such a picture, establishing one's own ends is not a matter of choosing from a menu of available possibilities, but one of discovering what one's ends really are or ought to be; and then my fundamental preference, in morality as well as politics, would surely be for the conditions of self-knowledge rather than the conditions of choice. In short, Rawls's voluntaristic emphasis in his picture of the self's relation to its ends excludes *a priori* certain alternative emphases which have a long tradition in moral and political thought; his conception of the self is thus neither neutral nor uncontroversial on this matter.

The second reason for Sandel's concern is more important, and has to do with how Rawls understands the ways in which a person might identify with the ends to which she is committed. If the self is antecedently individuated, then no matter how closely it identifies with a given end, that end can never become integral to the self's identity. The characterization of such values or interests must describe the objects that I seek, not the subject that I am; my identity is fixed in advance of my choice of ends, so that a certain distance between who I am and what I value must always remain.

> One consequence of this distance is to put the self beyond the reach of experience, to make it invulnerable, to fix its identity once and for all. No commitment could grip me so deeply that I could not understand myself without it. No transformation of life purposes and plans could be so unsettling as to disrupt the contours of my identity. No project could be so essential that turning away from it would call into question the person I am. Given my independence from the values I have, I can always stand apart from them; my public identity as a moral person 'is not affected by changes over time' in my conception of the good.[1]

Such a conception of the self rules out the possibility of being torn between several competing values in a way which I experience as the pull of competing identities within my self; in other words, it permits no intra-subjective understandings of the self. And by the same token, it limits Rawls's understanding of the relation between a self and any other-directed (in particular, any community-directed) end to which that self is committed. The problem Sandel detects here arises not because Rawls's conception fails to admit of the possibility that human beings may take as their goal or object the good of another or of a group of others; it arises because such ends must be held in a way that ensures that they can be no more than the interests of a person – they can at best be possessed by the self, they cannot be integral to it. Rawls thus excludes the possibility of purposes and ends held in common with others that inspire more expansive inter-subjective self-understandings, ones in which I identify myself with that community and regard my membership of it as essential to who I am.

In general, then, Rawls's conception of the self as antecedently individuated excludes any understanding of the relation between the self and its ends and circumstances that implies that the boundaries of the self might be disrupted, whether by personal commitment, by intra-subjective conflict or by intersubjective relationships. But human moral and political life and experience abounds with examples that can only be described in these ways. We need only think of people who build their lives around a cause and whose life is accordingly devastated by the failure of that cause; of people whose sense of themselves is torn apart by conflicting desires or aims; of our tendency to attribute responsibility and acknowledge obligations to family, tribe, class or nation as well as to individuals. What this suggests is that, if Rawls's conception of the self *is* an antecedently individuated conception, then it simply cannot account for some of our basic human experiences of, and attitudes towards, agency and self-reflection; it is incapable of coping with the full range of human moral circumstance and self-understanding.

Sandel's third reason for concern is in effect a more specific version of his second worry: this is his belief that Rawls's conception of the self commits him to an impoverished understanding of *political* community. As we have just seen, on Rawls's view a sense of community describes a possible aim of antecedently individuated selves, not an ingredient of their identity. Essentially communal goods thereby find their place only as one type of contender amongst many within the framework decided by the principles of justice. So, individuals who happen to espouse communitarian aims in the political sphere can pursue them, but only within a well-ordered society as defined by Rawls's theory of justice; they cannot question whether that society is itself a community in the constitutive sense. For Rawls, the good of political community is participation in a well-ordered system of cooperation for mutual advantage; the possibility of a public life in which the identity as well as the interests of the participants might be at stake is, according to Sandel, ruled out in advance. The idea that a political community might specify the subject as well as the objects of shared aspirations is thus excluded from any society that accords absolute priority to justice. Once again, this hardly seems to be a weak or uncontroversial assumption about society.

On Sandel's view, then, the constraints imposed by Rawls's conception of the self are multiple and significant. That conception commits Rawls to ruling out in advance anything other than a voluntaristic relation between a self and its ends, any end whose adoption or pursuit might engage with or transform the self, and any possibility that the good of community might consist in a constitutive dimension of this kind. This makes his conception of the self radically inadequate as a reflection of human moral circumstance; and as a result, it entails that any society constructed on Rawlsian principles of justice will be much less neutral between competing conceptions of the good than might have seemed to be the case.

Of course, liberals have never attempted to deny that a society organized according to its principles of justice would discriminate against *some* conceptions of the good that are held by its citizens; it would necessarily and explicitly exclude any such conception whose implementation would violate the rights of other citizens as specified by those principles. But this is essential if autonomy is to be upheld as a general value, for it alone can ensure that any citizen's exercise of her freedom does not interfere with the right of all citizens to exercise that same freedom; any given citizen's autonomy is in this respect limited only by the need to protect the autonomy of all citizens. Apart from this, people in a liberal society are free to choose and live according to any conception of the good that they please; and the structure and policies of that society would not be built upon, and could not be justified by invoking, any particular conception of the good. This does indeed seem to suggest that a liberal society would be maximally neutral between competing conceptions of the good. But Sandel is arguing that the *absoluteness* of the liberal respect for autonomy which underpins their commitment to this neutrality, the unqualified priority of justice which liberalism presupposes, can be justified only by presupposing a commitment to a certain conception of the person. And this commitment has consequences which might significantly alter our conception of the kind and degree of neutrality to which liberalism can validly lay claim.

These consequences are of two different kinds. First, Sandel claims, commitment to this degree of neutrality (between competing conceptions of the good) in the realm of politics is founded upon a surprisingly high degree, and a surprisingly implausible kind, of non-neutrality (about the nature of human selfhood) in the realm of metaphysics. And second, this metaphysical non-neutrality seeps back into, and materially diminishes the amount of neutrality displayed in, the realm of politics and morality. For if Sandel's claim to have identified a set of necessary presuppositions about personhood at the basis of liberal thinking is correct, then a far wider range of conceptions of the good than might have been supposed will in fact be discriminated against in a truly liberal society. Why? Because a vision of the self as antecedently individuated excludes any conception of the good which allows for or presupposes constitutive personal attachments to values, projects and communities; a society built with antecedently individuated selves in mind cannot provide a home for those whose conceptions of the good are built around such constitutive attachments and so founded upon a very different conception of the person.

In the first place, it cannot provide a home for those committed to strongly communitarian conceptions of politics, ones in which a person's membership of a given political community is understood to be a constitutive attachment, a vital aspect of their well-being and identity rather than an attribute or end which they merely happen to possess. According to Sandel, a Rawlsian polis would force its citizens to think of themselves as participants in a scheme of mutual cooperation, deriving advantages they could not have gained by their own efforts, but not tied to their fellow citizens by bonds whose severance or alteration would change their identity as persons. Moreover, the conception of the person that grounds this limited conception of politics also distorts our understanding of non-political social relationships – ones in which the relevant others stand to us not as citizens but as fellow party-members, religious believers or relatives. For example, antecedently individuated selves would be unable to develop and sustain constitutive attachments to members of their family: although a mother might have the good of her children as her primary goal in life, it would not be integral to her sense of her own identity – it could only be an end she happens to have, not an aspect of who she is. If a political community is shown to be founded on a conception of the self that has no room for such non-political attachments, it may thereby lose some of its attractiveness as a vision of politics; and it might also fail to provide a framework within which those who found their conception of human well-being upon such non-political relationships with others can flourish. In short, whether the bond in question is political or non-political, Rawls's theory of justice seems to offer little scope for those who understand their relationships with others as constitutive of their identity as persons.

Sandel is not claiming something that is palpably untrue, namely that liberals have never perceived that such consequences flow from their understanding of what justice requires; for example, the ways in which family structures differentially influence the opportunities of children is a familiar topic in liberal politics. Moreover, the liberal theorist has a justification for regarding such consequences as a price that ought to be paid; for she might, if she wishes, argue that these undeniable goods must be sacrificed to the greater good of justice and the protection of individual rights. Sandel's aim is rather to point out that the sacrifices demanded in the name of justice may be a great deal more significant and extensive than liberals tend to admit, and to argue that any such sacrifices are ultimately made in the name of a conception of the person as antecedently individuated (as metaphysically asocial) which may lack the coherence and attractiveness that the liberal moral claims that it supports seem to possess.

In short, according to Sandel, Rawlsian liberalism is subject to a sort of metaphysical myopia. A certain range of conceptions of the good will be unable to flourish in a truly liberal society because the individualist and asocial metaphysical foundations of liberal principles of justice generate an inability to perceive or acknowledge the varieties of human moral experience around which those conceptions of human good are crystallized and their true worth displayed. What this myopia entails is that the Rawlsian liberal's claim to preserve and maximize the area within which a person's autonomous will may be exercised conceals the imposition of strong and implausible restrictions upon the range of values, projects and conceptions of the good from which that person is permitted to choose. The prime virtue claimed by the proponents of justice as fairness seems to have been put under seige by Sandel's examination of its metaphysical presuppositions.

Liberalism and moral subjectivism

What the preceding section has attempted to demonstrate is that Sandel's critique of liberalism includes versions of three of the five themes or topics on our original agenda of issues. According to

Sandel, Rawls is committed to an incoherent conception of the person as antecedently individuated, and thus lacks any awareness of the ways in which our goods or ends contribute to the constitution of our identity as persons: this is a version of the first theme on our agenda. As a consequence, he believes that Rawls ignores the constitutive importance of social or communal human goods, of goods held in common through which people develop constitutive attachments to others, and so regards the political community in particular merely as a system of cooperation between mutually disinterested individuals rather than as a possible focus of constitutive attachments. This is a version of the second theme on our agenda, that of asocial individualism; but it is a version of only one of the two main strands of argument that we located under that general heading. For Sandel's point is not so much that Rawls ignores the social *origin* of our conceptions of the good (which would be a philosophical/sociological error about the importance of the social matrix for our acquisition of any of our individual ends or goals), but rather that he is blind to the constitutive importance of conceptions of the good whose *content* or focus is inherently social (which is a failure to see the true significance of those specific ends that regard our links to others as helping to fix our individual identity). And by making these two points Sandel casts doubt upon the liberal claim to maximal neutrality between competing conceptions of the good – which is the fifth theme on our agenda.

As we have seen, the source of all these liberal ills, for Sandel, is the Rawlsian conception of the person. The Rawlsian view of the relation between society and the individual, and the degree to which the Rawlsian state fails to live up to its claim to neutrality, are not just dispensable adjuncts to Rawls's central concerns but rather make manifest that which drives his theory as a whole; they result from the conceptual blinkers imposed upon that theory by its conception of the person as antecedently individuated and so incapable of constitutive attachments. In this section, we will trace out Sandel's reason for thinking that this conception of the self also leads Rawls into a particular picture of the process by which an individual chooses her ends or conception of the good – one in which such choices are seen as arbitrary expressions of preference, and which seems to imply that moral judgements in general are entirely subjective (the fourth theme on our agenda).

When Rawls discusses the question of how individuals would set about exercising the freedom that a liberal society provides for them – how they would choose a conception of the good, for example – his picture of the exercise of rationality in this domain is as follows:

> We can say that the rational plan for a person is the one (amongst those consistent with the counting principles and other principles of rational choice once these are established) which he would choose with deliberative rationality. It is the plan that would be decided upon as the outcome of careful reflection in which the agent reviewed, in the light of all the relevant facts, what it would be like to carry out these plans and thereby ascertained the course of action that would best realize his more fundamental desires. (*TJ*, p. 417)

Sandel fixes upon this final emphasis on desire, and interprets it as having two crucial consequences. In the first place, Rawls seems to be restricting the focus of deliberation to the self's desires without leaving room for deliberation about the self understood as the subject of these desires. Apart from conforming to the basic tenets of instrumental rationality (for example, employing more rather than less effective means to a given end), the full extent of the individual's decision-making process seems to amount to determining the various plans or goods that are available and their likely consequences, and establishing the existence and relative intensity of her own desires. If this is so, then the agent's self-reflection seems to go no further than a sort of introspection – in order to decide how to live, one need only weigh the relative intensity of one's existing wants and desires. In other words, although the self's desires and wants are to be inspected, the self as subject of those desires is not; we can reflect upon the kind of desires we have, but not upon the kind of selves we are. Self-reflection does not seem to extend to asking who we really are – it only involves asking what we really feel.

Sandel regards this emphasis as entirely to be expected, given Rawls's conception of the person. If the self is antecedently individuated, then the kind of beings we are is given entirely independently of any form of reflection or agency and so not subject to revision by them; indeed, if all of our ends, goals and beliefs are at best contingent attributes of the self (things that we possess or have rather than features that are integral to our identity), then there can be nothing in the self to reflect upon – it is barren of constituent traits. For Rawls, the identity of the subject can never be at stake in moments of choice or deliberation, for the bounds that define it are beyond the reach of the agency that would contribute to its transformation.

Sandel's second reason for focusing upon Rawls's picture of rational choice as a matter of weighing the relative intensity of desire is that it suggests to him that Rawls views the final stage of such deliberation as a matter of bare expressions of preference. This is a suggestion that seems to be supported by several remarks in *A Theory of Justice*. For example, according to Rawls, since the rational principles mentioned above do not specify a single best plan of life, 'a great deal remains to be decided . . . We eventually reach a point where we just have to decide which plan we most prefer without further guidance from principle . . . We may narrow the scope of purely preferential choice, but we cannot eliminate it altogether . . .' (TJ, pp. 449, 551, 552). Sandel points out that if decision is a matter of weighing existing desires and wants, then the process of choosing a life-plan is not really a matter of choice at all: the agent merely introspects, establishes the presence of a given desire and then acts upon it – it is a matter of taking a psychic inventory, not choosing the values she would profess or the aims she would pursue. Of course Rawls could allow for the presence of second-order desires on a given person's inventory – that is, an agent could find that she possesses desires about her desires, perhaps a desire that she have certain first-order desires rather than others. But this second layer will not really alter the situation, since the agent would still have only the fact of this second-order desire to establish and its intensity to assess; her only ground for justifying or defending this second-order desire would be its existence and force. In particular, she could not affirm it as essential to her own identity as an agent, since on Rawls's view (according to Sandel) the identity of the agent is barren of constituent traits and so it simply cannot be argued that a given desire is integral or essential to it.

The main thrust of Sandel's critique here should by now be a little clearer. Rawl's picture of deliberation rests upon the notion of a psychic inventory of present desires and wants; and his conception of the person as antecedently individuated relegates those desires and wants to the status of ultimately contingent attributes of the self. But if my conception of the good is based upon such essentially contingent facts about me, then my commitment to that conception has no more worth or validity than they do; as the product of my desires, that commitment is no less governed by contingency than they are, and so has no deeper basis than the sheer fact that I happen to hold them with a certain degree of intensity. In short, my choices of ends or conceptions of the good are arbitrary; they give expression to my preferences, but can be given no less subjective and no more rational a basis than that. According to Sandel, Rawls's conception of the self pushes him into a position of general moral scepticism, and one which fits well with the liberal commitment to neutrality. For, of course, if no given conception of the good can be assigned a more rational or objective justification than any other, then it would simply be crazy to attempt to construct a society based upon any such conception. For Sandel, Rawls's reason for asserting that the state should treat any individual's choice of conception of the good as if it were an expression of personal preference is not (or not merely) that to do otherwise would violate the state's neutrality; it is his belief that this is all that such choices really are. 'That we have one conception of the good rather than another is not relevant from a moral standpoint. In acquiring it, we are influenced by the same sort of contingencies that lead us to rule out a knowledge of our sex and class.'[2]

The difference principle

One might think that the four Sandelian criticisms so far touched on, if valid, are sufficiently damning in themselves to demonstrate at Rawls's theoretical edifice is radically flawed; but Sandel wishes to press his critique further. He argues that, as well as presupposing an inadequate and controversial metaphysical conception of the self as antecedently individuated, Rawls's theory of justice must at other points presuppose a very different conception of the self if its principles are to be regarded as valid. In short, he wishes to demonstrate that Rawls is committed to two contradictory conceptions of the self at one and the same time.

The need for an alternative conception emerges most clearly in Rawls's defence of the difference principle. As we saw in our Introduction, he argues that one of the key principles that would be agreed upon by parties to the original position is the following: that only those social and economic inequalities that work to the benefit of the least advantaged members of society will be permitted. Rawls defends the claim that such a principle determines a truly just distribution of social and economic resources by arguing that it would be unjust to permit a social system in which those endowed with social and economic advantages (wealth, status, power) or natural advantages (talents, abilities) benefit more than those who lack them. Such assets – whether social, cultural or natural – are not deserved by their possessors; the distribution of such assets is entirely a matter of contingency and so is wholly arbitrary from a moral point of view, no better than a lottery. No one deserves to be endowed with intelligence, any more than she deserves to be born into a wealthy or powerful family, or to be provided with high-quality education or training: 'There is no more reason to permit the distribution of income and wealth to be settled by the distribution of natural assets than by historical and social fortune' (*TJ*, pp. 73–4). Since my possession of these assets is arbitrary, it would be unjust to regard me as the rightful possessor of the rewards that flow from their employment; and the difference principle represents an agreement to regard the distribution of natural talents as a common asset, an agreement to share the benefits of this distribution whatever it turns out to be.

It is important to note that, if the notion of desert has no application to a person's assets, certain kinds of entitlement do play a role. Since it is in the general interest that I cultivate and exercise the talents I possess, so that society as a whole may benefit from their fruits, society is typically arranged so as to provide resources and incentives for their cultivation. Rawls is perfectly happy to say that I am entitled to my share of the resulting benefits when I have qualified for them under the terms specified. However, these claims are legitimate expectations created by institutions designed to elicit my efforts, not primordial rights based upon virtues I possess; they presuppose the existence of the cooperative scheme, and have no validity independently of those institutional arrangements. Rawls thus has a twofold reason for asserting that I do not deserve the fruits of my talents: to do so, I would have to possess the talent non-arbitrarily and have a pre-institutional right that society value this particular talent rather than some other one. On Rawls's view neither condition holds.

The possibilities opened up by this form of argument are worth contemplating; for example, Sandel notes in passing that it is often used – although not explicitly by Rawls – to justify policies of positive discrimination. With respect to this issue Dworkin has argued[3] that no individual can claim that her rights have been violated by an affirmative action programme that entails, for example, that some black candidates are admitted to medical school with lower qualifications than some white candidates who are excluded, because no one – black or white – *deserves* to go to medical school to begin with. Someone's possession of the relevant characteristics is a matter of good fortune and so simply does not constitute a basis for desert. At best, we can talk about entitlements or legitimate expectations; but these have no pre-institutional validity, and so cannot be determined independently of the existence and rationale of those institutions. No one is entitled to demand that medical schools reward any particular talent or characteristics they possess (for example, intelligence or medical aptitude), because what counts as a characteristic meriting such a reward depends solely upon the qualities deemed relevant to the social purposes the institution serves. In the case of medical schools, intelligence is clearly relevant to the purpose of saving lives, but a range of other characteristics may also be relevant to other purposes; and if it is decided that society wishes to utilize these institutions as means of increasing the number of blacks in socially strategic professions, then colour of skin will count as relevant as well. Just as whites are not excluded out of contempt but out of an instrumental calculation of the sort that justifies the more familiar criteria, so blacks are included not out of a belief that skin colour has intrinsic worth but out of the belief that in certain circumstances skin colour is a socially useful trait. This defence of affirmative action thus relies upon precisely the understanding of natural assets, desert and entitlement that underlies Rawls's defence of the difference principle.

According to Sandel, it is easy to see how this Rawlsian view of natural assets as failing to provide the basis of desert emerges very smoothly from a theory committed to a conception of the person as antecedently individuated. According to that conception, my specific talents, character and motivations are contingently given and wholly inessential attributes of my self – they are inessential to my being the particular self that I am. Such a self's identity is preserved by its invulnerability to transformation by experience or circumstance: if it is not defined or constituted by such things as its talents, then it cannot be transformed or redefined by their alteration or loss.

More specifically, a principle of distribution that regards those talents as common assets and redistributes their fruits to others cannot be said to violate the self by treating it as a means to social ends; for it is not persons but their attributes that are being so used. For a talent to constitute a basis for desert, it must be something that I possess in an undistanced, constitutive sense of possession: if I deserve a high grade in a course, for example, then it must be in virtue of some fact about me as a person. On Rawls's view, however, there are no such facts; there are no attributes I possess that are integral to my identity. And if there is nothing of that kind that I can be said to possess in the relevant sense, then nothing of that kind can provide me with a basis of desert. I do not deserve to benefit from the use of my natural or social endowments – not because they are arbitrarily given, but because they are non-constitutively possessed.

The fit between the difference principle and Rawls's conception of the self thus looks to be a very neat one. However, two immediate problems emerge if we follow Sandel and look a little more closely at the way these two claims hang together. In the first place, in order to defend his claim that people do not deserve the fruits of their talents, Rawls is forced to press very hard indeed on the distinction between persons and their talents, character, abilities and assets; he distinguishes so sharply between the self and its possessions that he risks falling into the Kantian trap of making the subject radically disembodied. The Rawlsian subject is so shorn of its empirical characteristics as to leave it little more than an abstract, pure consciousness that floats behind every one of its traits; and this seems incoherent. If the difference principle is indeed based upon such a conception of the self, this is hardly an argument in its favour. In the second place, even if we accept that the distinction between the self and its possessions does justify the conclusion that individuals do *not* deserve or possess their natural assets, it does not justify the conclusion that society *does*. After all, our bodily parts are in this sense natural assets and their distribution is arbitrary from a moral point of view; but we do not think that society has a right to redistribute them, for example to redistribute one eye from those lucky enough to have two to those unfortunate enough to have none at all. Is not the location of natural assets in the province of the community just as accidental and arbitrary from a moral point of view as their attribution to the subject? Why not simply regard them as unattached in advance to any particular subject?

In short, Rawls's conception of the self as antecedently individuated leaves the difference principle without an adequate justification and open to the charge of presupposing an incoherent account of personhood. The only way in which Rawls might justify his presumption that assets not possessed or deserved by individuals *are* possessed and deserved by society is by making use of a very different conception of the subject. Instead of claiming that the difference principle is justified because my assets rather than my person are thereby utilized for others, Rawls might question the sense in which those who share in 'my' assets are properly called 'others'. If Rawls allowed that the relevant description of the self might sometimes incorporate more than a single empirically individuated human being, he could then argue that these assets are common because they belong to a common subject of possession – the community. If my identity as an individual is partly constituted by my membership of the community, if I identify with it and my fellow members in a constitutive sense, then a redistribution of the fruits of my labours to other members of that community is not a case of using me as a means towards the ends of entirely distinct individuals. I will then not experience redistributive taxation as a violation of my integrity as a person because I have a sense of community that is strong enough (sufficiently integral to my sense of my own identity) to transcend such purely individualistic reactions.

Certain passages in *A Theory of Justice* suggest that Rawls is not unaware of the trend of his own thinking on this issue. Indeed, at one point he says: '. . . the difference principle represents, in effect, an agreement to regard the distribution of natural talents as a common asset and to share in the benefits of this distribution whatever it turns out to be' (*TJ*, p. 101). But Sandel's claim is that treating natural assets in this way can only be justified by invoking an intersubjective conception of the self and a constitutive conception of community – both of which Rawls is officially committed to rejecting.

Agreement in the original position

A similar need to invoke an intersubjective conception of the self also seems to emerge if we return to the original position and enquire more closely into the way Rawls imagines people coming to agreement on the principles of justice.

The original position is a dramatized expression of Rawls's contractarian approach to social and political issues; his principles of justice are defined as those that would be freely agreed upon by everyone behind the veil of ignorance. However, just as the original position is a device of representation rather than an actual location, so the contract which is the outcome of deliberation in the original position is a hypothetical rather than an actual contract. Like actual contracts, hypothetical ones presuppose the plurality and distinctness of the parties to the contract, and emphasize the element of choice involved in consenting to them. Unlike actual contracts, however, the Rawlsian hypothetical contract cannot turn out to be unfair: because of the veil of ignorance there can be no differences of power or knowledge amongst the parties, and there is no possibility that a hypothetical agreement might be implicated in the (possibly unfair or coercive) practices and conventions of a given actual society. If, then, the parties are in a situation such that no unfairness could result, the agreement reached in the original position will be an instance of pure procedural justice; its outcome is fair no matter what, purely by virtue of the fact that it is agreed to.

The important question for Sandel arises here; for if the original position is constructed so as to *guarantee* that any agreement reached in it is fair, then what scope is there for the exercise of choice by people in the original position? Although they are theoretically free to choose any principles they wish, their situation is such as to guarantee that they will wish to choose only certain principles, upon which they will unanimously converge. As Rawls puts it: 'The acceptance of these principles is not conjectured as a psychological law or probability. Ideally anyway, I should like to show that their acknowledgement is the only choice consistent with the full description of the original position. The argument aims eventually to be strictly deductive' (*TJ*, p. 121). Sandel argues that the implications of this remark are wide-ranging.

In the first place, it follows that no bargaining can be said to go on in the original position, because bargaining in any sense requires some differences in the interests or knowledge or power or preferences of the bargainers, whereas the veil of ignorance removes any such thing. Neither could any discussion coherently be thought to take place between people, all of whom are assumed to reason in the same way and draw the same conclusions and none of whom has perceptions or concerns that distinguish her from anyone else. And if bargaining and discussion are not possible, then agreement is not possible either; if everyone reasons in the same way and has identical interests and preferences, any given person need only reach a conclusion for herself in order to know that it has been reached by all. In effect, the agreement made in the original position is not a freely willed agreement made with others to abide by certain conditions, but an acknowledgement of the validity of a certain set of propositions (like coming to see that $2 + 2 = 4$). It is something we come to know rather than something we decide, agreement to a proposition rather than agreement with others; it is agreement in a cognitive rather than a voluntaristic sense.

If, however, Rawls's real emphasis in the original position is upon agreement in the cognitive sense, then our earlier assumption that the original position acknowledges and respects the plurality and distinctness of persons begins to look a little hasty. For the veil of ignorance removes every characteristic that distinguishes one person from another; and this means not that everyone is *similarly* situated but that they are *identically* situated – we have no means of distinguishing them one from another. There is no bargaining, discussion or agreement behind the veil of ignorance because the plurality of people which such notions presuppose is absent; what we find behind the veil of ignorance is not many persons but one subject – we find an intersubjective self of precisely the sort against which Rawls has officially turned his face.

Sandel summarizes his claim as follows:

> The secret to the original position – and the key to its justificatory force – lies not in what [the parties] *do* there but rather in what they *apprehend* there. What matters is not what they choose but what they see, not what they decide but what they discover. What goes on in the original position is not a contract after all, but the coming to self-awareness of an inter-subjective being.[4]

This may sound a great deal more ontologically speculative than it really is. Sandel is in essence arguing that Rawls's conception of the original position and its occupants – in other words, his conception of ourselves insofar as we are thinking about justice – seems to involve the attribution of a very strong (indeed, a constitutive) sense of community. Only if we think of ourselves as already bound to one another in our political community will it make sense for us to accept the constraints imposed upon us by the veil of ignorance and its associated features, and to deliberate within those constraints in the sorts of way that Rawls seems to imagine. In short, our propensity to accept the original position as an appropriately designed device of representation for deliberation about justice seems to presuppose an acknowledgement of moral ties binding us to others – ties of precisely the sort that we are forbidden to presuppose or draw upon *within* the original position, in which all parties are stipulated as being mutually disinterested.

This argument therefore precisely parallels Sandel's claim about the difference principle; in both cases he claims to detect a reliance within the Rawlsian theory upon a constitutive sense of community. And this sort of constitutive attachment to our community and to the other members of it, is of course precisely what Sandel thinks that Rawls's official conception of the person (upon which Rawls must rely if he is to justify the assignment of absolute priority to autonomy) forbids. As he puts it: 'We cannot be persons for whom justice is primary and also be persons for whom the difference principle is a principle of justice.'[5]

The limits of liberalism

With that final quotation, we can conclude this attempt to analyse the five main elements of Sandel's critique of Rawls. Having tried to establish Rawls's commitment to a conception of the self as individuated antecedently to its choice of ends and so incapable of constitutive social or communal attachments of any sort, Sandel has gone on to argue that this general commitment results in a conception of the political community as a system of cooperation between mutually disinterested persons, a conception of moral judgements as arbitrary expressions of preference, and a degree of neutrality between competing conceptions of the good that is significantly lower than it might appear. For good measure, Sandel adds the charge that features of Rawls's own theory presuppose the existence of constitutive attachments to the political community whose very possibility is denied by the terms of his official conception of the self.

It should now be clear why Sandel's criticisms of Rawlsian liberalism were labelled 'communitarian'. Rawls's conception of persons as antecedently individuated excludes the possibility that attachment to *any* good or end might ever be integral to one's identity as a person; but what Sandel particularly emphasizes is that it therefore excludes the possibility that any *communal* goods might have such a constitutive role – most specifically, that it commits Rawls to thinking of the *political* community as a scheme for the production and distribution of mutually advantageous benefits between mutually disinterested individuals, rather than as something with which such individuals might identify and through which they might develop and refine their sense of their own identity as individuals. The fundamental importance of such constitutive attachments to the political community is demonstrated, for Sandel, by the fact that some of the most intuitively attractive of Rawls's own political ideas can be seen to presuppose them. And this merely confirms what Sandel takes to be obvious in its own right, namely that our sense of identity is inseparable from an awareness of ourselves as members of a particular family or class or community or people or nation, as bearers of a specific history, as citizens of a particular republic; and that we look to participation in the political realm as a way in which we can develop and refine our sense of ourselves by developing and refining forms of community with which we can be proud to identify. In other words, the restrictions of Rawlsian theory ensure that '. . . it forgets the possibility that when politics goes well, we can know a good in common that we cannot know alone'.[6]

Of course, this does not mean that Sandel regards the values to which Rawls is so explicitly attached – the values of freedom and equality – as unimportant in politics. His worry is rather the degree to which Rawls's theory focuses so exclusively upon them, and the degree to which they are compatible. For, according to Sandel's critique, what commits Rawls to a conception of the self as antecedently individuated is his assignment of absolute priority to individual autonomy, to the individual's capacity to choose her own conception of the good; but Rawls's commitment to equality (for example as manifest in the difference principle) presupposes the very possibility of constitutive communal attachments that his official conception of the self prohibits. As Rawls himself acknowledges, his commitment to equality presupposes the existence and force of the value of fraternity amongst the members of the political community – he identifies the difference principle as an 'interpretation' of fraternity, of our capacity to identify with and care for other citizens (cf. *TJ*, pp. 105ff.); but according to Sandel, the absoluteness of Rawls's commitment to freedom (reflected in the lexical priority he attaches to the principle of equal liberties) prevents him from being able to accommodate that value – even in the lexically subordinate position he wants to give it. In short, Rawls's lexically secondary commitment to equality presupposes the very thing that his lexically primary commitment to freedom places under threat – fraternity. Moreover, setting equality aside, even if most of us would agree that it would be wrong to subordinate liberty entirely to fraternity (sacrificing individual freedoms in pursuit of the goods we can only know in common), it would surely be equally wrong entirely to subordinate fraternity to liberty. For Sandel, a balance must be struck which acknowledges them both; an absolute commitment to one cannot be the best response to the fact that such fundamental values can and do come into conflict in the arena of politics.

Perhaps the most important thing to note at the end of this consideration of Sandel's critique is the degree to which four of its five elements depend for their force upon the validity of the fifth element. We have quoted passages from *A Theory of Justice* that can, it seems, be read in ways that imply that Rawls holds a view of the political community as a cooperative scheme and a view of moral judgements as arbitrary expressions of preference; but a Rawlsian liberal might well dismiss these passages as lax formulations, or as views that are not at all essential to the main elements of Rawls's theory. From Sandel's perspective, what shows that such a dismissal is wrong – what shows that they manifest something integral to Rawls's theory – is primarily the fact that both views are a consequence of Rawls's commitment to a specific conception of the person. Similarly, Sandel's main ground for claiming that Rawlsian theory discriminates against conceptions of the good that focus upon constitutive attachments to projects, values and community is his claim that Rawls conceives of persons as antecedently individuated;

and the notion that Rawls's commitment to the difference principle conflicts with other elements of his theory depends upon the claim that one of those elements is a conception of the person as antecedently individuated. In short, any attempt to defend Rawls against Sandel's critique must focus upon Sandel's attribution of this conception of the person to Rawls: if that attribution can be justified, then the other four elements of Sandel's critique will be massively buttressed, and if it cannot, then the critique as a whole will lack foundations.

The questions that must be answered will, therefore, all focus upon this issue. Does Rawls's conception of justice presuppose a particular conception of the person, and if so is it a conception of the sort that Sandel claims, that is, is it a vision of the person as individuated antecedently to its acquisition of any ends (particularly communal or social ones), and does it function as a general metaphysical claim about the nature of personhood (as opposed, for example, to a conception of the person that is suited to political matters but not moral or metaphysical ones)? If Rawls is not committed to such a conception of the person, then what is it that justifies his assignment of absolute priority to the autonomy of the citizens in his liberal society? How else might he defend his claim that people have a highest-order (not merely a high-order) interest in this capacity – that the right is prior to the good in a way that brooks no compromise whatever? These are the questions that we shall address in chapter 5.

Notes

1 Sandel, *Liberalism and the Limits of Justice*, p. 62. The quotation from Rawls cited in this passage is from 'Kantian Constructivism in Moral Theory', pp. 544–5.
2 Rawls, 'Fairness to Goodness', p. 537.
3 See Dworkin, 'Why Bakke has no Case', in *New York Review of Books*, 10 November 1977, pp. 11–15, reprinted as 'Bakke's Case: Are Quotas Unfair?'.
4 Sandel, *Liberalism and the Limits of Justice*, p. 132.
5 Ibid., p. 178.
6 Ibid., p. 183.

2
MACINTYRE:
morality after virtue

Alisdair MacIntyre's work (in *After Virtue* and succeeding volumes)[1] operates at a much higher level of generality and involves a much broader sweep of moral and cultural history than does Sandel's work. MacIntyre's critical analysis is focused not on one text in contemporary political theory but on the origins, development and decline of Western moral and political culture; so any conclusions of his that might be thought pertinent to Rawlsian liberalism will have application just insofar as Rawls's work can be read as a specific symptom of much deeper and wider cultural movements and attitudes. This means that our exegetical presentation of MacIntyre's framework of thought will necessarily involve the examination of many issues in moral philosophy whose connection with contemporary political theory will not at first be obvious; and it also means that we will afterwards have to indulge in a much higher degree of speculative extrapolation in order to show how MacIntyre's work might be thought to constitute a critique of Rawlsian liberalism than we did with Sandel. On the other hand, MacIntyre does make some references to liberalism in general and to Rawls's work in particular, so the speculations that will follow our exegetical presentation will not entirely lack a concrete textual basis; and the details of that presentation are essential to any attempt to establish why MacIntyre can be regarded as a communitarian thinker.

Even at this stage, however, we can give the reader some preliminary indication of which strands in MacIntyre's analysis will support the claim that he can be read as a communitarian critic of liberalism, by signalling in advance the way in which his conclusions relate to our original agenda of issues. Like Sandel, MacIntyre accuses liberalism of presupposing an incoherent rather than unattractive conception of the person (first theme), and of being committed to a form of scepticism about the possibility of rationality or objectivity in moral matters (fourth theme); in addition, and again like Sandel, he holds that liberalism misrepresents and under-estimates the importance of communal life to the identity and integrity of the individual (second theme), and that liberalism is far less neutral than it claims between competing conceptions of the good life for human beings (fifth theme). However, the way in which MacIntyre sees these various criticisms as relating to one another differs significantly from that of Sandel; in particular, where Sandel regards the asocial individualism of liberalism as the result of its commitment to conception of the self as antecedently individuated, MacIntyre sees things the other way round – he sees the liberal conception of the self as a consequence of liberalism's failure to perceive the importance of the community in the moral life of the individual. And this in turn means that the sense in which MacIntyre is a communitarian thinker is significantly different from the sense in which Sandel can be so categorized.

At the moment, of course, these comparisons and contrasts may be difficult to appreciate; but they are simply designed to give the reader advance warning of the aspects of our exegetical summary that will turn out to be of most importance for our specific purposes.

The predicament of contemporary morality

According to MacIntyre, contemporary moral and political culture is in a state of confusion. He begins *After Virtue* by noting that modern liberal democracies are beset with arguments between people holding opposing moral positions on such issues as the rectitude of abortion, the justifiability of doctrines of deterrence in a nuclear age and the structure of truly just societies; and as yet no widely agreed answer to these questions has emerged. What MacIntyre takes to be worrying about this, however, is not the mere fact that such arguments occur or that they have not yet arrived at a conclusion; his worry is that the form these arguments take guarantees that they can *never* be brought to a rational conclusion.

This is because the moral positions of the participants are fundamentally incommensurable. When a proponent of abortion rights attempts to justify her view, it is of course perfectly possible for her to highlight more basic and general premises that lead her to it; and those premises can themselves be traced back to more fundamental beliefs and values, until we reach the propositions that ground her moral view as a whole. However, when those truly basic premises are brought up against the basic premises of her opponent, it proves impossible to evaluate their relative worth or validity; within the parameters of their own position, each person's opinion is rationally derivable from her more fundamental premises, but the premises themselves are incommensurable with one another. Each invokes concepts that cannot be translated into the concepts invoked by opposing points of view: premises that invoke rights are contrasted with premises that invoke universalizability or the notion of a soul, and there is simply no overarching framework in terms of which these concepts can be compared with one another and the rational superiority of one demonstrated.

This incommensurability entails that any person's choice of basic premises or frameworks cannot be justified against those of her opponent; within a given framework, conclusions follow from premises, but the premises themselves are by definition ungrounded – they are what permits rational justification, and so cannot themselves be rationally justified or undermined. The invocation of one premise or framework against another is thus not something susceptible to rational evaluation; so the argument between proponents of different frameworks is incapable of rational termination. Moreover, if one person's choice of framework cannot be justified to another, then that person cannot justify it to herself either. It is purely and simply unjustifiable – a matter of purely personal preference.

This perception of the arbitrary nature of contemporary moral debate is, however, masked by a feature of the language employed by those who attempt to explain and justify their moral views. For our discourse retains a contrast between personal and impersonal reasons for doing something, and the reasons we offer to others for doing what we think is morally demanded fall into the latter category. An example of a personal reason would be something like 'Do this because I want you to': by saying such a thing I have given my interlocutor no reason for doing what I ask unless she has some other reason for doing what I want – if, for example, I am in a position of authority over her, or she is a relative of mine. An impersonal reason would be something like 'Do this because it is your duty': in this case, whether the reason given for the action is a good one is entirely independent of particular facts about the person speaking or her relationship with her interlocutor – it presupposes the existence of impersonal criteria, of standards which apply to all people regardless of their circumstances, wishes or desires. It is language of this latter sort to which people typically appeal when justifying a particular moral judgement.

In short, according to MacIntyre, the actual processes of moral argument exemplify the clash of personal wills and their arbitrary commitments, but the language in which the arguments take place invoke the existence of impersonal standards by means of which such disputes might rationally be arbitrated. According to a school of moral philosophy called emotivism, this paradox is easily explained: the essence of moral judgements is and has always been that of giving expression to one's personal feelings or attitudes and attempting to do so in a way that will bring others to align their feelings with your own; and the use of language designed to invoke impersonal standards is spurious – it is simply an effective way of bringing about the sought-after realignment.

MacIntyre finds this account of the paradox inadequate. Understood as a thesis about the meaning of moral judgements it fails for the following reasons: first, it fails to explain in a non-circular way the precise nature of the feelings given expression by moral utterances. If one asks what kind of feelings are involved, it will not be sufficient to be told 'feelings of approval', since approval can be of many kinds; but the only way of further characterizing those feelings seems to be as 'feelings of moral approval', which simply reintroduces the term that this analysis was meant to explain. Second, emotivism seems to be engaged in a fruitless task from the outset, because its analysis conflates two kinds of expression whose function in the language (as we have seen) is determined precisely by the contrasts and differences between them. In effect, it collapses the difference between personal and impersonal reason-giving, and thus ignores what seems to be a significant difference in meaning. The reason for this error is to be found in the third of MacIntyre's criticisms, namely that emotivism confuses meaning and use.

Emotivism is a theory about the meaning of sentences, but the expression of feelings or attitudes is characteristically a function not of their meaning but of their use on specific occasions. A schoolmaster might express frustration by screaming '7 × 6 = 42!' at his class, but this has nothing to do with the meaning of the proposition he utters.

In short, emotivism is false if understood as a theory about the meaning of moral utterances, but true if understood as a theory about the use to which such utterances are put in contemporary moral culture. According to MacIntyre, what has happened is that, over time, the meaning and the use of moral utterances have become radically discrepant: at present, we use them as modes of expressing, our fundamentally arbitrary feelings and attitudes, but the meaning of the utterances we employ in this way retains traces of a prior historical period in which impersonal standards were available, and so their present use invokes those criteria in circumstances in which they can no longer be cashed out. Our present culture is indeed an emotivist culture, but it was not always like that.

It is this diagnosis that governs the structure of *After Virtue*; for it sets MacIntyre a twofold task. First, he must flesh out his claim that contemporary culture has become imbued with emotivist attitudes and practices; and second, he must investigate the history of that culture, in order to understand how it became emotivist and thereby to assess the possibility of restoring it to a state in which moral judgements might once again be able to claim real objectivity and impersonality.

The emotivist self

According to MacIntyre

> A moral philosophy . . . characteristically presupposes a sociology. For every moral philosophy offers explicitly or implicitly at least a partial conceptual analysis of the relationship of an agent to his or her reasons, motives, intentions and actions, and in so doing generally presupposes some claim that these concepts are embodied or at least can be in the real social world. (*AV*, p. 22)

In claiming that contemporary culture is emotivist, MacIntyre is therefore committed to claiming that this culture understands itself to be (and is, to some degree, in reality) structured in accordance with the sociology that this particular brand of moral philosophy presupposes.

MacIntyre argues that the social content of emotivism flows from its obliteration of the distinction between manipulative and non-manipulative personal relations. Emotivist moral philosophy regards all moral discussions as no more than attempts by one party to alter the preferences and feelings of another party so that they accord with their own; they involve using whatever means might be effective to bring about this goal. No distinction is drawn between reasons that will influence the person in the relevant way and ones that the person herself will judge to be good; there is no such thing as appeal to genuinely impersonal criteria whose validity the person must judge for herself regardless of her relationship to the speaker. By collapsing the distinction between personal and impersonal reasons, emotivism removes the possibility of treating persons as ends, as rational beings capable of making an independent assessment of what they take to be right; no moral debate can be anything other than an attempt to treat one's interlocutor as a means towards one's own goal, namely that of aligning her feelings to one's own.

If emotivist moral philosophy regards all moral discussion as an instance of a manipulative interpersonal relationship, then emotivist sociology will hold the same view of social relationships *per se*. We can see what the social world seen through emotivist eyes would look like by noting what MacIntyre calls the 'characters' of modern culture. A character is a fusion of a specific role with a specific personality type in a way that emblematizes certain moral and metaphysical ideas embedded in a culture; and the characters of modern emotivist culture are the Aesthete, the Manager and the Therapist. The Aesthete sees the social world as an arena for the achievement of her own satisfaction, a series of opportunities to gain pleasure and at all costs to avoid boredom; other people are the means by which she achieves this. The Manager's goal is to organize and direct her human and non-human resources in order to achieve her goals with maximum efficiency and effectiveness; but she explicitly eschews the task of fixing or evaluating the goals themselves – they are treated as givens (given to her by the market or her shareholders or her directors). The Therapist's concern is purely with the transformation of neurotic symptoms into energy that is redirected towards purposes deemed socially useful; like the Manager, her concern is with technique, efficiency and effectiveness, and she avoids the task of evaluating or advising her patients on the intrinsic worth of the ends they adopt. In short, modern characters agree in treating people as means towards others' ends and in regarding questions of ends as ultimately beyond systematic, rational or objective assessment.

It is by reference to role-models such as these that (MacIntyre claims) the modern individual works out her self-definition. This emotivist self cannot be unconditionally identified with any of the moral viewpoints it takes up; devoid of rational criteria for evaluating such viewpoints, it lacks any conception of limits to what can be evaluated – everything can be subject to criticism from the viewpoint it has adopted, including the viewpoint itself. To be a moral agent is thus to stand back from any and every situation in which one is involved and from every characteristic one may possess, and to regard them all as subject to judgement from a purely universal and abstract viewpoint, one detached from any social particularity. The capacity to be a moral agent is located in the self rather than in any of the social roles or practices that it adopts; the resources for the possession and exercise of moral judgement are to be found in that unencumbered self alone.

As a further consequence, any moral attitude or position that the self takes on must be seen as an expression of ultimately arbitrary and purely personal preference; since they cannot be justified by rational criteria, their only justification for the person who adopts them is the fact that she has freely chosen to do so. This entails regarding the self's relation to its ends as purely voluntaristic; and it also involves regarding that self's transitions from one position or end to another as an essentially arbitrary process. Such a person cannot be said to have a history; there is no way of telling an intelligible story of her movements through moral positions and through life – no narrative thread concerning the development or refinement of her self-understanding.

In effect, then, the modern self that hangs together with and is secreted from the social content of emotivism is fixed or bounded independently of any of its social embodiments or characteristics, and lacks a rational history. Neither its identity at any given time nor its identity over time are fixed by or dependent upon its attitudes, characteristics or life story; neither its personality nor its history are part of its substance; indeed, that substance assumes an abstract and ghostly character.

More generally, of course, this emotivist conception of the self is strikingly similar to the conception of the person as antecedently individuated that Sandel attributes to Rawls. At this stage of MacIntyre's argument, he makes no explicit reference to liberalism in general or Rawls in particular; but those references do emerge later, and it is easy to see why readers of Sandel should have assumed that MacIntyre's analysis of modern culture, and the critique that he builds upon that analysis, might converge with the analysis and criticisms of liberalism offered by Sandel. It seems clear that, for MacIntyre, contemporary forms of liberalism are simply further symptoms of the emotivist disease that he is attempting to diagnose and cure; the Rawlsian self is a version of the emotivist self.

The Enlightenment project

On MacIntyre's view, the emotivist self and the corresponding decline of moral debate into the conflict of arbitrary personal wills first became definitively established during the Enlightenment. More specifically, MacIntyre claims that the emotivist fate of modern culture was sealed when the Enlightenment project of providing a rational justification for morality failed. The attempts of Kierkegaard, Kant, Diderot, Hume and Smith were all uniformly unsuccessful; and although each of their attempts took its own form, MacIntyre is convinced that the reason for their failure was the same in every case.

All of these philosophers agreed to a surprising degree on the nature or content of the morality that they were attempting to justify; none denied that marriage and the family were fundamental moral structures, or that promise keeping and justice were inviolable values. Furthermore, they all largely agreed upon the form that a rational justification of such a morality would have to take: its key premises would characterize some feature or features of human nature, and the rules of morality would be justified as those that a being possessing such a nature would be prepared to accept. The trouble was that the moral rules that they were attempting to justify had originated in a historical and cultural context within which their function was very different from that imagined by those who had inherited the rules but lived in a very different environment.

Those rules had been developed within a wider moral scheme which had dominated the medieval period and had originated with Aristotle. Within that framework, there is a sharp and vital distinction between man-as-he-happens-to-be and man-as-he-could-be-if-he-realized-his-essential-nature; and ethics is seen as the science that enabled human beings to understand how to make the transition from the former to the latter state. What this presupposed is a distinction between potentiality and its fulfilment in reality (the sort of distinction we employ in order to relate an acorn to an oak tree, or a kitten to a cat), and an account of what the true end or fulfilment of human nature might be; it viewed human nature as initially discrepant with the precepts of ethics, and so in need of transformation through experience and the tutelage of practical reason until it fulfilled its potential (reached its telos).

It then follows, however, that the precepts that make up morality will require *both* a conception of untutored human nature *and* one of the telos or end of that nature in order to make any sense; they are intended to help people to achieve human-nature-as-it-could-be-if-it-realized-its-telos, to move them from their present state to a new one. But those Enlightenment philosophers we mentioned had (for a variety of reasons) dispensed with the idea of a human telos, and so of any sense that human nature as it happens to be might be discrepant or discordant with a higher or more fulfilled state. The abandonment of this notion left them with two elements of the older moral scheme whose relationship to one another inevitably became wholly unclear; for, since the moral injunctions that they wanted to justify were intended to alter, improve and reform human nature as it happened to be rather than to fit with it in its untutored state, it would never be possible to justify them by deducing them from or otherwise relating them to features of that present state. Indeed, it is much more likely that human nature thus understood would have a strong tendency to disobey the injunctions of morality. As MacIntyre puts it:

> . . . the eighteenth-century moral philosophers engaged in what was an inevitably unsuccessful project; for they did indeed attempt to find a rational basis for their moral beliefs in a particular understanding of human nature, while inheriting a set of moral injunctions on the one

hand and a conception of human nature on the other which had been expressly designed to be discrepant with each other . . . They inherited incoherent fragments of a once coherent scheme of thought and action and, since they did not recognise their own peculiar historical and cultural situation, they could not recognise the impossible and quixotic nature of their self-appointed task. (*AV*, p. 53)

We might put MacIntyre's conception of the importance of a human telos in the following way. He sees the concept as vital to morality understood as a rationally justifiable or objective enterprise, because it alone can license immediate transitions from statements of fact to statements of value or obligation – transitions from 'is' to 'ought'. We can move immediately from the knowledge that a knife is blunt and bent to the conclusion that it is a bad knife, and from the fact that it is sharp and evenly balanced to the judgement that it is a good knife, because we know that a knife is a tool for cutting things – we know, in other words, what the purpose or end (the telos) of such a thing is. Functional or purposive concepts thus seem to transform evaluative judgements into a species of factual statement; for then such judgements follow immediately from the object judged having, as a matter of fact, some particular characteristics. If we think of human nature as possessed of a telos, we can make similarly immediate transitions from 'is' to 'ought', since our grasp of the fulfilled or final state of human nature allows us to distinguish between character traits or behaviour patterns that do, and those that do not, contribute to the development and realization of that telos, and to regard the latter as 'bad' and the former as 'good'. We could therefore regard moral judgements as a species of factual statement as well.

So it seems that the reintroduction of the concept of a telos will be vital to any attempt to restore a sense of morality as an aspect of human life that can be said to be rational or objective in its content. This way of looking at human beings is of course central to Aristotelian ethics, but according to MacIntyre it is even older than that:

It is rooted in the forms of social life to which the theorists of the classical [Greek] tradition give expression. For according to that tradition to be a man is to fill a set of roles each of which has its own point or purposes: member of a family, citizen, soldier, philosopher, servant of God. It is only when man is thought of as an individual prior to and apart from all roles that 'man' ceases to be a functional concept. (*AV*, p. 56)

If one thinks of a person as a farmer, then one thinks of him as having certain purposes or ends by virtue of his role, and answers to the question of how he ought to behave – in relation to his animals, his crops, his fellow farmers and his fellow citizens – follow immediately from our grasp of the function it is his task to perform. For MacIntyre, then, the reintroduction of rationality to morality by means of the concept of a human telos can be brought about only by rejecting the abstract, ghostly emotivist self and regarding the person as necessarily implicated in and defined by her social, cultural and historical circumstances. These three elements (moral judgements as factual, a human telos, and the encumbered self) were central to the moral understanding of Ancient Greece, and formed the original and sense-conferring context for the incoherent fragments of morality with which modernity is left; so it is to that context that MacIntyre turns for advice on how to reconstruct such a framework within modern culture.

Aristotle and the virtues

In the Homeric world to which Aristotle's ethical system is a reaction, individuals were regarded as having a fixed role or status in virtue of the position they occupied in a well-defined and highly determinate social structure. As a consequence, knowing how any given individual ought to behave in a given situation followed immediately from knowledge of their role; in knowing that, we know what he owes to and what he is owed by others whose relationship to him is determined by the position they occupy in the same hierarchies of kinship, household and society. The concept of the virtues enters here as a term denoting those excellences of character that permit a man to carry out the duties incumbent upon him and that are manifested in his actions when he fulfils those duties. Furthermore, in knowing how he ought to behave, in knowing the role he occupies, the Homeric individual knows who he is; the idea of rejecting or distancing himself from that role could make no sense, since it amounted to the sloughing off of his identity.

Thus, right action flows immediately from an individual's identity, and since that identity is defined by his social role, in Homeric society morality and social structure amount to one and the same thing; in other words, the emotivist self is no self at all, and evaluative questions are questions of (social) fact.

Aristotle understands himself as part of the Homeric tradition; the points just mentioned provide the framework of his ethical enquiry, but they do not so much fix its precise shape as form the landmarks in terms of which he will sketch his own significantly different map of the terrain. For example, Aristotle detaches the concept of the virtues and of morality from any tight connection with specific social roles, but not from all connection with any role; for him, the relevant role is that of 'human being' rather than 'king' or 'son'. Human beings are understood as having a specific nature which sets them certain aims and goals; and the virtues are those excellences of character that allow them to move towards that specifically human telos. However, those virtues are not merely a means towards the achievement of an independently specifiable end state:

> For what constitutes the good for man is a complete human life lived at its best, and the exercise of the virtues is a necessary and central part of such a life, not a mere preparatory exercise to achieve such a life. We thus cannot characterize the good for man adequately without already having made reference to the virtues. (*AV*, p. 140)

Moreover, the virtues as Aristotle understands them cannot be exercised outside the political community; their development and implementation in a complete human life requires that such a life be lived out in the polis, together with others all engaged in a common project of attempting to live the good life. Only the material and cultural resources of the city state allow this project to be implemented; and virtues such as courage, fidelity and friendship constitute both the framework conditions for any such community to maintain itself and an essential part of the form of life at which those in the community are aiming. This is the sense in which Aristotelian man is necessarily a political animal.

This exceedingly brief summary of MacIntyre's version of Aristotle identifies themes that will be vital if we are to understand his attempt to provide a reconstructed version of Aristotle's conception of ethics, in particular the central role accorded to the virtues and the need for a communal context for the living of the good life. However, MacIntyre has (at least) two main reasons for thinking that his prescription for modern morality must be a heavily reconstructed version of Aristotle. In the first place, Aristotle's own understanding of the human telos was dependent upon his metaphysical biology, and those proto-scientific theories are now entirely discredited – indeed, it was the discredit into which they had fallen that partly explained the Enlightenment's rejection of the very idea of a human telos. MacIntyre must therefore show that such a teleological understanding of human nature is justified or necessitated without relying upon such metaphysical presuppositions. Secondly, Aristotle places great emphasis on the constitutive role of the polis for morality, but the Athenian city state was a historically and culturally specific form of life which could not conceivably be revived in the twentieth century; so MacIntyre must find a way of invoking the concept of a community in morality without presupposing entirely utopian social and political changes.

His reconstruction attempts to meet both these challenges by deploying three central concepts – that of a practice, that of the narrative unity of a human life, and that of a tradition: the first and third of these in particular are, as we shall see, inherently social in nature, and all three are together intended to provide a rational framework for morality in which the concept of a virtue retains a central place. We shall look at each of these three concepts in turn.

The concept of a practice

According to MacIntyre, a practice is

> . . . any coherent and complex form of socially established co-operative human activity through which goods internal to that form of activity are realised in the course of trying to achieve those standards of excellence which are appropriate to, and partially definitive of, that form of activity, with the result that human powers to achieve excellence, and human conceptions of the ends and goods involved, are systematically extended. (*AV*, p. 175)

This requires a lot of clarification; but some of its implications are relatively obvious. For example, on this definition, noughts and crosses is not a practice (insufficiently complex) but chess is; kicking a football is not a practice (although it may be a component of a practice of playing football); planting turnips is not a practice insufficiently complex or self-contained) but farming is.

The import of other terms in the definition is much less obvious, in particular the notion of a good that is internal to a practice. Internal goods are ones that cannot be achieved by engaging in any activity other than the practice itself; external goods are ones that can be derived from participating in the given practice, but that can also be derived from participating in other practices. Take chess as an example: power, fame and wealth can be achieved through excellence in chess playing, but they are external goods because they can also be achieved in other ways – they are not practice-specific; whereas certain highly particular kinds of analytical skill, strategic imagination and competitive intensity achievable by playing chess are goods internal to that practice, for they cannot be achieved in any other way. No activity that lacks internal goods can count as a practice; and those goods are the fulcrum of MacIntyre's first definition of the virtues:

> A virtue is an acquired human quality the possession and exercise of which tends to enable us to achieve those goods which are internal to practices and the lack of which effectively prevents us from achieving any such goods. (*AV*, p. 178)

This definition therefore links the possession and exercise of the virtues to participation in practices; and although MacIntyre's definition allows a wide range of things to count as practices, participation in any of them will necessarily have a certain character. In the first place, participation in the practice requires acceptance of the authority of the standards and paradigms operative in the practice at the time. If we stick with chess as an example: unless I begin by accepting correction from those more versed in the game and regarding certain games and certain players as paradigmatic of chess excellence, I can never hope to achieve even a modest version of that excellence in my own play and so cannot hope to achieve the internal goods of chess. In short, I must subject my own preferences, tastes and attitudes to the communal standards and authorities that currently define the practice.

It is this feature of MacIntyre's notion of a practice that has been taken to show that he is committed to a form of conservatism, to the view that criticism of the status quo within a given practice is ruled entirely out of court. But this is a misreading of his position: for the fact that entry into a practice demands the subjection of my personal preferences to the standards prevailing in it does not entail that, subsequent to my entry, I must unquestioningly accept every judgement made by the community of other practitioners. MacIntyre is happy to admit that such judgements will often be disputed, and will sometimes be disputed at a fundamental level; after all, practices have a history within which the participants' perception of its paradigms and standards (and so of its internal goods) will change, and such disputes are the motor of that change. The point is that such disputes will be subject to certain constraints.

For example, it will not be enough merely to *assert* that Capablanca was a better chess player than Karpov, for any such judgement must be justifiable by reference to the standards and paradigms that govern and partly constitute the practice. I must argue, for example, that Karpov's end-game play lacks a certain fluidity, that he is prone to loss of nerve at crucial points in his matches, that even his best games display a strategic imagination very limited in comparison with Capablanca at his best. Of course, my interlocutor might disagree, arguing that Capablanca's imagination is insufficiently disciplined, as his 1946 game in Paris demonstrated and so on; it may even be the case that the two of us never resolve our disagreement. But our debate can be said to be a rational one because its progress has a logic: the process of grounding and disputing our differing judgements is governed by certain shared canons of relevance. We might disagree about the limitations of Karpov's strategic imagination, but we agree that the quality of that imagination is vital in any assessment of his claims to chess greatness; we might disagree over Capablanca's status relative to Karpov, but we agree that it is against the likes of Capablanca that Karpov's claim to chess greatness must be measured.

The same point holds for any attempt on the part of participants in a practice to alter the direction or self-understanding of that practice: such criticism may be radical, but it must nonetheless make reference to some one or other of the practice's paradigms and standards, on pain of being unrecognizable as a piece of chess criticism at all. Anyone who accepted that a given player lacked all strategic imagination, analytical skill and competitive intensity, but continued to claim that the player was a new brand of chess genius, would not be demonstrating a very different conception of chess greatness – he would be displaying complete incompetence in the practice of chess. In other words, the standards of the practice, together with the players and games regarded as paradigmatically great, provide a framework within which reasoned argument may be conducted and agreement may emerge (although, of course, agreement is not guaranteed). The framework itself is subject to change, but not all at once and not in any way the reformer pleases; for that framework serves to constitute the practice, and its total rejection would constitute the total obliteration of the practice rather than a change in its trajectory. Even the revolutionary critic must be a participant.

Judgements within practices therefore cannot be regarded as purely subjective or arbitrary; they cannot be given an emotivist analysis. It is not up to the individual to determine in an entirely abstract and ultimately criterionless way what she will regard as the achievement of chess excellence. Although she can decide to place more importance on certain chess-playing virtues than on others, she cannot pluck any old character trait out of the air and transform it into such a virtue; although she is not forced to agree with every judgement made by her fellow practitioners, she cannot decide for herself what will count as a relevant ground for such a judgement or what will count as a relevant response or counter to the ground she invokes. This framework of agreed modes of argument and shared canons of relevance allows us to achieve an objectivity and impersonality of judgement that transcends purely personal expressions of preference.

It seems, then, that participation in such shared projects, acceptance of such communally and historically determined standards, initiates the individual into forms of life in which human judgements of worth are immune to the threat of emotivism. Moreover, the fact that there can be many and varied practices, and so a wide variety of internal goods and virtues, signifies a healthy pluralism in MacIntyre's conception of what is valuable in human life. However, that same multiplicity of practices also raises a worry: for, granted that within a given practice questions about value and worth can be settled in non-arbitrary ways, what of questions about the relative value and worth of practices themselves? The fact that there are so many practices makes it likely that any given individual will participate in several at the same time, and the demands they make upon her will inevitably come into conflict; the demands of practising to become a chess Grand Master will conflict with the demands of being a good parent and spouse, the demands of the artist's life will conflict with those of the sportswoman. But no single practice can provide an overarching framework within which the question of which demands should take precedence can be given a rational or objective answer; arbitrary retentions and renunciations of allegiances seem inevitable. In short, MacIntyre must face the threat that these competing allegiances will fracture the life of the virtues. His response is his account of the narrative unity of a human life.

The narrative unity of a human life

Human behaviour cannot be understood simply as stretches of bodily movements. In order for such movements to count as actions at all, we must characterize them in relation to the intentions, desires and goals of the person whose bodily movements they are (even if only by saying that what was done was unintentional); and if we are to make sense of those intentions, we must relate them to what MacIntyre calls the setting of the action. He takes the case of a man digging his garden. Such an action can be rendered intelligible by explaining it either as the result of his intention to prepare the garden for winter, or as the result of his desire to please his wife; in the former case, the action is related to a particular type of household-cum-garden setting, in the latter to the setting and history of a marriage. Of course, any piece of behaviour may relate to more than one setting at the same time: the digging could be embedded in both of the settings invoked by my explanations of it; and if we wish to know exactly what the agent is doing, we will need to find out which of these settings is primary for him. Would he, for example, continue to perform the action if he discovered that his absences in the garden irritated his wife? In other words, we will need to identify his short-term intentions about the digging, their relation to one another, and their relation to his longer-term intentions concerning his marriage and his garden. In effect, we relate the agent's history to the history of the settings to which it belongs.

It seems, then, that rendering an action intelligible is a matter of grasping it as an episode in the history of the agent's life and of the settings in which it occurs; we come to view it as another instalment in a nesting of narratives. In other words, narrative history of a certain kind is the basic genre for the characterization of human action. This holds both for our characterization of other's actions and for our characterization of our own; in offering an explanation of what we are doing, we relate it to our own intentions and thereby present it under the aspect of a further episode in the narrative of our lives. This is what explains the fact that both short- and long-term stretches of our lives can be and are characterized in terms appropriate to literary works. Events ranging from conversations through chess games, courtships and seminars to marriages and careers are all capable of having dramatic shape: they have beginnings, middles and ends, they are subject to dramatic reversals and eleventh-hour reprieves, they develop and decline, they have digressions and subplots, they belong to genres (the tragic, the comic, the farcical). And in the absence of such patterning, they become alienating and unintelligible, both to those participating and to those observing. Because action has a basically historical character, our lives are enacted narratives in which we are both characters and authors; a person is a character abstracted from a history.

Of course, we are not entirely sovereign authors. We are subordinate characters in the dramas of others, the settings in which our actions must take place are and have been shaped in ways not fixed by us, and the future will always be ultimately unpredictable. Despite such constraints and unpredictability, however, the narrative form of our lives gives them a certain teleological character (without invoking metaphysical biology):

> We live out our lives, both individually and in our relationships with each other, in the light of certain conceptions of a possible shared future, a future in which certain possibilities beckon us forward and others repel us, some seem already foreclosed and others perhaps inevitable. There is no present which is not informed by some image of some future, and an image of the future which always presents itself in the form of a *telos* – or of a variety of ends or goals – towards which we are either moving or failing to move in the present. Unpredictability and teleology therefore coexist as part of our lives; like characters in a fictional narrative we do not know what will

happen next, but nonetheless our lives have a certain form which projects itself toward our future . . . If the narrative of our individual lives is to continue intelligibly – and either type of narrative may lapse into unintelligibility – it is always the case both that there are constraints on how the story can continue *and* that within those constraints there are indefinitely many ways in which it can continue. (*AV*, pp. 200-1)

It is this narrative form that provides the framework within which we can attempt to make rational choices concerning the conflicting demands of different practices. In effect, MacIntyre is saying to the person trying to decide between spending more time playing chess and spending more time with her family: 'Don't think of this as a choice which is made in a vacuum, as if you have to decide whether chess *per se* is more worthwhile than family life *per se*. This is a choice that is being made by a particular person at a particular stage in her particular life – one in which it may be clear that you have exceptional chess potential and that your marriage is in a stage of terminal decline, or in which it is clear that the years of your married life have transformed a once obsessional commitment to chess into a satisfying but ultimately secondary subplot. Ask yourself not "Which internal goods are best?" but rather "Which matter most to me?" or "Which decision will introduce or maintain the shape or form which my life has begun to develop?"; ask yourself "Who am I really – a chess player or a spouse?" This shift of perspective will not *necessarily* isolate the one right thing for you to do, but it might do so; and even if it doesn't, it provides a context within which both you and anyone who knows you can distinguish between better and worse options. Perhaps your decision will never come to seem clearly right or wrong, or perhaps it will do so only in retrospect; but what allows such clarity of vision will be the shape that your life took (its unity, depth and coherence) as a result of that decision.'

Of course, in urging that we approach such dilemmas by asking 'How best may I live out the narrative unity of my life?', MacIntyre is arguing that the asking of the question is at least as important to an individual's success in living the good life for human beings as the specific answers which may or may not emerge. Systematically asking the question, and attempting to answer it in word and deed, are what provide the moral life with its unity – the unity of a narrative quest for the good. For embarking on such a quest amounts to embarking upon a search for a conception of the good life that will enable us to order the other goods in our lives and to extend our understanding of the virtues; but the goal of the quest is not separable from the quest itself, in the sense that it is only in the course of the quest and in the course of coping with the events that threaten such a project that its goal is finally to be understood.

It is because a quest educates the person engaged upon it, about herself as well as about what she is seeking, that MacIntyre can define the good life for human beings as a life spent searching for the good life for human beings, and not be accused of leaving an empty circularity at the heart of his definition. And he is now able to offer a second, revised definition of the virtues:

> The virtues are therefore to be understood as those dispositions which not only sustain practices and enable us to achieve the goods internal to them, but which will also sustain us in the relevant quest for the good by enabling us to overcome the harms, dangers, temptations and distractions which we encounter, and which will furnish us with increasing self-knowledge and increasing knowledge of the good. (*AV*, p. 204)

The concept of a tradition

Of course, the shape of this quest for the good life is not the same for all individuals everywhere. To begin with, the historical specificity of practices means that the good life for an Athenian general will not be the same as that of a medieval nun or a seventeenth-century farmer.

> But it is not just that different individuals live in different social circumstances; it is also that we all approach our circumstances as bearers of a particular social identity. I am someone's son or daughter, someone else's cousin or uncle; I am a citizen of this or that city, a member of this or that guild or profession; I belong to this tribe, that clan, this nation. Hence what is good for me has to be what is good for one who inhabits these roles. As such I inherit from the past of my family, my city, my tribe, my nation, a variety of debts, inheritances, rightful expectation and obligations. These constitute the given of life, my moral starting-point. This in part is what gives my life its moral particularity. (*AV*, pp. 204–5)

The fit with MacIntyre's narrative conception of the self is obvious in effect, he is claiming that the possession of a historical identity and the possession of a social identity coincide. The idea is not that one cannot rebel against that identity; it is rather that in so doing one is adopting one mode of acknowledging it, and that after doing so one will be in no less particular a set of circumstances: *pace* the emotivist self, there is no way of finding a realm of truly abstract and universal principle which holds only of human beings *per se*. MacIntyre is thus stressing a central part of what makes us less than wholly sovereign authors of our lives, and which provides a texture and framework within which we might make better and worse decisions about how to carry those narratives forward.

One central part of this social inheritance will be a person's membership of what MacIntyre calls a tradition. A tradition is constituted by a set of practices and is a mode of understanding their importance and worth; it is the medium by which such practices are shaped and transmitted across the generations. Traditions may be primarily religious or moral (for example Catholicism or humanism), political (for example Marxism), economic (for example a particular craft or profession, trade union or manufacturer), aesthetic (for example modes of literature or painting) or geographical (for example crystallizing around the history and culture of a particular house, village or region). The communal understanding embodied in such traditions is neither hegemonic nor static; on the contrary, in a healthy tradition that understanding will be the subject of continuous debate at any given moment and across time. So, when an institution (for example a church, a university, a hospital, a farm) is a bearer of such a tradition, its common life will be partly constituted by a continuous argument as to what a good church or university or hospital or farm might be – an argument that is constrained by that tradition's best self-understanding but that can move forward in an indefinite number of ways.

Insofar as persons must be understood as partly individuated by their membership of traditions, the history of their lives will be embedded in the larger narrative of a historically and socially extended argument about the good life for human beings. Most importantly of all, this background will determine that individual's resources for making rational decisions about how to pursue her quest for the good, for it will be in terms of that tradition's best understanding of itself (both of its practices and of the ways in which those practices might be evaluated and criticized) that she will evaluate and criticize her own efforts to live the good life. Part of developing a conception of the good life for human beings is developing a conception of how one might evaluate and criticize one's attempts to enact and extend that conception; and just as the former is open to revision and redefinition, so the standards by which such revisions are justified and rendered intelligible are themselves open to reshaping. For MacIntyre, the view that there is an ahistorical, timelessly applicable mode of practical reasoning to which all individuals can or must commit themselves is no more intelligible than the idea that there is a universally applicable evaluation of an internal good, or a timeless essence of the self.

However, this third stage in MacIntyre's reconstruction of morality seems to leave us prey to relativistic worries of precisely the sort that arose with respect to practices. For contemporary culture contains a multiplicity of traditions, and even if we are born into one of them we can only regard a decision to remain within it or to leave it for another as a rational one if there is some way of evaluating the relative validity of one tradition with respect to its rivals. If, however, the only available conceptions of practical reasoning are tradition-specific, then we must either rely upon one of those conceptions and beg the question against rival ones, or be reduced to an arbitrary (because criterionless) choice between traditions.

In *Whose Justice? Which Rationality?*, MacIntyre attempts to allay these worries. He argues that the relative worth or cogency of a tradition can be settled by examining its performance when it meets an *epistemological crisis*. Any tradition has its own internal standards for assessing the degree to which it is progressing and deepening its own understanding of its doctrines and conceptions of the good, or alternatively failing to transcend its previous achievements and finding it impossible to reduce the number of unresolved difficulties left on its agenda. When a tradition tends towards the latter pole – riven by sterile conflicts and reiterating old formulae – it is in a state of epistemological crisis. It can overcome the crisis only by developing a new set of concepts or a new synthesis of old doctrines and ideas, a framework that meets the following three conditions: it allows the tradition to solve its outstanding problems, to explain how they arose and why they had not hitherto been solved, and to do so in a way that exhibits fundamental continuity between the old and the new synthesis.

The internal availability of such a conceptually innovative synthesis is never guaranteed, and yet no tradition can be immune from the possibility of crises that require it for their valid or rational resolution. So it is possible that a tradition may not only decline but definitively founder as a result of such a crisis. Alternatively, however, its proponents may experience such a crisis, be unable to transcend it from within, and perceive that a rival tradition has the resources to construct concepts and theories that – by the standards of the tradition in crisis – both permit the solution of the critical problems and provide an account of the emergence of the crisis. Of course, these solutions and explanations are discontinuous with the tradition's old synthesis; but that merely confirms that the rival tradition has established its rational superiority over the tradition in crisis. The proponents of the latter are obliged, by virtue of their commitment to their own standards, to admit that the alien tradition is superior in rationality and in respect of its claims to truth.

If the reader is interested in looking in more detail at specific examples of traditions coping or failing to cope with such crises, *Whose Justice? Which Rationality?* provides a wealth of historical information, concentrating in particular upon Aquinas's synthesis of Christianity and Aristotelianism. Of course, MacIntyre's particular interpretations of these historical episodes are highly controversial, as is his general notion of an 'epistemological crisis'; but we have no space to explore these matters in any depth here. What matters most for our concerns is that, from MacIntyre's perspective, he has the resources needed to establish that traditions as a whole *are* open to rational assessment: 'It is in respect of their adequacy or inadequacy in their responses to epistemological crises that traditions are vindicated or fail to be vindicated.'[2] And when there is no crisis, then *ex hypothesi* there is no good reason for any member of any tradition to put his allegiance to it in question, and every reason to continue within it.

MacIntyre and liberalism

The central weight that MacIntyre places upon the interrelated concepts of a practice, the narrative unity of a human life and a tradition should at least make it clear that he is a fundamentally communitarian thinker; for on his view, the very possibility of sustaining rationality and objectivity in the arena of moral and political evaluation depends upon locating individuals and their arguments with other individuals within an overarching and nested set of inherently social matrices. This gives the concept of 'community' a much broader and more vital role than it has in Sandel's work. On the latter's view, the liberal myopia about the possibility of individuals developing constitutive attachments to their ends entailed a failure properly to acknowledge *one* important sort of human good – the sort that is strongly communal in content, and so can only be achieved through constitutive attachments to the community. But on MacIntyre's view, failing to recognize the way in which human beings can be and are constitutively attached to their communities entails an inability to give a coherent account of the circumstances necessary to achieve *any* kind of human good (whether communal in content or not), for in the absence of such constitutive communal frameworks, the very idea of morality as a rational or intelligible enterprise drops out.

The important question for our purposes, however, is whether liberalism in general and Rawlsian liberalism in particular can or should be read as ignoring or denying the communitarian claims that MacIntyre makes. Why does MacIntyre think that liberalism – as opposed, say, to emotivism – is a legitimate target for his critique? In short, why and in what ways does he think that liberalism is a species or variant of emotivism?

We claimed earlier that MacIntyre criticizes liberalism under four of the five headings mentioned on our original agenda of issues. To begin with, he accuses liberals of being committed to an incoherent emotivist-style conception of the self as unencumbered, and – as a consequence – to the view that the moral judgements made by such a self are inherently arbitrary and subjective rather than being capable of rational or objective justification. In *After Virtue*, he clearly thinks that these two criticisms apply to liberalism generally, and so must presumably think that Rawls's theory of justice is vulnerable to them as well; but he provides little textual evidence to back up this claim. It therefore seems that those who wish to coopt MacIntyre as a critic of Rawls will here have to take advantage of the fact that MacIntyre's versions of these two criticisms parallel those of Sandel. In other words, a communitarian might plausibly argue that Sandel's detailed textual arguments for the presence and import-ance in Rawlsian liberalism of a conception of the self as

antecedently individuated themselves constitute the main grounds
for concluding that Rawls falls under MacIntyre's critical fire.
MacIntyre's unencumbered emotivist self and Sandel's antecedently
individuated self are so similar that they stand and fall together. If
Rawls can be shown to hold the latter, he can be taken to hold the
former; and if he can be shown not to hold the latter, then he cannot
be taken to hold the former.

Of course, as we noted at the very beginning of this chapter,
although MacIntyre and Sandel both criticize liberalism for its
conception of the person and its commitment to moral subjectivism,
they differ in their diagnosis of the reasons for liberalism's
commitment to these views. For Sandel, the liberal conception of
the person is the defining characteristic of that mode of moral and
political theory, and its commitment to moral subjectivism is a
consequence of its cleaving to that conception. But for MacIntyre,
both that conception of the person and the commitment to moral
subjectivism are consequences of a more fundamental liberal
myopia, namely their inability to comprehend or accommodate
the importance of the community in maintaining the objectivity of
all moral thought and the integrity of human identity. In short, a full
comprehension of MacIntyre's first two criticisms will lead us on to a
third charge – the claim that liberalism is essentially a form of asocial
individualism in politics and morality. But in this respect as well, his
attack on liberalism is different from Sandel's: for whereas, under
this heading, Sandel restricts himself to the charge that liberalism is
blind to the importance of human goods (both political and non-
political) whose *content* is social or communal, MacIntyre's view is
that liberalism is a reflection in politics of the general modern
inability to perceive that every human good or end (whether
communal in content or not) has its *origin* in social matrices – that all
human goods derive from a framework of overlapping communal
practices and traditions. And here MacIntyre does attempt to argue
explicitly that Rawls's conception of politics and political theory is
vulnerable to his attacks.

His ground for accusing Rawls of endorsing a political variant of
this asocial individualism seems to be the role of the original
position in Rawls's argument, and in particular the fact that this
device of representation is a modern-dress version of the social
contract, which encourages us to think of the structure of society as
something about which people who already possess certain interests

can come together and negotiate under certain other conditions of voluntarily imposed ignorance about themselves.

> For . . . Rawls a society is composed of individuals, each with his or her own interest, who then have to come together and formulate common rules of life . . . Individuals are thus . . . primary and society secondary, and the identification of individual interests is prior to, and independent of, the construction of any moral or social bonds between them. (*AV*, pp. 232–3)

MacIntyre's claim is thus that, by positing the original position as an appropriate device of representation for thinking about justice, Rawls reveals his view that entry into society ought ideally to be envisaged as the voluntary act of rational individuals with prior interests whose question is 'What kind of social contract is it reasonable for me to enter into with these others?' Such a vision would, MacIntyre claims, entirely exclude the possibility that society is or might be a community whose primary bond is a shared understanding both of the good for human beings and of the good of that community, and within which individuals identify their primary interests by reference to those goods. It is, he thinks, a possibility that Rawls cannot envisage because of what MacIntyre calls his explicit presupposition that '. . . we must expect to disagree with others about what the good life for man is and must therefore exclude any understanding of it that we may have from our formulation of the principles of justice' (*AV*, p. 233).

But, of course, from MacIntyre's perspective, it is only by working to establish and maintain precisely the sort of shared communal understandings of the good that Rawls explicitly excludes from our deliberations about justice that we can confer any rationality or objectivity upon the course of those deliberations. For it is only by introducing a conception of desert in relation to the common tasks of the community in pursuing shared goods that we can provide the basis for rational judgements about social virtue and social injustice. In the absence of the strong social bonds that create space for such a conception of desert, MacIntyre argues that Rawls's task of developing a conception of justice upon which we can all agree is doomed to failure; and he asserts that Rawls's inability to justify the importance he attributes to a principle of equality with respect to needs against competing basic premises (for example Nozick's principle of entitlement) merely exemplifies the incommensurability that descends upon such matters when they are shorn of their communal matrix.

So, for MacIntyre, Rawls's asocial individualism ensures that he will be incapable of giving his theory of justice the rational grounding it requires, and his theory will accordingly be incapable of forming the substance of a political consensus in his society – of filling the very vacuum that leads him to forbid himself any reference in his political theorizing to specific conceptions of the good. MacIntyre thus associates Rawls with a long tradition of individualistic political thought, in which it seems as if '. . . we had been shipwrecked on an uninhabited island with a group of other individuals, each of whom is a stranger to me and to all the others' (*AV*, p. 233). The question of how far this characterization accurately reflects Rawls's position and how far it merely caricatures it is one that, technically at least, we will be leaving open until chapter 5; but even at this stage, it is worth pointing out something of which MacIntyre seems to take no account. As we suggested in our Introduction, whilst the structure of the original position does show that Rawls places a great deal of emphasis upon the individual, and upon that individual's social structures being ones to which he or she might be thought freely to consent, it does not necessarily embody the claim that individuals are in some chronological or logical sense prior to society, and so that their conceptions of the good are not necessarily social in origin. It is meant to be a device of representation, a way of thinking about justice in which people already in a society ignore certain information about their social identity without having to imagine that they could actually be divested of their membership of society and still remain capable of the sort of thinking in which they are at present engaged. It therefore seems at least possible that the original position is not so much an attempt to represent society as a collection of individuals essentially lacking any social bonds, but rather an attempt to represent precisely the common assumptions about an individual's primary interests that constitute the bonds that hold our particular liberal society together. In short, it may well be that Rawls has designed the original position to reflect the high importance that our political community attaches to the liberty and equality of its citizens; in particular, his exclusion of specific conceptions of the good may be designed to reflect the importance we attach to (what might be expressed in MacIntyre's terms as) the capacity freely to search for the good life for human beings without the state discriminating against certain forms of answer to that question.

We will take up this matter in more detail in later chapters, but it is worth raising at this point because it seems likely that an appreciation of this possibility on MacIntyre's part led him to alter the fundamental orientation of his attack upon liberalism in the seven years between the publication of *After Virtue* and that of *Whose Justice, Which Rationality?* In the earlier book, as we have seen, MacIntyre treats liberalism as a mode of thought whose pre-suppositions are such that it is incapable of understanding the true nature and source of morality and human identity, and so cannot really be thought of as a genuine *moral* position at all. In the later book, however, MacIntyre's conception of liberalism and his criticisms of it are placed in a much more detailed historical perspective, and he ends by claiming that contemporary liberalism is in fact a genuine and viable moral and political tradition. Of course, this does not make him any more enthusiastic about the elements that go to make it up; but now his criticism of it primarily takes the form of suggesting that the tradition-bound nature of liberalism ensures that it cannot be as neutral between competing conceptions of the good as it might appear to be – which is, of course, his fourth criticism of it, and a version of the fifth theme from our original agenda of issues.

The story MacIntyre tells is of a moral tradition that has its historical origins in the Enlightenment attempt to develop a morality that transcends tradition. He locates liberal political theory as part of a historical project of founding a social order in which individuals could emancipate themselves from the contingency and particularity of traditions by appealing to genuinely universal, tradition-independent norms. Initially the liberal claim was to provide a political, legal and economic framework in which assent to one and the same rationally justifiable principles would enable those who espouse widely different and incompatible conceptions of the good life to live peaceably together within the same society. According to MacIntyre, however, this goal necessarily entailed proscribing any attempts to reshape the life of the community in accord with any one particular conception of the good:

And this qualification of course entails not only that liberal individualism does indeed have its own broad conception of the good, which it is engaged in imposing politically, legally, socially and culturally wherever it has the power to do so, but also that in so doing its toleration of rival conceptions of the good in the public arena is severely limited.[3]

What MacIntyre includes under this broad liberal conception of the good, and claims to locate in contemporary representatives of this tradition such as Rawls, are such elements as the following: a distinctive conception of a just order (a primarily procedural one), of the modes of practical reasoning that are permitted within that order (treating moral beliefs as expressions of purely personal preference), and of the good life for human beings (one in which a variety of goods is pursued, each appropriate to its own sphere, with no overall good supplying any overall unity to life). It might seem surprising to think of Rawls's position as including the third of these elements; but MacIntyre cites a passage from *A Theory of Justice* that confirms that it does so: 'Human good is heterogeneous because the aims of the self are heterogeneous. Although to subordinate all our aims to one end does not strictly speaking violate the principles of rational choice . . . it still strikes us as irrational or more likely as mad. The self is disfigured' (*TJ*, p. 554). Moreover, for MacIntyre these elements are not only present in theories such as that of Rawls: they are embodied, debated and carried forward through the medium of a specific set of social, legal and cultural institutions – the institutions of a distinctively liberal social order. In other words, what began (with Kant and others) as an attempt to found morality upon tradition-independent principles which any human beings could accept insofar as they were rational, ended with the creation and perpetuation of one more moral tradition: 'Liberal theory is best understood, not at all as an attempt to find a rationality independent of tradition, but as itself the articulation of a historically developed and developing set of social institutions and forms of activity, that is, as the voice of a tradition.'[4]

At first sight, however, it seems the very reverse of a radical criticism of liberal political theorists to tell them that they are proponents of a specific political tradition. Representing a tradition is, on MacIntyre's own terms, an inevitable consequence of taking any evaluative stance, and so cannot be seen as a weakness; and it is difficult to imagine that contemporary liberal theorists (as opposed, say, to their historical forebears) would be surprised to be told that the continued sustenance of a distinctively liberal political order was their overriding goal. As we saw in our Introduction, when liberals such as Rawls claimed to be neutral between competing conceptions of the good, they could never have meant that they were neutral between liberalism and other forms of politics; and they have never denied that they will proscribe any conception of the good whose pursuit interferes with the equal right of other citizens freely to pursue their own conception of the good. What they distinctively claim is a neutrality of justification which forbids them from invoking any conception of the good in defence of state policies and actions, even if those policies and actions will inevitably have non-neutral effects. In short, it seems that MacIntyre's criticisms of liberal neutrality cannot be taken seriously in the extreme form in which they are stated, since those statements seem to amount to accusing liberals of being liberal.

There may, nonetheless, be a grain or two of truth in the point that he makes. First, it is all very well to say that contemporary liberal political theorists have always known that they are beginning from liberal starting-points; but that fact may not have been so obvious to many people in contemporary society whose primary awareness of liberalism is likely to be precisely its claimed neutrality between competing conceptions of the good. It may not be inconsistent for liberalism to acknowledge the true extent of its neutrality and toleration; but such an acknowledgement might well alter non-academics' views about its attractiveness as a social ideology.

The second grain of truth emerges if we acknowledge that the liberal tradition's distinctive refusal to employ conceptions of the good to justify state actions is of course one that operates only within the realm of politics: individuals are perfectly free to act in accordance with such conceptions in other areas of their lives. In other words, a split between political and non-political matters, between the spheres of public and private morality, is central to liberal thought. But MacIntyre's neo-Aristotelianism rejects that split: it is founded upon a conception of the political community as a fundamental arena within which our understanding and imple-mentation of the good life for human beings can be developed, and so integrates politics more closely with considerations that liberalism restricts to the realm of private morality. And MacIntyre's position is not the only one to contest this matter: we might think here of many traditions of religious thought.

What this makes clear is that establishing and maintaining a separation of the political and private spheres is a tradition-specific idea; it is itself a matter of real controversy. And according to MacIntyre, justifying and defending it against its opponents will involve drawing upon specifically liberal conceptions of practical reasoning and of human life more generally; it will involve drawing upon a wide range of other elements in the general liberal moral tradition. If this claim could be justified, it would seem to follow that any attempt to maintain a liberal political order is no less dependent upon the invocation of a general conception of the good life for human beings than is MacIntyre's own position. In short, the neutrality that liberals do typically claim for their conception of politics may be far less significant than it appears.

Of course, whether this criticism, together with the other three criticisms mentioned earlier, should be held to be valid of liberalism in general and of Rawls in particular is a matter which we must leave to later chapters; but it should at least be clearer why MacIntyre thinks that Rawls falls into his target area. Before concluding our discussion of his position, however, it is absolutely vital that we make it clear just what MacIntyre takes to follow from his multiple criticisms of liberal political theorizing; in particular, and perhaps surprisingly, it must be emphasized that MacIntyre is *not* advocating the reintroduction of a neo-Aristotelian conception of politics at the level of the contemporary Western nation-state.

As we saw earlier, MacIntyre certainly believes that Rawls's project of constructing a theory of justice applicable to modern societies must fail, because no coherent form of political community can be established in the absence of a shared conception of the good to which the community is committed, and Rawls's theory explicitly eschews reliance upon any such conception. However, MacIntyre doesn't think that the problem would be solved simply by reintroducing such a conception of the good into contemporary political theorizing. For such theories are concerned with political arrangements at the level of the nation-state, and MacIntyre also believes that the specific character of the modern nation-state ensures that any attempt to introduce a shared conception of the good at that level will do far more harm than good (for example, encouraging totalitarian and other evils). In this respect, MacIntyre sides with the liberal theorist against those contemporary communitarian thinkers in America and elsewhere who argue that governments should give expression to some shared vision of the human good; as he puts it, this debate is one 'in which from my own point of view communitarians have attacked liberals on one issue on which liberals have been consistently in the right'.[5]

However, the conclusion MacIntyre draws from this is not that shared visions of the human good should have no role to play in politics at all; it is rather that, since there can be no proper politics without a shared vision of the good, the proper focus of politics should shift from the nation-state to smaller, more local forms of community, in which such a shared vision can be established and maintained without the evils of oppression or bureaucratic stultification. For him a 'genuinely Aristotelian conception of the polis . . . has to be a relatively small-scale and local form of political association. And when practice-based forms of Aristotelian community are generated in the modern world, they are always, and could not but be, small-scale and local.'[6] A fishing village on the Newfoundland coast, a college or university, a hospital or church – these are the communities that MacIntyre regards as the only feasible loci for a genuine, morally contentful and humanly fulfilling, form of political interaction; 'the nation state is not and cannot be the locus of community'.[7] In other words, despite important shifts in the focus of his critique of liberal political theorizing in his later writings, MacIntyre still cleaves to the almost-apocalyptic vision of modern moral culture with which *After Virtue* is imbued; he sees no reason to withdraw that book's concluding remark – that what we need most is the arrival of another St Benedict, a founder of exemplary local, practice-based communities: someone to lead us out of a moral Dark Ages.

NOTES

1 The three volumes that are pertinent to our concerns are: *After Virtue* (hereafter *AV*), *Whose Justice? Which Rationality?* and *Three Rival Versions of Moral Enquiry.*
2 MacIntyre, *Whose Justice?*, p. 366.
3 Ibid., p. 336.
4 Ibid., p. 345.
5 A. MacIntyre, 'A Partial Response to my Critics', in *After MacIntyre*, eds J. Horton and S. Mendus (Oxford: Polity Press, 1994), p. 302.
6 Ibid., p. 302.
7 Ibid., p. 303.

3

TAYLOR:

the sources of the liberal self

Unlike Sandel and like MacIntyre, Charles Taylor's work in the domain of political theory[1] is integrated into a sweeping analytical account of the development of Western moral and political culture from Plato to post-modernism;[2] and in this account, Rawls appears only fleetingly whilst liberalism has a role primarily as one central strand of modern culture rather than as the sole focus of Taylor's concerns. Moreover, and unlike either Sandel or MacIntyre, Taylor is not inclined to reject liberalism *per se*; on the contrary, he thinks that some of its central claims are worthy of very serious consideration, but only if they can be detached from various erroneous or incoherent ways of elucidating or defending them. Our key question must therefore be whether Rawlsian liberalism counts as one such erroneous defence of liberal values; and this question can be answered only by determining in some detail what sort of errors and incoherences Taylor is concerned to eradicate – errors that relate to the form and scope of moral evaluation in general. In short, before we can determine whether Taylor's work furnishes material for a critique of Rawls, we must follow his exploration of what may seem to be very abstract issues in moral philosophy.

We can at least, however, state in advance the main aspects of Taylor's framework of thought that have suggested to many of his readers that he has constructed a communitarian critique of liberalism. This suggestion is based upon Taylor's view that human beings are self-interpreting animals, creatures whose identity as persons depends upon their orientation and attachment to conceptions of the good which they derive from the matrix of their linguistic community. If such a communitarian view of human beings is correct, then it would clearly reveal the incoherence of any political theory that embodied a conception of persons as antecedently individuated and/or occluded the necessarily social origin of people's ends – the first and second themes on our original agenda of issues. Another aspect of Taylor's work is his view that moral judgements and intuitions are essentially capable of rational elucidation or articulation, a process that requires the invocation of fundamental and wide-ranging evaluative frameworks, also deriving from the community; these claims imply that Taylor will be hostile to any form of moral subjectivism or scepticism (the fourth theme on our agenda), and deeply suspicious of any political theory that claims not to rely upon anything other than a thin theory of the good (the fifth theme). However, in order to see whether Taylor's views are worthy of respect, we must examine them in more detail.

The status of moral intuitions

According to Taylor, our ordinary and widely shared moral intuitions – for example, a respect for the worth and dignity of others which emerges in instinctive reactions of horror and pity when that dignity is violated – have a dual aspect. On the one hand, they seem fundamental and purely instinctual, like reactions of nausea to certain tastes; on the other, they are articulable in accounts of what elicits them: agents manifesting them are often capable of explaining just what it is about human beings that merits or deserves the reaction. We might, for example, claim that human beings possess a dignity that deserves respect because they are children of God, or rational choosers of ends; in other words, we articulate our intuitions by developing a particular ontology of the human.

It is vital to see that this second aspect of moral intuitions completely distinguishes them from brute reactions such as nausea or delight at certain tastes. In the latter case, we simply do not acknowledge that there is anything to articulate or argue about. If someone is made nauseous by the taste of vodka, there is no question of asking him for an explanation of this or of attempting to persuade him that his reaction is ill-judged; the connection between the substance's properties and the reaction is just a brute fact. In the case of the moral intuition, we also react to a particular property of a given object, but here the property marks the object as one *meriting* the reaction. In this case there is a question as to the fitness of our response to the object; there is room for reasoning and argument about whether our reaction is the correct or most appropriate one, and for charges of inconsistency between our reactions. In short, in those arguments we invoke descriptions of the object whose criteria are independent of our given reactions; we are dealing with an instance of what Taylor has called 'strong evaluation' – discriminations of right and wrong in terms of standards that are independent of our given desires and preferences and that allow us to evaluate their worth.

In effect, then, our moral reactions implicitly acknowledge claims made upon us by their objects, and the various ontological accounts mentioned above are attempts to articulate those claims. Moreover, those accounts cannot simply be regarded as ornamental rhetoric which must be discarded if we are to reach a truly objective understanding of the validity of the reactions themselves; for the account and the reaction are internally related. The terms of the account specify the character or identity of the reaction: in characterizing the property of the object that merits the reaction, they are specifying what the reaction is a reaction *to* and so telling us precisely what reaction it is. If we dispense with the ontological account, there would be no space for an argument at all because the terms of that account are the only possible terms for that argument; in dispensing with it we would thus lose from view precisely what we were arguing about, and transform the reaction into (rather than revealing it to be) something akin to reactions of nausea. Moral growth may require that we repress or alter some of our reactions and develop others, but it could never require us to prescind from our reactions altogether; they are 'our mode of access to the world in which ontological claims are discernible and can be rationally argued about and sifted' (*SS*, p. 8).

Taylor thinks of moral intuitions and moral thinking in general as having three axes. The first has to do with our relations to other human beings – our sense of their worth and dignity, of what we owe them; the second has to do with our conceptions of the good life for human beings in general – our sense of what a full or flourishing human life consists in; and the third has to do with our sense of our own dignity or status – of the characteristics by which we command or fail to command the respect of others. Since all three axes presuppose some conception of the nature or status of human beings, this way of organizing the articulation of moral intuitions emphasizes the point that an ontological account is an essential part of that articulation. It also makes it clear that moral frameworks developed around those three axes will necessarily involve the notion of strong evaluation. For example, people asking themselves what the good life for human beings might be are well aware that their present desires could lead them to answer the question wrongly and waste or otherwise destroy their lives. In other words, any such framework incorporates a crucial set of qualitative distinctions; judging within them involves having the sense that some actions, modes of life or inflections of feeling are incomparably higher than those that might be more readily available to us. Such ends are worthy or desirable in a way that cannot be measured on the same scale as our ordinary desires and ends; they are not just quantitatively more desirable, but rather possess a qualitatively different status, one that commands our respect, admiration and awe.

It is Taylor's claim that no system of moral thinking can avoid engaging in such strong evaluation, even if only implicitly, since if it failed to do so, it would not constitute an ethic at all. In particular, systems such as utilitarianism, which pride themselves on denouncing more traditional moralities such as the honour ethic or the monastic ideal for perversely downgrading or denying the worth of ordinary human satisfactions, are (Taylor argues) themselves committed to distinguishing between different modes of achieving those ordinary satisfactions. An ordinary human life of irrationality, alienation or slavery – in other words, one that ignored or repressed the importance of instrumental reason – could not be regarded by utilitarians as an admirable, worthy or higher life. More generally, the notion that *whatever* we do might be acceptable is untenable simply because that could never be an intelligible basis for a conception of human dignity. In other words, strong evaluation is inescapable in the world shaped by our moral responses.

The self in moral space

So far, Taylor has been arguing that our moral reactions presuppose an ontological account of some sort: we cannot explicate what makes sense of our moral responses without articulating a framework along the three axes outlined above. This already provides strong reasons for rejecting moral subjectivism, where that is understood as the claim that moral intuitions and reactions are no more than the essentially arbitrary expression of preference; for such a claim fails to acknowledge the responsibility we have to articulate the *grounds* of our intuitions insofar as we present those intuitions as moral ones. The next stage of his argument is designed to show that developing, maintaining and articulating such intuitions is not something that human beings could easily or even conceivably dispense with; for the evaluative frameworks whose existence is presupposed by moral argumentation are also presupposed by our concept of personhood. According to Taylor, we cannot make sense of human agency if we dispense with the strong, qualitative discriminations that such frameworks embody.

> Moreover, this is not meant just as a contingently true psychological fact about human beings, which could perhaps turn out one day not to hold for some exceptional individual or new type, some superman of disengaged objectification. Rather the claim is that living within such strongly qualified horizons is constitutive of human agency, that stepping outside these limits would be tantamount to stepping outside what we recognize as integral, that is, undamaged human personhood. (*SS*, p. 27)

Taylor's claim is that a vital part of knowing who I am is knowing where I stand; my identity is defined by the commitments and identifications that provide the horizon within which I can determine from case to case what is valuable, good or worth doing. People who define their identity in terms of their commitment to a church or political party, or their membership of a nation, class or tribe, are not merely claiming that they have a strong feeling of attachment to certain values or views; they mean that such identifications provide an evaluative framework without which they would no longer know what the significance of a wide range of things was for them, without which they would be at sea. Our moral orientation is thus an essential part of our sense of our own identity.

But why should this be so? Taylor's claim is that the question 'Who are you?' is asked to place someone as a potential interlocutor in a society of interlocutors; we answer it by giving our name, our relationships to others ('I'm John's sister'), our social role ('I'm the President'), our commitments ('I'm an anarchist, a Quebecois etc.'). So, someone who qualifies as a potential object of this question is someone with her own standpoint or role amongst others, each of whom has their own standpoint or role – she is someone who can speak for herself. But to be able to answer such a question, to answer for oneself, is to know where one stands – to know what one wants to answer; and that is in part a matter of knowing one's fundamental moral orientation. An agent free of all frameworks would be in the grip of an appalling identity crisis, unable to know where she stood on a variety of fundamental issues, unable to answer for herself on them; and one who did not suffer this absence as a lack would be in the grip of a frightening dissociation, a pathological condition far beyond the range of what we would normally describe as shallowness. Since our identity is what allows us to define what is, and what is not, important to us, it could not be entirely without strong evaluations; so the notion of an identity defined by some mere *de facto*, not strongly valued preference is incoherent.

Thus, the idea that the adoption of a moral framework is optional is fundamentally wrong; a moral orientation is inescapable because the questions to which the framework provides answers are themselves inescapable.

> . . . to speak of orientation is to presuppose a space-analogue within which one finds one's way. To understand our predicament in terms of finding or losing orientation in moral space is to take the space which our framework seeks to define as ontologically basic. The issue is, Through what framework-definitions can I find my bearings in it? In other words, we take as basic that the human agent exists in a space of questions. And these are the questions to which our framework-definitions are answers, providing the horizon within which we know where we stand, and what meanings things have for us. (*SS*, p. 29)

Finding my bearings is something I do in a space that exists independently both of me and of my success or failure in orienting myself within it. Taylor's spatial metaphor thus brings out the objective status of the questions to which moral frameworks provide answers, the fact that the space that those questions define is no more a human fiction than physical space itself; we can no more imagine a human life that fails to address the matter of its bearings in moral space than we can imagine one in which developing a sense of up and down, right and left was regarded as an optional human task.

Selves and self-interpretations

One way of summarizing the claims that Taylor makes about the relation between human identity and the possession and deployment of a moral framework would be to say that the identity of the human self is bound up with and partially constituted by that self's sense of the meaning or significance of the objects and situations he encounters in his life. If we rephrase the matter in this way, we can see more clearly that the views Taylor develops in *Sources of the Self* are based upon a fundamental idea which he articulated almost 20 years before, in a paper entitled 'Interpretation and the Sciences of Man'. This idea was that human beings must be thought of as self-interpreting animals, as beings whose nature and identity is not specifiable independently of their self-interpretations; and it is worth looking in more detail at its relation to the later claims we have been examining.

In that early article, Taylor pointed out that a certain notion of meaning had a vital place in any attempt to characterize human behaviour; this is the sense in which we speak of a situation, an action, a demand, a prospect having a certain meaning for a person, for example talking of a terrifying situation or an attractive prospect. Our actions are ordinarily characterized by the purpose sought and explained by reference to desires, thoughts, and emotions; but the language by which we describe those goals and feelings or emotions is also that used to describe the meaning of a situation for an agent. The vocabulary defining such meaning ('terrifying', 'attractive') is closely linked with that describing feeling ('fear', 'desire') and that describing goals ('safety', 'possession').

Moreover, these three sets of terms are so closely related that we can only understand one of them by grasping their relation to the others; as Taylor puts it, they form a hermeneutic circle. For example, an emotion such as shame essentially refers us to a certain sort of situation (a 'shameful' or 'humiliating' one) and to a certain sort of response to it (hiding, covering up and so on); and it is essential to this emotion's being identifiable as shame that it be tied up with situations of this sort and give rise to dispositions of this type. But shameful situations can only be identified as situations that provoke shameful feelings; and the disposition is to a goal that similarly cannot be understood except by reference to the feelings experienced – the hiding in question is one that will cover up my shame, not one that is appropriate to being hunted by an armed enemy.

Just like moral reactions, then, a wide range of human feelings and actions are not brute phenomena (such as nausea), but can be appropriate or inappropriate to their situation: we can feel ashamed of things that another would argue are not genuinely shameful, and fail to respond appropriately to situations that genuinely are shameful ones. More importantly, however, the characterization of human feelings and purposes – and so their specific identity – is inseparable from the vocabulary the agent employs to characterize the meaning or significance of the situations in which he finds himself. And it follows that human behaviour itself (which cannot be understood as action unless related to a background of desire, feeling, emotion and purpose) can only be characterized in terms of the meaning that the situation in which the action occurs possesses for the agent concerned.

At this point, Taylor reminds us that the vocabulary that we employ to characterize the experiential meaning of situations has its particular significance only as part of a semantic field, a set of related but contrasting concepts. Each term in the field derives its meaning from the contrasts that exist between it and other terms in the field. For example, describing a situation as 'fearful' will mean something different according to whether the contrasts available in my vocabulary include such terms as 'terrifying', 'worrying', 'disconcerting', 'threatening', 'disgusting' or not; the wider the field of available contrasts, the finer are the discriminations that can be made by the choice of one term as opposed to another, and the more specific the significance of each term becomes. Thus, the use the same term as part of two different semantic fields, or its use before and after the introduction of a new term into its semantic field, will result in a change of that term's meaning; and this will in turn effect a change in the experiential meaning of the situations it characterizes, and in the feelings or purposes that are internally related to those situations.

More generally, however, this means that the significance of the situations in which an agent finds herself, and so the import and nature of her emotions and goals, is determined by the range and structure of the vocabulary available to her for their characterization.

She cannot feel shame if she lacks a vocabulary in which the circle of situation, feeling and disposition characteristic of shame is absent; and the precise nature of that feeling of shame will alter according to the range of the semantic field in which that vocabulary is embedded (shame as opposed to what?). Of course, the relation between feeling and available vocabulary is not a simple one. It is not just a matter of the vocabulary corresponding more or less adequately to pre-existing feelings, for we often experience how gaining access to a more sophisticated vocabulary makes our emotional life more sophisticated. On the other hand, neither is it a question of thinking making it so, for not any definition can be forced on us, whether by others or by ourselves; and some that we gladly take up can be judged inauthentic, self-deluded and wrong-headed. Nonetheless, however careful we must be in avoiding these opposing errors, it remains true that the relationship between a person's inner life and the vocabulary available to him for characterizing or interpreting it is an intimate one.

Taylor draws the following conclusions from this analysis:

> If this is so, then we have to think of man as a self-interpreting animal. He is necessarily so, for there is no such thing as the structure of meanings for him independently of his interpretation of them; for one is woven into the other. But then the text of our interpretation is not that heterogeneous from what is interpreted; for what is interpreted is itself an interpretation; a self-interpretation of experiential meaning which contributes to the constitution of this meaning. Or to put it another way: that of which we are trying to find the coherence is itself partly constituted by self-interpretation.[3]

This passage makes rather heavy weather of a relatively clear point. Taylor's claim is that to be an agent is to experience one's situation in terms of certain meanings; and this can in a sense be thought of as a sort of proto-interpretation, which is in turn interpreted and shaped by the language in which the agent lives these meanings. Moreover, if this is true at the fundamental level of feelings and reactions such as shame and fear, it will be even more pertinent at the level of a person's sense of her own character, her conceptions of the good life and her conception of her own nature. In short, a person's identity – both as a specific individual and as a type of agent – is partly (perhaps primarily) constituted by internalized self-interpretations.

Or, as Taylor puts it in his most recent writings, the identity of the human self is bound up with that self's sense of the significance and meaning of the objects and situations it encounters in life.

The self and the community

However he puts it, Taylor is clearly opposing any conception of the self that regards human beings as the sorts of entities whose nature and identity is fixed, and so can be studied independently of any descriptions or interpretations offered of it by human beings. In contrast with the objects of scientific study, to ask what a person is in abstraction from his self-interpretations is to ask a fundamentally misguided question.

> We are not selves in the way that we are organisms, or we don't have selves in the way we have hearts and livers. We are living beings with these organs quite independently of our self-understandings or interpretations, or the meanings things have for us. But we are only selves insofar as we move in a certain space of questions, as we seek and find an orientation to the good. (*SS*, p. 34)

And for Taylor, this essential relation between selves and self-interpretation entails an equally essential relation between selves and other selves – a relation to the community. We can see this in two ways. First, gaining access to self-interpretations is a matter of gaining access to a vocabulary that embodies them, and according to Taylor a language only exists in a language community. Second, if my self-definitions are thought of as answers to the question 'Who am I?', and this question finds its original sense in the interchange of speakers, then I can define who I am only by defining my relations to other selves, by establishing where I speak from in the family tree, in social space, in my intimate relations to the ones I love, and so on. Both ways of looking at the matter entail that one is a self only amongst other selves.

Moreover, these two views of the matter are interconnected. On the one hand, Taylor claims that being initiated into a language is a matter of entering into ongoing conversations between those who bring us up; the first meanings of the words I learn are the meanings that they have for me and my conversation partners together. But

such talk is primarily talk *about* something, and will serve to
characterize the significance of that something for the talkers. So I
can only learn what anger, love, anxiety etc. are through my and
others' common experience of their significance for us – that is, for
people with a particular role or status in the web of relationships
that make up our community.

Later, of course, I may innovate, developing an understanding of
myself and human life that is in sharp disagreement with my family
and background; there is no reactionary exclusion of change or
criticism in Taylor's position. But he does want to stress that such
innovations can only take place from a base in our common
language, and their significance can only be understood if they are
placed in relation to (even if only in sharp contrast with) the vision
and conceptions of others. The very confidence that we know what
we mean depends upon what is in effect a conversation (even if only
an imaginary or possible conversation) with human interlocutors.

> This is the sense in which one cannot be a self on one's own. I am a self
> only in relation to certain interlocutors: in one way in relation to those
> conversation partners who were essential to my achieving self-
> definition; in another in relation to those who are now crucial to my
> continuing grasp of languages of self-understanding – and, of course,
> these classes may overlap. A self exists only within what I call 'webs
> of interlocution'. (*SS*, p. 36)

In short, the full definition of someone's identity usually involves
not only her stand on moral and spiritual matters but also some
reference to a defining community. This is why any attempt to
comprehend the integrity and identity of human beings in what
Taylor calls atomistic terms, to regard society as merely an
aggregation of such antecedently individuated atoms in the absence
of which human beings would still be human, is incoherent. In terms
of the two main strands we distinguished under the second heading
of our agenda, Taylor's position places him primarily in opposition
to philosophical rather than to substantive asocial individualism; if
people are self-interpreting animals, they need not give most
importance to conceptions of the good whose *content* is strongly
communal, but their self-interpretation must be able to acknowledge
the necessarily social *origin* of any and all of their conceptions of the
good and so of themselves. It was no accident that our earlier

answers to the question 'Who am I?' made reference to family relationships and memberships of certain cultures, traditions and nations. Identifying oneself as an Armenian or a Quebecois is an essential part of identifying where one is speaking from and who one is speaking to – it is essential to one's self-interpretations.

Orientation and narration

So far, we have tried to show the strong sense in which Taylor's view of human beings as self-interpreting animals commits him to the view that the individual's relation to her community is constitutive of her identity. What we must demonstrate now is how this generally communitarian framework of thought leads him to other specific conclusions about the nature of human selfhood which we have already seen developed by other communitarian thinkers (in particular by MacIntyre).

As we saw earlier, Taylor's inclination to speak of moral frameworks as means of achieving orientation in a certain space of questions carries the implication that the relevant space exists independently of our ability or inability to find our bearings within it; it is an aspect of human ontology as fundamental as the need to establish our bearings in physical space. Now we must turn to another crucial implication of the metaphor of orientation in space, one that flows from the fact that orientation has two aspects: that there are *two* ways in which we can fail to have it. We can be ignorant of the lie of the land around us, lacking a map of the major landmarks and their relationship to one another; or we can possess a map, and yet not know where to place ourselves upon it. By analogy, our orientation in relation to the good requires not only some framework that defines the shape of the qualitatively higher but also a sense of where we stand in relation to this evaluative landmark. And if it is fundamental to our status as agents that we place ourselves in a space defined by certain qualitative distinctions, then where we stand in relation to those distinctions must matter to us: 'Not being able to function without orientation in the space of the ultimately important means not being able to stop caring where we sit in it' (*SS*, p. 42). Taylor's point here, with its presumption of the possibility and importance of constitutive attachments to goods, has a very Sandelian ring. His claim is that the goods that define our spiritual orientation are the ones by which we will measure the worth of our lives (the second of Taylor's axes); and this concern with the worth or meaningfulness of our lives is best thought of as a concern with how we are situated or placed in relation to those goods – whether we are in contact with them or not, whether we are *rightly* placed with respect to them. And, as the spatial metaphor further suggests, this issue can arise for us in two different senses. First, we can ask ourselves how close we are to those goods – to what degree my life manifests and embodies the domestic harmony or artistic achievement to which I am committed; and second, we can ask whether we are pointed in the right direction in the first place – however far away I am from the domestic harmony I crave, I can at least know that my basic stance and commitment to that good, my determination to live a life focused upon it, is firmly set.

In other words, the issue for beings like us is not just where we are but where we are going: and the direction in which our life is moving is important to us precisely because our lives are such that they have direction – they move. Taylor is in effect echoing a central theme of MacIntyre's work, the notion that my sense of the good, of qualitative discrimination, has to be woven into my understanding of my life as an unfolding story. The space of moral questions within which I must orient myself is part of a larger space of questions which only a coherent narrative can answer: an answer to the question 'Who am I?' involves answers to the questions of how I have become who I am and where I am going. In other words, the concepts of orientation towards the good and of the narrative unity or 'quest' structure of a life are mutually implicating and internally related:

> My underlying thesis is that there is a close connection between the different conditions of identity, or of one's life making sense, that I have been discussing. One could put it this way: because we cannot but orient ourselves to the good, and thus determine our place relative to it and hence determine the direction of our lives, we must inescapably understand our lives in narrative form, as a 'quest'. But one could perhaps start from another point: because we have to determine our place in relation to the good, therefore we cannot be without an orientation to it, and hence must see our life in story. From whichever direction, I see these conditions as connected facts of the same reality, inescapable structural requirements of human agency. (*SS*, pp. 51–2)

Hypergoods and practical reasoning

We mentioned at the beginning of the chapter that Taylor was not only hostile to moral subjectivism, to any notion of an unencumbered or antecedently individuated self, and to certain versions of asocial individualism; he was also committed to an attack upon the idea that specific moral or political principles could be defended without invoking anything more than a thin conception of the good for human beings. Having examined his grounds for the first three claims, we can now examine the fourth in more detail, and in particular we must elucidate Taylor's notion of a hypergood.

For, having established the importance of conceptions of the good to the identity of human agents, Taylor goes on to complicate the picture by reminding us that there are many goods in human life, and that they may sometimes (or even very often) come into conflict with one another. What this entails is that any given individual will need to rank the many goods that she recognizes to be worthy of pursuit in her life; and in some cases, this will involve regarding one of them as being of supreme importance relative to the others. Someone may, for example, recognize the value of self-expression, justice, the worship of God and family life, but she may consider one of them – perhaps worship of God – as of overriding importance. Such an individual, whilst recognizing a whole range of qualitative distinctions or moral frameworks, recognizes a qualitative discontinuity between one such framework and all the others; in short, she imposes a higher-order qualitative distinction in order to segment goods which are themselves defined in terms of lower-order distinctions. Taylor calls such higher-order goods *hypergoods*.

Hypergoods are generally a source of conflict, for the obvious reason that they presuppose an ultimate intolerance of the goods to which they assign lower rank. More interestingly, however, they have usually arisen through a historical supersession of earlier, less adequate views; they present themselves as steps to a higher moral consciousness. For example, the principle of equal respect is held as a hypergood by many people today; but those people recognize that it was not always dominant, that it arose through a process of conflict and development in which it gradually replaced earlier and more restricted ethics, and that it continues to find new applications by challenging other ethics even today (for example with respect to relations between the sexes). Such transvaluations of values – the complete rejection of goods previously treated as hypergoods themselves – are inherently conflictual.

Of course, examining such transvaluations raises the question of practical reason: for, even if a given hypergood establishes its dominance so that a culture moves away from a previously dominant ethic towards it, how can we be sure that the transition is a justifiable or rational one? Why should we accept the judgement that the previously dominant good is more restrictive or less worthy than the new one, when such judgements are inevitably made from within the framework of the new hypergood? For Taylor, the very feature of hypergoods that raises this worry also reveals the way to dissolve it; for human practical reason is precisely designed to cope with situations such as these – it is a reasoning in transitions.

Practical reasoning does not aim to establish that some position is correct absolutely, but rather that some position is superior to some other position; and it does so by demonstrating the epistemic gain that flows from making the transition from position A to position B. We can do this by showing that moving from A to B resolves a contradiction in A or a confusion that A relied on, or by acknowledging the importance of some factor that A screens out or obscures, and so on.

This picture of rationality is strongly reminiscent of MacIntyre's picture of the ways in which the rationality or validity of a given moral tradition might be vindicated against the claims of others by means of its capacity to cope with epistemological crises. It is therefore unsurprising to discover that Taylor sees this form of argument as having its source in biographical narrative:

> We are convinced that a certain view is superior because we have lived a transition which we understand as error-reducing and hence as epistemic gain. I see that I was confused about the relation of resentment and love, or I see that there is a depth to love conferred by time, which I was quite insensitive to before. But this doesn't mean that we don't and can't argue. Our conviction that we have grown morally can be challenged by another. It may after all be illusion. And then we argue; and arguing here is contesting between interpretations of what I have been living. (*SS*, p. 72)

Taylor's point, then, is not that claims to moral growth (whether at the personal or the cultural level) as a result of the transition from one hypergood to another are incontestable, or guaranteed to convince everyone. The point is that there are, and can be, no criteria for deciding the moral superiority of a given hypergood that do not themselves presuppose some moral framework or other. Any individual's perspective is and must be defined by the moral intuitions she has, the articulations by means of which she grounds them, and the considerations that move her morally; if she abstracts from this, she does not achieve moral objectivity: she becomes incapable of understanding any moral argument at all. A moral agent can be convinced only by changing her reading of her moral experience, and in particular her reading of her life story, of the transitions she has lived through (or refused to live through). Even if my moral framework is grounded in a belief in God, a being who infinitely transcends my moral experience, it is a belief in which I can have rational confidence only if it is itself grounded in considerations that take account of my moral experience.

In effect, then, Taylor's claim that practical reasoning is transitional amounts to the claim that any evaluations of practical reasoning will necessarily involve the invocation of conceptions of the good. Specific moral decisions and positions can be assessed as rational or irrational only by reference to one's own concrete moral experience and intuitions, and the conceptions of the good that they presuppose; and it will also entail the higher-order ranking of competing goods. The rationality of an agent will therefore be judged in *substantive* terms, according to whether her answer is right or not; being rational just is getting it right. So, just as one cannot comprehend the nature of human agency and morality without comprehending their intimate relation to conceptions of the good, so one cannot grasp the nature of the moral reasoning engaged in by such agents without appreciating that it is similarly indebted.

However, many modern ethical theories cleave to a procedural rather than a substantive conception of practical reasoning. For them, the rationality of the agent is assessed by reference to how she thinks rather than to the correctness of the answers she reaches; rationality is a matter of observing the correct procedures. This approach necessarily involves sidelining conceptions of the good; for redefining the value of practical reasoning in terms of its observation of a certain style or method entails that this value can and must be assessed entirely independently of the substantive worth of the conceptions of the good that are thereby chosen. It follows that, from

Taylor's perspective, there are two problems with any such conception of practical rationality. First, any such doctrine will be officially committed to denying the existence of a connection (between evaluations of practical rationality and the invocation of values and goods) which is an inevitable part of making judgements of rationality in ethics; and second, since the doctrine nonetheless constitutes one way of making such judgements (of assessing moral decisions and positions as rational or irrational), it must itself invoke certain values or goods despite its official commitments.

In the case of procedural conceptions, these values are not hard to unearth. Emphasizing the style or method of one's reasoning rather than its conclusions is a way of giving primacy to the agent's own desires and will; it highlights the importance of free and autonomous choice. Furthermore, it implicitly denies the existence of an objective order in nature or the universe, for such an order would determine that some conceptions of the good are right and others wrong and thus lead us towards a substantive conception of practical reason. Procedural conceptions of rationality in morals are designed for a disenchanted universe in which subjects are free to choose not only their way of life but also the standards in terms of which they shall measure the worth of those lives. In effect, they are committed to the hypergoods of modernity, the values identified by Sandel and MacIntyre as their main targets (although not under that title).

On Taylor's view, however, these substantive commitments are ones that the proponents of such conceptions are driven by the demands of their own theory to deny and repress. If they are to preserve the goods to which they are committed, they must ensure that the pursuit and achievement of practical rationality is assigned a certain primacy as against other pursuits; and they can achieve this only by asserting the priority of the moral domain over other aspects of human life. At the same time, however, their official aversion to the invocation of conceptions of the good ensures that they cannot offer an account of the reasons they have for asserting this priority, for that would transform their emphasis on procedure into an ultimate reliance upon arguments of substance. In short, according to Taylor, the protagonists of procedural reason face a dilemma. They must segregate the domain of the moral without being able to explain why; they must defend an absolute boundary without being able to account for its absoluteness.

It seems that they are motivated by the strongest moral ideals, such as freedom, altruism and universalism. These are amongst the central moral aspirations of moral culture, the hypergoods which are distinctive to it. And yet what these ideals drive the theorists towards is a denial of all such goods. They are caught in a strange pragmatic contradiction, whereby the very goods which move them push them to deny or denature all such goods. They are constitutionally incapable of coming clean about the deeper sources of their own thinking. (*SS*, p. 88)

The priority of right

The pragmatic contradiction in which proponents of procedural conceptions of practical reasoning find themselves is, in Taylor's view, also the inevitable fate of those who assign an absolute priority to the right over the good in their moral and political theorizing. And this, of course, is the point at which these seemingly abstract issues in moral philosophy make contact with the concerns of *A Theory of Justice*. Assigning priority to the right is perfectly justifiable, and indeed demanded, if this is meant to signify a rejection of utilitarianism or other consequentialist theories; for then it simply signifies a first-order substantive insistence that morality ought not to be conceived simply in terms of outcomes, but should also include notions of intrinsic worth or duty. But it can also be used to signal a particular second-order ethical view; in that context, it indicates not a rejection of the homogeneous good of desire-fulfilment around which utilitarianism is based, but rather a rejection or downgrading of the relevance of any conception of the good. It is in effect an attempt to argue for a moral view without invoking any of the qualitative distinctions that Taylor has argued are inseparable from the elucidation of any moral view whatsoever.

Taylor here takes Rawls as an example. The Rawlsian theory of justice is held to avoid reliance upon any particular conception of the good; for if it did not, then the social institutions that it advocates would effectively impose that conception upon all those who lived their lives within them, and their autonomy would be violated. If, however, we are to assess the principles of justice that emerge from that theory, we must assess them against our moral intuitions – this is what Rawls admits is integral to his method of reflective equilibrium. And if we are to articulate the frameworks and ontological accounts that do and must underlie those intuitions – if, in other words, we are to engage in practical reasoning about them – we would necessarily start spelling out a very substantive theory of the good. Even if we do not spell it out, we are necessarily relying upon a complex and sophisticated sense of the good when we advocate those principles; and the claim, essential to Rawls's understanding of his project, that no such conception is at stake is simply an instance of repression or denial.

Taylor summarizes his point as follows:

> Where 'good' means the primary goal of a consequentialist theory, where the right is decided simply by its instrumental significance for this end, then we ought indeed to insist that the right can be primary to the good. But where we use 'good' in the sense of this discussion, where it means whatever is marked out as higher by a qualitative distinction, then we could say that the reverse is the case, that, in a sense, the good is always primary to the right . . . the good is what, in its articulation, gives the point of the rules which define the right. (*SS*, p. 89)

In other words, Taylor's claim, both with respect to procedural conceptions of practical reasoning and to deontological conceptions of justice, is that their official prohibition on the invocation of anything more than a thin theory of the good is necessarily incoherent. We cannot do without the wide-ranging and funda-mental qualitative distinctions which go to make up a thick theory of the good because in their absence we have no way of articulating the moral point of the actions and feelings that our moral intuitions enjoin upon us or present as admirable. They may not always be explicit or clearly articulated in our everyday moral life, but if they were not there to be articulated – or if we are forbidden from drawing upon them – we would be left with nothing that we could recognize as morality. Our moral intuitions would lack the very feature that distinguishes them from brute reactions such as nausea, and that is integral both to the identity of a recognizably human self *and* to the narrative unity of a recognizably human life: they would lack any relation to conceptions of the good.

Taylor and the communitarian critique of Rawls

In his own presentation of the views that we have been examining above, Taylor does not explicitly name Rawls as the target of his critique except when discussing the priority of the right over the good. Rather, he defines his position in opposition to much more general and pervasive strands of cultural thought, such as naturalism and utilitarianism, thus implying that he has bigger fish to fry than a specific contemporary political theorist. Nonetheless, people did regard Taylor as participating in a communitarian critique of liberalism; and it is the purpose of this section to examine the validity of that perception.

In the first place, it is clear that there is a genuine family resemblance between Taylor's work and that of the writers we have examined in previous chapters. More precisely, Taylor's general conclusions and those of Sandel and (more particularly) MacIntyre exhibit a striking degree of convergence. Like both Sandel and MacIntyre, Taylor claims that commitments or orientations towards the good are integral to or constitutive of the identity of the self; moreover, like MacIntyre, he claims that the life of a human being can only be understood in terms of its narrative form – the narrative of that individual's progress towards (or away from) the good. In addition, Taylor argues – just like MacIntyre – that the very notion of morality as a rational enterprise presupposes this view of the person and of a human life, since only they can allow room for a substantive conception of practical reasoning as a reasoning in transitions that must always be rooted in concrete moral experience and a particular moral framework. And of course, Taylor concludes by arguing (again, like MacIntyre) that any moral or political theory that claims to dispense with or to be neutral between conceptions of the good will find itself embroiled in a pragmatic contradiction, forced to rely upon value commitments of a kind, and claiming a degree of generality, that it has officially prohibited.

In addition, underlying and unifying these specific positions we can see in Taylor an essentially communitarian conception of moral frameworks and of the self, but one which more closely resembles MacIntyre's than it does Sandel's. For in Taylor's view, any adequate conception of morality, of the self and its narrative unity, and of practical reasoning must acknowledge the foundational importance of moral frameworks or qualitative distinctions; and all such frameworks are essentially communal in nature: they can be established, maintained and acquired only through membership of a language community. This constitutes a profound attack upon asocial individualism, but an attack upon its philosophical rather than its substantive variants, since it amounts to criticizing moral and political theories for ignoring or repressing the dependence of all conceptions of the good and of the self upon social matrices rather than for ignoring or repressing the importance of conceptions of the good that are strongly communal in content. In this respect, Taylor's affinities are once again with MacIntyre rather than Sandel. And of course, this communitarian inflection in Taylor is in the last resort a consequence of his conception of the self. For if human beings are self-interpreting animals, and the linguistic and experiential resources for such self-interpretations are only to be found in the context of a community of other selves, then Taylor is committed to the view that community is a structural precondition of human agency and selfhood.

What, however, justifies the claim that Taylor's communitarian critique is applicable to Rawlsian liberalism – that Rawls is incapable of acknowledging any of these points? Here, it is worth recalling the way in which we located his criticisms on our original agenda of issues. As we mentioned at the beginning of this chapter, Taylor's conception of human selfhood is such as to generate a critique that is applicable to any political theory committed to an unencumbered or disembodied conception of the self (first theme), to some philosophical versions of asocial individualism (second theme), to certain variants of moral subjectivism (fourth theme) and to any claim to have dispensed with the invocation of a substantial theory of the good (fifth theme). Apart from this fourth and final point, Taylor never explicitly claims that Rawls is propounding a theory that exemplifies these errors. So it seems that Taylor can only be seen as a critic of Rawls under the first three of our headings if Sandel and MacIntyre are right in their belief that Rawls is committed to an unencumbered or emotivist view of the self, one that regards the self as individuated prior to its choice of ends and its participation in communities. The identity of such a self would not depend upon her choice of conceptions of the good, and the course of her life would have no narrative logic; her practical reasoning would be procedural, and her moral frameworks would lack any ultimate rational status. Moreover, anyone committed to such a view of the self would seem to be committed to some form of atomism or asocial individualism, since antecedently individuated selves are logically prior to and so essentially independent of any society of which they might be members. In short, a theory committed to such a conception would be vulnerable to every facet of the argument Taylor has developed under the first three headings of our agenda; and its vulnerability would be a consequence of its fundamentally non-communitarian understanding of the nature of selfhood. But it must be noted that Taylor's work does not, and is not intended to, support the claim that such a conception of the self is one to which Rawls really is or must be committed.

What Taylor's work *does* directly support is the weaker conclusion that Rawls must be committed to *some* particular conception of the self. For according to him, any moral or political theory must rely upon an implicit set of qualitative distinctions and an ontological account of human nature. If that theory is to count as a contribution to moral debate, it will draw upon a sense of the good that must be articulable; and any such articulation will involve an attempt to explain what it is about human beings that entails that they be treated in the way that the theory demands. Taylor's point is thus not the trivial one that any given theory about the just treatment of persons will involve some conception of the person; it is the stronger, dual claim that such a theory can only be defended if the theorist is prepared substantively to endorse a very general conception of the nature of human beings and the worth of their lives. Taylor would thus seem to support the conclusion that Rawls can refuse to engage with his opponents at this fundamental level only on pain of abdicating from the arena of moral debate altogether; there seems to be no half-way house. Rawls's conception of the person may not be what Sandel thinks it is, but he must nonetheless be relying upon some particular ontology of the human.

It might also be thought that Rawls is directly vulnerable to Taylor's critique of procedural conceptions of practical reasoning. For Rawlsian justice as fairness is presented to us as the product of reasoning that takes place in the original position; and in that position, no reliance upon knowledge of a particular conception of the good is permitted. Rather, the observance of certain principles and prohibitions whilst deliberating is held to guarantee the validity of the outcome of that deliberation; in short, a pure procedural conception of justice is at stake. To think that this makes Rawls vulnerable to Taylor's critique would, however, be a mistake; and it is a mistake that Taylor explicitly counsels his reader against making (cf. *SS*, p. 87, n. 60). For, of course, although reasoning *within* the original position is procedural, the reasoning that leads us to *accept* the original position and its constraints as appropriate to questions of social justice is not. On the contrary, restricting reasoning in the original position to a purely procedural form is presented by Rawls as necessary for the maintenance of certain substantive goods – in particular, as reflecting our concern to respect the freedom and equality of all citizens. So Rawls cannot be held to involve himself in a pragmatic contradiction of the sort that Taylor diagnoses in other attempts to defend a procedural conception of justice.

This leaves us with the only direct criticism of Rawls to which Taylor does commit himself – the one that relates to the fifth heading on our agenda. As we saw earlier, Rawls figures explicitly in Taylor's work only as a proponent of the priority of the right over the good, a principle regarded by Taylor as equivalent to the claim that Rawlsian liberalism embodies a view of justice that is not dependent upon anything other than a 'thin' theory of the good. Taylor argues that if the grounds for accepting the priority of the right are fully articulated, they will be found to constitute a very substantive sense of the good, one in which a set of qualitative distinctions hangs together with a particular ontological account of human nature.

What this criticism amounts to is the claim that Rawlsian liberalism cannot be as neutral between competing conceptions of the good as it aspires to be. The absolute priority assigned to the right over the good reflects Rawls's assignment of absolute priority to the value of autonomy; it reflects the fact that autonomy is the Rawlsian hypergood. Reliance upon a hypergood is not in itself a flaw in any moral theory; it is rather *de rigueur*. And Taylor is happy to admit that the liberal hypergood is one that has many attractions. But, according to his arguments about the nature of moral evaluation and debate, it is merely self-delusive for liberals to attempt to defend their values by claiming that they – unlike their opponents – make use of a minimal array of evaluative assumptions about the good life for human beings and about human nature. In effect, Taylor agrees with the main thrust of MacIntyre's argument that, in order to defend its claim about the right way to organize the sphere of political life (that is, separating it from that of ethics or morality more broadly understood by forbidding the invocation of conceptions of the good life for human beings within politics), liberalism must draw upon the conceptions of human good and the general ontology of the human that make up the broad liberal ethical tradition of which this conception of politics is merely a part.

This claim about the wide-ranging roots of liberal political theory has its counterpart with respect to liberal political practice. For Taylor also claims that the goal of developing, protecting and maintaining human beings in their full autonomy as citizens requires a great deal more than the sustenance of a liberal political system; it requires the maintenance of a distinctively liberal society. This follows from his understanding of persons as self-interpreting animals. For such an animal could only *be* an autonomous chooser of ends in a society whose institutions and culture embodied and presupposed a conception of persons as autonomous choosers of ends; it could not otherwise have the conceptual resources to interpret itself in that way and so to be a person of that sort. So the institutions and practices of modern liberal democratic societies (for example negotiations and contracts, public debate on moral and political issues, voting systems, universities) are absolutely vital in ensuring that its members regard themselves as, and so become, people whose interpersonal relations are willed, who have an identity distinct from that of other individuals, who are capable of autonomously choosing and revising their conceptions of the good.

In other words, although it may be a trivial truth that any being recognizable as a human agent must be possessed of a will and be capable of exercising it, it is not a condition of human status that one interpret oneself as being most fundamentally and essentially an autonomous chooser of ends: that will happen (if it happens at all) only in an appropriately liberal social matrix. And two important conclusions follow from this. First, it implies that an individualist political tradition such as liberalism, one that places emphasis upon the right of each human being to a measure of freedom and equality, must not express its concern for the preservation of those rights in ways that ignore or conflict with its need simultaneously to preserve the social structures that underpin them. If, for example, liberals were to present the institutions and procedures that embody its individualist values as purely instrumental affairs, as merely the means by which individuals defend themselves against others, then they may weaken the sense of a common allegiance to those institutions without which they will be unable to carry out their instrumental work, and the society that they help to make up would lose its cohesion. In short, even someone committed to values or goods that are essentially individual in content must also be committed to defending the communal structures underpinning those individualist values.[4]

The second conclusion we can draw depends upon seeing that the communal structures that the liberal is committed to defending are pervasive elements in our social life; universities, modes of negotiation and genres of public debate seem to be 'political' structures only in a rather broad understanding of that term. But then it may be misleading for liberal political theory to present itself as something that could *either* be argued for without drawing upon values that apply far beyond the realm of party politics *or* implemented otherwise than as part of a generally liberal social order. In other words, Rawlsian liberalism in politics may only be defensible as one component in a more general project to establish and maintain a society that embodies a very specific conception of the human good. Taylor thinks that this will involve a significant alteration in the Rawlsian self-interpretation. If Taylor is right, then by adopting this mode of defining itself Rawlsian liberalism will be altering its identity: it will be altering its self. And even if Taylor is wrong about Rawls's self-understanding, it might nonetheless be the case that a wider appreciation of this point about the true degree of liberal neutrality will significantly alter the image of liberalism that occupies the minds of many people in contemporary society.

Notes

1 His most important contributions to that field can be found in the two volumes of his *Philosophical Papers*.
2 An account to be found in his most recent book *Sources of the Self* (hereafter *SS*).
3 Taylor, 'Interpretation and the Sciences of Man' (page reference is to the 1985 collection).
4 This is the point that is central to Taylor's worries about atomism, and to his own analysis of Sandel's critique of Rawlsian liberalism in 'Cross-Purposes'.

4

WALZER:

justice and abstraction

Michael Walzer's critique of Rawlsian liberalism is pitched at a level significantly different from that of the other three communitarian thinkers we have already examined. Unlike Sandel, Walzer is not primarily concerned with criticizing the Rawlsian conception of the person; and unlike MacIntyre and Taylor, he is not interested in presenting a sweeping historical account of Western culture from which certain criticisms of liberalism in general and Rawls in particular can be deduced. The position put forward in *Spheres of Justice (SJ)* focuses rather upon the question of what *methodology* is appropriate to the business of political theory; Walzer wants to know how one should go about constructing and defending a theory of justice. More specifically, he concentrates upon how we should understand the goods for which a theory of justice seeks to articulate distributive principles, and attacks the understanding of this matter that he identifies in Rawls's theory.

The essence of Walzer's argument may be had from his claim that 'different social goods ought to be distributed for different reasons, in accordance with different procedures, by different agents; and all these differences derive from different understandings of the social goods themselves – the inevitable product of historical and cultural particularism' (*SJ*, p. 6). We should note from the outset that this brief quotation contains two distinct strands of argument. On the one hand, there is the substantive claim that 'different social goods ought to be distributed for different reasons', which we will refer to as the 'differentiated substance' of the theory. This is the idea, contained in the title of his book, that different goods constitute different distributional spheres within which specific distributive arrangements are appropriate, and that justice consists in autonomous distributions, whereby the distribution of a good such as, for example, health care, is in accordance with the principles peculiar to that good and not corrupted by goods, such as money, that properly belong to other spheres. On the other hand, there is the quite distinct point that these differences derive from different 'understandings of the social goods themselves' and that such understandings are 'the inevitable product of historical and cultural particularism'; we will call this the 'particularistic methodology' of the theory. This is the idea that the way to see how particular goods should be distributed is to look at how those goods are understood in the particular culture in question. As this last sentence suggests, and as we shall see in this chapter, Walzer is objecting to two distinct kinds of abstraction, and insisting upon two distinct kinds of particularity or specificity. The political theorist should recognize both that distributive principles must be good-specific and that good-specific principles must be culture-specific. Rawls is deemed to be deficient on both counts.

It is Walzer's particularistic methodology that shows how his critique of liberalism should be placed on our agenda of issues; for the idea that the principles of justice must be culture-specific entails a hostility to any political theory that embodies claims to universality (the third theme on our agenda). Moreover, like Sandel, Walzer is careful to offer specific arguments and references to Rawls's theory that are intended to validate his claim that Rawlsian liberalism is insufficiently particularistic in its methodology; so we can spell out the sense in which Walzer's work is intended as a critique of Rawls simply through our exegetical summary of that work. What may be less clear is the degree to which Walzer's critique resembles that of the other writers we have been considering. In particular, his writings are good-rather than person-oriented; he makes no mention of a conception of the person underlying those aspects of Rawls's theorizing to which he objects, and focuses rather upon the meanings that certain goods have for the persons to whom they are to be distributed. This might suggest that his approach would better be regarded as concerned with the distributive aspects of Rawlsian liberalism than with the emphasis on the freedom of the individual in relation to her community, which we have claimed to be the distinctive concern of the communitarian critique. Nonetheless, as we shall see, Walzer's focus on goods and the principles appropriate for their distribution does involve a claim about the importance of the community as the repository of value and thus, implicitly, about the priority of the community over the individual; and the key elements of his critique can be restated in terms that relate them more directly to a conception of the person and of what is in their interests or constitutes their well-being. Moreover, it will also become clear that the presuppositions of Rawls's approach to distributive matters to which Walzer takes exception are in fact a consequence of the distinctive Rawlsian concern for the freedom of the individual – as epitomized in his prohibition on the invocation of conceptions of the good in the sphere of politics.

So much for preliminary orientation. Now we must outline the main elements of Walzer's critique, beginning with his attack on methodological abstraction.

Rawls's methodological abstraction

Walzer is most emphatic in his insistence that the political theorist should not seek to transcend the contexts constituted by cultural particularity and difference. As he puts it:

> My argument is radically particularist. I don't claim to have achieved any great distance from the social world in which I live. One way to begin the philosophical enterprise – perhaps the original way – is to walk out of the cave, leave the city, climb the mountain, fashion for oneself . . . an objective and universal standpoint. Then one describes the terrain of everyday life from far away, so that it loses its particular contours and takes on a general shape. But I mean to stand in the cave, in the city, on the ground. Another way of doing philosophy is to interpret to one's fellow citizens the world of meanings that we share. (*SJ*, p. xiv)

Rather than trying to detach herself from the society in which she lives and assessing it from a vantage-point above the contingencies of culture, the philosopher should seek to articulate those very shared 'meanings' that constitute that culture.

Walzer is explicit that it is theories like Rawls's that are the target here. Referring not only to *A Theory of Justice* but also to works by Habermas and Ackerman[1] which share the structural features to which he objects, he writes that today the system of distributive justice 'is commonly described as the one that ideally rational men and women would choose if they were forced to choose impartially, knowing nothing of their own situation, barred from making particularist claims, confronting an abstract set of goods' (*SJ*, p. 5). In the case of Rawls, this is particularly clear; for the things of which justice demands the principled distribution are 'primary goods'. That is:

> Things which it is supposed a rational man wants whatever else he wants. Regardless of what an individual's rational plans are in detail, it is assumed that there are various things which he would prefer more of rather than less. With more of these goods men can generally be assured of greater success in carrying out their intentions and in advancing their ends, whatever these ends may be. The primary social goods, to give them in broad categories, are rights and liberties, opportunities and powers, income and wealth. (*TJ*, p. 92)

The presentation of Rawls's theory in our introductory chapter should have made clear why he was to invoke some such generalized or abstract conception. The people in the original position are denied knowledge of their particular conceptions of the good and must be motivated rather by 'the thin theory of the good' which defines a person's good in suitably non-committal terms as 'the successful execution of a rational plan of life' (*TJ*, p. 433). With appropriate caveats about the difficulties involved in the term 'neutrality', we might say that the point about primary goods is that they are in some sense neutral between the different conceptions of the good that people might actually choose to frame and pursue. As Rawls puts it:

> I suppose that it is rational to want these goods whatever else is wanted, since they are in general necessary for the framing and execution of a rational plan of life. The persons in the original position are assumed to accept this conception of the good, and therefore they take for granted that they desire greater liberty and opportunity, and more extensive means for achieving their ends. (*TJ*, p. 433)

In short, abstraction from particularity is essential to Rawls's understanding of the goods with which his theory is concerned because it is an integral aspect of the abstraction from particular conceptions of the good that he imposes in order to protect the autonomy of those to whom these goods are to be distributed. Distributive questions here make contact with questions of individual freedom in a way that ensures that Walzer's critique of matters relating to the former can be construed as pertinent to matters relating to the latter. In other words, his goods-based critique of Rawls is by no means as distant from the autonomy-focused critiques of the other three communitarian critics of liberalism as it might appear.

So far, however, we have simply pointed out reasons for thinking that Rawls will be in the target area of Walzer's critique of methodological abstraction. We have not even begun to explore the question of what Walzer thinks is damaging about such abstraction. What is wrong with suggesting that questions of social justice ought to be considered under conditions that minimize the making of particularist claims about the relevant goods?

The problem is not that one will not reach a singular conclusion, for Walzer recognizes that, if they are suitably constrained, rational people will choose a particular distributive system. Nor is the problem that particularism of interest that might lead people to disregard the 'rational' or 'impartial' conclusion because it does not suit them as they actually are in real life. For Walzer, people *can* set aside their own particular interests for the public good. The failure of this approach is rather its lack of attention to a different kind of particularity:

> The problem is with the particularism of history, culture, and membership. Even if they are committed to impartiality, the question most likely to arise in the minds of members of a political community is not. What would rational individuals choose under universalizing conditions of such and such a sort? But rather, What would individuals like us choose, who are situated as we are, who share a culture and are determined to go on sharing it? And this is a question that is readily transformed into. What choices have we already made in the course of our common life? What understandings do we (really) share? (*SJ*, p. 5)

Why should people who necessarily conceive themselves, and the goods that make up the social world in which they live, in 'thick' culture-laden ways disregard that cultural particularity and adopt a 'thin' conception of 'rationality' when thinking about principles to govern the distribution of goods in their society? The abstraction that Rawls's theory requires involves, for Walzer, a disattention to the choices that people have already made and that are embodied in their culture's own particular understandings of the goods that are to be distributed. What we must now examine are Walzer's grounds for condemning such disattention.

Against methodological abstraction: the conceptual argument

The first argument Walzer provides takes a purely conceptual form, in that it follows from his analysis of the very concept of a good. The opening proposition of his 'theory of goods' states that 'all the goods with which distributive justice is concerned are social goods' (*SJ*, p. 7) and it is the various implications of the term 'social' here that underpin his whole approach. Above all, its force is to assert that the meaning and value that goods have are derived from the communities whose goods they are. On the one hand, goods do not have brute 'natural' meanings: they only acquire their significance through a process of interpretation and understanding, of 'conception and creation'. On the other, that process is always and necessarily a social and not an individual one. 'A solitary person could hardly understand the meaning of the goods or figure out the reason for taking them as likable or dislikable' (*SJ*, pp. 7–8). Here we see Walzer giving his own application of the communitarian thought, already observed in Taylor and to some extent in MacIntyre, that points to the inherently social nature of concepts and language. Goods do not come into the world with their meanings attached to them, or if they do, it is only because they have been conceived and created in a manner that is irreducibly social.

And if the meanings of goods are necessarily social, they will have different meanings in different societies. Take an apparently basic pre-interpretive good such as bread; surely here is a good whose 'meaning' is not a matter of social or cultural construction but of biological necessity. Not for Walzer: 'Bread is the staff of life, the body of Christ, the symbol of the Sabbath, the means of hospitality, and so on' (*SJ*, p. 8). While it may be the case that, if it came to the distributive crunch, the first bread-as-the-staff-of-life use would take precedence, even this is not certain. We can easily imagine cultures in which any conflicts that might arise between nutritional uses of bread and religious uses of it could as easily be settled in favour of the latter. We might think perhaps also of those religious sects that understand the meaning of health care, and of the divine will, in such a way that they would rather watch their children die than allow them to receive medical attention. The same 'things' may mean quite different things to different cultures.

What is most important for Walzer about such culture-dependence of meaning is that the meaning of a good and an understanding of the way in which it should be distributed go together, and thus the latter is as inherently social as the former. As he puts it:

> . . . it is the meaning of goods that determines their movement. Distributive criteria and arrangements are intrinsic not to the good-in-itself but to the social good. If we understand what it is, what it means to those for whom it is a good, we understand how, by whom, and for what reasons it ought to be distributed. All distributions are just or unjust relative to the social meanings of the goods at stake. (*SJ*, pp. 8–9)

An example may make the force of this point clearer. Take the social good of health care: a Walzerian could argue that, in our society, anyone who understands what health care is (that is, grasps its social meaning) will know that its primary or essential purpose is the treatment of illness and the restoration and maintenance of physical well-being. But it immediately follows from this understanding that this particular social good should be distributed in a certain way, namely to those who are in need of it, to those who are ill or unhealthy. Anyone who failed to see this would simply have failed to grasp the meaning of this particular good; and although it might be possible to argue that practical political and social constraints will bring other considerations into the picture when a particular health care system is being set up, the onus of argument is upon those who wish to introduce distributive principles other than those already inherent in the meaning of the good itself.

The difficulty for a Rawlsian approach would seem to be clear: There is no single set of primary or basic goods conceivable across all moral and material worlds – or, any such set would have to be considered in terms so abstract that they would be of little use in thinking about particular distributions' (*SJ*, p. 8). Questions of social justice do not arise about primary goods; they arise about specific goods with specific and often radically different meanings in specific societies. But Rawls's principles of justice are intended to apply to the distribution of primary goods, and so will possess a degree of abstractness which will make it impossible for them to be usefully applied to particular goods in particular societies; they will bear as distant and opaque a relation to those goods as does the notion of a primary good itself. If, however, the requisite initial and detailed attention is paid to the social meaning of those specific goods, then they will be found already to contain specific distributive principles. And, given that the meaning of the good is where any theory of justice must begin its analysis and argument, then the distributive principles that are an essential aspect of that meaning must similarly be regarded as the unavoidable starting point and essential bench-mark of deliberations about the just distribution of that good. In short, the particularity of the social meanings of all human goods seems to entail that the methodological abstraction that generates Rawlsian principles of justice will make them either useless or superfluous.

Against methodological abstraction: the democratic argument

Although the conceptual argument against methodological abstraction is important to Walzer's approach in *Spheres of Justice*, there are grounds for thinking that a more substantive argument is also at work. For example, on the penultimate page of that book Walzer writes that 'There is a certain attitude of mind that underlies the theory of justice . . .: we can think of it as a decent respect for the opinions of mankind' (*SJ*, p. 320). Here, Walzer's worry seems to be that the kind of political philosophy that seeks detachment from social meanings and so from the particular community of which the philosopher is a member will not only result in principles of justice that are impossible to apply to concrete cases; it will also fail to accord proper weight to the opinions of the philosopher's fellow citizens as those are embodied in the present social meanings of specific goods. And in so doing it will reveal the sense in which that kind of political philosophy is undemocratic, or at least prone to undemocratic application.

If we draw on his fuller presentation of this strand of argument in an article that predates *Spheres of Justice* by a couple of years,[2] we can see that for Walzer it is the fact that philosophy aims at truth that gives it its undemocratic implications. For in order to reach 'truth' the philosopher must detach himself from his particular time and circumstances, from the particular ways of thinking prevalent in his culture, rising above such contingency to achieve an objective standpoint. As Walzer puts it, and his terminology makes clear that Rawls and Habermas are again the targets,

> The truths he commonly seeks are universal and eternal, and it is unlikely that they can be found from inside of any real and historic community. Hence the philosopher's withdrawal: he must deny himself the assurances of the commonplace . . . To what sort of a place, then, does he withdraw? Most often, today, he constructs for himself . . . an ideal commonwealth, inhabited by beings who have none of the particular characteristics and none of the opinions and commitments of his former fellow-citizens. He imagines a perfect meeting in an 'original position' or 'ideal speech situation' . . .[3]

For Walzer, taking seriously Wittgenstein's observation that 'the philosopher is not a citizen of any community of ideas',[4] the withdrawal of the philosopher to his original position represents an attempt to leave behind the role of citizen, to achieve the kind of standpoint that gives one's conclusions a status, as 'truths', superior to the mere opinions of the other members of one's political community.

Democracy, however, is not about truth. The justification of democratic government is not that it is likely to yield right decisions, where rightness can be understood as something that could have been arrived at by other means (such as philosophical argument), but that it yields decisions that embody the will of the citizenry. The people's claim to rule rests not upon their knowledge of truth but upon who they are: citizens who can only freely be bound by laws if they themselves make them. 'On the democratic view, it is right that they make the laws even if they make them wrongly.'[5] Since law should be a function of popular will and not of reason, the philosopher's commitment to the latter is likely to be problematic.

Now, even if we accept that understanding of his role that has him seeking heroic detachment from the opinions of his fellow citizens, it does not immediately follow that the truth-seeking philosopher must be aiming to subvert the democratic process. If he presents his arguments in the right spirit, if he simply invites the people to revise their own conclusions in the light of his work, then there is no problem. 'At the moment of publication, at least, he is a proper democrat: his book is a gift to the people.'[6] Nor does Walzer think that the results of philosophical 'objective' thinking are necessarily irrelevant. He does not doubt that the aspiration to realize universal truths is one by means of which particular communities can improve themselves. What worries him is rather that the philosopher will claim for his conclusions a different status from that which he accords to the opinions of his fellow citizens, and, finding that the latter resist some or all of those conclusions, seek to bypass the democratic arena and have them directly instituted in law.

It is here that Walzer's argument becomes clearly aimed at the doctrine of judicial review as that is practised in the United States, where the Constitution accords people certain rights and entrusts the judiciary with the task of interpreting that Constitution and reviewing legislation to ensure that it does not infringe them. The anti-democratic bent of such a procedure should be obvious: indeed it is precisely as a means of protecting individuals against the will of majorities (or, to put it more controversially, the will of the community) that rights may best be understood. Whether or not one can provide a justification of rights that appeals to the same values as those that ground one's commitment to democracy and thus attempt to resolve the tension,[7] it is clear that the basic function of constitutional rights, and of the doctrine of judicial review which serves to protect them, is precisely to act as constraints on the democratic will. Walzer is worried that the philosopher will persuade those judges whose task it is to interpret the Constitution that detached reasoning demonstrates that people have an extensive list of rights. Since 'the more rights the judges award to people as individuals, the less free the people are as a decision-making body',[8] this is subversive of democracy. Indeed, for Walzer this philosophical list of rights invites judicial activity that is radically intrusive on what he calls 'democratic space' as soon as it extends beyond bans on legal discrimination and political repression.

Because the whole point of his detachment is to achieve a standpoint from which he can transcend the particularity of his own community, and because communities will differ in the answers that they reach, it follows that the political success of the philosopher 'would have the effect of enforcing a singular over a pluralist truth',[9] of overriding those cultural differences constituted by citizens' own 'traditions, conventions, and expectations'.[10] Moreover, and more closely connected to the democratic principle:

> It is not only the familiar products of their experience that the people value, but the experience itself, the process through which the products were produced. And they will have some difficulty understanding why the hypothetical experience of abstract men and women should take precedence over their own history . . . They might well choose politics over truth, and that choice, if they make it, will make in turn for pluralism. Any historical community whose members shape their own institutions and laws will necessarily produce a particular and not a universal way of life. That particularity can be overcome only from the outside and only by repressing internal political processes.[11]

Thus the argument for keeping the democratic space free from interference from philosophy is simultaneously an argument for pluralism over singularity and particularity over universality.

Clearly, the substantive issue of the extent to which the rights of individuals should be permitted to constrain the will of the people is too large to be addressed in a satisfactory manner in this context. What is important for our purposes, and what will take us back towards the kind of argument that is central to Walzer's *Spheres of Justice*, is the observation that the case in favour of 'a decent respect for the opinions of mankind' is distinct from that against the incorporation of extensive individual rights in the law. The latter is a particular instance of the much more general former, for clearly the opinions that the philosopher might be urged decently to respect might include ones other than those implying policies that infringe rights.

This distinction is important because it reveals that in this earlier article Walzer is really objecting to two separate aspects of Rawls's theory, which he takes together. On the one hand, what he dislikes is the general failure to attend to cultural particularity, the attempt to transcend his fellow citizens' 'conventions, traditions and expectations'. On the other, the specific focus of his objection is the way in which such disattention leads to a political theory framed in terms of rights which then serve to limit the scope available for popular decision-making. While each of these strands can be formulated in terms of the charge that Rawls fails to recognize the importance of community, the force of such a charge is importantly different in the two cases. In the first case the problem is that Rawls, in seeking a universal standpoint and a single right answer, does not attach proper importance to the values and practices of particular communities. Here it is the pretensions to universality that neglect the importance of community. In the second it is rather that the particular theory that he articulates is one which, in framing itself as a theory of justice and rights, gives priority to the individual over her community. Here it is the liberal framework that is the enemy of community.

It is the first strand rather than the second that feeds into *Spheres of Justice* and that is part of Walzer's distinctive contribution to the communitarian critique. For, as we have said, what is novel about his position is the extent to which it focuses not on the standard problematic of the relation between the individual and her community but on the rather different issue of how we should think about those goods that it is the aim of a theory of justice to distribute. What Walzer is above all concerned to point out is the variety of ways in which different cultures understand the different goods and distributive principles that together make up their social world, and his claim is that a theory of justice must be true to those understandings. We have already seen that the force of this 'must' is partly conceptual in nature: not being true to those understandings condemns one's theory to uselessness. Now we can see that the force of this 'must' is also substantive, that we must be true to those understandings on pain of being undemocratic, of failing to *respect* those whose understandings they are.

What is particularly interesting about Walzer's two-pronged methodological critique is that he is happy, on occasion, to couch it in terms of a general conception of the person. For example, he poses the following rhetorical question:

By virtue of what characteristics are we one another's equals? One characteristic above all is central to my argument. We are (all of us) culture-producing creatures; we make and inhabit meaningful worlds. Since there is no way to rank and order these worlds with regard to their understanding of social goods, we do justice to actual men and women by respecting their particular creations. And they claim justice, and resist tyranny, by insisting on the meaning of social goods among themselves. Justice is rooted in the distinct understandings of places, honors, jobs, things of all sorts, that constitute a shared way of life. To override those understandings is (always) to act unjustly. (*SJ*, p. 314)

In other words, what Walzer thinks matters about people is their capacity to 'make and inhabit meaningful worlds', to endow the natural world and brute objects with significance and value – a view that resembles Taylor's vision of human beings as self-interpreting animals. What is communitarian about this claim, and what is signified by the insistence that the world they create is 'social', is the fact that meanings and values are irreducibly communal and cannot be created by individuals acting alone. So, where the liberal identifies people's highest-order interests as being in their capacity as individuals to frame, revise and pursue conceptions of the good, Walzer directs us rather to the point that such processes are necessarily parasitic upon cultural constructions that are essentially communal.

Of course, and as we have already hinted, the pretensions to universality that Walzer identifies in Rawls's theory – and that must be there if his methodological critique of Rawlsian liberalism (in whatever terms it is couched) is to succeed – may be more apparent than real, and this suggestion applies to its understanding of goods as much as to its other aspects. In our chapter on the new Rawls we shall in fact argue that his conception of primary goods is not as abstract or as universal as it seems. For now, having established that two separate lines of argument converge in Walzer's affirmation of methodological particularism in political theory, we can consider some of the objections and difficulties to which this methodological approach seems to be open.

The relativity of social meanings

The fundamental issue raised by Walzer's arguments against methodological abstraction, epitomized in his claim that 'All distributions are just or unjust relative to the social meanings of the goods at stake' (*SJ*, p. 9), is that of relativism. Does it imply that there is no basis upon which we can criticize the social meanings of another culture? No trans-cultural standards to which we can appeal when defending our own and rejecting the distributive practices of other societies? Or that there is no basis upon which we can criticize the understandings of goods conventional in our own society? No place for the political theorist as social critic? Is the political theory that results from the application of such a methodology necessarily conservative, perhaps even failing to see that 'social meanings' are themselves ideological in content, serving to conceal or to justify relations of power and exploitation? If these are the implications, are they acceptable, or should we rather seek a different methodological approach which might involve less counter-intuitive assertions? There are here big questions of interpretation ('What exactly is Walzer's position?') and of argument ('Is it tenable?'), and, in concentrating on the former, we do not aim to do more than indicate the kinds of move that might be made on either side of the relativism debate.[12]

It cannot be doubted that there is a significant relativistic strand in Walzer's position: 'Justice is relative to social meanings . . . There are an infinite number of possible lives, shaped by an infinite number of possible cultures, religions, political arrangements, geographical conditions, and so on. A given society is just if its substantive life is lived in a certain way – that is, in a way faithful to the shared understandings of the members. (*SJ*, pp. 312–13) Consider, to take an extreme example which Walzer himself uses, a society with a well-defined caste system, where a person's position in terms of religious purity, itself a function of one's birth and blood, determines her access to a variety of other goods. As long as the social meanings supportive of that system are genuinely shared, then justice consists in being true to those meanings. However much they may offend against our beliefs about the equal status of all human beings, about the rights of individuals to equality of opportunity, even about the criteria (such as need or ability) relevant to the distribution of particular goods (such as health care or education), we must adopt the relativistic position that says that justice is internal to social meanings, and hence that a grossly unequal distribution of goods, and one that gives little or no weight to the criteria *we* consider relevant, is just. As Walzer says, 'In a society where social meanings are integrated and hierarchical, justice will come to the aid of inequality' (*SJ*, p. 313).

The example of the caste society makes particularly clear the distinction between Walzer's general methodological injunction to respect social meanings and the more specific claim he makes about our society (which we will examine later), namely that different goods should be distributed for different reasons; for the point about a caste society is that their meanings are not distinct. Rather, '. . . the system is constituted by an extraordinary integration of meanings. Prestige, wealth, knowledge, office, occupation, food, clothing, even the social good of conversation: all are subject to the intellectual as well as to the physical discipline of hierarchy. And the hierarchy is itself determined by the single value of ritual purity . . . Social meanings overlap and cohere' (*SJ*, p. 27). In other words, whilst Walzer's theory implies differentiation of distributive principles for us, this is only because he reads our social meanings as committing us to such differentiation, and in a caste society things will be very different. Of course Walzer is quite able to recognize that in such a society the meanings supportive of pervasive and systematic inequality may not really be shared, and members of the lower caste may actually feel anger and indignation. In that case justice would demand attention to their understandings also, for 'social meanings need not be harmonious' and sometimes 'provide only the intellectual structure within which distributions are debated' (*SJ*, pp. 313–14). But then the basis for criticism would still be 'local', internal to the meanings of the society itself, not an appeal to any external or universal principles; and if the meanings really were endorsed by all members of the society, then there would be no basis for criticism at all.

The extreme relativism apparently espoused in *Spheres of Justice* attracted a great deal of criticism, and in his more recent works *Interpretation and Social Criticism*, *The Company of Critics* and *Thick or Thin*, Walzer has been concerned to make clear that his methodological insistence on attention to particularity and to cultural meanings does not commit him to a denial of the possibility of radical social criticism. Properly understood, his argument involves a rejection not so much of social criticism *per se* as of a particular model of the way in which it may appropriately be conceived and presented. What matters is that such criticism be 'internal' or 'connected', recognizing its relation to the culture that it seeks to address and not presenting itself as deriving from an external and universal vantage-point quite detached from that culture. And where our fundamental moral beliefs lead us to reject the practices of another culture, we may be justified in preventing them from being true to their own meanings even if we have to appeal to principles that make little sense to their practitioners.

In terms of one's own culture, political theory as the interpretation of social meanings is not only consistent with the possibility of radical social criticism but in some ways invites it. Even if one grants Marx's claim that social meanings are 'the ideas of the ruling class',[13] those ideas are necessarily such as to leave room for critical manoeuvre. Marx's observation that every ruling class is compelled to present itself as a universal class makes criticism a permanent possibility:

> This self-presentation of the rulers is elaborated by the intellectuals. Their work is apologetic, but the apology is of a sort that gives hostages to future social critics. It sets standards that the rulers will not live up to . . . One might say that these standards themselves embody ruling class interests, but they do so only within a universalist disguise. And they also embody lower-class interests, else the disguise would not be convincing. Ideology strains towards universality as a condition of its success.[14]

The Italian Antonio Gramsci is the Marxist who first articulated this understanding of the social critic as 'connected'. Arguing that in order to establish hegemony – intellectual and moral leadership – over subordinate groups the ruling class must make some sacrifices to those groups, and hence that the ruling ideas will inevitably contain contradictions, he urges the radical critic to initiate 'a process of differentiation and change in the relative weight that the elements of the old ideologies used to possess. What was previously secondary and subordinate . . . is now taken to be primary and becomes the nucleus of a new ideological and theoretical complex.'[15] In contrast to Lenin and the Bolsheviks, whose theoretical framework bore little or no internal relation to that society they used it to shape, the Gramscian social critic can be understood as rearticulating ideas already in the culture, bringing to the fore what was hitherto only latent.

What emerges above all from this strand of Walzer's argument is that he takes 'social meanings' to be loose and interminably subject to interpretation. Any concrete culture will contain a variety of different, even contradictory, conceptual threads which it is the task of the political theorist to articulate into as coherent a whole as possible. Social meanings, it would seem, are by no means closed but yield resources to apologists and critics alike. This in turn suggests that the task of the political theorist is more creative or active than that of merely 'reading off' the meanings of the various goods in her society, and it makes clear a way in which an interpretive meanings-based methodology need not automatically be conservative. While it raises difficult issues, more usually associated with the study of literature, concerning what makes one interpretation better than another – in terms of what criteria are we to choose between the different interpretations offered to us by apologist and critic? – this understanding of the political theorist's task at least involves her in more than merely holding a mirror up to the society and its existing practices. There may, for example, be a pervasive understanding in our society that housework or childcare is a good that is done by women and without pay, but the critic can point to other, equality-based threads in our culture which imply alternative distributive principles, and suggest that we are being truer to our social meanings overall if we change our current practice.

Nor is Walzer committed to a denial of the possibility of criticizing alien cultures by invoking our own values. Already in *Spheres of Justice* he makes it clear that it is perfectly appropriate for us to attempt to convince those who believe them that the doctrines supportive of the caste system are in fact false, and this shows that his relativism is not so extreme as to remove any basis upon which we can assess or judge the social meanings of other cultures. What is prohibited is not the attempt to persuade other cultures to change their understandings but the overriding of those understandings without changing them. We can perhaps identify here readings of Walzer's position that make it weak but plausible. It would seem to be a necessary condition of persuading someone to see things differently that one be intelligible to that person, that one make some sense to her. But in that case it is obviously necessary that one's criticism appeal to the 'social meanings' of her own culture if these are understood to mark the bounds of intelligibility. If one attempts to persuade someone of a value system that in no way maps onto her current beliefs, then one will simply fail to make sense to her, will seem to be talking nonsense. Even if we think that this particular reading renders Walzer's claim too weak to be of interest, for it is reduced now to the idea that one cannot change someone's mind without speaking a language she understands, it is highly plausible to think that one's chances of success will relate closely to the extent to which one is able to appeal to ideas already present in her culture. The critic must 'connect' in a very weak sense in order simply to be intelligible, but it may well be that there is a stronger kind of connection needed if one is actually to change people's minds.

Furthermore, in *Interpretation and Social Criticism* Walzer suggests that there may even be justified grounds for intervening in the practices of another culture even where the attempt at persuasion, and thus at the appeal to understandings latent in the other culture, has failed. For there he posits 'a kind of minimal and universal moral code',[16] one that stands to a thickly constituted moral culture as a hotel room does to a home, constituting a basic framework too thin and spare to provide the detail one might need to know how to live, but nonetheless standing as trans-cultural constraints on shared meanings. Since such a minimal code derives its validity from the fact that it arises, or is discovered, universally, societies that fail to respect it must necessarily be rare exceptions. But when they do, then others may be justified in intervening to prevent its contravention.

> Consider the example of the Spaniards in Central America, who claimed sometimes to speak for Catholicism, sometimes only for natural law. They had, to be sure, a Catholic understanding of natural law, but they may still have been right to oppose human sacrifice, for example, not because it was contrary to orthodox doctrine but because it was 'against nature'. The Aztecs probably did not understand, and yet the argument did not have the same degree of externality as did arguments about the blood and body of Christ (and it may well have connected with the feelings, if not the convictions, of the sacrificial victims).[17]

As the last two clauses suggest, it may well be that some trace of the minimal code was to be found in Aztec culture and that not all members of the society really did share those understandings embodied in the practice of human sacrifice, and to that extent the social critic might regard herself as appealing to currently subordinate strands in the culture. But in this passage that thought is secondary, for Walzer clearly thinks that intervention in the name of the minimal code, here understood as the natural law, would be justified in any case. If we feel that a fundamental value is being violated by members of an alien culture, then we can be morally justified in acting to prevent that violation even when the violaters cannot understand our reasons. Where social meanings run out, where bases for rendering ourselves intelligible are unavailable, we can no longer seek to persuade; but, on some occasions, the seriousness of the issue at stake may nonetheless warrant intervention.

Moreover, there is, implicit within Walzer's approach but not articulated by him, a further possible trans-cultural principle, which he seems not to regard as part of the minimal code but which nonetheless seems to yield a basis upon which we might legitimately criticize another culture even if failing to connect with that culture's own self-understandings. We emphasized above that one principle underlying Walzer's meanings-based methodology was a decent respect for the opinions of mankind. This it is that leads him to advocate social change by persuasion, a process necessarily involving some degree of internality between critique and culture criticized as a prerequisite both of intelligibility and of success, rather than simply by overriding existing social meanings. Recall his rhetorical question: 'By virtue of what characteristics are we one another's equals? One characteristic above all is central to my argument. We are (all of us) culture-producing creatures; we make and inhabit meaningful worlds' (*SJ*, p. 314). Since what grounds the respect for cultural particularity that leads to the relativistic strand in his theory is the principle that we are all equally culture-producing creatures, we might think that our respect for other cultures' ways of doing things need not extend to those cultures which themselves do not recognize this principle. If a society is failing to allow people equally to create the cultural constructions by which they live, then the idea that drives Walzer's argument would seem to justify intervention, not restraint.

This suggestion of course raises a number of difficulties. How are we to know whether a group of people is being excluded from the process of cultural construction? Isn't it a plausible analysis of the caste system that this is just what has happened to the untouchables? Or to women in fundamentalist Muslim communities? We cannot, it would seem, ask people we suspect to be excluded what *they* think, since their acceptance or endorsement of their position might be interpreted either as evidence of their non-exclusion or of the great extent to which they have internalized an identity from the construction of which they have been barred. We might be inclined to think that people accorded equal status in the process of cultural creation would never create cultures that gave them subordinate status, and suspect that those regarded as inferior must have been excluded from the process of creation. But perhaps this is mistakenly and unjustly to apply our own conceptions of what it would be reasonable for people to do in a way that Walzer's anti-universalism and respect for cultural particularity is precisely seeking to avoid.

Although it hardly resolves all the difficulties raised by the question of relativism, it does seem both that Walzer provides at least the suggestion of a trans-cultural critical principle, and, especially interesting given our thematic agenda, that it consists in a conception of the person. We said at the beginning of this chapter that Walzer's contribution to the debate was distinctive in focusing rather on goods than on persons, and this remains valid, but it is worth emphasizing here that his theory can be read as presupposing a particular understanding of what is important about people.

Whatever the merits of this final thought, the evidence of Walzer's later writings suggests that some of the more extreme consequences deduced by his critics from the relativistic strand in *Spheres of Justice* were neither intended nor entailed by his invocation of social meanings. If anything, what emerges is an impeccably liberal emphasis upon the need to respect alien cultures and to give priority to persuasion rather than force when political disputes arise – an attempt to create a space for tolerance without allowing that tolerance to paralyse action on truly fundamental matters. And even given these qualifications, Walzer's original emphasis upon the priority of social meanings remains undiluted; the conceptual argument that Rawlsian methodological abstraction condemns Rawlsian principles of justice to inapplicability, and the substantive argument that it amounts to a failure to respect democratic values, remain.

Complex equality

Now we can turn from the particularistic methodology Walzer espouses to the positive theory of justice (a theory of 'differentiated substance') that emerges when he applies that methodology to contemporary society. This substantive element of Walzer's argument, which we referred to earlier as the 'different goods for different reasons' strand, is relatively straightforward, so our presentation can be correspondingly brief.

According to Walzer's interpretation of the social meanings of the goods produced and distributed in our society, those meanings are distinct; and

> when meanings are distinct, distributions must be autonomous. Every social good or set of goods constitutes, as it were, a distributive sphere within which only certain criteria and arrangements are appropriate. Money is inappropriate in the sphere of ecclesiastical office; it is an intrusion from another sphere. And piety should make for no advantage in the marketplace, as the marketplace has commonly been understood. (*SJ*, p. 10)

What is wrong with the conversion of money into the 'sphere' of ecclesiastical office is that this offends against the social meanings of the two goods in question, and it should be clear how this relates to the methodological considerations that we have been discussing hitherto. Respect for cultural particularity requires attention to the ways in which a community understands its goods, and such understandings carry implications for the way that those goods are distributed. If one good exchanges for another whose meaning is distinct, then this is a violation of the cultural constructions involved.

So, whilst there remains, of course, a concern that goods be distributed in accordance with their own meanings, the thrust of Walzer's theory is such as to focus attention not so much on the distribution of goods considered one by one as on the prevention of exchanges between them. Thus, putting it very crudely, what is unjust about capitalist society is not so much the unequal distribution of money as the fact that money is able to bring its possessor goods, such as health care or education, that properly belong to different distributive spheres. In Walzer's terminology, what is wrong is that money is a 'dominant' good, one that 'tyrannizes' over others. And the mistake in focusing on the more equal distribution of money rather than the prevention of exchanges between it and other goods is that of pursuing 'simple' rather than 'complex' equality.

Let us try to clarify the meanings of these terms, beginning with Walzer's distinction between 'dominance' and 'monopoly':

> I call a good dominant if the individuals who have it, because they have it, can command a wide range of other goods. It is monopolised whenever a single man or woman, a monarch in the world of value – or a group of men and women, oligarchs – successfully hold it against all rivals. Dominance describes a way of using social goods that isn't limited by their intrinsic meanings or that shapes those meanings in its own image. Monopoly describes a way of owning or controlling social goods in order to exploit their dominance. (*SJ*, pp. 10–11)

This distinction allows him to contrast two sorts of demand for justice: first, the claim that the dominant good, whatever it is, should be redistributed so that it can become equally or at least more widely shared (this amounts to saying that monopoly is unjust); and second, the claim that the way should be opened for the autonomous distribution of all social goods (this amounts to saying that dominance is unjust). Walzer's argument is for the latter rather than for the former, that is for the autonomous distribution of goods, distribution in accordance with the good-specific meanings of each, rather than for the more equal distribution of whatever good happens to be dominant.

This distinction between monopoly and dominance leads to another between 'simple' and 'complex' equality: 'Imagine a society in which everything is up for sale and every citizen has as much money as every other. I shall call this the 'regime of simple equality'. Equality is multiplied through the conversion process, until it extends across the full range of social goods' (*SJ*, p. 14). Here one good is dominant – money – but that good is distributed equally. The problem with this, for Walzer, is that it is unstable, for free exchange from an equal starting-point will soon lead to new inequalities, and the only means of sustaining simple equality over time would be a dangerously strong state (that is, a state strong enough to break up incipient monopolies and repress forms of dominance), which would then become the focus of new competitive struggles.

But if simple equality is not viable, does that mean that equality as such is out of the picture? Not at all. We should be thinking rather in terms of complex equality.

> I want to argue that we should focus on the reduction of dominance – not, or not primarily, on the break-up or constraint of monopoly. We should consider what it might mean to narrow the range within which particular goods are convertible and to vindicate the autonomy of distributive spheres . . .
>
> Imagine now a society in which different social goods are monopolistically held – as they are in fact and as they always will be, barring continual state intervention – but in which no particular good is generally convertible . . . This is a complex egalitarian society. Though there will be many small inequalities, inequality will not be multiplied through the conversion process. Nor will it be summed across different goods, because the autonomy of distributions will tend to produce a variety of local monopolies, held by different groups of men and women. (*SJ*, p. 17)

From this perspective what's wrong is not inequality as such – 'monopoly is not inappropriate within the spheres' (*SJ*, p. 19) – but what Walzer call 'tyranny': the disregard of the distinctness of the principles internal to each distributive sphere. The regime of complex equality

> is the opposite of tyranny. It establishes a set of relationships such that domination is impossible. In formal terms, complex equality means that no citizen's standing in one sphere or with regard to one social good can be undercut by his standing in some other sphere with regard to some other good. Thus citizen X may be chosen over citizen Y for political office, and then the two of them will be unequal in the sphere of politics. But they will not be unequal generally so long as X's office gives him no advantages over Y in any other sphere – superior medical care, access to better schools for his children, entrepreneurial opportunities, and so on. (*SJ*, pp. 19–20)

In short, the way to achieve justice is vigilantly to patrol the barriers between goods, preventing conversions between goods whose meanings, and hence principles of just distribution, are distinct.[18]

Since he is methodologically committed to the rejection of general distributive principles, it is not surprising that the one that Walzer ends up with is 'open-ended', stating that 'no social good x should be distributed to men and women who possess some other good y merely because they possess y and without regard to the meaning of x' (*SJ*, p. 20). The force of such a principle is to direct our attention towards the study of the way different goods are indeed understood in different societies, and, if our specific concern is with justice in our own society, to the interpretation of our own social meanings. The bulk of *Spheres of Justice* consists of the carrying out of just these two tasks, and it is by concrete illustration as much as by abstract argument that Walzer makes the case for his particularistic approach to thinking about justice. He richly portrays the sheer variety of ways in which different cultures have conceived the goods they have created and distributed, and argues persuasively that the proper interpretation of our own social meanings of a host of goods, from money and education to hard work, commits us to certain distributive principles. That the strength of his position should lie in its culture- and good-specific detail is of course as Walzer would wish it, but it does not lend itself to summary of the kind required here. If the reader doubts the validity of the approach when presented in its abstract form, she may be more persuaded by its particularistic exemplification and should read the central chapters of the book, for this is certainly how Walzer would wish to persuade her.

Before moving on to consider some of the critical issues raised by Walzer's substantive ideas about justice, it may be helpful to add two further observations on these ideas. First, we should be able to see the connections between them and both aspects of the methodological strand of Walzer's argument. Justice requires that each good be distributed in accordance with its own sphere-specific principles, which are discovered through interpretation of its social meaning. A society is tyrannical if one good dominates others, if it violates those meanings; for in so doing it fails decently to respect the opinions of those who conceive the goods, the process, necessarily social, of cultural creation that endows the goods with meanings in the first place. The open-ended distributive principle and the regime of complex equality which it implies, because they alone give proper weight to social meanings, are thus the only approaches to justice that observe the methodological injunctions discussed above.

Second, it should now be even clearer why Walzer must reject Rawls's conception of primary goods. For it is not only, as we have already seen, that the latter's apparent attempt to come up with a list of 'basic' goods that can be applied cross-culturally fails to respect cultural difference and seeks an abstraction from meaning that renders goods meaningless. It is also that, even with respect to a single culture such as Rawls's own, the apparent lumping together of a range of different goods into a single list neglects the fact that different goods should be distributed for different reasons. The whole idea that people in the original position might think usefully about how to distribute goods whilst neglecting their distinct meanings must, for Walzer, be fundamentally misguided.

The desirability of complex equality

The idea that different goods should be distributed for different reasons, and that we should prevent conversions between goods whose meanings are distinct, has a great deal of intuitive plausibility. There are specific conversions that our society does not permit: we do not, for example, allow people to buy and sell votes, or political offices. Similarly, there are several goods, such as education and medical care, that we tend to regard as so important, so qualitatively different from straightforward commodities, that they should not be distributed in accordance with ability to pay. We may well feel that there is something more unjust about the ability of the wealthy to purchase superior or quicker health care than there is about their ability to purchase superior or quicker cars. Of course, given Walzer's claim to have derived his substantive conclusions via interpretation of the social meanings that we share, it would be surprising if they did not have a certain *prima facie* plausibility. What matters is whether such first appearances survive critical analysis, and we may undertake this, and simultaneously suggest a sense in which Walzer's position might be understood as communitarian, by observing how it relates to those arguments that point rather to the value of the individual's being free to make her own choices about what she does with her resources.

One way to approach this kind of argument is to think about how many of those worries we might have about conversions between different goods would disappear if there were an equal distribution of resources in the first place. Suppose everybody had the same amount of money. Would we still feel that there was something wrong with people using their money to buy health care? Should it not be up to them to decide how to allocate their resources? If they would prefer to take an expensive holiday, or buy a TV satellite dish, than to take out health insurance, it might seem that this is their decision. What makes us think otherwise is not, perhaps, anything about the social meaning of health care that demands that it not be purchased for money. Rather it is a concern that people should equally have access to medical treatment and that the currently unequal distribution of money tells against this; or, putting it another way, that the unequal distribution of purchasing power will mean that the distribution of health care does *not* reflect the free choices of individuals but is distorted in favour of the better off. In a situation of equal resources, the distribution of health care would genuinely reflect the choices of individuals as to how they would like to spend their money, there would be equal access, and in that case there might seem to be nothing wrong in principle with permitting exchanges of this kind.

The argument, which is essentially about the freedom of the individual to choose for herself, can be extended to more extreme cases. We are inclined to think that people should not be permitted to sell their kidneys for money. But if a particular individual would prefer a certain cash sum to the kidney, and another would prefer the kidney to the cash sum, what reason do we have to stop them both doing what they want? Our immediate response is to think that nobody could really freely choose to sell his kidney, that she must be desperate, forced by poverty or analogous circumstance to do something she does not really want to do. Empirically this is doubtless overwhelmingly the case. But we could imagine a situation where someone already comfortably off could, by selling her kidney, earn enough extra to buy herself the Steinway piano she has wanted all her life. If that is her choice, why should she be prevented?

We do not mean to suggest that there are no answers to such questions. The connection between the freedom of the individual and the free market is a very big issue, and those who are suspicious of the latter have many arguments at their disposal. For a choice to be 'free', must the person who makes it have full information? Perhaps we can justify taking health care out of the market on the grounds that individuals are not competent accurately to assess the real likelihood of their falling ill, and so will buy less insurance than would be rational. Does this mean that a choice is only free if it is 'rational'?[19] And who then decides what is and isn't rational? Or might it be the case that lots of choices freely made by individuals aggregate to produce unintended consequences that nobody wants? If so, here again restrictions on individual freedom might be justified. These are just some of the questions central to a full assessment of the case for and against the market, and we cannot pursue them here. All that we hope to have shown is the way in which Walzer's injunction to block exchanges between goods with different meanings involves constraining the individual's freedom to do as she will with what she has.

However we may choose to specify and qualify it, and it is important to recognize that different kinds of liberal accord the market different roles in their political theories, the general shape of the connection between liberalism and the market should be clear. The idea that people should be free to make their own choices about how they live their lives sits neatly with an economic system based upon free exchange. Indeed, there are more sophisticated arguments which claim that the way in which the market determines prices, as a function of supply and demand, has the great virtue of not involving any substantive judgements about the value of particular goods but rather simply reflects the relative value accorded to them by the different people in the economy. In a sense, then, and again on the hypothetical assumption of an equal distribution of resources, the free market can be seen to embody that anti-perfectionist strand, perhaps even that neutrality between conceptions of the good, that we have seen to be central at least to some strands of liberal thought.[20]

The sense in which Walzer's substantive argument might be considered distinctively communitarian can now also be seen. The preventing of free exchanges – of what, echoing Nozick,[21] we might term voluntary acts between consenting adults – in the name of the autonomy of the different distributive spheres, involves the overriding of individuals' choices in the name of the 'social meanings' of the goods in question. Since the force of that 'social' is to remind us that those meanings are necessarily created and conceived communally, this implies a clear prioritization of the community over the individual. Walzer is explicit that the 'opinions of mankind' that he is exhorting us to respect are 'Not the opinions of this or that individual, which may well deserve a brusque response: I mean those deeper opinions that are the reflections in individual minds, shaped also by individual thought, of the social meanings that constitute our common life' (*SJ*, p. 320). For the liberal, concerned to guarantee the individual's freedom to pursue her own way of life, this may seem unhelpfully vague, especially if she suspects that there is real and significant disagreement within her culture about what the social meanings of goods actually are. Indeed, to hint further at a thought that we shall develop in a later chapter, might not liberalism plausibly be regarded as a response to circumstances characterized precisely by the fact that people do *not* agree about how people should live their lives or how particular goods should be distributed? And might not this be an accurate empirical description of contemporary advanced industrial socie-ties? In such circumstances, the doctrine that people should be free to make up their own minds about how they live their lives and what they do with their resources may look particularly persuasive, and an anti-perfectionist state and a free market might be thought to be the social institutions that embody such a doctrine.

Walzer contra Rawls

Whatever the qualms we might have about certain aspects of Walzer's substantive theory of justice, it is clear that his co-option as a communitarian critic of Rawlsian liberalism depended much more upon his arguments about the methodology that is appropriate to theorizing about social justice in general. In this respect, his critique falls squarely under the third heading on our agenda of issues, for what he identifies in Rawls and condemns in general is any mode of political theorizing that fails to pay attention to the cultural particularity of the contexts within which such theorizing must have application. In brief, it is Rawls's emphasis upon primary goods and the resulting appearance of universal scope attaching to his conclusions that falls foul of Walzer's claim that any theory of justice must base itself upon a careful reading of the particular social meanings of the goods whose distribution is at issue, on pain both of failing to respect democratic values and of failing to be utilizable in any concrete social circumstances. Whether this appearance of

Rawlsian anti-particularism accords with reality is a matter we defer to the next chapter.

What gives Walzer's distinctively methodological critique its communitarian bias is the central place it allots to social meanings: the distribution of goods cannot be decided apart from a grasp of the specific meanings of those goods, and those meanings are inherently social – constructed by, derived from and maintained by the community and its practices and institutions rather than by the thoughts and deeds of any individual. Thus, Walzer's work pre-supposes a conception of the individual's relation to her community, of the importance of communal frameworks and so of the inherent worth of communal practices and institutions, that aligns him very closely with the work of MacIntyre and Taylor. Most strikingly of all, Walzer's vision of human beings as culture-producing creatures is strongly reminiscent of Taylor's claim that human beings are self-interpreting animals.

It may, however, be worth pointing out that Walzer's criticisms of Rawls do not entail that he opposes liberalism *per se*, or at least does not entail that he is hostile to certain central strands of typically liberal political thinking. Walzer is clearly opposed to political theories that give *undue* emphasis to enshrining individual rights in law in a way that seriously encroaches upon the democratic process; and insofar as the Rawlsian emphasis upon primary goods is a manifestation of the general liberal attempt to be maximally neutral between competing conceptions of the good, Walzer is opposed to that attempt. On the other hand, his demand that the political theorist attend to the particularity of social meanings reflects a commitment to the values of tolerance and respect for alien cultures that is impeccably liberal; and insofar as liberal ideas and values have permeated the institutions and practices of our society, then a Walzerian respect for the social meanings that our goods now carry may well result in recognizably liberal conclusions. After all, although his emphasis upon preventing conversions between goods seems to conflict with Rawls's attempt to give absolute priority to individual freedom, the general idea of a separation of spheres has a respectable liberal ancestry. It is, after all, liberals who are keen to insist on the separation, and separability, of church and state, of the economic and the political, and, more generally, of private and public.[22] In this respect, the example of Walzer reinforces the point we made in the previous chapter about

Taylor: being a communitarian critic of liberalism by no means entail a wholesale rejection of liberalism and liberal values.

Notes

1 Habermas, *Legitimation Crisis*; Ackerman, *Social Justice and the Liberal State*.
2 Walzer, 'Philosophy and Democracy'.
3 Ibid., pp. 388–9.
4 Wittgenstein, *Zettel*, no. 455.
5 Walzer, 'Philosophy and Democracy', p. 386.
6 Ibid., p. 389.
7 As is argued by Dworkin, 'Rights as Trumps'.
8 Walzer, 'Philosophy and Democracy', p. 391.
9 Ibid., p. 393.
10 Ibid., p. 394.
11 Ibid., p. 395.
12 Dworkin, 'What Justice Isn't', is a clear statement of objections to the relativism of Walzer's theory. This is a reprint of a piece in the *New York Review of Books*, 14 April 1983, pp. 4–6, and the reader may be interested in the subsequent exchange between Walzer and Dworkin in that journal, 21 July 1983, pp. 43–6.
13 Marx, *The German Ideology*, p. 64.
14 Walzer, *Interpretation and Social Criticism*, p. 41.
15 Gramsci, *Selections from the Prison Notebooks*, p. 195.
16 Walzer, *Interpretation and Social Criticism*, p. 24.
17 Ibid., p. 45.
18 This vision is assessed from a sociological perspective in Swift, 'The Sociology of Complex Equality'.
19 A classic essay that considers the different ways in which the concept of liberty has been understood, and in particular its relation to that of rationality, is Berlin, 'Two Concepts of Liberty'.
20 Here, as earlier in our Introduction, we massively simplify the approach of Dworkin, 'What is Equality?', which we consider in more detail in chapter 9.
21 Cf. Nozick, *Anarchy, State and Utopia*, p. 163.
22 For a fuller discussion on this point see Walzer, 'Liberalism and the Art of Separation'.

Concluding summary

We have now examined each of the writers who have been held to contribute to the communitarian critique of liberalism. But the task of summarizing their views, explaining why they might be thought to conflict with Rawlsian liberalism and elucidating the sense in which each writer might deserve the label 'communitarian' has entailed covering a lot of complex and detailed ground. So it seems advisable to provide a retrospective overview of this material, one which might be thought of as providing an answer to the question 'To what degree do the communitarians form a coherent group?' Since this coherence will be manifest – if at all – on two levels, namely whether their criticisms of liberalism are interrelated, and whether the four are 'communitarian' in the same sense, we will examine them in turn, beginning with the former.

Family resemblances: the criticisms of liberalism

Our treatment of this matter can most helpfully be organized around the agenda of issues with which we began this book, and it will take the following form. Under each of the five headings on that agenda, we shall specify which of the four communitarians develop views that are opposed to the one attributed to Rawls, and which of them explicitly argue that Rawls holds the view they oppose.

The conception of the person

Here, the focus is on a conception of the person as antecedently individuated or unencumbered, a conception that allows no room for the possibility that the attachments that individuals develop to their chosen ends, values, conceptions of the good and communities might become a constitutive part of their identity. Sandel, MacIntyre and Taylor develop views about personhood that attempt to undermine this conception; and Sandel and MacIntyre explicitly argue that Rawls is committed to it.

Asocial individualism

Two separable issues come under this heading: the philosophical error of assuming that any individual's ends, values and identity (regardless of their content) can be thought of as existing independently of the wider communities of which she is a member; and the substantive error of failing to acknowledge the true significance of those particular human goods whose content or focus is inherently communal (in particular the good of political community). MacIntyre and Taylor develop arguments that attempt to undermine the philosophical version of asocial individualism, and MacIntyre explicitly argues that Rawls is committed to it; Sandel develops arguments against the substantive version of asocial individualism, and explicitly argues that Rawls is committed to it.

Universalism

Here, the issue is whether Rawls's theory of justice is intended to apply universally and cross-culturally, with no attention paid to the culture-specificity of the subject-matter of such theorizing. Walzer develops a view that attempts to undermine any such conception of political theory; and he also explicitly argues that Rawls is committed to that conception.

Subjectivism/objectivism

The focus of debate here is the view that individuals' choices of ends, values and conceptions of the good are arbitrary expressions of preference, essentially incapable of rational justification. MacIntyre and Taylor develop views that attempt to undermine this position; and Sandel and MacIntyre explicitly argue that Rawls is committed to it.

Anti-perfectionism and neutrality

Under this heading, the accusation is that Rawls's theory of justice is far less neutral between competing conceptions of the good than might appear to be the case. It is argued that the theory, which prohibits the invocation of 'thick' conceptions of the good in the political arena, must itself draw upon just such a conception in its own defence; and that the liberal society that would result from implementing the theory might discriminate against conceptions of the good held by its citizens in ways other than those explicitly sanctioned by the need to protect the autonomy of all citizens. Different versions of this criticism are developed and pressed against Rawls by Sandel, MacIntyre and Taylor.

This way of summarizing the communitarian critique makes two important points very clear. First, as the distribution of names suggests, the third of the communitarian criticisms seems much less tightly connected with the other four than the latter are with one another. Walzer's criticism of the methodological abstraction he identifies with Rawlsian liberalism is not directly supported by the work of the other three critics; and their opposition to the Rawls's conception of the person, his asocial individualism, his moral subjectivism and his claims to neutrality is not paralleled in Walzer's work. The reason for this should by now be evident. As we stressed in the previous chapters, anyone committed to a conception of the person as antecedently individuated is likely to be drawn to defend certain versions of asocial individualism and moral subjectivism, and consequently will be relying upon a strongly non-neutral set of presuppositions in her moral and political thinking; but these beliefs neither entail, nor are entailed by, a particular conception of the methodology of political theorizing. To put it crudely, the former beliefs specify the substantive content of a theory and the latter conception specifies its scope; and the question of whether one's theory should have universal application is largely (if not entirely) independent of its content.

Second, within the main group of three critics, it is clear that we are given more reason to oppose the views to which they object than to attribute them to Rawls in particular or to liberalism in general. Whereas Sandel, MacIntyre and Taylor all develop positions that lead them to oppose views that have been attributed to Rawls, Sandel does more to defend the legitimacy of those attributions than MacIntyre, who himself does more in this respect than Taylor. This means that much of the weight of the communitarian attack, understood as an attack upon Rawls, depends upon the textual analysis and interpretations discussed in the first two chapters of this part of the book. If they can be defended, then Rawls is open to a multiplicity of mutually supporting criticisms; but much of the material we have examined is devoted to the general task of undermining the putatively erroneous views than to the more specific one of justifying their attribution to Rawls.

Family resemblances: the communitarianism of the critics

The best way to approach this question is to remind ourselves of the sense in which each critic of liberalism was seen to be a 'communitarian', and then to highlight the similarities and differences between them.

Sandel

Sandel's communitarianism is manifest in his concern to rehabilitate a possibility that a conception of the self as antecedently individuated seems to exclude. Insofar as such a self has an integrity that is given prior to and independently of its choice of ends, it is incapable of developing attachments to those ends that are partly or wholly constitutive of its identity. One such type of constitutive attachment upon which Sandel places great (but not exclusive) emphasis is to the community or communities of which the self is a member, and in particular to the political community.

MacIntyre

On MacIntyre's account of the relationship of the individual to the community, any attempt to give a coherent account of the person and of morality understood as a rational enterprise must make reference to the participation of individuals in essentially social phenomena such as practices and traditions. Here, communal membership is not merely essential to one sort of human good, but is integral to the possibility of attaining any sort of human goods whatever.

Taylor

Taylor argues that any adequate conception of morality, practical reasoning and the person must invoke qualitative frameworks which can be established, maintained and acquired only through member-ship of a linguistic community. If human beings are self-interpreting animals, and the languages needed for such self-interpretations are essentially social phenomena, then community is a structural precondition of human agency (including moral agency).

Walzer

For Walzer, the meanings – and so the very nature – of the goods for which any theory of justice must establish distributive principles cannot be grasped independently of the specific and widely-varying socio-cultural contexts within which they are produced, encountered and utilized. Since their meanings are social meanings, the goods with which justice is concerned are social goods; and as a consequence, both the practice of political theorizing and the very concept of social justice itself must be understood as embedded within and relative to communal frameworks.

If we organize our retrospective overview around these four extremely condensed summaries, then we can see that, at first blush, the four critics of liberalism whose work we have examined utilize the concept of the community in three significantly different ways. MacIntyre and Taylor embody one such way, regarding reference to the community as integral to any account of human selfhood, agency and practical reasoning; but Sandel's claims are much more limited, amounting only to the view that constitutive attachments to the community are *one* important species of human good; and Walzer invokes the community solely in order to give an adequate account of practical reasoning about justice – and about the objects rather than the subjects of justice at that. From this perspective, we might say that MacIntyre and Taylor are the most fully-fledged communitarians, with Sandel and Walzer instantiating two variants of that central type which are different in focus and more restricted in scope.

This initial appearance of diversity is, however, misleading; for it could be argued that all four communitarians are alike in basing their work upon a particular, communally oriented conception of the person. In the case of MacIntyre and Taylor this is clear: Taylor's fundamental view of human beings as self-interpreting animals in linguistic communities is very similar to MacIntyre's neo-Aristotelian view that human beings can only make sense of themselves as persons and moral agents through the concepts and standards bequeathed to them by practices and traditions. As we suggested in chapter 4, much of Walzer's work on the methodology of political theorizing depends in a very similar way upon his view that human beings are essentially culture-producing and culture-inhabiting creatures. And Sandel's concern to rescue and re-emphasize the possibility of constitutive attachments to the community can easily be reinterpreted as a way of highlighting the degree to which the identity of human beings is bound up with their inhabitation of and identification with the smaller and larger communities of which they are members. From this perspective, all four communitarians are united around a conception of human beings as integrally related to the communities of culture and language that they create, maintain and inhabit.

This way of characterizing their communitarianism has the added advantage of relating it very closely to their criticisms of Rawls; for, as we have already noted, a large part of the case for accusing Rawls of asocial individualism, moral subjectivism and insufficient neutrality between conceptions of the good depends upon attributing to his work a conception of the person as antecedently individuated. Such a conception of the person is clearly fundamentally opposed to the one that we have claimed underlies the work of the communitarians: for if selves are antecedently individuated, then the possibility of developing constitutive attachments to the community is excluded and the idea that the creation, inhabitation and maintenance of communal frameworks might be integral to one's personhood cannot be adequately acknowledged. And of course, seeing the fundamental opposition between liberals and communitarians in terms of competing conceptions of the person underlines the central role in this debate of the charge that Rawls is committed to one such conception; for if this charge does not stick, then many of the other putative criticisms of Rawls will not stick either.

If, however, we wish to characterize the dispute between liberals and communitarians in a more abstract or value-oriented way, then we might venture the following formulation. Sandel's most fundamental reason for thinking that Rawls is committed to a metaphysical conception of the person as antecedently individuated is that it would account for the absolute priority that Rawls attaches to protecting the autonomy of the individual; in this sense, therefore, the role Sandel attributes to that conception of the person reflects his perception of the primacy of autonomy in the liberal framework. And of course, one of the key consequences of developing a conception of the person as culture-creating and culture-inhabiting is that emphasis falls upon capacities that the individual can only exercise by acting in concert with other human beings. Culture and society are the creations of human communities: they cannot be produced or maintained on an individual basis, and the resources they provide which are so essential to human selfhood and agency are bequeathed to the person by his or her community. Thus, the communitarian conception of the person opposes the classic liberal emphasis upon individual autonomy by stressing the degree and extent of that individual's necessary dependence upon the community.

What this formulation suggests is that there need not be a flat opposition or contradiction between these differing liberal and communitarian emphases. More specifically, the communitarian stress upon the ways in which an individual should not be thought of as autonomous of his or her community does not entail that individual autonomy should be altogether scrapped or entirely downgraded as a human good. It is rather designed to question the absoluteness of the priority and the universality of the scope that liberals are prone to assign to that good; it serves to suggest that both the priority and the scope should be modified or restricted. This is why, of all the communitarians, only MacIntyre is explicitly and almost unqualifiedly hostile to liberalism as a general moral tradition; Taylor is explicitly concerned to attack certain ways of defending liberalism rather than to attack the tradition as a whole, many of Walzer's methodological recommendations have a strongly liberal ring to them, and Sandel is explicitly concerned merely to suggest that liberalism has limits. In this sense, the communitarian critique of liberalism might be thought of in Sandelian terms: it is an attempt to identify the limits of the attractiveness and worth of autonomy, not an attempt to deny that attractiveness and worth altogether.

PART II

RAWLS'S RESPONSE

Introduction to Part II

Rawls's liberalism, the conception of justice as fairness and its purported theoretical presuppositions and implications, has, we have seen, been the target of a variety of distinct but interrelated communitarian criticisms. The question now arises of whether those criticisms have correctly perceived their target. Does Rawls believe what the communitarians attack? Is a Rawlsian liberal really committed to a conception of the person as unencumbered and antecedently individuated, to a view of the individual as prior to society, or to the belief that moral commitments are no more than subjective expressions of preference? In methodological terms, is he seeking an inappropriately universal or abstract conception of justice? Does his liberalism rely upon a conception of the good rather thicker than that claimed?

It will take us no fewer than three chapters to answer these questions; for matters are made less than straightforward by the fact that Rawls has published a second book – *Political Liberalism* (hereafter *PL*) – in which he presents his position in a way that, by his own admission, differs from the way it was presented in *A Theory of Justice*. Justice as fairness is now to be understood as a distinctively *political* version of liberalism. As he says:

> The distinction between a comprehensive doctrine and a political conception is unfortunately absent from *Theory* and while I believe nearly all the structure and substantive content of justice as fairness

... goes over unchanged into that conception as a political one, the understanding of the view as a whole is significantly shifted. (*PL*, p. 177)

It is the task of our first chapter to explain what is involved in this shift to the political. As this quotation suggests, what has changed is not the conception of justice as fairness itself but the way we should understand that conception: its status, what other views it relies upon, the shape of the argument for it; in sum, what kind of theory it is. This implies, of course, that Rawls is no longer putting forward the same kind of theory as that on which communitarians have focused their attack; a fact that necessarily complicates any assessment of its accuracy.

In the second chapter, we attempt to show that it is the claim to be distinctively political that gives Rawls's position the resources to respond to some of the communitarian objections we have outlined; indeed, the structure of this book reflects our judgement that it is illuminating to read the later Rawls in the light of that critique. It is important in this context to register the following two caveats. First, we do not seek to dispute Rawls's own view that the changes in his position are not replies to criticisms raised by communitarians (or others) but rather arise from, and all follow from the solution to, a problem internal to the argument of *A Theory of Justice*. Our concerns are not biographical but analytical. The issue, for us at least, is not whether communitarian criticisms motivated the changes, which is what we take Rawls to deny, but how the changes relate to the criticisms. Nor, however, do we argue that it is *only* by shifting to his distinctively political conception of liberalism that Rawls has acquired the resources that enable him to reply to communitarian objections – we will see that some of these were already available to him in *A Theory of Justice*.[1] But the task of identifying those responses that do and do not depend upon his change of position can only be carried out when we have a sense of what that change amounts to.

That leaves, of course, the question of whether Rawls's shift to the political – and hence the responses that it makes available – can be sustained; this is the matter of our third chapter. Having set out the essence of Rawls's political liberalism, and having considered its relation to the communitarian critique, we turn to the job of investigating whether that position stands up to critical assessment. The reader who stays with us through this second part of the book will find us arguing that Rawls's liberalism, as he would now have us understand it, is not susceptible to that critique as it was originally formulated, and indeed itself contains significantly communitarian ideas; but that the theory in its current incarnation avoids some communitarian objections only by relying on claims that are themselves doubtful.

Notes

1 For the view that the communitarian critique of liberalism rested almost entirely on misunderstandings of the latter see S. Caney, 'Liberalism and Communitarianism: A Misconceived Debate'. Our 'Liberalisms and Communitarianisms: Whose Misconception?' responds to that view and is followed by Caney's reply to our response.

5

Rawls's political liberalism

Rawls's *Political Liberalism* is a long, complex and difficult book, and it is not our aim in this initial exegetical chapter to provide more than the barest outline of its key ideas, sufficient only to give the reader a sense of his overall vision and without much of that attention to the details of formulation that would be needed to make good one nuance of interpretation rather than another. Those concerned at the sketchiness of our presentation may be mollified to learn that things get more complicated in the next two chapters, where we engage in further exegesis as necessary first to set out the relation between Rawls's position and the communitarian critique and then to consider whether his crucial claim to be presenting a merely political conception of liberalism can indeed be sustained. We think it best, then, to proceed slowly, gradually increasing the depth and detail of our exposition chapter by chapter; but we recognize, of course, that matters of interpretation cannot be avoided even at this early stage. The reader should be aware that different parts of the Rawlsian jigsaw can be made to fit together in different ways, and sometimes seem to be put together differently even by Rawls himself – perhaps reflecting the way in which he has arrived at his latest statement only after a multi-staged trek through various published papers that appeared during the 1970s and 1980s.

We hope in general to avoid getting bogged down in the fascinating but tortuous issue of the precise relation between *Political Liberalism* and *A Theory of Justice*, but one aspect of it is sufficiently important to be worth getting clear from the outset. Rawls regards his political liberalism as a general conception and one that is not simply equivalent to the particular theory of justice that he presented in *A Theory of Justice*. For him, ' "justice as fairness" is but one example of a liberal political conception; its specific content is not definitive of such a view' (*PL*, p. 226). People agreeing on the *kind* of liberalism he puts forward may nonetheless disagree about the content that it implies, indeed Rawls thinks that it is inevitable and even desirable that this will happen. He does, however, think that in order to qualify as a liberal political conception any theory will have to share certain basic features with justice as fairness – it is on distributive matters, which we have deliberately chosen to ignore, that there seems to be most room for political liberals to differ. And since he clearly regards his later project as that of providing a more complete justification and understanding of the particular theory put forward in 1971, that is how we will present it in what follows.

The relation between the positions put forward in the two books is thus potentially confusing. On the one hand, someone could accept the arguments for a distinctively political brand of liberalism but reject justice as fairness, perhaps thinking that the latter fails to meet the conditions of acceptability laid down by the former. On the other, some have been attracted to the substance of justice as fairness but have understood Rawls's move to the political to involve a weakening of its justification that they would disavow. Some, then, accept the later Rawls but reject the earlier, while others defend the earlier against the later. And all this in a context where Rawls himself regards both as valid and the one as supporting the other.

How political?

Granting that, from its presentation in *A Theory of Justice*, justice as fairness might seem to be embedded in a comprehensive moral doctrine, Rawls is keen to insist that it is not, that it is intended rather as a political conception, and, as we have seen, he acknowledges that this makes a significant difference to the way that his theory should be understood. Clearly, then, our initial task must be to see what he means by calling it 'political', and how this is distinct from the reading that his original book encouraged.

At their most succinct, the three distinguishing features of a political conception of justice are:

> that it is framed to apply solely to the basic structure of society, its main political, social, and economic institutions as a unified scheme of social cooperation; that it is presented independently of any wider comprehensive religious or philosophical doctrine; and that it is elaborated in terms of fundamental ideas viewed as implicit in the public political culture of a democratic society. (*PL*, p. 223)

In this section we shall unpack these three features in turn, leaving until later the crucial issue of why Rawls should want a conception that is 'political' in these senses. While the two questions are intimately related, it is rather more straightforward to see what makes a conception political for Rawls than it is to see why he should seek such a conception, and we shall begin with the easy bit.

First, then, is the point that the theory is intended to apply to a specific subject, what Rawls calls 'the basic structure'. The essential point here is that the conception of justice as fairness is not intended to be general in its scope: it is not supposed to tell us what justice requires in all situations, nor how all institutions must be organized if they are to be just. The two principles apply quite specifically to the basic political, social and economic institutions of society; how churches, universities and hospitals, for example, institutions not belonging to the basic structure, are justly to distribute the goods with which they are concerned are questions on which justice as fairness is silent. While these other forms of association must be bound by the constraints that arise from the principles of justice, so that, for example, liberty of conscience demands that religions cannot burn heretics, only excommunicate them, the special aims and purposes of these different forms mean that quite different principles of justice may apply within them.

The first respect in which the conception is political, then, is in its *scope* or *subject*; it applies specifically to the political sphere, as long as this is understood broadly, as it is in ordinary usage, to include not only political but also major social and economic institutions. The second concerns rather what we might call its *status*. The idea that a political conception of justice can be 'presented independently of any wider comprehensive religious or philosophical doctrine' takes us to the heart of the later Rawls.

His point here is that the various claims built into his conception of justice as fairness, those ideas embodied in the thought experiment of the original position and the principles of justice that are derived from it, do not rely upon any full-blown claim about how people should lead their lives in general, in private as well as in their political conduct. In contrast to utilitarianism, for example, which, as a comprehensive moral doctrine, is usually taken to indicate to its adherents what they ought to do in all aspects of their lives, Rawls's specifically political conception is intended to stand independently of, and not to presuppose, any particular expansive understanding of moral, religious or philosophical values or ideals. We have already noted that this is the shift from the presentation of the theory in *A Theory of Justice* that Rawls is most ready to acknowledge; in that work, he admits, justice as fairness is regarded as a comprehensive, or partially comprehensive, doctrine. It is crucial for Rawls, for reasons we shall address shortly, that justice as fairness does not in fact rely upon any particular comprehensive doctrine but can be presented independently as a freestanding and specifically political conception. According to him, one does not have to be committed to any particular comprehensive moral ideal in order to accept the moral claims, including the identification of people's highest-order interests, that are built into the characterization of the original position.

The third respect in which the conception is political, which we may think of as concerning its *method* or *source*, is that 'it is elaborated in terms of fundamental ideas viewed as implicit in the public political culture of a democratic society'. Justice as fairness should be understood not as the elaboration of a particular comprehensive ideal but rather as the systematic articulation, the 'working up' into a coherent pattern, of intuitive ideas that, because they are embedded in our society's main institutions and the public traditions of their interpretation, can be regarded as implicitly shared. Whether the conception can be extended to other societies, with quite different political cultures, is a separate question.

Society as a fair system of cooperation between free and equal citizens

Before moving on to the crucial question of why Rawls should want his conception of justice to be 'political' in the ways sketched out above, it may be helpful briefly to spell out how the various features of justice as fairness do indeed fit this characterization. The key points here, and those in terms of which these three features of the political interrelate, can be expressed in two stages. First, the original position, which, as we have seen, can be regarded as the embodiment of the various substantive normative claims that lie at the heart of justice as fairness, is intended to represent the idea that society should be regarded as a fair scheme of cooperation between citizens conceived as free and equal. It models what we regard as 'fair conditions under which the representatives of free and equal citizens are to specify the terms of social cooperation in the case of the basic structure of society' (*PL*, pp. 25–6). Second, that very idea, that understanding of how we should regard society and its members, is itself taken to be relevant only to matters concerning the basic structure, to be implicit in our public political culture and not to presuppose the validity of any comprehensive ideals. As Rawls says, 'the fundamental organizing idea of justice as fairness, within which the other basic ideas are systematically connected, is that of society as a fair system of cooperation over time, from one generation to the next. We start with the exposition of this idea, which we take to be implicit in the public culture of a democratic society' (*PL*, p. 13). The original position, then, models the normative claims not of a comprehensive moral, religious or philosophical doctrine but of a distinctively political conception of society and the person.

We will consider in the next chapter the ways in which these claims provide Rawls with the means to accommodate or rebut communitarian objections, but it may be helpful even at this stage to give an indication of the kind of move it makes available to him. Consider, for example, the significance of the claim that the conception of the person modelled by the original position is of the person as citizen and can be affirmed as appropriate to political contexts by people holding a variety of comprehensive conceptions of the good. While in the initial presentation of the theory it looked as if you had to be committed to a liberal understanding of what is important about people all the way down, as it were, or to a claim about the metaphysical essence of people, Rawls now maintains that one can hold a liberal conception of people as citizens, one that regards people as free and equal in the senses represented by the original position, without being liberals in a fuller or more comprehensive sense. One does not have to regard autonomy or individuality as a comprehensive moral or philosophical ideal in the manner of Kant or Mill in order to think that the capacity to form, revise and rationally pursue conceptions of the good, a highest-order interest in which is attributed to the parties to the agreement in the original position, is important in politics.

Why political?

Although we have gone some way towards understanding the sense in which Rawls would have us read his conception of justice as political, we have still not broached the question of what it is that leads Rawls to insist upon the specifically political nature of his theory. The issue of what motivates the search for a conception with these three features can no longer be avoided.

This is not straightforward. Rawls himself presents his shift to the political as initially motivated by a recognition that justice as fairness, or any other liberal conception, would not be stable, or at least not stable in the right way, if it relied upon the validity of a comprehensive philosophical doctrine, as it had been presented in *A Theory of Justice*. In Rawls's view, members of democratic societies are inevitably going to espouse a variety of comprehensive conceptions of the good, and a version of liberalism that insisted that it was the one true comprehensive doctrine would not be able to provide the kind of social stability that is part of Rawls's conception of a truly just, well-ordered society. This is the sense in which, on his account, the 'political' aspect of his theory began as the solution to an internal problem rather than being motivated by the communitarian critique.

Even on Rawls's own account, however, it is clear that its providing a solution to the problem of stability by no means exhausts the significance of that aspect. In his preface Rawls acknowledges that 'this change in turn forces many other changes and calls for a family of ideas not needed before' (*PL*, p. xvii), and throughout the book he repeatedly insists that the proper exposition of his argument proceeds in two stages, with questions of stability secondary:

> Justice as fairness is best presented in two stages. In the first stage it is
> worked out as a freestanding political (but of course moral)
> conception for the basic structure. Only with this done and its
> content – its principles of justice and ideals – provisionally on hand do
> we take up, in the second stage, the problem whether justice as
> fairness is sufficiently stable. (*PL*, pp. 140–1)

The need for his theory to be 'political' may first have become
apparent because of his concern that it be stable; but the idea that it
is a freestanding view, 'an account of a political conception of justice
that applies in the first instance to the basic structure and articulates
two kinds of political values, those of political justice and of public
reason' (*PL*, p. 64), clearly comes in at the first stage and informs its
content from the start.

There has been a deal of disagreement over what exactly the shift
to the political involves, and we will suggest, in chapter 7, that
Rawls's own presentation in *Political Liberalism* contains a couple of
significant difficulties, as if his thinking were still on the move and
the position put forward in that book unhappily containing strands
of different and incompatible kinds of argument. All this makes
clear exegesis very difficult, but our best attempt will take the
following form. We begin by showing that what motivates Rawls's
concern for a political conception of justice is the importance of its
being publicly justifiable to the members of a society that is
characterized by what he calls 'the fact of reasonable pluralism'. This
will involve us in explaining both his crucial notion of public reason
and why he adopts the method of political constructivism. Asking
why he should want his conception to be justifiable in this way, we
will point to his commitment to the liberal principle of legitimacy,
stressing the extent to which this commitment makes him, despite
some appearances, thoroughgoingly liberal. We will then go on to
consider how questions of stability fit into this account, doing our
best to explain what Rawls might mean by insisting that his theory is
best presented in the two stages outlined above, but stressing the
sense in which they seem to coincide.

Public justifiability and public reason

Rawls seeks a conception of justice that is political in the three senses identified because he wants something that can be publicly justified to all members of a society whose members endorse a variety of conflicting comprehensive views. For Rawls, it is inevitable that modern democratic societies will contain a diversity of incompatible yet reasonable comprehensive religious, philosophical and moral doctrines. This is not a mere historical condition that is likely to pass away, rather it is 'the normal result of the exercise of human reason within the framework of the free institutions of a constitutional democratic regime' (*PL*, p. xvi). This, for Rawls, is the 'fact of reasonable pluralism', a pluralism that is reasonable in the following sense: it is not simply the upshot of self- and class interest, or of people's tendencies to view the world from a limited standpoint; neither can it be solely attributed to failures of rationality or logical errors. Even those who conscientiously and correctly exercise their powers of reason and judgement in the ordinary course of moral and political life face ineradicable obstacles to the attainment of agreement on such comprehensive questions; these obstacles are what Rawls calls 'the burdens of judgement'. They include such factors as the following: the evidence bearing on the case is complex and conflicting; the weight to be attached to any given piece of evidence is contestable; our concepts are vague and subject to hard cases; and our judgements are imponderably but decisively and differently influenced by the whole course of our individual moral experience. These sources of disagreement (unlike such factors as self-interest, irrationality and wilfulness) are compatible with the full reasonableness of all parties involved; so when human reason and judgement is exercised within the framework of free institutions (which prohibit attempts to overcome these burdens by coercion or other less direct forms of undue influence), support for a plurality of reasonable comprehensive doctrines is the inevitable outcome.

We will explore the issues raised by these claims in some detail in chapter 7. For now what matters is to see that it is the requirement of public justifiability, when combined with his view that citizens will inevitably and reasonably disagree over comprehensive doctrines, that makes it crucial that Rawls's conception of justice is free-standing. Given this fact of reasonable pluralism, any conception that presupposed one comprehensive doctrine would necessarily conflict with some others, precluding the possibility of agreement between citizens quite reasonably committed to those alternative views. We should also be able to see how another feature of the political fits in: the method of looking to intuitive ideas implicit in the public political culture makes sense because those ideas can be regarded as implicitly shared, as available to all citizens whatever their own particular comprehensive views. As Rawls puts it:

> Justice as fairness aims at uncovering a public basis of justification on questions of political justice given the fact of reasonable pluralism. Since justification is addressed to others, it proceeds from what is, or can be, held in common; and so we begin from shared fundamental ideas implicit in the public political culture in the hope of developing from them a political conception that can gain free and reasoned agreement in judgment . . . (*PL*, pp. 100–1)

We have already pointed out that Rawls regards the conception of society as a fair scheme of cooperation between free and equal citizens, a conception modelled by the original position, as just such a 'shared fundamental idea'. It is thus, for Rawls, something that can be justified to all members of society despite the fact of reasonable pluralism; despite the fact that they will be committed to conflicting and incommensurable comprehensive doctrines.

We should now be able to see the relation between the wish to avoid controversial claims, claims that presuppose the validity of any particular comprehensive conception, and the exclusion of reasons that is represented by the veil of ignorance and the original position. In denying the people in the original position knowledge of their particular comprehensive conceptions of the good, Rawls is representing the idea that appeals to those conceptions are inappropriate when it comes to thinking about justice. What can distinctively be remarked upon here is the connection between this exclusion of reasons and the desire for a conception of justice that can be publicly justified, that can be justified by appeal only to what Rawls calls 'public reason', and can be acceptable to citizens committed in their private non-political lives to quite different moral, religious and philosophical beliefs.

If the basic structures and arrangements of a society are to be justifiable to all its members regardless of their particular comprehensive conceptions of the good, then strict limits must be placed upon the kinds of considerations that such justifications might legitimately draw upon; and those limits in effect specify a highly distinctive subset within the set of all possible reasons for taking decisions about fundamental political issues – the realm of public reason. Public reason is thus public in three senses: it is the reason of persons in their public role (i.e. as citizens), its subject is the public good and matters of fundamental justice, and its nature and content is public (i.e. transparently based on publicly available ideas and principles).

It follows that public reason is to be contrasted with reasoning of other kinds. Deliberations in which we engage *qua* members of non-political associations such as churches, universities or families (even when they relate to political questions) will all have limits of a kind very different from those imposed by public reason, since they will be determined by the very different kinds of constraints and considerations appropriate to the concerns of the particular association (although, of course, all will share that reliance upon principles of inference and rules of evidence without which they would be indistinguishable from rhetoric or mere persuasion). Such ways of reasoning can be thought of as non-public in a certain sense, but they must not be thought of as private, for they are perfectly public with respect to fellow members of the association concerned; for Rawls – as for Kant – there is no such thing as private reason, only ways of reasoning that are non-public with respect to one's fellow citizens.

When, however, we venture to address fellow citizens in a public forum, fellow citizens who do not necessarily participate in the same associations of civil society as we do, we must respect the way of reasoning that is appropriate to the political realm, the limits of public reason. And according to Rawls, the same constraint applies in a special way to those who hold political office, and to the judiciary – those who he thinks of as being, in effect, officers of the government. It applies to legislators when they speak on the floor of parliament, and to the public pronouncements and actions of those who wield executive power; and it applies with particular force to the judiciary, and above all to a supreme court in a constitutional democracy with judicial review, since the justices on such a court must account for all their decisions in terms of their understanding of the constitution and relevant statutes and precedents. Here, Rawls's familiarity with the American political and legal system comes to the fore; it leads him to declare that the special role of a supreme court makes it 'the exemplar of public reason' (*PL*, p. 216). But even in societies that do not follow the American system of dividing political power between the judiciary, the legislature and the executive, the limits of public reason still apply to debates and decisions concerning the exercise of coercive state power, and they do so because they reflect the division between pertinent considerations with which our fellow citizens can, and those with which they cannot, reasonably be expected to agree. We can therefore think of Rawls's talk of public reason as one way of giving forceful expression to his fundamental concern with the limits of public justifiability.

Political constructivism

This same fundamental concern is what leads Rawls to emphasize that, in his presentation of his political liberalism, he relies upon a method of political theorizing that he calls 'political constructivism'. By this he means that he represents the principles of political justice as the outcome of a procedure of construction – one in which certain basic, purely political conceptions of the person and of society are utilized to generate a conception of a just constitutional regime that might then be used to guide our political endeavours. Unlike theorists whom he labels 'rational intuitionists', he does not assume that the principles of justice that emerge from this procedure form part of an independently existing order of moral principles and values, or that human beings cognize them by a species of perception or intuition (supplemented by theoretical reflection). Neither, however, does the political constructivist deny these rational intuitionist claims, or assert views that imply their falsity. In particular, political constructivism does not assume, as does what Rawls calls 'Kantian moral constructivism', that moral (including political) principles and values are actually constituted or created by the exercise of human practical reason. Political constructivism restricts itself to purely political principles, and assumes only that they can be represented or regarded *as if* they were the outcome of a procedure of construction. It therefore neither denies nor asserts that these principles are in reality constituted by human beings and their rational capacities.

In short, Rawls adopts political constructivism because it is a method of political theorizing whose authority does not depend upon our accepting a particular, controversial metaphysical doctrine about the nature of moral and political values.

[G]iven the fact of reasonable pluralism, citizens cannot agree on any moral authority, whether a sacred text, or institution. Nor do they agree about the order of moral values, or the dictates of what some regard as natural law. We adopt, then, a constructivist view to specify the fair terms of social cooperation . . . [I]f the procedure can be correctly formulated, citizens should be able to accept its principles and conceptions along with their reasonable comprehensive doctrine. (*PL*, p. 97)

In other words, political constructivism represents principles of justice in a manner which leaves as few hostages as possible to the outcome of ongoing metaphysical disputes about the nature of moral and political value. It offers, in effect, a way of presenting those principles that is compatible with a wide range of different metaphysical views; from the perspective of each such comprehensive doctrine, political constructivism does not tell anything like the full story about the nature of value, but neither does it assume anything which conflicts with that full story. Rawls's method of political theorizing is thus, in effect, publicly justifiable; the materials employed in his constructive procedure (certain conceptions of the person and of society) are purely political, and the procedure itself begs as few controversial metaphysical questions as possible. He can therefore reasonably expect that the political conception of justice which results from its employment will be endorsed by those who cleave to any reasonable comprehensive doctrine.

The liberal political ideal

We have attempted to flesh out what Rawls means by claiming his conception to be publicly justifiable, or justifiable by appeal to public reason, and have laid out the relation between this and his politically constructivist method. Why does he want his theory to be publicly justifiable in the first place?

Despite the complexity and elegance of Rawls's system, the answer to this key question is surprisingly simple. The justification for restricting political debate over fundamental matters to the realm of public reason, for excluding controversial truths from the original position, for going to fundamental intuitive ideas implicit in the public political culture, lies in the liberal political ideal that since political power is the coercive power of free and equal citizens as a corporate body, this power should be exercised, when constitutional essentials and basic questions of justice are at stake, only in ways that all citizens can reasonably be expected to endorse in the light of their common human reason (*PL*, pp. 139–40)

The concern for public justifiability, the fundamental reason to seek a conception of justice with the three features outlined, derives from a straightforward and substantive moral conception of the nature of political power in a liberal democracy. In such a society, political power is held jointly by free and equal citizens, and it is wrong for some to use that power against others in ways that cannot be justified by appeal to reasons they can all accept. Given the fact of reasonable pluralism, the permanent existence of a plurality of diverging and conflicting comprehensive doctrines that are reasonable in the sense of being subject to the burdens of judgement (and hence reasonably disagreed with), such a conception must not presuppose the truth, or falsity, of any particular ones. Rather, if public justifiability is to be achieved, it is important that the conception appeals only to public reason, to ideas that are implicit in the public political culture. The idea of society as a fair scheme of cooperation between free and equal citizens, an idea modelled by the original position, satisfies this condition.

Two related features of this line of argument are especially worthy of comment, since these, when combined, have tended to lead to misunderstanding. The first is the extent to which it is wholeheartedly or thoroughgoingly liberal; the goal of public justifiability presupposes a distinctively liberal understanding of the nature of politics and the proper relation between the individual and the state. The second is the fact that the conception of the person as free and equal thus plays something of a dual role; it is both what leads Rawls to seek a conception of justice that is publicly justifiable and what he finds when he goes to the public political culture in order to do just that.

That Rawls's position is grounded in thoroughly liberal premises has already been seen in the passage cited above, but the point is so central that it bears repetition and warrants a further quotation. Given that coercive political power is the power of free and equal citizens as a collective body, and given the fact of reasonable pluralism, Rawls asks:

when may citizens by their vote properly exercise their coercive political power over one another when fundamental questions are at stake? Or in the light of what principles and ideals must we exercise that power if our doing so is to be justifiable to others as free and equal? To this question political liberalism replies: our exercise of political power is proper and hence justifiable only when it is exercised in accordance with a constitution the essentials of which all citizens may reasonably be expected to endorse in the light of principle and ideals acceptable to them as reasonable and rational. This is the liberal principle of legitimacy. (*PL*, p. 217)

Here is the undeniably liberal essence of Rawls's theory. At the heart of his approach is an avowedly liberal conception of the political relationship and of what makes a regime legitimate. What leads Rawls to espouse a methodology constraining him to the working up of ideas implicit in the public political culture is a distinctively liberal understanding of the proper relation between the individual and the state, and one that he himself formulates in terms of the claim that as citizens we are free and equal, reasonable and rational. His theory is thus liberal from the very bottom up.

The reason why it is necessary to emphasize this point is that it has looked to some as if Rawls were attempting to deny that his theory is liberal in any respect other than that it is a theory articulating the ideas to be found in a public political culture that happens to be liberal. This appearance results from the dual role played by the liberal conception of the citizen as free and equal. On the one hand, as we have just seen, it is what leads him to seek public justifiability in the first place. On the other, it is also part of the content of the public political culture to which he restricts himself in seeking a conception that is publicly justifiable. Indeed, it was in this second way that we first introduced the idea of people as free and equal citizens earlier in this chapter; it entered the theory, was modelled by the original position, because it was implicit in the public political culture. It is not surprising, then, that there has been misunderstanding, for an understanding of people as free and equal citizens is both what leads Rawls to seek public justifiability and what is publicly justifiable. In insisting, partly in response to critics like Sandel, that one can get to justice as fairness without presupposing the validity of any particular comprehensive doctrines, Rawls has been at great pain to stress the latter, that the

conception of the person as free and equal citizen can be derived
from the public culture alone, and, as we saw above, this can give
the impression that it enters the theory solely for that reason and not
at all because Rawls is committed to it. Once we see that the reason
to accord weight to what is publicly justifiable, to the content of our
public political culture, is that this follows from his fundamental
commitment to the liberal political ideal (or principle of legitimacy),
we will no longer be tempted to read Rawls's theory as liberal only
because our political culture is so. Far from indicating the disowning
of essentially liberal premises, Rawls's stress on public justifiability
and public reason is actually a manifestation of them.

There is a sense, then, in which the viability of Rawls's political
liberalism rests upon a fortunate coincidence, and the conditions of
its success are rather stringent. If the liberal political ideal, which
presupposes an understanding of people as free and equal citizens, is
to fulfil its commitment to the public justifiability of principles to
govern the political domain, then it is essential that that understanding of people itself be publicly justifiable – a component of the
public political culture – rather than relying on any particular, and
reasonably disputable, comprehensive views. The criteria for political
legitimacy imposed by such an understanding can only be met if that
understanding is itself public. To see the serendipity involved we
need only think about those societies in which what is publicly
justifiable is something other than the conception of the person that
leads Rawls to seek public justifiability. There political institutions
cannot fully satisfy the ideals of Rawls's liberalism since they cannot
meet the criteria of justification that it lays down for them.

The role of stability

Our account of Rawls's shift to the political has so far involved no
reference to considerations of stability; what leads him to the realm
of public reason and the fund of shared ideas implicit in the public
political culture is the liberal political ideal just outlined. Yet we
have seen that Rawls regards that shift as initially made necessary
by a recognition that, if presented as part of a comprehensive
doctrine, as it had been in *A Theory of Justice*, his conception of justice
as fairness would not be stable. Have we then made some error in
our exegesis? To see why not, we need to explain the *kind* of stability

that Rawls is concerned to secure. This is easily enough done, but leaves us with the residual problem of making sense of his insistence that his theory is best presented in two stages, with questions of stability arising only after the content of the conception is provisionally on hand.

Rawls's concern that his conception be stable is not the mere desire to avoid futility. It is quite common for us to organize our political thoughts into two parts: first we think about how society ought to be, then we think about whether that aim is practically realizable, and if so how. This is not how Rawls organizes his political thoughts. He is not interested simply in avoiding a conception of justice that turns out to be futile because it cannot be realized.

> [T]he problem of stability is not that of bringing others who reject a conception to share it, or to act in accordance with it, by workable sanctions if necessary, as if the task were to find ways to impose that conception once we are convinced it is sound. Rather, justice as fairness is not reasonable in the first place unless in a suitable way it can win its support by addressing each citizen's reason, as explained within its own framework. . . . A conception of political legitimacy aims for a public basis of justification and appeals to public reason, and hence to free and equal citizens viewed as reasonable and rational. (*PL*, pp. 143–4)

This, of course, is to couch the issue of stability in terms identical to those in which we presented the liberal political ideal that lies at the heart of Rawls's vision. As he says

> The kind of stability required of justice as fairness is based . . . on its being a liberal political view, one that aims at being acceptable to citizens as reasonable and rational, as well as free and equal, and so as addressed to their public reason. (*PL*, p. 143)

The stability to which Rawls's theory aspires, then, coincides with the conception of legitimacy in terms of which we initially presented his reason for seeking public justifiability. It is in order that it can be stable in the right, liberal, way that it matters that it satisfy the liberal ideal of legitimacy: being presentable as a freestanding conception, independent of any particular comprehensive doctrines, appealing only to public reason, and so on.

When we presented the heart of Rawls's argument in a way that did not refer to questions of stability, we can be read as simply taking seriously his own claim that it is best to present justice as fairness in two stages, with questions of stability arising only when the principles of justice are already on hand; those principles being presented in the first stage as freestanding and the articulation of the values of political justice and public reason. Since, however, the sort of stability he is after clearly involves reference to precisely the conceptions of the citizen and of public reason in terms of which the political conception is to be articulated at his first stage of exposition – the conditions that a conception must satisfy in order to be provisionally on hand after the first stage seem identical to the conditions that it must satisfy in order to be stable in the right way – his repeated urging of the two-stage presentation may seem less than helpful.

The best way to make sense of that exhortation, we would suggest, is to see it as concerned specifically to allay the worry that his concern for stability makes his theory political in the wrong way. In his 1985 paper, 'Justice as Fairness: Political not Metaphysical', which is widely read because of its inclusion in a popular edited collection on these issues,[1] Rawls emphasized the sense in which the aim of his theory is practical, and this emphasis, together with his initial article-length exposition of the idea of an overlapping consensus,[2] led some to see it as merely pragmatic – as if his task were simply that of conflict-avoidance, identifying whatever it is that people can agree to despite their differences. It is, we think, in order to stress the extent to which this pragmatic reading was based on misunderstanding that Rawls has thought it best to insist on the two-stage presentation of his theory.

There are, for Rawls, two distinct questions relating to stability. First, will people who grow up under just institutions acquire a normally sufficient sense of justice so that they will comply with those institutions? His affirmative answer to this depends upon what he calls a 'moral psychology' that appeals ultimately to the claim that reasonable people will want to realize the liberal ideal of citizenship. Second, given that people disagree over comprehensive doctrines, can the political conception be the focus of an overlapping consensus of such doctrines? Can, that is, those who advocate diverse and conflicting comprehensive doctrines nonetheless unite in affirming the same political conception of justice?

We will examine in the next chapter Rawls's reasons for thinking that they can. Very roughly, they rely, first, on his belief that the political values expressed by his political conception are so great as normally to outweigh those non-political values that make up people's comprehensive doctrines with which they might come into conflict and, second, that anybody who disagrees with this judgement as to their overwhelming weight is unreasonable. But it is important for present purposes to see that what Rawls has in mind by an overlapping consensus is a situation in which citizens unite in affirming the same political conception *on the basis of their own comprehensive doctrines*. This is why an overlapping consensus is not a mere *modus vivendi*, something to which people agree because the balance of power is such that it is not in their interests to violate it:

> An overlapping consensus . . . is not merely a consensus on accepting certain authorities, or on complying with certain institutional arrangements, founded on a convergence of self- or group-interests. All those who affirm the political conception start from their own comprehensive view and draw on the religious, philosophical, and moral grounds it provides. The fact that people affirm the same political conception on those grounds does not make their affirming it any less religious, philosophical or moral, as the case may be, since the grounds sincerely held determine the nature of their affirmation. (*PL*, p. 147)

If his political conception of justice will serve as an object of consensus it will be as a moral conception and, unlike a *modus vivendi*, its stability will not depend upon any particular distribution of power between those espousing different comprehensive views.

The point, then, of Rawls's two-stage mode of exposition is that it allows him to explain clearly that the content of his principles of justice

> is not affected in any way by the particular comprehensive doctrines that may exist in society. This is because, at the first stage, justice as fairness abstracts from the knowledge of citizens' determinate conceptions of the good and proceeds from shared political conceptions of society and person . . . So while a political conception of justice addresses the fact of reasonable pluralism, it is not political in the wrong way: that is, its form and content are not affected by the

existing balance of political power between comprehensive doctrines. Nor do its principles strike a compromise between the more dominant ones. (*PL*, pp. 141–2)

The fact that Rawls's theory is not merely pragmatic is worthy of emphasis, not just in order to correct misperceptions of Rawls's earlier statements of his own position, but also because its serving as a *modus vivendi* can seem to some the essence of liberalism more generally. Rawls's conception of justice represents a development in the contract approach to political theory and of course one important strand of thought within the contract tradition is the Hobbesian idea of the state as something to which people agree out of self-interest, because they wish to avoid the nasty, brutish and short life characteristic of the state of nature that would result from the lack of contractual agreement. Once Rawls places the fact of reasonable pluralism at the heart of his argument for political liberalism, it can easily look as if he is a liberal of the Hobbesian brand, with willingness to tolerate differences simply the necessary condition of social stability. We have seen, however, that, for him, the reason to tolerate each other's differences, to exclude controversial matters from politics, is not simply that their inclusion would necessarily lead to conflict and social disorder but rather that such a political framework expresses great values and can be stable in the specific sense of being supported by, and affirmed on grounds provided by, a range of reasonable comprehensive doctrines.

That said, we do think that his repeated insistence on the two stages is more confusing than illuminating. Since the kind of stability required of justice as fairness is based on its being a liberal political view, addressed to the public reason of citizens conceived as free, equal, reasonable and rational, it seems to us somewhat misleading to insist that questions of stability arise only at a second stage, after the content of the conception, which has been developed at the first stage as an articulation of the political values of political justice and public reason, is provisionally on hand. As we suggested above, the conditions that a conception must satisfy in order to be provisionally on hand after the first stage seem identical to the conditions that must be met if it is to be stable in the right way.

Concluding summary

Despite our insistence on its complexity and difficulty, the core argument of *Political Liberalism* is almost disarmingly straightforward. In order to respect one another's freedom and equality as reasonable and rational, citizens of constitutional democracies should not use the coercive power of the state against their fellow citizens except in ways that those subject to that coercion might reasonably be expected to endorse. Since citizens can reasonably disagree about the truth of a plurality of comprehensive religious, moral or philosophical doctrines, any use of state power that is justified by appeal to such a doctrine violates this principle of legitimacy. Instead, appeal must be made only to public reasons – to values and ideas that all share, or can share, despite their other and deeper disagreements, and that can serve as a public basis of justification. These are to be found in the public political culture, which yields, amongst other things, the idea that society is a fair system of cooperation over time between free and equal citizens. This idea, which is freestanding in that it does not presuppose the validity of any particular comprehensive doctrine, is worked up via the construct of the original position into the substantive theory of justice as fairness. Since it is a necessary condition of a political conception's being justified that it be stable in an appropriately liberal way, it matters also that this theory be such that those who grow up under its institutions are normally motivated to comply with them and that it can be the focus of an overlapping consensus of (rather than conflicting with) those reasonable comprehensive doctrines likely to persist over time.

One feature of this argument is worthy of emphasis. The idea of citizens as free and equal enters the story twice. On the one hand, it generates 'the liberal principle of legitimacy' that leads Rawls to the public political culture, in search of fundamental ideas that members of liberal democracies share despite their disagreements over comprehensive doctrines. On the other, it is one of the ideas that this search uncovers, and which (in combination with the idea of society as a system of fair cooperation over time) can then be worked up into a substantive, political, theory of justice. The centrality to his position of the former indicates Rawls's commitment to those liberal premises that his insistence on the latter has sometimes made it look as if he wished to avoid.

This apparent coincidence also makes clear the significance of *Political Liberalism*: it brings the methodology that is to underpin liberal politics into line with its substance. Kant and Mill argued for liberal values in politics, but they did so, in Rawls's view, in a way that itself contradicted the liberal ideal, invoking elements of comprehensive doctrines that free and equal citizens, who affirm a diversity of reasonable comprehensive doctrines, could reasonably reject. To be true to its content, Rawls's trajectory implies, liberalism has to retreat methodologically – away from claims involving controversial metaphysics, theories of value or wide-ranging conceptions of the good, and onto that common, political, ground that can alone satisfy the demands of public reason. In short, where Locke urged religious toleration, Rawls seeks to 'complete and extend the movement of thought that began three centuries ago' and to 'apply toleration to philosophy itself' (*PL*, p. 154).

Whether this self-proclaimed status as grand historical climax is justified depends crucially upon whether the claim to do without philosophy – in the shape of comprehensive doctrines – can indeed be sustained. His premises may be liberal, but Rawls would maintain that they are only politically so. Is Rawls's theory really only political and not at all comprehensive? We will address this question in chapter 7, after we have assessed the relation between political liberalism and the communitarian critique. As we will see in the next chapter, its answer is relevant also to an assessment of that relation.

Notes

1 Avineri and de-Shalit (eds), *Communitarianism and Individualism*.
2 Rawls, 'The Idea of an Overlapping Consensus'.

6

Political liberalism and the communitarian critique

Now that we have offered a general interpretation of the position Rawls develops in *Political Liberalism*, we can go on to spell out in more detail the ways in which it might be utilized in responding to his communitarian critics. We will then be able to determine whether the perceived disagreement between them really exists, and, if it does, which party to the dispute is right. So in this chapter we will evaluate the state of the argument with respect to each of the five thematic headings we established at the outset, in each case attempting to answer on Rawls's behalf the array of interrelated questions that we posed under those headings in our Introduction. As we will see, there are not only significant ways in which Rawls's position is immune from the communitarian critique but some in which he can be regarded as communitarian himself. Since we were at pains in the previous chapter to stress the extent to which his position was thoroughgoingly liberal, this should be sufficient to suggest that the two views are by no means as mutually exclusive as some have thought. Chapter 7, however, suggests reasons for thinking that the theoretical assumptions grounding some of those Rawlsian answers may not be as clear, or as reliable, as they seem, so the reader need not fear a happy resolution of all differences.

It is important to appreciate at the outset that a Rawlsian liberal might well feel that many of the communitarian criticisms of Rawls could adequately be rebutted without the new family of ideas embodied in *Political Liberalism*. As we suggested in the introduction to this part of the book, it is plausible to argue that some of those criticisms rested either upon misreadings or upon an imperfect grasp of certain elements of *A Theory of Justice*; and Rawls's 1980 Dewey Lectures – published before the main texts associated with the communitarian critique – provide further material for such an argument. Important as these matters are, we nevertheless feel that an exhaustive treatment of them is beyond the scope of our project. Of course, we cannot see the distinctiveness of Rawls's shift to the political without devoting some time to distinguishing those responses to the communitarians that presuppose the new concepts associated with political liberalism from those that presuppose only the ideas utilized in earlier presentations of his theory; and as we work through our agenda of issues, we will underline this distinction. But since Rawls explicitly describes *Political Liberalism* as an attempt to recast the ideas developed in his Dewey Lectures and the sequence of articles he published during the 1980s into a unified, coherent and clear form (cf. *PL*, pp. xiii–xiv), we feel that justice can best be done both to him and to the significance of his ideas in the debate between liberals and communitarians by focusing exclusively upon that recent synthesis. We regard the (undeniably interesting) task of tracing the history of the various stages, false starts and insights through which this synthesis was constructed as falling under the purview of Rawlsian textual scholarship, which is not our concern here.

The conception of the person

Under this heading, we declared at the outset that Rawls would never have denied that his theory of justice as fairness was built around some particular conception of the person. For that theory explicitly embodies the claim that, when it comes to matters of justice, people should be regarded as distinct from their particular natural endowments, social position and ends, but possessed of a highest-order interest in their capacity to frame, revise and rationally pursue their conceptions of the good – and such a claim amounts to an assessment of what is important about people, what constitutes their well-being. What is controversial about Rawls's conception of the person is not its existence or relevance, but rather its scope, its source or origin, its status, its validity and coherence, and its desirability. We shall examine each of these five questions in turn.

In Rawls's more recent writings, he takes his conception of the person to be a political conception. This means that it is a conception of the person *qua* citizen, one that is implicit in the public political culture of constitutional democracies and stands free of any particular comprehensive moral or philosophical doctrine. On this understanding, we can quickly summarize its scope: it applies to the person only in so far as she is a member of the public political realm, and not to any other aspect of her life. It is, Rawls insists, 'part of a conception of political and social justice. That is, it characterizes how citizens are to think of themselves and of one another in their political and social relationships as specified by the basic structure' (*PL*, p. 300).

Its source and status are more difficult to determine. It is formulated in terms of the shared resources of the public political culture, so it is tempting to regard this public culture as its source. But when we think about why it matters to Rawls that the conception of the person be formulated in this way, we see that to regard it in this way is somewhat misleading. The reason is not that Rawls believes that only theories relying upon such shared conceptions could provide social blueprints whose implementation was practically feasible; his turn to the public political culture is not driven by pragmatism. It is rather that he attaches great importance to the public justifiability of a political theory. For him, a society whose political arrangements can be justified to all its citizens is one possessed of great moral value, and his political theory can only provide such a justification if it restricts itself to public and shared political conceptions and values. This restriction means that Rawls's theory cannot depend upon the truth of a philosophical doctrine of the self, or upon any moral or political doctrines that have application beyond, or invoke values or conceptions that are not available in, the public political realm (what Rawls calls general and comprehensive moral conceptions); for any such doctrines would, by definition, be controversial, and his theory could not then be publicly justifiable.

But the conception of the person does not enter Rawls's theory *solely* because it is publicly justifiable. That would imply that what matters to him is attaining agreement regardless of the content of that agreement, and so that his reliance upon the resources of the public political culture to work up his conception of the person indicates a wish to dissociate himself from a commitment to its validity. But this is manifestly not the case: that conception enters Rawls's theory because he substantively endorses it as the way one *ought* to conceive of the person as citizen. Indeed, his view that the public justifiability of his theory is a good thing depends upon his having a respect for citizens as free and equal (as requiring political arrangements they can all freely endorse regardless of their particular conceptions of the good), and this respect amounts to a substantive commitment to the very conception of the person as citizen that he claims to find in our public political culture. So, although Rawls's conception of the person can be formulated in terms that derive from the public political culture, and although its capacity so to be formulated is something that this conception demands of itself, its real source or ultimate justification – and so its true status – is not sociological but moral. It could not form part of any *comprehensive* moral doctrine, since it would then fail the test of public justifiability, but it remains a substantive doctrine for all that. In short, Rawls is not merely building with whatever materials are at hand; he is endorsing his political edifice and its constituent values and conceptions from top to bottom.

On this understanding of the scope, source and status of Rawls's conception of the person, how are we to view the communitarian attacks upon it? Broadly speaking, they focus upon its validity – its accuracy as a general account of our moral experience and its coherence as a philosophical account of human nature. In particular, they suggest that it allows no room for the possibility that the attachments that individuals develop to their chosen ends, values, conceptions of the good and communities might become a constitutive part of their identity. But if Rawls's claim that persons ought to be regarded as detached from their particular natural and social endowments and conceptions of the good is restricted to the domain of politics, then it need not imply that we can *generally* step back from each and every one of our value-commitments, or that we are metaphysically detached from them. In fact, Rawls explicitly concedes the validity of Sandel's claims about the phenomenology of our moral experience:

It can happen that in their personal affairs, or in the internal life of associations, citizens may regard their final ends and attachments very differently from the ways the political conception presupposes. They may have, and often do have at any given time, affections, devotions and loyalties that they believe they would not, and indeed could not and should not, stand apart from and evaluate objectively. They may regard it as simply unthinkable to view themselves apart from certain religious, philosophical and moral convictions, or from certain enduring attachments and loyalties. (*PL*, p. 31)

Rawls is happy to see such modes of self-understanding flourish in the context of families, churches and scientific societies; what he denies is that this way of regarding ourselves is appropriate for the purposes of politics. For him, our public or institutional identity, our identity as citizens, should remain the same whatever changes we may undergo in our personal commitments, in our moral or non-institutional identity; this is what is captured in his conception of citizens as being independent from, and capable of revising on reasonable grounds, their conception of the good. If it were otherwise, if our identity as citizens was instead permitted to turn upon whether or not we established or maintained a particular personal or moral identity (so that, for example, professing a certain religious belief was treated as a precondition for the state's recognition of our political rights), then coercive political power would be deployed in the service of a particular comprehensive doctrine that could not be publicly justified. So, for Rawls, political liberalism allows room for Sandelian modes of self-understanding in the non-political spheres of life; it excludes such self-understandings only in the political sphere, where they would impose morally unjustifiable demands on one's fellow citizens.

We should note, however, that even without Rawls's recent attempts to distinguish between purely political and comprehensive modes of liberalism, a different but perhaps equally effective response to the communitarian critique would still have been open to him – one that requires only the resources available in *A Theory of Justice*. To see what we have in mind, it may be helpful to distinguish between the metaphysical and the comprehensive, and to note that Rawls has changed his terminology: in 1985 he was arguing that justice as fairness is 'political not metaphysical', only later did he abandon this formulation in favour of the distinction between the political and the comprehensive. The point is that, even if the conception of the person involved in justice as fairness did indeed involve a comprehensive moral or philosophical doctrine, such as a fundamental commitment to autonomy in all areas of life, still this might not commit advocates of the theory to any genuinely metaphysical claim – where 'metaphysical' refers to ontological claims about the essence of human beings. To Sandel's objection that the original position presupposes an unencumbered subject, a shadowy self detachable from all its ends, the liberal might reply directly that it does no such thing: the original position simply models the claim that what is important about people is their capacity to reflect upon and revise the attachments that they happen to have, and one can think this important without holding that people can detach themselves from all their values at the same time. Of course the process of reflection and revision goes on against a background of other values or commitments; we cannot detach ourselves from everything at the same time, for then there would be no basis on which to make a judgement. But the original position does not presuppose that we can so detach ourselves: Sandel fails to see that it is intended only as a 'device of representation', a means of presenting a certain understanding of people's interests and capacities.

Of course, such a reply to Sandel concedes less than the one that Rawls adopts. Since it makes no use of the distinction between political and comprehensive doctrines, its advocates cannot allow (as Rawls can) that the importance liberals attach to a person's capacity to choose and revise conceptions of the good applies only within the sphere of politics. They must (as Rawls need not) be prepared to come into conflict with those comprehensive doctrines that attribute great significance to the human capacity to form constitutive attachments to ends, values and communities. Whether this makes their position more or less attractive than Rawls's own is not a matter we can explore in any detail here: for our purposes, it is only important to note that it is a mode of response to the communitarian critique that Rawls could have adopted purely on the basis of the resources of *A Theory of Justice*, and that he did not in fact do so.

One further question about Rawls's conception of the person remains – the issue of its desirability. For even if we accept that it involves no incoherent metaphysical or comprehensive presuppositions, it is still open to us to question its attractiveness as a substantive moral conception of persons as citizens. For example, Rawls's political liberalism sharply distinguishes between the political and the personal in the life of every citizen; it is a requirement of citizenship in a Rawlsian society that each individual, when thinking about justice, should normally restrict herself to considerations arising from a conception of herself as a free and equal person participating with others in a fair system of social cooperation, and exclude those considerations arising from the comprehensive moral or religious beliefs that may give her non-political life its integrity and meaning. This distinction between public and private self-understandings will of course be entirely acceptable to anyone cleaving to a comprehensive moral doctrine that supports a commitment to political liberalism, and while Rawls's claim is that all reasonable comprehensive doctrines will overlap in affirming this view of the political, it is hard not to suspect that, for many, living in accordance with such a conception of politics will involve a greater or lesser degree of what might be called schizophrenia, a bracketing off or suspension of their vision of the good.

This worry about the desirability of a Rawlsian polity is widespread (for example, it forms an important part of Ronald Dworkin's rejection of Rawls's shift to the political, as we shall see in chapter 9). But an assessment of its true significance depends upon getting clear about how political liberalism might respond to such criticisms; and, as we shall see in the following chapter, this involves a critical examination of Rawls's view that any comprehensive doctrine requiring that the very great values of the political be trumped by non-political considerations thereby reveals itself to be an unreasonable doctrine, asking for more than can in justice be demanded from citizens who do not cleave to its conception of what is of value in human life. We must therefore defer any final judgement upon this specific accusation until we look more closely at Rawls's conception of the burdens of judgement in the context of reasonable pluralism.

With this qualification in mind, we can sum up the present state of play under this heading of our agenda. If the communitarians are to renew their attack upon the Rawlsian conception of the person, they seem to have two options. First, they can contest Rawls's claims about the true scope, source and status of that conception: for if it is not restricted to the domain of the political in the ways Rawls claims, then the communitarians' original criticisms of its validity and coherence might retain some of their force. Second, they can question the desirability of the conception, even given its restricted status: they can, for example, defend the view that it posits a split between the political and the personal that seems to require those holding non-liberal comprehensive doctrines to do so in a rather half-hearted (perhaps even liberal) way, and it accords a priority to the political over the personal that gives the value of autonomy a primacy it may not fully deserve. We shall examine these two possible avenues in more detail in the following chapter – when we assess Rawls's claim to be presenting an exclusively political version of liberalism.

Asocial individualism

Under this heading, the communitarian criticisms focused upon Rawls's contractual approach to political theory, arguing that this approach (as exemplified in the original position) embodies the belief that people's ends are formed independently of or prior to society, which is regarded as the outcome of negotiation between individuals whose ends are already given. For the communitarians, such an asocial individualist view embodies two different sorts of mistake. It denies the important philosophical or sociological truth that people's conceptions of the good and of themselves are dependent upon a social matrix; and it ignores or represses the importance of human goods whose content is communal, in particular the significance of the good of political community – for by regarding politics merely as an arena within which people cooperate with others solely in order to pursue their private advantage, Rawls ignores the possibility that the bonds of fellow-citizenship can function as a (or as the most) significant constitutive attachment in people's lives.

A Rawlsian response to these two criticisms could begin by stressing something that was evident even in *A Theory of Justice* – that the original position is a device of representation whose function is to dramatize and articulate a particular substantive conception of the person. It therefore aims to embody no particular sociological or philosophical claims about the relative priority of the individual to society, but rather forms part of an argument for the development and maintenance of a type of society within which people accord a particular moral status to one another. Rawls's shift to the political allows him to strengthen this point by characterizing the substantive position that the original position dramatizes as a purely political one: it concerns the person understood as citizen, regulates her relation to other persons only *qua* fellow citizens, and avoids drawing upon any comprehensive conceptions. In short, the substantive underpinning of the original position is designed to be freestanding; it floats free of support from any particular, even liberal, comprehensive doctrines. But does this allow it to float free of charges of asocial individualism?[1]

The constitutive role of social matrices

Of all the communitarian objections to Rawls's theory, that alleging that he fails to acknowledge the constitutive role of social matrices seem most obviously to overlook, or discount, aspects of his thought that had already been made clear before those objections were formulated. In *A Theory of Justice* itself Rawls had already dismissed as a truism the view that 'social life is a condition for our developing the ability to speak and think, and to take part in the common activities of society and culture'. 'No doubt,' he continued, 'even the concepts that we use to describe our plans and situations, and even to give voice to our personal wants and purposes, often presuppose a social setting as well as a system of belief and thought that is the outcome of the collective efforts of a long tradition' (*TJ*, p. 522). In a paper published in 1977 – 'The Basic Structure as Subject' – moreover, he had made it clear that the context of a social contract must allow for the fact that we cannot know what we would have been like had we not belonged to society, observing parenthetically that 'perhaps the thought itself lacks sense' (p. 162). It is clear, then, that a Rawlsian liberal, even one who has not presented her liberalism as political rather than comprehensive, can accept the point stressed by Taylor in his critique of the liberal tendency to give priority to the individual over her community – namely, the extent to which it is the community in which people live that, by providing the conceptual resources in terms of which they come to understand who they are, shapes who they are and the values that they have. In this context, it is perhaps worth recalling that while both MacIntyre and Taylor argue that liberalism has a tendency to perpetrate this strand of asocial individualism, only MacIntyre claims that Rawls himself is guilty of it.

In fact, Rawls not only acknowledges this point, but regards it as integrally related to the question of public justifiability which, though it first emerged in the Dewey Lectures (1980) – in which the following passages first appear – is clearly central to his political liberalism.[2] For he spells out that idea of public justifiability partly in terms of what he calls the full publicity condition. Justice as fairness must be public not only in the sense that it builds upon ideas implicit in the public political culture (so that its principles can be mutually acknowledged by all citizens), but also in the sense that its very justification can be mutually recognized. The theory itself – its whole justificatory background, everything discussed in the previous chapter and more – must itself be publicly available to citizens. But why?

Rawls offers two arguments. First, he claims that

> publicity ensures, so far as practical measures allow, that citizens are in a position to know and accept the pervasive influences of the basic structure that shape their conceptions of themselves, their character and ends . . . that citizens should be in this position is a condition of their realizing their freedom as fully autonomous, politically speaking. It means that in their public political life nothing need be hidden. (*PL*, p. 68)

Only if social institutions are transparent can the fact that such arrangements influence people's self-understandings be rendered compatible with their freedom. This is an implication of the idea that if the individual is to be free, she must be aware of all those processes influencing her. It is precisely because (as Taylor claims) the community precedes the individual in this sense that freedom requires that the basic structure of that community be publicly justifiable to the individuals who live in it.

His second argument rests on the idea that, if public, justice as fairness fosters the very conception of the person upon which it builds. For Rawls, once a moral conception is public, it assumes a wide role as part of public culture:

Not only are its first principles embodied in public and social institutions and public traditions of their interpretation, but the derivation of citizens' rights, liberties and opportunities invokes a certain conception of the person. In this way citizens are made aware of and educated to this conception. They are presented with a way of regarding themselves that otherwise they would most likely never have been able to entertain. To realize the full publicity condition is to realize a social world within which the ideal of citizenship can be learned and may elicit an effective desire to be that kind of person. (*PL*, p. 71)

In other words, justice as fairness itself plays an educative role in helping people to see themselves as free and equal, as having the capacities for a sense of justice and to frame, revise and pursue conceptions of the good. Thus, this second argument for full publicity again recognizes that people will to a great extent form their understanding of themselves as citizens from their public political culture and from the conceptions of the person and society within it; it further demonstrates Rawls's sense of the importance of a particular social milieu to the ideal of liberal citizenship and political autonomy.

The importance of communal goods

Rawls's response to the second, substantive strand of the communitarian critique of liberal asocial individualism takes various forms. It is true that his political liberalism begins precisely from the denial that community of the kind after which communitarians seem to hanker is possible or desirable at the level of political society. As he says

justice as fairness does indeed abandon the ideal of political community if by that ideal is meant a political society united on one (partially or fully) comprehensive religious, philosophical or moral doctrine. That conception of social unity is excluded by the fact of reasonable pluralism; it is no longer a political possibility for those who accept the constraints of liberty and toleration of democratic institutions. (*PL*, p. 201)

What motivates Rawls's concern that his liberalism be distinctively political, having the three features that we outlined near the beginning of this chapter, is precisely the claim that democratic societies are inevitably and permanently characterized by a plurality of different and conflicting conceptions of the good and that the only way to ensure agreement on any conception would be by the oppressive use of state power. Liberalism, on this understanding, is a response to the lack of any morally acceptable possibility of any more substantive or specific form of political community. Rawls's position, then, is a direct rejection of (the morally acceptable possibility of) communitarian demands for a political society built around a shared comprehensive conception of the good.

While this is the essence of Rawls's response to the communitarian critique, it is important to see that it leaves room for two ways in which he can recognize the importance of distinctively communal goods that his communitarian critics charge him with neglecting. In the first place, along lines similar to those relied upon in the reply to Sandel cited above, it is quite acceptable to the political liberal that communal goods be realized at the non-political level:

> Note that what is impracticable is not *all* values of community (recall that a community is understood as an association of society whose unity rests on a comprehensive conception of the good) but only political community and its values. Justice as fairness assumes, as other liberal political views do also, that the values of community are not only essential but realizable, first in the various associations that carry on their life within the framework of the basic structure, and second in those associations that extend across the boundaries of nation-states, such as churches and scientific societies. (*PL*, p. 146)

It is wrong to pursue communal values at the political level because, for Rawls, a community only exists where there is a common comprehensive doctrine. Given the fact of reasonable pluralism, this could not be achieved without the oppressive use of state power that failed to respect citizens as free and equal, reasonable and rational. But citizens are perfectly able to realize the values of community in this sense within, or across, political societies.

Furthermore, although his definition of the term means that he would not accept the description, it seems to us that Rawls's political liberalism itself embodies a particular understanding of community, in that what motivates the exclusion from politics of reasons appropriate to people's non-public lives is precisely a shared aim, a conception of community and a recognition of the value of goods that can only be realized communally. Responding to those who charge liberalism with being excessively individualistic and instrumental in its understanding of politics, who claim that it regards society as nothing more than the outcome of an agreement between individuals or associations cooperating solely to pursue their pre-social individual or associational advantage, Rawls emphasizes both that his political conception of justice does involve a commitment to a shared goal and that this goal can become an important part of an individual's identity. As he says:

> in the well-ordered society of justice as fairness citizens share a common aim, and one that has a high priority: namely, the aim of political justice, that is, the aim of ensuring that political and social institutions are just, and of giving justice to persons generally, as what citizens need for themselves and want for one another. It is not true, then, that on a liberal view citizens have no fundamental common aims. Nor is it true that the aim of political justice is not an important part of their noninstitutional or moral identity. But this common aim of political justice must not be mistaken for (what I have called) a conception of the good. (*PL*, p. 146)

A society well-ordered by justice as fairness is not a private society, in which individuals or associations cooperate to pursue their private advantage, it is one that recognizes a common aim and indeed gives that aim priority over the personal interests that people may have, for these latter can only be pursued within the constraints of a just framework.

We must recall that his general emphasis on public justifiability derives not from a pragmatic concern with stability but is morally driven, as is the conception of the person that is to be justified. The vision of society that this entails, a society in which each citizen acknowledges the freedom and equality of all other citizens and is committed to maintaining the institutions and practices that preserve it, does not reduce the social to an arena for the extraction of egoistic benefit. It is of course good for the individuals within it, since it allows them to develop and exercise their two moral powers; but it is also a genuinely social good – only realizable through joint activity based on a shared final end.

In fact, much of this vision of the substantive and common good embodied in a well-ordered society was already laid out in *A Theory of Justice*. In the section devoted to 'The Idea of Social Union', Rawls distinguished in some detail between private societies, in which individuals combine as a means to their personal ends, and social unions, through which individuals aim at shared ends and in which they value their common institutions as good in themselves; examples of the latter would include families, parishes, scientific and artistic communities. He then characterizes his vision of a well-ordered society as 'a social union of social unions': in it, members of society would participate in any number of different sub-societal social unions, but as free and equal members of the political community within which they conduct these activities, they would aim at the shared final end of establishing and maintaining just institutions, and would prize those institutions as good in themselves. It therefore cannot be argued that Rawls is only able to accommodate the idea of a common good at the societal level because of the family of new ideas associated with his recent turn to the political, although it is probably fair to say that that turn has involved a significant change in the way that he understands the content of that common good. Indeed, in 1971 Rawls was happy to regard the public realization of justice as a 'value of community' (*TJ*, p. 529) – a view that is of course consistent with both his current definition of community and his acknowledgement that in 1971 justice as fairness was presented as a comprehensive, or at least partially comprehensive, doctrine.

That his critics overlooked these communitarian aspects of his original theory is perhaps not altogether surprising, for Rawls has admitted that the presentation of some other parts of the argument was misleading insofar as it seemed to suggest that justice as fairness was a theory for individualistic egoists:

> A remark in *Theory*, p. 16, where it is said that the theory of justice is a part of the theory of rational decision . . . is simply incorrect. What should have been said is that the account of the parties, and of their reasoning, uses the theory of rational decision, though only in an intuitive way. The theory itself is part of a political conception of justice, one that tries to give an account of reasonable principles of justice. There is no thought of deriving those principles from the concept of rationality as the sole normative concept. I believe that the text of *Theory* as a whole supports this interpretation. (*PL*, p. 53 n. 7)

What Rawls here means by 'the reasonable' is the constraints that form the framework within which rational choice is exercised. In this sense, 'the rational' is a specification of how the people in the original position are motivated, but 'the reasonable' is a specification of how the original position is set up in the first place. Since this means that the reasonable is prior to the rational, and embodies a variety of moral concerns, including claims about what sort of political community is worthy of allegiance, then we have no grounds for regarding Rawls's use of rational choice machinery as a sign that he is an asocial individualist in the substantive sense.

Nonetheless, the common good that Rawls seeks in politics is undeniably an individualistic good; the highest-order interests that we possess as citizens are interests that we have as individuals, and for Rawls it would be unacceptable for our community to deprive us of them. In particular, it would be unjust for a political community to be founded on a comprehensive conception of the good – whether liberal or otherwise; so in this sense, Rawls is deliberately setting his face against certain strong readings of the good of political community. This is an issue to which we will return under the fifth heading of our agenda, when we examine Rawls's attribution of priority to the right over the good; and any further discussion of the issues it raises must wait until then. But we can at least say that this would seem to be one point upon which any renewal of the communitarian critique under this heading could focus.

Universalism

Under this heading, the communitarian critique argued that Rawls's theory of justice was designed to apply universally and cross-culturally, and thus failed to attend to the ways in which different cultures embody different values and practices, a fact with significant consequences for the intelligibility and/or justifiability of claims about social justice. More specifically, Walzer criticized Rawls's use of primary goods for neglecting the fact that different goods must be distributed for different reasons; and he attacked Rawls's supposed attempt to construct a universal vantage point from which to derive principles of justice as failing to recognize the importance of 'social meanings', of a culture's own particular understandings of its goods. Readers of *A Theory of Justice* could be

forgiven for thinking that justice as fairness had such universalist
pretensions: its final paragraph claimed that to see our place in
society from the perspective of the original position was to see it *'sub
specie aeternitatis'* (*TJ*, p. 587), Rawls's account of his primary goods
does not go out of its way to exclude such an interpretation, and the
remark (quoted above) that his theory of justice was part of a theory
of rational choice implies exactly the kind of ahistorical conception
of human rationality (and so of human beings) of which Walzer was
suspicious. However, the new Rawls's response to this criticism is
both clear and powerful: by emphasizing that his conception of the
person is derived from the public political culture of constitutional
democracies, he shows that his general theory of justice as fairness is
importantly culture-specific. The abstraction from people's particular natural and social endowments and from their particular
conceptions of the good that is embodied in the original position
is an expression of our particular culture's conception of the person
as citizen; it is therefore an abstraction resulting rather from Rawls's
attending closely to cultural particularity than from his failure to do
so. We must examine these matters in more detail.

Rawls and Walzer: abstraction and cultural particularity

In the first place, Rawls's primary goods are by no means as abstract
as they look. Far from being an undifferentiated mass of things that
people might want, they are actually rather carefully related to the
principles proposed for their distribution in just the way that Walzer
demands – for they are internally related to the specifically political
conception of the person. For Rawls, primary goods specify the
needs of people *qua* citizens – needs which flow from their particular
political role and status.

> The requirements, the needs, of citizens as free and equal persons are
> different from the needs of patients or of students, say . . . In effect, the
> political conception of the person and the idea of primary goods
> specify a special kind of need for a political conception of justice. (*PL*,
> p. 189 n. 20)

It appears, then, that Rawls and Walzer have rather similar views about the importance of relating principles of justice to the particular goods which they are to distribute. The difference is only that where Walzer talks of principles being good-specific, Rawls conceives the point rather in terms of their being 'role-specific' or 'conception of the person-specific'. If we think of primary goods as 'citizen-goods', of health care as 'patient-goods' and education as 'student-goods', and acknowledge Rawls's point that different principles may be appropriate in these different contexts, then the similarity becomes rather striking.

It is the internal relation of justice as fairness to the basic structure and the conception of the person as citizen that enables a specifically political understanding of Rawls's theory to avoid the first of Walzer's criticisms. And it is that theory's derivation from the public political culture that renders it immune to his second charge – that of seeking universality and abstracting from cultural particularity. For nothing could be more in line with Walzer's injunctions to respect social meanings than Rawls's claim that the content of a political conception of justice 'is expressed in terms of certain fundamental ideas seen as implicit in the public political culture of a democratic society' (*PL*, p. 13). Far from representing an attempt to transcend cultural particularity and to reach a perspective from which one can construct a theory of justice that applies universally, the original position is a device for representing an explicitly culture-specific understanding.

> In a democratic society there is a tradition of democratic thought, the content of which is at least familiar and intelligible to the educated common sense of citizens generally. Society's main institutions, and their accepted forms of interpretation, are seen as a fund of implicitly shared ideas and principles. (*PL*, p. 14)

Justice as fairness starts from within that political tradition, and finds in the fund a particular understanding of society and its members. The original position is an attempt to present that understanding in a clear and unified way. So here too, rather than seeking distance from the political community, Rawls does precisely what Walzer would have him do: he articulates our shared social meanings.

Indeed, a Rawlsian might even want to argue that Rawls's method is not only consistent with Walzer's approach but more successful –

that Rawls is truer to our shared meanings than is Walzer. For Rawls (it might be said) recognizes how little we do share. What motivates his search for a specifically political conception of justice is a recognition of the fact of reasonable pluralism – the fact that there are (and will continue to be, in the absence of oppressive uses of state power) a diversity of conflicting comprehensive conceptions of the good. Given this fact, all that we can agree to – and what therefore gets embodied in the original position – is an understanding of politics, a conception of political society and of the person as citizen, that leaves people free to frame, revise and pursue whatever conceptions of the good they choose. Whereas Walzer seems to suppose that beneath our apparent differences of opinion we all actually share an understanding of the way in which particular goods should be distributed, Rawls's liberalism starts from the acknowledgement that we do not, that the citizens of a democratic society will espouse quite different understandings of how people should live their lives and how goods should be distributed. If it is Walzer who insists that different cultures will understand their goods in different ways, it is Rawls who recognizes that different members of our culture will do so.

One might say that Rawls abstracts not from our culture, as Walzer supposes, but from those particular comprehensive doctrines of the good espoused within it; and he does so because that is the way to be true to our particular culture and those meanings that we do indeed share. The work of abstraction 'is not gratuitous: not abstraction for abstraction's sake. Rather, it is a way of continuing public discussion when shared understandings of lesser generality have broken down' (*PL*, pp. 45–6). The abstraction involved in Rawls's conception of primary goods does not, then, represent an abstraction from our particular culture and social meanings, but rather a careful attention to the abstraction from particular conceptions of the good that precisely characterizes that culture and those meanings. Political liberalism must abstract from particular comprehensive conceptions of the good because that abstraction is itself demanded by the understandings (of higher generality) that we do actually share.

In a (significantly) parenthetic remark in *Spheres of Justice*, Walzer makes the following observation on what should happen if there is disagreement on social meanings:

A given society is just if its substantive life is lived in a certain way – that is, in a way faithful to the shared understandings of its members. (When people disagree about the meaning of social goods, when understandings are controversial, then justice requires that the society be faithful to the disagreements, providing institutional channels for their expression, adjudicative mechanisms, and alternative distributions.) (*SJ*, p. 313)

'Being faithful to the disagreements' seems to us a remarkably accurate description of Rawls's political liberalism. If he is right in thinking that the meanings that we share are those of a society as a fair scheme of social cooperation between free and equal citizens, whilst we disagree about comprehensive doctrines, then, methodologically, it is Rawls who is the true Walzerian.

However, we must not give undue weight to these parallels. In particular, we must recall the relative importance that Rawls assigns to public justifiability and to the political conception of the person. Rawls is substantively committed to the conception of the person as citizen that he claims to find in our public political culture, and the respect for public justifiability that drives his turn towards that culture is itself motivated by that same commitment (by his belief that citizens deserve to have political arrangements they can all freely endorse). So his commitment to public justifiability is only one aspect of his wider substantive view that a society arranged in accord with his theory of justice is the best sort of society for human beings to inhabit. There is, then, a crucial respect in which Rawls's approach differs from Walzer's: it is not at all that Rawls is committed to the idea that justice is the articulation of shared meanings whatever they may be. On the contrary, it seems that he is only able to present his theory as the working up of the public culture because it happens that the content of that culture coincides with the very conception of society and of the person as citizen which leads him to pursue that method. While it is indeed important that his conception of justice be publicly justifiable to the citizens whom he seeks to address, and in this respect he would endorse Walzer's concern with the world of meanings that we share, this interest in public justifiability follows from a commitment to a liberal conception of people as free and equal, and does not require Rawls to accept the relativistic aspects of Walzer's position.

This implies that, if Rawls were to find himself in (or, more generally, to find himself considering) a non-liberal society whose public political culture did *not* embody his conception of the person, then the impossibility of providing a public justification of liberalism would not in itself *oblige* him to refrain from advocating and working towards the liberal reconstruction of that society in other ways. In other words, if the course of action dictated by his commitment to public justifiability and that dictated by his commitment to the conception of the person as citizen ever diverged, then Rawls could perfectly consistently sacrifice the former value to the latter; he could argue that his primary commitment was not to whatever ideas happen to be publicly justifiable, but to the ideas embodied in his political conception of the person. In short, in societies where the shared political culture is itself illiberal, Rawls need not regard justice as truth to that culture.

Rawls has not as yet provided a detailed and explicit articulation of his position on this matter. He has, however, clarified his position on an issue that has an obvious bearing on it, and that also falls under this heading on our agenda – the question of how a state committed to political liberalism might relate to non-liberal cultures.

Rawls and international justice

In his Amnesty lecture on 'The Law of Peoples', 1993 Rawls argues that the scope for establishing and maintaining just relationships between (rather than within) nation-states is not restricted to those states which fully accept the tenets of political liberalism, but can also include what he calls 'well-ordered hierarchical societies'. Such societies do not apply the principles of justice as fairness, or indeed any other version of political liberalism, to their own basic institutions; but their systems of law are sincerely and not unreasonably regarded by their members as guided by a common good conception of justice – one that takes impartially into account what are regarded as their fundamental interests, and which treats all citizens with formal equality (e.g. treating similar cases similarly). Further, their political systems must embody a reasonable consulta-tion hierarchy – a family of representative bodies or assemblies that look after the important interests of all society's members, giving everyone the right to express dissent and to have that dissent taken seriously, and treating everyone as bearers of moral duties and obligations to one another. Thus, although they do not view all citizens as free and equal in the full liberal sense (for example, they do not assign them an extensive right to free speech), these assemblies do secure for all citizens a right to life, to freedom from slavery and serfdom, and to property. In short, a well-ordered hierarchical society respects human rights without respecting the full schedule of rights at the core of political liberalism.

One example of such a society would be that sketched by Hegel, in which the basic institutions of political decision-making allocate differing degrees of influence to different classes or estates of society, but in which no estate is entirely deprived of influence; and we might also imagine theocratic or caste-based variants of that Hegelian model – although any such variant must admit a measure of liberty of conscience, not denying any non-established religion the right to be practised in peace. If such societies are also essentially peaceable, respecting the integrity of other societies, then their representatives can legitimately enter with representatives of liberal democracies into an international original position, in which they are symmetrically situated behind a veil of ignorance concerning their territorial size and strength, their natural resources, and their economic development, but in which they are aware of the specific conception of justice ordering their domestic arrangements. Rawls then argues (more precisely, he has space only to assert) that both liberal democracies and well-ordered hierarchical societies would agree on a familiar set of principles of international law, including duties of non-intervention, respect for treaties and the honouring of human rights.

Even this brief sketch of Rawls's view might lead us to question the clarity and plausibility of his preliminary determination of the threshold at which a non-liberal society might be deemed to be well-ordered and hierarchical. We might further question whether, on a sufficiently stringent determination of that threshold, any non-liberal states in the real world will cross it. But what is clearly critical for him in his attempt to define a category of non-liberal but nonetheless legitimate forms of political community is that the arrangements of such communities at least embody a substantial analogue to the liberal conception of citizens as free, even if they do not treat them as fully equal. For example, members of differing Hegelian estates are not equally well-placed with respect to influencing the political process and lack the right to free speech (as that is understood in liberal states), but every member is represented in the political process, and all must be free to express dissent and have it taken seriously in that process. Such societies at least treat their citizens as bearers of moral duties and obligations, and so as responsible and cooperating members of society. So, Rawls's willingness to tolerate deviations from political liberalism is strictly limited, and in ways that are recognizably rooted in the principle of tolerance that is the core of political liberalism; we can have no moral grounds for acknowledging as a member of the international community a society which lacks *any* substantial analogue to a vision of its citizens as free.

But it is also clear that, for Rawls, the mere fact that another state has rejected political liberalism does not entail that it cannot be permitted to enter into just relationships with states that are committed to political liberalism. In the case of hierarchical societies, their partial acknowledgement of their citizens' rights to freedom and equality justifies our acknowledgement of them as an equal member of the community of nations with the freedom to determine their own basic institutions. In other words, when political liberalism's commitment to the principle of toleration within nation-states conflicts with its commitment to the principle of toleration between nation-states (the former implying a refusal to acknowledge an unjust regime as legitimate, the latter implying an acknowledgement of the fact of international political pluralism), there can be circumstances in which working towards the very great good of a more nearly just international community takes priority over working towards the very great good of greater justice within non-liberal members of that community. In effect, then, political liberalism's conception of the person both is and is not functioning as a cross-culturally applicable standard of justice. Any state that falls short of its demands is to that degree imperfectly just, and no state that entirely disowns it is politically legitimate; but any non-liberal state whose public political culture embodies a substantial analogue to the liberal conception of the person deserves the respect and toleration of all liberal states.

Let us try to sum up Rawls's position on the issues pertaining to this heading on our agenda. His conception of the person is an elaboration of resources implicit in the public political culture of liberal democracies, and is designed to apply solely to the sphere of politics. But it is not necessarily designed to apply to the sphere of politics solely in societies whose public political culture contains that conception of the person – that is, to the politics of liberal democracies. Rawls's commitment to public justifiability is not the consequence of a Walzerian belief that social justice is nothing other than truth to the social meanings prevalent in the given society. It is a further expression of his belief that the conception of the person prevalent in the public political culture of liberal democracies embodies the right understanding of social justice. This does not mean that Rawls *must* regard his theory of justice as having universal cross-cultural validity and application, but neither does it mean that Rawls *must* restrict its validity and application to those cultures in which the resources for elaborating that theory are publicly available. As far as can be judged from his recent writings on international law, in which he appears prepared to acknowledge the legitimacy of states whose domestic arrangements manifest only an etiolated version of liberal respect for persons, Rawls takes his conception of the person as citizen to specify a cross-culturally applicable ideal of political justice, but not a necessary precondition of political legitimacy.

Subjectivism/objectivism

The communitarian critique under this heading accused Rawls of a commitment to a philosophical scepticism about the rationality and objectivity of value judgements. Rawls's fundamental concern for a neutral state and his specific invocation of a veil of ignorance in the original position were held to derive from a belief that either moral judgements in general or judgements about conceptions of the good in particular were arbitrary expressions of preference, inherently incapable of being rationally justified.

The new Rawls makes it clear that his reason for excluding comprehensive considerations from the sphere of politics is that the value of a political community that can be publicly justified to all its citizens is so great as to give us a strong moral reason to exclude such considerations even if we believe them to be objectively valid. We do not exclude them because we doubt that they are true:

> Properly understood . . . a political conception of justice need be no more indifferent, say, to truth in philosophy and morals than the

principle of toleration, suitably understood, need be indifferent to truth in religion. Since we seek an agreed basis of public justification in matters of justice, and since no political agreement on those disputed questions can reasonably be expected, we turn instead to the fundamental intuitive ideas we seem to share through the public political culture. From these ideas we try to work out a political conception of justice congruent with our considered convictions. (*PL*, pp. 150–1)

One can believe in the truth of a particular comprehensive doctrine and still hold that its truth is irrelevant or inappropriate to questions of justice. The Rawlsian liberal can argue for an anti-perfectionist state, can endorse the exclusion from politics of reasons arising from comprehensive doctrines, whilst being committed *qua* private individual to the truth of any such doctrine. What matters is that she should recognize that her reasons for believing in her doctrine are not of the kind that can serve as a public basis of justification. It would, indeed, be self-contradictory if Rawls's political liberalism did presuppose subjectivism or any form of moral scepticism, for that would amount to a reliance upon a controversial philosophical doctrine, and so to the violation of his commitment to public justifiability.

For exactly the same reason, Rawls is very careful to stress that political liberalism's use of what he calls a constructivist method in political theorizing does not commit him to any controversial views about the nature of political values or the objectivity or truth of political judgements. At first sight, this claim may seem difficult to sustain, since – as we saw in the previous chapter – Rawls explains what he understands by political constructivism by distinguishing it from rational intuitionism on the one hand, and from Kantian moral constructivism on the other; and he draws these distinctions precisely in terms of the three positions' differing views on the nature of moral and political values, principles and judgements. For example, the rational intuitionist is defined as regarding correct moral judgements as true statements about an independent order of moral values whose existence is established or cognized by perception or intuition supplemented by theoretical reflection. By contrast, the political constructivist regards such judgements as the outcome of a procedure of construction, in which certain basic conceptions of the person and of society are utilized to generate a set of principles which determine a just political order. It therefore relies primarily upon practical rather than theoretical reason, by which Rawls means that it is concerned not with attaining knowledge of objects that are already given, but with the production of objects according to a conception of those objects (in this case, the object is a genuinely just political order); and it judges between candidate principles solely in terms of whether or not the political construction they determine is reasonable, not in terms of whether or not it is true to an independent order of moral values. Although of course heavily Kantian in inspiration, political constructivism is distinguished from Kantian moral constructivism primarily because of its restricted scope; it does not rely upon a comprehensive moral view, but utilizes only purely political conceptions of the person and of society in order to establish a purely political agreement. Furthermore, according to Rawls, whereas Kantian transcendental idealism claims that the order of moral values is actually constituted or brought into existence by the principles of practical reason, political constructivism makes no such claim.

What we must remember is that although political constructivism stakes out a distinctive view of political values and the nature of political judgements, it is one which is compatible with a wide range of views about those topics. For example, although political constructivism does not affirm the rational intuitionist view that there is an independent order of moral values, that is not because it affirms a view which conflicts with that of the intuitionist; in particular, it does not affirm the contrary, Kantian constructivist view that this order of values is constituted by human practical reason. By saying that principles of justice can be regarded as the outcome of a procedure of construction, Rawls is not asserting that this is how they, and other moral values, come into being; both a Kantian moral constructivist and a rational intuitionist could agree that these principles *can be regarded* in this way, whilst thinking that the full story about their nature and origins is very different (and whilst fleshing out that story in very different ways, according to their very different comprehensive views). In other words, political constructivism is the method of political theorizing that is best suited to Rawls's desire to eschew controversy over metaphysical doctrines – it offers an approach that might constitute common ground between a number of competing comprehensive perspectives.

This is also why political constructivism restricts itself to judging the acceptability of a theory of justice purely in terms of whether or not it is reasonable; doing so enables it to dispense entirely with the question of whether or not the theory is true, and thus to escape the responsibility of providing and defending one particular, and thus highly controversial, elucidation of that troublesome concept – whether in Kantian or intuitionist terms. However, this aspect of its avoidance of controversy raises a worry that is particularly pertinent to this heading of our agenda; for if political constructivism dispenses with the concept of truth, how can it account for the idea of a political principle or judgement's being objective – how can it distinguish between theories which appear to be, and those which really are, correct? In particular, how can it show that Rawls's judgement of the superiority of justice as fairness has a claim to objectivity? Rawls believes that his concept of the reasonable provides all that is needed to perform this, admittedly essential, task. For of course, what makes a theory reasonable is a matter of mutually recognized criteria and evidence; it is not a matter of its rhetorical persuasiveness, and neither is it determined by whether any given agent might happen to think it is reasonable. For political constructivism (as for any theoretical method that is worthy of the name), thinking that something is reasonable does not make it so – only the ability to present your conclusions as emerging from an appropriate procedure of construction in the right kind of way can show that. But this means that political constructivism can retain a notion of objectivity whilst entirely dispensing with the concept of (moral and political) truth; Rawls can retain the conceptual machinery he requires in order to make sense of the idea that we can discriminate better political judgements from worse, whilst reducing to the barest minimum the controversial philosophical commitments about the nature of truth that this machinery might carry with it.

A further question remains, however. If a political constructivist attempts to do without the concept of truth, is it therefore impossible for Rawls to argue that his version of political liberalism – justice as fairness – is true? We can only provide the bare outline of an answer here. On the one hand, as we have seen, political liberalism aims for reasonableness rather than truth, since reasonableness is the appropriate standard of correctness given the aim of establishing a public basis of justification in the context of reasonable pluralism. 'Holding a political conception as true, and for that reason alone the one suitable basis of public reason, is exclusive, even sectarian, and so likely to foster political division' (*PL*, p. 129). On the other, Rawls's idea of overlapping consensus, in which reasonable comprehensive doctrines have their own reasons for affirming the same political conception, means not only that we may speak of the moral truth of a political conception when we assess it from the point of view of our comprehensive doctrine, but also that:

> if any of those reasonable comprehensive doctrines supports only true moral judgments, the political conception is itself correct, or close thereto, since it is endorsed by a true doctrine. Thus the truth of any one doctrine in the consensus guarantees that all the reasonable doctrines yield the right conception of political justice, even though they do not do so for the right reasons as specified by the one true doctrine . . . *[i]f one of their doctrines should be true, all citizens are correct, politically speaking: that is, they all appeal to a sound political conception of justice. (PL,* p. 128)

Although officially committed to claiming only reasonableness for his conception, Rawls ends his discussion of this issue with a string of rhetorical questions strongly suggesting that the very fact that reasonable comprehensive doctrines coincide in affirming political liberalism is good evidence for its being true after all.

It therefore seems clear that Rawls takes himself to be well-equipped to regard moral and political judgements as capable of objectivity, and to regard his own political theory as not only reasonable but true. Nevertheless, there remains an element of what might be called quasi-scepticism in his most recent writings. For if his defence of his exclusionary principle in political debates relies upon his commitment to public justifiability, then the main reason for excluding comprehensive doctrines from the realm of politics must be that such doctrines are extremely controversial and so not available as a freely agreed basis for moral judgements between citizens. But this in turn at least seems to imply that if agreement upon all or at least a significant part of the answers to such questions were ever reached, then there would be no basis for excluding reference to such matters in the realm of politics, and Rawls's objections to a non-neutral, sectarian state would disappear.

Rawls has not explicitly addressed this hypothetical question; and part of his reason for doing so seems to be a deep scepticism about the likelihood of the question ever becoming a real one. In *Political*

Liberalism, he lays great stress upon pluralism as a permanent feature of modern culture, one that is unlikely to change because it is *reasonable* for people to disagree about comprehensive conceptions of the good. So, in order to assess the nature and import of this scepticism, we must examine more closely what Rawls's notion of reasonable disagreement actually means – a task that we can best perform in the following chapter.

Anti-perfectionism and neutrality

The fifth and final heading under which the communitarians attacked Rawls has to do with what we called the latter's anti-perfectionism. From the outset, Rawls has argued that, rather than seeking to act on those ideals that often guide people when they live their individual lives and pursue their own conceptions of the good, the state should deliberately refrain from acting on any such comprehensive considerations and seek only to provide a neutral framework within which people can make their own individual choices. Rawls has typically given expression to this political anti-perfectionism by claiming that his political theory makes the right prior to the good. The liberal state must act to protect the rights that people have to revise and pursue their conceptions of the good, and so must rule out any conceptions of the good whose pursuit would violate those rights. But beyond this, whenever constitutional essentials and matters of basic justice are at issue, the state must refrain from acting on the basis that one conception of the good is more valuable than another. The communitarian attack has been devoted to suggesting that this claim to neutrality is an illusion; such a liberal state, by upholding a framework of rights and refraining from any further action, is in effect presupposing the validity of a distinctively liberal conception of the good. Rawls can only justify the assignment of priority to the right over the good by invoking a distinctively liberal understanding of how people should live; the exclusion of conceptions of the good from the domain of politics itself presupposes a particular conception of the good.

In his recent writings, Rawls has dealt explicitly with this issue. In Lecture V of *Political Liberalism*, he makes it clear that his idea of the priority of the right is such that it is compatible with the utilization of no less than five different ideas of the good in the overall theory of justice as fairness. The relevant sense in which justice as fairness is nonetheless significantly neutral between conceptions of the good is that it does not presuppose any particular *comprehensive* religious, philosophical or moral doctrine. It applies only to the sphere of politics and is elaborated from ideas implicit in the shared public political culture, and so does not form part of, or depend upon the truth of, any particular conception of what human life as a whole – outside as well as inside the realm of politics – ought to be. It is neutral, then, in the sense of building on ground that is common as between the range of reasonable comprehensive doctrines that citizens might and do endorse. These claims clearly require more detailed examination.

The five ideas of goodness in the theory of justice as fairness are: the idea of goodness as rationality, the idea of primary goods, the idea of permissible comprehensive conceptions of the good, the idea of political virtues, and the idea of the good of a well-ordered political society. The first two ideas together form what Rawls earlier called his 'thin' theory of the good. The first amounts to the assumption that all participants in discussions about justice will acknowledge certain values such as the fulfilment of basic human needs and purposes and the possession of a rational plan in terms of which individuals order and organize their lives. The second, as we saw when discussing Walzer's critique of primary goods, constitutes a minimal specification of what resources persons understood as citizens (and so as free and equal persons) can be presumed to require regardless of which particular life-plan or conception of the good they may adopt. Taken together, these two ideas provide content for the deliberations which take place in the original position; they give those deliberating behind the veil of ignorance something to deliberate about.

The third idea, that of permissible conceptions of the good, simply underlines the priority Rawls attaches to the right: his liberal state will obviously and necessarily discriminate between those conceptions of the good whose pursuit is compatible with a respect for the rights of all citizens to do likewise, and those whose pursuit violates those rights – and it will prohibit the latter. In this sense, such a state is not neutral between all possible conceptions of the good – it could hardly do otherwise and still be a recognizably liberal state; but it is nonetheless neutral in another important sense, for its prohibition of certain conceptions of the good is not itself based upon considerations that derive from any particular conception of the good. As Rawls would now put it, the grounds for these prohibitions are not derived from a comprehensive religious or moral doctrine, but from a purely political one. In addition, of course, a Rawlsian state will be neutral in the sense that it will secure equal opportunity to advance any *permissible* conception of the good; as we saw in our Introduction, liberal state institutions must not be intended to favour any particular permissible comprehensive doctrine, although it is not sociologically possible for them to have neutral effects, for example, upon which permissible comprehensive doctrines secure, and which lose, adherents over time.

The final two ideas of the good help to bring out an element in Rawls's thinking which, although clearly present, was not foregrounded in his earlier writings. His concept of the political virtues is a way of characterizing those forms of judgement and conduct that are essential to sustain fair social cooperation over time between citizens regarded as free and equal; they are the character traits that specify the ideal of a good citizen of a democratic liberal state. As such, the state is perfectly within its rights to foster and strengthen these virtues in its citizens; for example, it can legitimately act in such a way as to encourage the virtues of toleration and mutual trust (e.g. by discouraging certain sorts of racial and religious discrimination) without thereby becoming a sectarian state, because such virtues are not ones that characterize ways of life belonging to comprehensive religious and philosophical doctrines. The same is true of Rawls's conception of the good of a well-ordered political society – which we examined under the second heading of our agenda earlier in this chapter. This is the good that citizens realize in maintaining (partly by the exercise of the political virtues) a just constitutional regime and in conducting its affairs justly. In such a society, citizens have ends in common – in particular, the substantive and valuable end of supporting just institutions and treating one another justly. Since, however, the resulting communal good is specified solely from within a political conception of justice, since the vision of the political community that embodies it is not based upon a comprehensive doctrine, state actions designed to realize it do not fall foul of the state's duty to remain neutral.

Rawls defines the extent of his political communitarianism by drawing a distinction between classical republicanism and civic humanism. Both are conceptions of the good of political community, but the former embodies the view that the preservation of democratic liberties requires the active participation of citizens possessed of those virtues needed to maintain a constitutional regime, whereas the latter advocates political participation on the grounds that this is the privileged locus of the good life for human beings. Rawlsian justice as fairness is entirely compatible with classical republicanism, and it is happy to permit individuals to seek the good life in political activity; but it is opposed to civic humanism in just the way that it is opposed to reliance upon any particular comprehensive conception of the good in politics. If it is to a civic humanist conception of politics that communitarians like Sandel and MacIntyre are inclined, then they are right to think that Rawls excludes it, but wrong to imagine that he does so by oversight; rather, he explicitly rejects such a strong conception as a threat to the rights of citizens in a context of moral and political pluralism. In short, if this is what is meant by their accusation that Rawls propounds a substantive asocial individualism, that he fails sufficiently to emphasize the importance of constitutive attachments to the political community, then he will be happy to plead guilty to the charge.

Rawls the communitarian?

We have seen, then, a number of ways in which Rawls's theory can accommodate, and in some cases already and explicitly had accommodated, what communitarians took to be objections to liberalism in general or to his theory of justice as fairness in particular. His conception of the person admits the possibility of Sandelian constitutive attachments in non-political contexts, and the common aim of political justice is itself an important part of an individual's moral identity. MacIntyre's and Taylor's insistence that the social matrix is sociologically or philosophically prior to the individual is dismissed as a truism, and explains why the publicity of Rawls's theory is so important. Values of community can be realized in sub-political associations, and the polity itself is by no means a private society but rather realizes a common good as Sandel would have it do: the shared final end of establishing and maintaining just institutions. Far from seeking a culture-free vantage point, political liberalism seeks to articulate ideas implicit in the public political culture of constitutional democracies, and can be regarded as more faithful to our shared meanings than is Walzer's own execution of his methodological injunctions. Sandel and MacIntyre are wrong to think that the veil of ignorance in the original position embodies the claim that judgements as to how people should live are arbitrary expressions of subjective preference, it represents rather the view that such judgements lack a public basis of justification, and thus are inappropriate grounds for principles of justice.

On the first four issues of our agenda, then, there are reasons to regard Rawls as himself significantly communitarian. While some of these depend upon his theory being distinctively political, some do not. The fifth issue – that of neutrality and anti-perfectionism – is the one where Rawls's response to communitarian worries most clearly depends upon its being so. To the objection that his claims to neutrality are unjustified, that his attribution of priority to the right over the good itself conceals a conception of the good, Rawls's move is to acknowledge no fewer than five senses of the good that play a role in his theory but to insist that these are compatible with neutrality in the specific sense of not presupposing the validity of any particular comprehensive religious, moral or philosophical doctrine. They are political ideas of the good only, applying specifically to politics, justifiable by appeal only to public reason, and so to citizens endorsing a range of reasonable comprehensive doctrines. Whether he can sustain this distinction between the political and the non-political without himself invoking aspects of a comprehensive liberal doctrine is thus crucial. It is to an assessment of this question that the next chapter is devoted.

Notes

1 We have written at greater length on both these strands of critique and response in 'The Social Self in Political Theory: The Communitarian Critique of the Liberal Subject'.
2 These lectures – 'Kantian Constructivism in Moral Theory' – can be seen as a key transitional stage in Rawls's gradual move towards his current understanding of his theory as distinctively political. Although publicity and the importance of social agreement on justice plays an important part in those lectures, as does the constructivist method upon which Rawls still relies, he had not at that stage distinguished between moral and political constructivism.

7

Political liberalism: political or comprehensive?

We mentioned in the previous chapter, under the first heading on our agenda, the anxiety that a separation between the sphere of the political and that of the non-political of the kind that Rawls's liberalism imposes in effect calls for a rather schizophrenic attitude on the part of those citizens whose comprehensive conception of the good is not one that embodies such a vision of politics. The idea of such a separation is of course integral to some comprehensive moral doctrines, and so its implementation would contribute to the unity and integrity of the lives of those cleaving to such doctrines; but those whose life is given its shape and meaning by comprehensive doctrines that do not contain such an idea are in effect being asked to bracket off these fundamental beliefs in the political domain. Of course, Rawls can and does argue that this bracketing-off is imposed for the sake of substantial and genuine goods, both individual and corporate; conforming to the liberal conception of the person as citizen confers real and lasting moral gains, and most members of liberal democracies are likely to recognize the value of the goods upon which Rawls has placed such emphasis. But Rawlsian liberalism does not simply require that people recognize the goods of a well-ordered liberal polity to be something whose attractions ought to be acknowledged in calculations about how to live one's life within such a polity. It further requires that, when these political goods conflict with other goods drawn from comprehensive moral and religious conceptions, all citizens must normally allow the political goods to triumph over – to trump – those other goods.

Before we go any further along this line of argument, however, we must note two important qualifications on the priority Rawls attaches to his political goods. First, he constantly emphasizes that the values of political liberalism are intended to have priority solely with respect to what he calls 'constitutional essentials and questions of basic justice'. These concern both the basic freedoms of citizens – their equal basic rights and liberties and the maintenance of just political procedures; – and social and economic inequalities – the background institutions of social and economic justice appropriate to citizens as free and equal. When political debate concerns issues that do not fall under either of these headings, political liberalism does not require that they be settled by appeal to political values alone; and this class of issues is not small.

> Many if not most political questions do not concern those fundamental matters, for example, much tax legislation and many laws regulating property; statutes protecting the environment and controlling pollution; establishing national parks and preserving wilderness areas and animal and plant species; and laying aside funds for museums and the arts. Of course, sometimes these do involve fundamental matters. (*PL*, p. 214)

In short, the exclusion of non-political values demanded by Rawlsian political liberalism has a more restricted scope than might otherwise appear. Furthermore, and this is the second qualification, even with respect to issues lying within its scope, the priority Rawls attaches to political over non-political values is never exceptionless or unconditional; throughout the text of *Political Liberalism*, he is careful to say that, with respect to fundamental matters, political values *normally* or *typically* outweigh non-political values with which they may conflict. He is thus, at least in principle, prepared to recognize that there are circumstances in which, even with respect to constitutional essentials and matters of basic justice, non-political values might trump political ones.

The scope of the priority of the political

It is, however, far from easy to evaluate the true significance of these two qualifications to the priority of the political. Take his declaration that political values have priority only with respect to constitutional essentials and matters of basic justice. Rawls offers no detailed discussion of how the distinction between such fundamental matters and other, less fundamental ones might be drawn; we are offered no principles or criteria of fundamentality, but rather a list of examples of non-fundamental matters (the one quoted above). Rawls is, of course, conscious of this lacuna and its importance, for he continues:

> A full account of public reason would take up those other questions and explain in more detail than I can here how they differ from constitutional essentials and questions of basic justice and why the restrictions imposed by public reason may not apply to them; or if they do, not in the same way, or so strictly. (*PL*, pp. 214–15)

It remains unclear whether Rawls has no such full account to give, or whether he simply lacks the space to develop it; but this passage strongly suggests that he is convinced that a principled distinction of some kind does exist – that is, that a significant range of political issues are not ones that require that we restrict ourselves to purely political values when deliberating about them.

However, as we saw in the previous chapters, political liberalism's basic justification for this restriction is that it prevents citizens from exercising political power, the coercive power of free and equal citizens as a corporate body, in ways that they cannot justify publicly to their fellows. The apparent problem for Rawls's current position is that that power is exercised whenever the state implements its decision, whether or not that decision involves constitutional essentials or matters of basic justice. Tax legislation, for example, is based on deploying threats of financial penalties or imprisonment against those who refuse to pay their taxes – so anything done by the state with income it derives from taxation would seem to involve coercive political power. Accordingly, the question arises: why not say that *all* political questions involving such uses of political power should be considered purely in terms of political values? Why should it ever be admissible to go beyond that range? The logic of Rawls's own argument seems to commit him to a more extensive restriction to public reason than he is ready to accept.

It is interesting to note that, in *A Theory of Justice*, Rawls was rather more sensitive to this kind of anti-perfectionist argument:

> the principles of justice do not permit subsidizing universities and institutes, or opera and the theater, on the grounds that these institutions are intrinsically valuable, and that those who engage in them are to be supported even at some significant expense to others who do not receive compensating benefits. (*TJ*, p. 332)

Nevertheless, he did permit two other possible modes of justification. First, once a given state had fully implemented the two principles of justice as fairness, its citizens could authorize further taxation-funded expenditure on public goods such as museums and art galleries when the level of such provision by market mechanisms would not match their true aggregate preferences; but they could do so after achieving approximate unanimity on the means of covering the costs (in a representative public forum not subject to the veil of ignorance that Rawls calls 'the exchange branch' of government). This first option plainly regards the public goods of culture as luxuries from the viewpoint of basic justice, so that state funding should be directed towards them only after the claims of justice have been met, and only when the coerciveness of taxation procedures has been overcome; as Rawls puts it, 'the coercive machinery of government is used in this case only to overcome the problems of isolation and assurance, and no-one is taxed without his consent' (*TJ*, p. 331). The second possibility is very different; it amounts to establishing that state subsidy for culture might legitimately be regarded as maintaining the background conditions for justice. As Rawls expresses it, 'taxation for these purposes can be justified only as promoting directly or indirectly the social conditions that secure the equal liberties and as advancing in an appropriate way the long-term interests of the least advantaged' (*TJ*, p. 332).

The first of these strategies brings out very clearly the extent to which Rawls's original theory sought to eliminate perfectionist considerations in politics. Those who want public goods like art galleries and museums can get together via their representatives in the exchange branch to overcome market imperfections and provide them for themselves, but they cannot appeal to the intrinsic value of those goods to justify imposing the costs of that provision on others who do not share their preferences. The second raises the question of what considerations might permit us to regard access to art galleries as a condition for advancing the basic interests of all citizens without implicitly invoking a belief in the intrinsic importance of culture for individual well-being? We shall return to this question when we examine Dworkin's strikingly parallel justification of liberal state expenditure on the arts in chapter 9. At the moment, however, our primary concern is with how Rawls chooses to respond to the basic question this issue raises in the context of his later writings; how can it ever be acceptable for a political liberal to go beyond purely political values when considering any exercise of coercive political power?

In *Political Liberalism*, Rawls takes a very different, and much more cautious, approach. Posing to himself the question at hand: 'why not say that all questions in regard to which citizens exercise their final and coercive political power over one another are subject to public reason? Why would it ever be admissible to go outside its range of political values?', he answers:

> my aim is to consider first the strongest case where the political questions concern the most fundamental matters. If we should not honour the limits of public reason here, it would seem we need not honour them anywhere. Should they hold here, we can then proceed to other cases. Still, I grant that it is usually desirable to settle political questions by invoking the values of public reason. Yet this may not always be so. (*PL*, p. 215)

Though more than a little obscure, Rawls's inclination seems to be to reduce as much as possible the range of political questions whose consideration can legitimately invoke non-political values. So this first qualification on the scope of the priority he attaches to political values may not be as definite or as unalterable as it sometimes seems.

Justifying the priority of the political

What, then, of the second qualification? How are we to understand Rawls's insistence that political values *normally* trump non-political ones? What is to count as an abnormal or atypical case, in which that priority does not hold? Since what might count as justifying

exceptions to a general rule depends upon what justifies the general
rule itself, we can best approach Rawls's answer to this question by
examining how he justifies his claim that political values can normally
outweigh whatever other values are likely to conflict with them.

In his lecture on the idea of an overlapping consensus, Rawls
actually offers two arguments in defence of the priority of political
values; we shall examine them in turn, and in some detail. It may
therefore help the reader to follow this rather complicated discussion
if we summarize in advance its general shape. Rawls's first
argument turns on the very great value of fair social cooperation,
but runs into difficulties when confronted by those who, while
perhaps acknowledging that value, judge that it might in some cases
be outweighed by certain non-political ones. His second argument
turns on establishing the limits and the permanency of reasonable
disagreement over comprehensive doctrines; however, the precise
content of Rawls's conception of 'the reasonable' suggests that this
seemingly separate line of argument ultimately amounts to a
restatement of the first, and opens him to a charge of circularity.
Moreover, as the final section of this chapter will attempt to
demonstrate, his stress upon 'the reasonable' also threatens to
destabilize other aspects of the structure of his theory of justice.

The value of fair social cooperation

The first argument Rawls offers is that

> the virtues of political cooperation that make a constitutional regime
> possible are . . . very great virtues. I mean, for example, the virtues of
> tolerance and being ready to meet others halfway, and the virtue of
> reasonableness and the sense of fairness. When these virtues are
> widespread in society and sustain its political conception of justice,
> they constitute a very great public good, part of society's political
> capital. Thus, the values that conflict with the political conception of
> justice and its sustaining virtues may be normally outweighed
> because they come into conflict with the very conditions that make
> fair social cooperation possible on a footing of mutual respect. (*PL*, p.
> 157)

Here, Rawls is in effect claiming that political values should trump those values with which they might conflict because assigning priority to the latter would work against the virtues of political cooperation by returning divisive issues to the political agenda, and would thus make fair social cooperation impossible.

Understood against the background of this argument, Rawls's claim that the priority of political values is something that obtains only 'normally' or 'typically' must mean that it obtains 'except when furthering certain real but non-political goods is sufficiently valuable to outweigh the value of fair social cooperation on a footing of mutual respect'. But then it seems that a political view or doctrine can come into conflict with political liberalism even if it accepts that, with respect to constitutional essentials or matters of basic justice, political values normally trump non-political ones. For it is, after all, relatively easy to think of issues pertaining to fundamental political matters about which apparently reasonable people, who accept that political values are great enough *normally* to trump comprehensive considerations, none the less conclude that on this particular issue comprehensive considerations are sufficiently important to win out. State prohibition of abortion or pornography (perhaps also state endorsement of heterosexual marriage, or prohibitions of sado-masochistic sexual practices), would certainly seem to affect citizens' basic liberties, and may well be justified by reference to elements of comprehensive moral and religious conceptions of the good. If, however, their proponents defend them (as many appear to do in reality) by arguing that, in these specific cases, the costs in terms of the value of fair social cooperation are outweighed by the benefits that will accrue from implementing certain non-political values, Rawls can have no objection to the general shape of their justification. They would in effect be accepting that the value of the political virtues generally or normally outweighs non-political values, and their policy proposals would amount to exceptions acknowledged within a general attribution of priority to the political, exceptions of a kind that Rawls seems explicitly to allow for in his emphasis on the word 'normal'. Yet, allowing cases such as these to count as exceptions would have the effect of draining his theory of justice of its substance. After all, in what sense would a polity be maintaining its citizens' freedom and equality if the state prohibited certain publications, or withdrew public provisions for abortion, on non-political grounds? How many such exceptions could a liberal polity make without losing its specifically liberal identity?

Not surprisingly, there are clear indications in the text of *Political Liberalism* that Rawls is in fact not prepared to regard issues of the kind we have just mentioned as legitimate exceptions to the general rule of attributing priority to the political. About abortion, for example, he has this to say:

> Suppose . . . that we consider the question in terms of three important political values: the due respect for human life, the ordered reproduction of political society over time, including the family in some form, and finally the equality of women as equal citizens . . . Now I believe any reasonable balance of these three values will give a woman a duly qualified right to decide whether or not to end her pregnancy during the first trimester . . . [At] this early stage of pregnancy the political value of the equality of women is overriding, and this right is required to give it substance and force . . . Any comprehensive doctrine that leads to a balance of political values excluding that duly qualified right in the first trimester is to that extent unreasonable; and depending on the details of its formulation, it may also be cruel and oppressive; for example, if it denied that right altogether except in the case of rape and incest. (*PL*, pp. 243–4 n. 32)

Regardless of how sympathetic we find Rawls's position on this particular issue, his tone suggests that he envisages very few exceptions to his general attribution of priority to political values; and someone who, whilst committed in general to the virtues of tolerance, reasonableness and fairness, regards abortion at any stage of pregnancy as the destruction of a human life, might be forgiven for wondering what sort of issue she might count as an acceptable exception to that commitment if not one such as this.

Clearly, no polity that regarded non-political values as normally or even frequently outweighing political ones could establish or maintain the widespread exercise of such virtues as tolerance or a sense of fairness; citizens whose freedom to pursue their own conception of the good was being systematically or regularly disrupted by those pursuing other conceptions would have no reason to continue acting tolerantly, and so an important condition of fair social cooperation on a footing of mutual respect would disintegrate. So Rawls can get some mileage from emphasizing the importance and value of that form of cooperation against those who might be inclined to hold that priority should normally be given to the non-political values arising from their comprehensive doctrines.

However, this point has little force against those who accept the general value of the political virtues, but believe that a specific exception to that priority carries with it a countervailing non-political benefit that outweighs whatever political costs it inflicts.

Moreover, the argument presupposes that those to whom it is addressed are committed to treating their fellow citizens with respect *as that is understood within political liberalism*. Within such a society, someone pursuing a non-liberal comprehensive conception of the good has a reason to support structures of mutual toleration that permit her to live out her comprehensive beliefs; but she could perfectly consistently view the disappearance of such a society and its replacement by one founded on her own less tolerant conception as something that would benefit not only herself but all her fellow citizens (helping to turn them away from erroneous comprehensive doctrines). From this perspective, and this is one that we will consider in more detail in chapter 10 on Raz, it will perhaps seem odd to 'respect' others by ignoring the necessary conditions of their true flourishing. The existence of a well-ordered liberal society is only a condition for the pursuit of a valuable life in which a liberal understanding of politics plays some part; for those from whose comprehensive conception such an understanding is absent, such a society may even appear as an obstacle not only to their own flourishing but also to that of other people. And in that case, pointing out that a systematic abrogation of the priority of political values will undermine such a society may actually constitute a further reason in favour of such a policy.

In short, this first Rawlsian line of argument will not be successful against opponents whose comprehensive convictions assign a degree of significance to the non-political benefits resulting from a limited abrogation of the priority of the political with which he might disagree; *a fortiori*, it will carry little conviction with those who reject his general vision of the political realm altogether, for reasons grounded in their acceptance of a fundamentally non-liberal comprehensive conception of the good. What of his second line of argument?

Reasonable pluralism and the burdens of judgement

The second answer Rawls offers for how a political conception of

justice can express values that normally outweigh whatever other
values are likely to conflict with them is that

> severe conflicts with other values are much reduced. This is because
> when an overlapping consensus supports the political conception, this
> conception is not viewed as incompatible with basic religious,
> philosophical and moral values. We need not consider the claims of
> political justice against the claims of this or that comprehensive view;
> nor need we say that political values are intrinsically more important
> than other values and that is why the latter are overridden. Having to
> say that is just what we hope to avoid, and achieving an overlapping
> consensus enables us to do so. (*PL*, p. 157)

The previous response envisaged conflicts between political and non-
political values, and argued that the former were great enough
normally to win out. This second response makes the different,
apparently contradictory, move of arguing that, when an overlapping
consensus obtains, such conflicts are reduced and there is no need to
appeal to the intrinsically greater importance of political values.

This seems problematic in several respects. First, it implies a rather
puzzling answer to the question of what Rawls means when he
claims that political values 'normally' trump non-political ones. For
the justification that he here offers for this trumping holds only on
the assumption that an overlapping consensus obtains; it therefore
implies that the justification fails, and so that exceptions to the
general rule it supports can be made, when no such overlapping
consensus exists. In other words, it suggests that when Rawls says
that political values normally trump their competitors, he means
that they do so only when an overlapping consensus obtains. But
this is not an attractive position to adopt. It would mean, in effect,
that a condition for the applicability of a liberal view of politics, one
in which political values have a trumping role, is that there be a pre-
existing social agreement upon just that view.

What this puzzle about Rawls's 'normality condition' suggests at
a more general level is that his second response seems rather to beg
the question it is supposed to answer. It may well be that there is
little or no conflict when comprehensive doctrines coincide in
affirming political liberalism, for then the comprehensive doctrines
themselves imply a liberal approach to politics; what we need to
know is why comprehensive doctrines would or should so coincide.

To make sense of this second answer to the crucial question, we need to know Rawls's grounds for supposing that he can 'uncover a sufficiently inclusive concordant fit' (*PL*, p. 158) between his political values and the comprehensive doctrines espoused by members of his society. These grounds are to be found in Rawls's account of the fact of reasonable pluralism and the burdens of judgement.

As we saw in chapter 5, Rawls thinks both that there is a diversity of reasonable comprehensive religious, philosophical and moral doctrines at present found in modern societies and that this is not a mere historical condition that will soon pass away, but a permanent feature of the public culture of democracy. Rather, it is a result of the 'burdens of judgement' – sources of disagreement that are compatible with the full reasonableness of all parties involved. The implication that Rawls draws from this claim about the reasonableness of disagreement is then as follows:

> Since many doctrines are seen to be reasonable, those who insist, when fundamental questions are at stake, on what they take as true but others do not, seem to others simply to insist on their own beliefs when they have the political power to do so. Of course, those who do insist on their beliefs also insist that their beliefs alone are true: they impose their beliefs because, they say, their beliefs are true and not because they are their beliefs. But this is a claim that all could equally make; it is also a claim that cannot be made good by anyone to citizens generally. So, when we make such claims others, who are themselves reasonable, must count us unreasonable. And indeed we are, as we want to use state power, the collective power of equal citizens, to prevent the rest from affirming their not unreasonable views.
>
> To conclude: reasonable persons see that the burdens of judgement set limits on what can be reasonably justified to others, and so they endorse some form of liberty of conscience and freedom of thought. It is unreasonable for us to use political power, should we possess it, or share it with others, to repress comprehensive views that are not unreasonable. (*PL* p. 61)

So, Rawls's ground for thinking that adherents of the main competing comprehensive doctrines in his society will respect the limits of the political, his reason to believe that he is conversing with the converted, is that he pays them the compliment of assuming that they (and their doctrines) are reasonable. And what he has to say to the unconverted, his response to any remaining external critics of political liberalism, is simply to remind them that they are being unreasonable. Whether such a critic utilizes elements of her comprehensive doctrine to justify a local or a global rejection of the normal priority of the political, he points out that those who disagree with that doctrine may well be doing so reasonably, and claims that it would as a consequence be unreasonable to impose that doctrine upon them. Such a response appears to fulfil Rawls's desire to respect the limits of the political; for by attempting to rebut the non-liberal position as unreasonable, he is not necessarily rejecting as incorrect the comprehensive doctrine upon which it is based, and neither does he seem to be invoking part of a comprehensive doctrine himself. He seems simply to be invoking an uncontroversial fact.

There do, however, appear to be problems with this line of reasoning. First, it can be argued that it is too strong for its own good. After all, if the burdens of judgement apply to all exercises of human reason with respect to fundamental moral and political matters, they must apply both to judgements about comprehensive doctrines and to judgements about purely political ones. So, if it is unreasonable to expect one's fellow citizens to accept the imposition of comprehensive doctrines with which they might reasonably disagree, why is it not equally unreasonable to impose political liberalism upon those who disagree with it? Of course, some of these disagreements might be based upon self-interest or logical error; but why assume that all of them are? After all, Rawls explicitly acknowledges that more than one theory of justice might meet the constraints set by political liberalism, and accepts that people might reasonably disagree with the theory of justice as fairness that he propounds; and that concession alone would seem to make it unreasonable to impose either his own or any other purely political theory of justice on a political community. By contrast, he is plainly not prepared to accept that people might reasonably disagree with his judgement that any acceptable theory of justice must respect the restriction to purely political values that is the hallmark of political liberalism; but it is not at all clear that every objection to those limits must be based upon an error or failure of reasoning. In the absence of some further ground for making that assumption, it would appear that the burdens of judgement would make it unreasonable for Rawls either to construct a political community based on his own theory of justice as fairness, or to restrict the class of acceptable theories to those permitted by political liberalism.

It is also possible to argue that Rawls's defence of political liberalism is too weak to achieve its purpose – that Rawls takes the burdens of judgement to be more burdensome than they are. When, for example, he says that reasonable pluralism is 'the *inevitable* outcome of free human reason' (*PL*, p. 37: our italics), it sounds as if he takes reasonable disagreement on such matters to be guaranteed – as if the goal of establishing reasoned agreement on comprehensive doctrines is *necessarily* chimerical. But the points he adduces as comprising the burdens of judgement do not license this conclusion. They do show that disagreement about conceptions of the good can be (and perhaps is often likely to be) reasonable; but this is not equivalent to showing that such disagreement could never be overcome, that there could never be such a thing as reasonable agreement about such matters – to say that disagreement is to be expected is not to say that it is inevitable. To put the point at its most abstract: where reasonable disagreement is possible, so is reasonable agreement.

What this suggests is that Rawls's quasi-scepticism about agreement on comprehensive matters is really founded upon an empirical belief that the fact of pluralism is permanent rather than upon an irrefutable demonstration that it is intrinsically impossible to establish reasonable agreement on comprehensive doctrines, or elements of them. But then there is scope for his critics to question whether this sceptical conclusion is as unavoidable as Rawls seems to think. It may, for example, be implausible to claim that there will ever be rational society-wide agreement upon the truth of a single comprehensive doctrine taken as a whole – for example, a particular religious doctrine; although nothing about the burdens of judgement licenses us to exclude that possibility in all conceivable circumstances, such an eventuality is highly unlikely given the history and actual circumstances of late-twentieth-century Western democracies. But it is rather more plausible to imagine that rational social agreement might be established on *elements* of a comprehensive doctrine. We can, for example, easily imagine a society that acknowledges the goods of a well-ordered liberal polity, but which comes to an agreement, based upon rational but comprehensive considerations, on the intrinsic immorality of pornography, and resolves to sacrifice the autonomy of its citizens in this specific respect for the sake of discouraging people from indulging in such practices. In such circumstances, the burdens of judgement would demonstrate only that a reasonable person *might* disagree with that decision; but if the vast majority of citizens in fact do not, why should they place more weight upon an unrealized possibility of dissent than upon an actualized, general and reasonable agreement?

There are, however, grounds for thinking that Rawls would regard both of these lines of criticism as based upon a misunderstanding of his conception of 'the reasonable'. Our suggestion that the burdens-of-judgement argument is too strong supposes that reasonable disagreement is possible over the very great worth of his political values; and our suggestion that the argument is too weak supposes that there could be a reasonable social agreement to violate the normal priority of those political values. Further elements of the theory presented in *Political Liberalism* imply that both suppositions involve misuses of the term 'reasonable'. For Rawls, any citizen who rejects the normal priority of his political values is, by that token, acting unreasonably; and any comprehensive doctrine that fails to cede priority to political values when a potential conflict with non-political values arises is, by that token, an unreasonable doctrine.

When he introduces his conception of the reasonable, Rawls specifies that it has two basic aspects as a virtue of persons. The second is, of course, a willingness to recognize and accept the consequences of, the burdens of judgement; but the first is elucidated before we are introduced to those burdens, and provides the background in terms of which we must interpret their significance.

> Persons are reasonable in one basic aspect when, among equals say, they are ready to propose principles and standards as fair terms of cooperation and to abide by them willingly, given the assurance that others will likewise do so . . . The reasonable is an element of the idea of society as a system of fair cooperation . . . Reasonable persons . . . desire for its own sake a social world in which they, as free and equal, can cooperate with others on terms all can accept. (*PL*, pp. 49–50)

What this makes clear is that, on Rawls's understanding of the term, no one can be reasonable unless they accept the conception of the person and of society that is the irreducible core of political liberalism. As Rawls himself later puts it:

> Observe that here being reasonable is not an epistemological idea

(though it has epistemological elements). Rather, it is part of a political ideal of democratic citizenship that includes the idea of public reason. The content of this ideal includes what free and equal citizens can require of each other with respect to their reasonable comprehensive views. (*PL*, p. 62)

In other words, the notion of 'the reasonable' does not mark out a set of epistemological constraints that must be respected in the way Rawls outlines by anyone on pain of irrationality or ignorance of uncontroversial facts; rather, it contributes to the specification of a set of moral constraints that partly determine what it is to live up to the duties and obligations imposed by participation in a fair system of social cooperation based on mutual respect.

From Rawls's point of view, then, our two lines of criticism of his 'burdens of judgement' argument go wrong because they assume that reasonable constraints are purely epistemological rather than being crucially moral in nature. The burdens of judgement are indeed purely epistemological phenomena, but it is only when conjoined with certain moral assumptions that they deliver his full account of the reasonable; and his views, first, that there cannot be reasonable disagreement over the political values and, second, that there cannot be reasonable agreement upon (elements of) comprehensive doctrines, will remain incomprehensible if they are taken independently of those moral assumptions. If, however, we see that it is part of what it means to be reasonable that one views society as a system of fair cooperation between free and equal citizens, then it follows immediately that it is (morally) unreasonable to violate the general priority of political over non-political values; for both that view of society and that view of the limits of the political are simply two aspects of the freestanding doctrine of political liberalism.

Acknowledging the moral aspects of Rawls's account of 'the reasonable' means that we cannot make the two criticisms of his burdens-of-judgement argument in the form developed earlier; it leaves him, however, vulnerable to a further, and fundamental, criticism. For, as we saw, the accusation of 'being unreasonable' was needed to form an independent line of argument in defence of the priority Rawls attaches to the political values against those who reject both it and the importance he attributes to maintaining a system of fair social cooperation. But now it appears that recognizing the burdens of judgement will only result in the right sort of respect for the priority of the political if one views society as just such a system of fair cooperation. In short, this seemingly separate argument adds no independent weight to Rawls's earlier claims about the very great value of the political virtues; and, regardless of whether one makes the argument in terms of the political virtues or in terms of the limits of the reasonable, it is entirely circular. By defining 'the reasonable' as including a commitment to a politically liberal vision of society, Rawls defines anyone who queries or rejects that vision as 'unreasonable'; but he offers no independent reason for accepting that morally driven and question-begging definition.

In fact, matters may be even worse than this, for in his only direct treatment of the issue that interests us here – that of how he might respond to someone who rejects the limits of the political realm as he defines them – he acknowledges that 'in affirming a political conception of justice we may eventually have to assert at least certain aspects of our own comprehensive religious or philosophical doctrine' (*PL*, p. 152). The case he discusses is that of a religious believer who insists that the truth of her comprehensive doctrine, that the religious salvation of a whole people depends upon their conforming to her understanding of the divine will, is so fundamental as to justify civil strife. Rawls says:

> At this point we may have no alternative but to deny this, or to imply its denial and hence to maintain the kind of thing we had hoped to avoid.
>   To consider this, imagine rationalist believers who contend that these beliefs are open to and can be fully established by reason (uncommon though this view may be). In this case the believers simply deny what we have called 'the fact of reasonable pluralism'. So we say of the rationalist believers that they are mistaken in denying that fact; but we need not say that their religious beliefs are not true, since to deny that religious beliefs can be publicly and fully established by reason is not to say that they are not true. Of course, we do not believe the doctrine believers here assert, and this is shown in what we do. Even if we do not, say, hold some form of the doctrine of free religious faith that supports equal liberty of conscience, our actions nevertheless imply that we believe the concern for salvation does not require anything incompatible with that liberty. Still, we do not put forward more of our comprehensive view than we think needed or useful for the political aim of consensus. (*PL*, pp. 152–3)

Why does Rawls regard his assertion of the fact of reasonable pluralism as equivalent to asserting certain aspects of his own (at least partially) *comprehensive* religious or philosophical doctrine?[1] After all, the reason for introducing the fact of reasonable pluralism was supposed to be that of avoiding any such assertion – as Rawls puts it in this passage, to say that the relevant religious doctrine cannot be publicly justified is not to pronounce upon its truth. The answer is that no one who believed that doctrine would attach the weight Rawls attaches to the fact of reasonable pluralism, so Rawls's supposedly purely political contestation of the doctrine implicitly denies its truth and so amounts to his putting forward an element of his own comprehensive view. Thus, Rawls's own analysis suggests that the significance of reasonable pluralism cannot be determined independently of our comprehensive commitments. It implies that the burdens of judgement do not constitute a value-free, or even a purely political, point of leverage upon comprehensive doctrines that might contest the limits Rawls imposes upon public reason. In short, the argument from the burdens of judgement and the reasonableness of disagreement does not succeed in respecting Rawls's self-imposed limitation to a purely political defence of his political liberalism. He cannot avoid invoking aspects of his own (partially) comprehensive doctrine.

Of course, the particular case Rawls is here considering is that of the rationalist believer – someone who contends that her beliefs can be fully established by reason; she therefore flatly denies the fact of reasonable pluralism. But it is difficult to see why the same problem that Rawls acknowledges in this case should not also arise when he is faced with opponents who, whilst accepting the fact of reasonable pluralism, still insist that their view should prevail over other, equally reasonable ones. Recall the case we discussed in the previous section – that of the religious believer who is opposed to abortion. She need not deny that reasonable pluralism is a fact; but she may well believe that its real moral significance is outweighed by the moral significance of murder. Rawls's line of argument against such a person – as we quoted it earlier – does not explicitly deny that abortion (in the circumstances specified) is murder; but it is plain that no one who actually believed that abortion was murder would attach the same weight to the values his argument invokes as he does. In other words, his position with respect to those who merely contest the degree of significance to be attached to the fact of reasonable pluralism inevitably (even if implicitly) invokes elements of his own comprehensive doctrine, just as it does when he opposes those who flatly deny the fact of reasonable pluralism. Even when dealing with people whose disagreement with political liberalism is far less radical than in the case of the rationalist believer, Rawls cannot avoid overstepping the bounds of the purely political.

The structural integrity of political liberalism

In the previous section, we examined the question of whether Rawls's concept of 'the reasonable' can successfully perform one of the key tasks he allots to it. But it is also worth pointing out that, whether successful or not in that respect, its prominence may well have a damaging impact on the structural integrity of political liberalism as a whole; for its role has implications that seem to be inconsistent with other, seemingly independent, parts of that theoretical edifice.

The two stages of justification

In the first place, if Rawls's notion of 'the reasonable person' is a political or moral rather than a purely epistemological conception, then the same must be true of his conception of 'reasonable pluralism' and a 'reasonable comprehensive doctrine'. A condition of reasonable pluralism must be understood as one composed of a diversity of reasonable comprehensive doctrines, and each of those doctrines must, *qua* reasonable, accept the normal priority of the political values, and the vision of the citizen and of society that underlies it. But then it is not at all clear how Rawls can continue to maintain the distinction between two stages by means of which he explicitly develops his theory of justice, even in the rather specific sense that we attributed to that distinction in chapter 5. As you will recall, in the first stage that theory is worked out as a freestanding political (and so moral) conception for the basic structure of society; only after this is done, does he take up the question of whether justice as fairness is sufficently stable in being able to form the kernel of an overlapping consensus. In our initial exegesis, we pointed out the apparent coincidence between the conditions that a conception needed to satisfy in order to pass the first stage and the conditions it needed to meet in order to be stable in the right way. Our worry here is even more radical.

Rawls makes it clear in his lecture on that topic that the kind of overlapping consensus he seeks is

> a consensus of reasonable (as opposed to unreasonable or irrational) comprehensive doctrines. The crucial fact is not the fact of pluralism as such, but of reasonable pluralism . . . (*PL*, p. 144)

At first glance, this seems perfectly sensible: why concern oneself with those whose disagreements with political liberalism are based upon irrationality or unreasonable judgements? Second thoughts, however, suggest that there is something peculiar going on: if part of what it means for a comprehensive doctrine to be reasonable is that it accepts the normal priority of the political over the non-political, then there can be no need to *seek* an overlapping consensus between them, since their reasonableness simply guarantees it by definition.

This is not to deny that, after the first stage of Rawls's argument is complete, issues that might be thought of as questions of stability will arise. It remains to be demonstrated, for example, that the patterns of behaviour that will be encouraged under the institutions generated by political liberalism will be such as to support rather than undermine those institutions. This is the aspect of the stability question that Rawls answers by 'setting out the moral psychology in accordance with which citizens in a well-ordered society acquire a normally sufficient sense of justice so that they comply with its just arrangements' (*PL*, p. 141). But he defines the second and final aspect of this question in the following way:

> whether in view of the general facts that characterize a democracy's political culture, and in particular the fact of reasonable pluralism, the political conception can be the focus of an overlapping consensus. I assume this consensus to consist of reasonable comprehensive doctrines likely to persist and gain adherents over time with a just basic structure . . . (*PL*, p. 141)

Since, however, a society in the condition of reasonable pluralism contains (by definition) a diversity of reasonable comprehensive doctrines, and since (again, by definition) no such doctrine is reasonable unless it recognizes the burdens of judgement and the normal priority of political values, there can be no separate question as to whether the political conception can be stable in the sense of being the focus of an overlapping consensus of reasonable doctrines. Its stability in that sense is guaranteed.

This means that the second stage of Rawls's two-stage presentation of his theory is more vestigial even than it may have seemed from our interpretation in chapter 5. Apart from the question of moral psychology, and perhaps the empirical question of just how many comprehensive doctrines with broad support in a given society are reasonable by Rawls's definition, there is simply no theoretical work to be done under this heading.

The two faces of public justifiability

This same stress on 'the reasonable' has a second (and related) consequence for the structural integrity of Rawls's theorizing. For if this concept really does have the kind of foundational role it appears to have in his theory, then it can be used to define the limits of public justifiability; and what role, if any, is then played by the idea of turning to the public political culture for the substance of any legitimate, purely political theory of justice?

The problem is this. One of Rawls's three criteria for a theory of justice being purely political in nature is its being elaborated in terms of ideas viewed as implicit in the public political culture of a democratic society; and we suggested in chapter 5 that Rawls's turn to that culture was not pragmatic but was driven rather by a commitment to the value of public justifiability. If his theory is to be publicly justifiable, then it must presuppose only ideas that – being implicit in the public political culture – all members of society can reasonably be expected to endorse, regardless of their particular comprehensive commitments. As he says,

> Justice as fairness aims at uncovering a public basis of justification on questions of political justice given the fact of reasonable pluralism. Since justification is addressed to others, it proceeds from what is, or can be, held in common; and so we begin from shared fundamental ideas implicit in the public political culture in the hope of developing

from them a political conception that can gain free and reasoned agreement in judgment . . . (*PL*, pp. 100–1)

This suggests that what is available in the public political culture establishes the limits of the publicly justifiable, of what reasonable citizens can be brought to accept.

However, as we have been emphasizing in this chapter, Rawls also has a substantive conception of what is and is not reasonable that emerges directly from his conception of the significance of the burdens of judgement for anyone who views society as a fair system of cooperation between free and equal citizens. In other words, he can fully flesh out the limits of what is publicly justifiable in a way that flows immediately from the conjunction of an epistemological insight with his political conception of the person as free and equal. But then he has no need to take a detour via the public political culture in order to determine what is publicly justifiable.

In fact, if we give the concept of the reasonable the prominence it now appears to have in Rawls's theory, we seem to have no reason to attribute any significance at all to what is or is not implicit in the public political culture. For either it supports our independently given understanding of what a citizen can reasonably be expected to accept (in which case we have a happy coincidence); or it is in conflict with it (in which case we must reject it as violating the independently given limits of the reasonable). If, for example, we discovered that the public political culture contained an implicit agreement on the overriding importance of some element of a comprehensive doctrine (e.g. the immorality of abortion or pornography), that would not, on Rawls's understanding of the term, make it reasonable for a state to engage in political action predicated on the truth of that view, since (present or future) citizens might reasonably disagree with it. Whereas if we discovered that the public political culture did not embody an implicit commitment to a conception of citizens as free and equal, that would not make a theory of justice which centred around just such a conception any less reasonable, since no citizen could reasonably refuse to accept the limits it imposes upon the legitimate grounds of state action. In this respect, at least, Rawls's political liberalism would then be far less significantly culture-specific than it would if the limits of the publicly justifiable were set by reference to whatever is implicit in the public political culture. This would certainly weaken his defence against Walzerian charges of abstraction and universalism; but of course, for those who regard Walzer's predilection for cultural particularity as a recipe for relativism, this consequence of Rawls's recent stress on 'the reasonable' may not count as an objection to it.

In short, once the concept of 'the reasonable' comes to take centre stage in Rawls's theory, the third element of his initial definition of the sense in which his theory is purely political seems to drop out as irrelevant. The theory will, of course, remain purely political in the first two senses: its subject will be the basic structure of society, and it will be a freestanding theory, presentable independently of any particular comprehensive doctrines. Moreover, its freestandingness will still be driven by a concern for public justifiability. But now 'what can serve as a public basis of justification' will be understood to mean 'what reasonable people have in common'; and that will be determined by the consequences of the burdens of judgement for those who view society as a fair system of cooperation between free and equal citizens, not by an interpretation of the public political culture. Naturally, the public political culture of Western democracies, in which (Rawls claims) reasonable pluralism is well-entrenched, will contain all the elements Rawls needs to work up his purely political conception of the person and of society, and so the two different ways of defining the limits of the publicly justifiable will here coincide. But that will be at best a coincidence: even though an interpretation of the public political culture will in these circumstances give the right answer to the question of what is publicly justifiable, the fact that it is derivable in that way does not play any role in determining why that answer is the right one. That task is performed by an assessment of the consequences of acknowledging the burdens of judgement in a context of reasonable pluralism.

As far as we can see, there is no obvious way to resolve the tension between these two aspects of Rawls's presentation of his theory in *Political Liberalism*; he appears to have two different accounts of what he means by 'public justifiability', and the two accounts cannot be made to coexist with one another. It is perhaps worth pointing out that, in the development of Rawls's thinking through the 1980s, the role he accorded to a turn towards the public political culture appeared very early (in his 1985 article on 'Justice as Fairness: Political not Metaphysical'), whereas his account of the burdens of judgement, and the limitations they impose on reasonable citizens, emerged later (in his 1989 article 'The Domain of the Political and Overlapping Consensus'). So the fact that these two apparently incompatible elucidations of the concept of 'public justifiability' both appear in *Political Liberalism* may best be explained by assuming that at this point Rawls's thinking is still in a process of transition – that he began with a (broadly sociological) understanding of what determines the limits of public justifiability, then developed an alternative (moral and philosophical) understanding of those limits, perhaps in response to certain misinterpretations of the first position that took it to imply a purely pragmatic orientation on his part; and he has not yet fully acknowledged that the second position makes the first essentially superfluous.

Whatever the truth of these structural and developmental matters (which may well be of interest only to Rawlsian scholars), the issue that most concerns us is whether his presentation of the burdens of judgement argument provides him with a purely political defence of the normal priority of political over non-political values, one that will be effective against those who reject it for reasons rooted in their non-liberal comprehensive convictions. The results of our exploration suggest that it does not. Since Rawls's conception of what a reasonable response to the burdens of judgement might be is morally rather than epistemologically determined, and acceptable only to those who already view society and its citizens in the way demanded by political liberalism, his defensive strategy certainly seems to be purely political in nature; but for that very reason, it will carry no conviction with those who are in effect denying the validity of that vision of self and society. Indeed, since mounting even this defence implies – on Rawls's own admission – denying the truth of any comprehensive convictions that contest the reality or significance of the fact of reasonable pluralism, it appears that how we acknowledge the burdens of judgement is in fact a function of our comprehensive convictions. In that case, Rawls's latest defence of the limits of the political itself fails to respect those limits; the purely political Rawlsian state must inevitably base itself upon elements of a comprehensive doctrine, and so fails to live up to its own claims to neutrality.

Notes

1 According to Rawls, a partially comprehensive doctrine differs from a
   fully comprehensive one as follows: the latter covers all recognized
   values and virtues within one rather precisely articulated scheme,
   whereas the former comprises at least some non-political values and
   virtues, and is rather loosely articulated. Nevertheless, both types of
   doctrine are comprehensive rather than purely political.

PART III

LIBERALISM, POLITICS AND NEUTRALITY

Introduction to Part III

In this part of the book, we widen the focus of our investigation: after spending a great deal of time examining Rawls's theory of justice as fairness, we now turn to three other significantly different contemporary variants of liberal political thought – those advanced by Richard Rorty, Ronald Dworkin and Joseph Raz. However, this widening of focus does not, we hope, amount to a dissolution of our book's unity of theme. In the first place, since the communitarian attack is as much directed at the liberal tradition as a whole as at one representative of it, and since other liberal theorists might have resources for responding to communitarian objections that Rawls is not in a position to deploy, becoming aware of the variety of positions that are subsumed under the label of 'liberalism' is vital to an understanding of the overall state of play in the debate between the two schools of thought. Moreover, the respects in which the positions put forward by Rorty, Dworkin and Raz differ from, and resemble, Rawls's political liberalism enable us to get clearer on two key aspects of Rawls's own thought. It might help to orient the reader in this final part of the book if we develop these claims in a little more detail.

In chapter 5, we saw that the species of liberalism that Rawls now propounds is both anti-perfectionist and purely political: it excludes from political debate and decision (about constitutional essentials and matters of basic justice) considerations that quite properly guide people in their personal lives, and it attempts to justify that exclusion without drawing upon any comprehensive moral doctrines. In chapter 6, we spelt out in some detail the ways in which Rawls might respond to communitarian criticisms, and the sense in which it was a faithful observation of the limits of the political that enables him to deal with some of them; but in chapter 7, we argued that his attempts to defend his anti-perfectionism seem vulnerable to a charge of circularity, and (even by his own admission) appear to violate the limits of the purely political. This suggests that, if Rawls wishes to maintain his commitment to a split between political and private morality, he must confront his communitarian critics on the terrain which they seemed to assume that he occupied from the outset – that of competing (at least partially) comprehensive conceptions of the good; he must be prepared to defend the value of individual autonomy, not just as a primary concern in politics, but as a central value in human life more generally.

The liberal might make two responses to this chain of reasoning. One would be to urge Rawls to develop another way of defending his anti-perfectionism whilst observing the limits of the purely political. Our arguments were directed against the two types of justification that he has hitherto offered, but there may be other ways of articulating a purely political liberalism that avoid the difficulties we detected in Rawls's own version. This is where Rorty comes in: for in recent years, he has been applying his general philosophical anti-foundationalism to the sphere of political theory, and propounding a form of liberalism which – in his own words – stays on the surface, eschewing controversial and fruitless philosophical, metaphysical and religious arguments without abandoning the value of autonomy in politics. Rorty's liberalism without foundations seems to have captured the imagination of many, and so merits consideration in its own right. Since, however, it might also provide Rawls with an alternative way of observing the limits of the purely political, and since Rorty himself has presented his political liberalism not only as an interpretation of Rawls's new position but as a riposte to Rawls's communitarian critics, we have more immediate reasons for exploring Rorty's views in more depth. That will be our task in chapter 8.

But the difficulties in which Rawls finds himself embroiled might lead to a second, very different response. They might give liberals reason to doubt whether a purely political anti-perfectionism is the best way of understanding what a commitment to individual autonomy demands in the sphere of politics. Such doubters could, however, distance themselves from Rawls's position in two very different ways. They might reject his self-denying restriction to purely political considerations in justifying his anti-perfectionist view of the best arrangements for the political arena, holding it to be legitimate to draw upon comprehensive considerations when developing such substantive views. Or they might reject his anti-perfectionism, in favour of the view that states can and should act upon judgements about the relative merits of the different conceptions of the good espoused by their citizens. This suggests that, in principle, we might locate different versions of liberalism in a four-cell matrix, as in figure 1.

	Anti-perfectionist	Perfectionist
Political	Rawls Rorty	
Comprehensive	Dworkin	Raz

Figure 1 Versions of liberalism

The headings across the top of the matrix specify different kinds of view about the structure and the concerns of the sphere of politics, according to the kinds of consideration that are deemed relevant when making decisions about the exercise of coercive political power by the state. The headings at the side of the matrix refer rather to different kinds of view about how a particular vision of the role of the state might itself be defended or justified, according to the kinds of consideration that are deemed relevant when making decisions about the proper structure and concerns of the sphere of politics. It is easy to see how the two dimensions of comparison might be run together, since both in effect involve specifying the limits of legitimate justification, and both are primarily concerned with the relevance of comprehensive moral and philosophical considerations to the issue in question. But we can home in on the difference between them by considering their different objects of justification: one concerns the proper conduct of politics, the other concerns the proper conduct of political theorizing. In short, this matrix allows us to locate species of liberalism according to their political substance (perfectionist or anti-perfectionist) and their theoretical method (political or comprehensive).

Rawls himself appears in the top-left cell, as a purely political anti-perfectionist – as does Rorty, who offers a very different kind of purely political defence of an anti-perfectionist liberalism. Ronald Dworkin appears in the bottom-left cell, as a comprehensive anti-perfectionist liberal. For whilst he shares Rawls's view that governments should be neutral between the different and often conflicting convictions that citizens have about the right way to live, he defends that view by drawing upon a specific comprehensive conception of the nature of the good for human beings. We will explore his position in chapter 9. Joseph Raz appears in the bottom-right cell. For him, it is the proper role of the state to promote the well-being of its citizens, and that promotion may require it to act upon judgements about the relative value of different ways of life in its laws, but, in certain kinds of society at least, individual autonomy remains an essential component of human flourishing. He is, in short, a comprehensive perfectionist liberal, and his position is examined in chapter 10.

We will not, however, be looking at any example of a thinker, liberal or otherwise, who could be placed in the top-right cell of our matrix, for we know of no theorist, contemporary or otherwise, who could be described as a purely political perfectionist. This is not surprising, since the advocate of such a view would believe that a state could legitimately draw upon its judgements about the good life for human beings, and yet defend that vision of politics in a way that did not draw upon any comprehensive considerations. It is difficult to see what might justify such a schizophrenic or masochistic position, in which the theorist denies herself resources that she allows to the politician. There are, to be sure, theorists, such as Aristotle, who hold that human beings achieve self-realization through political activity, and in other contexts they might sensibly be termed political perfectionists. But, as we saw at the end of chapter 6, Rawls's reason for rejecting a civic humanist under-standing of the good of political society was precisely that it invoked a comprehensive doctrine of the kind that his political method required him not to presuppose. In terms of our matrix, then, such a position would be comprehensive rather than political. So the fourth cell of that matrix stands empty.

Naturally, we hope that classifying the various species of liberal theorist in terms of this matrix will help to illuminate the complex issues that have arisen through the communitarian critique of liberalism. In particular, we hope that the distinction between the two classificatory axes (between what one might call political neutrality and political-theoretical neutrality) will further clarify the difficult question of the nature, and the legitimacy, of the neutrality to which any given species of liberalism might lay claim – the question that is the fifth heading of our agenda. To aid this clarification, for the sense in which the liberal state might or might not be neutral is an issue that causes a great deal of confusion, it may be helpful for us to respond here to the following objection.

By placing Dworkin on the left-hand side of our matrix, we classify him as an anti-perfectionist liberal. This is because he agrees with Rawls that the state should not act on judgements as to the relative merits of the ways of life espoused by its citizens. However, he is a *comprehensive* anti-perfectionist: he justifies the neutrality of his state on the grounds that it best promotes a certain comprehensive conception of human well-being. It could therefore be objected that Dworkinian state neutrality, being in the service of a comprehensive conception of the human good, is not neutral at all and ought more properly to be called a species of 'perfectionism'. We are calling a state anti-perfectionist, or neutral, if it does not act upon judgements as to the relative merits of the different ways of life espoused by its citizens. But we are conceding that the reasons for it not to do so may lie, as we will see that they do for Dworkin, in a comprehensive doctrine about the nature of well-being. Surely this makes the claim to neutrality a sham? Surely in this case the state's actions are motivated by a distinctively liberal comprehensive conception of the good, and one that might properly be termed 'perfectionist'? It might thus be argued that our distinction between the kinds of reason the state can use to justify its actions and the kinds of reason the political theorist can use to justify its understanding of the proper role of the state serves primarily to maintain what can only be an illusion: that the state can be neutral in any sense.

In order to grasp the true force of this objection to comprehensive anti-perfectionist liberalism, we must first remind ourselves of the kind of neutrality to which anti-perfectionist liberalism of any kind aspires. It is, of course, true that the vision of an anti-perfectionist state is justified by appeal to certain, distinctively liberal values; it could hardly be otherwise, since no political position could be justified without appealing to some value or other (that is just what 'justifying one's position' means), and no recognizably liberal political position could be justified without appealing to recognizably liberal values (that is just a tautology). But the anti-perfectionist's claim to neutrality is not intended to imply that she can or should justify her position without making reference to values of any kind. The only neutrality to which she lays claim is contained in her belief that the state should not act on the basis of its judgements as to the relative merits of the particular conceptions of the good espoused by its citizens – that it should be neutral, in justificatory terms, between the particular values and ways of life that its citizens might choose. She can happily acknowledge that what justifies this view is her commitment to a classically liberal value – for example, the value of individual autonomy, the importance of people being free to choose their ways of life for themselves. If she was not committed to such a value, she would have no reason to object to a state which, by acting on the basis of its judgements about the relative merits of competing ways of life, effectively interfered with its citizens' exercise of that freedom.

We might think of this, not uncommon, defence of liberal anti-perfectionism as invoking a distinction between two different senses in which one might talk about 'a conception of the good'. In the first sense, this refers to an abstract or general conception of human well-being – one which might, for example, attribute fundamental importance to the human capacity for autonomy; in the second, it refers to more concrete conceptions of how to live, amongst which people choose when exercising their autonomy – for example, the choice of a particular career or religious faith or leisure activity. The anti-perfectionist state is justified by appeal to a conception of the good in the first sense but remains neutral on conceptions of the good in the second sense. What leads to anti-perfectionist conclusions is simply that what is claimed to be good for people in the first sense is autonomous choice. This is neutral as between conceptions of the good in the second sense, since it requires that the state eschew actions that are based on judgements of the relative worth of the particular ways of life amongst which its citizens choose.

It would therefore seem that there is no inconsistency in an anti-perfectionist liberal advocating a certain kind of neutrality for the state whilst offering a value-driven justification of that neutrality. If any vision of politics must be grounded in some particular values or conception of what is important to human well-being – since the only alternative to such a grounding is that one have no reason for advocating that vision of politics in the first place – then a liberal commitment to state neutrality cannot be shown to be illusory, or to be a species of perfectionism in disguise, simply by pointing out that it is justified by reference to a certain, distinctively liberal, conception of human well-being. On the contrary: the anti-perfectionist liberal might argue that, since all visions of politics must be grounded in a conception of human well-being, the only way in which such a vision might conceivably be neutral is in its substance rather than its theoretical grounding – by, for example, demanding that political power not be exercised on the basis of judgements about the relative merits of the particular ways of life espoused by citizens. And of course, that is precisely the demand that is characteristic of the anti-perfectionist liberal. In this sense, anti-perfectionists might feel justified in thinking of themselves not as duplicitously laying claim to a kind of neutrality that they cannot possess, but rather as committed to as much neutrality in politics as it is possible to have.

However, the plausibility of this defensive response by the anti-perfectionist liberal appears in a very different light as soon as we introduce Rawlsian political liberalism into the picture. For this allows us to distinguish between two, very different, species of anti-perfectionism, and to claim that one lacks a kind of neutrality that the other possesses – in other words, to claim that there is a further kind or level of neutrality that some species of anti-perfectionism fail to achieve, and so that there is a clear sense in which they are not as neutral as they might be. The crucial distinction is, of course, between comprehensive and purely political varieties of anti-perfectionism; and the distinction is drawn in terms of the way in which liberal values are invoked in justifying their commitment to state neutrality.

For example, Dworkin's anti-perfectionism qualifies as 'comprehensive' in Rawlsian terms because (as we shall see) it is grounded in a particular comprehensive conception of human well-being, one that applies to far more than the political sphere. In other words, its theoretical foundations are not neutral as between the competing comprehensive doctrines espoused by the citizens to whom its neutral political arrangements apply. By contrast, Rawlsian political liberalism claims that liberal justifications of state neutrality should themselves be neutral – they should not rely upon the validity of any particular comprehensive doctrines. His political anti-perfectionism claims, in effect, to be doubly neutral: its justification for state neutrality with respect to the particular ways of life that citizens might choose still builds upon values, but upon values that are common, or neutral, as between the comprehensive doctrines those citizens espouse. Dworkinian liberalism therefore offends against Rawls's principle that political power should only be used in ways acceptable to citizens committed to a range of comprehensive doctrines; *in comparison with political liberalism*, any such comprehensively liberal anti-perfectionist state is indeed sectarian or unjust, because its avowed neutrality is insufficiently thoroughgoing or radical.

The significance of whether Rawls's shift to the political can be sustained should now be clear. If it can, then the anti-perfectionist state could be neutral as between conceptions of the good in *both* of the senses we have distinguished. Not only would the political arrangements that it advocates be neutral, in aim, between the particular ways of life that people subject to those arrangements might choose, but its justification of that state neutrality, the kinds of value that it invokes in its own defence, would be neutral as between the comprehensive doctrines espoused by citizens. It would then make sense to accuse comprehensive anti-perfectionists of lacking that second kind of neutrality, and so of being less non-sectarian than they might be. However, in our critical analysis of Rawls's political liberalism in chapter 7, we have attempted to cast some doubt on its claims to be neutral in the second sense of that term. Insofar as this attempt succeeds, it suggests that the second kind of neutrality is not in fact attainable, and so that the first kind of neutrality, the kind that comprehensive anti-perfectionist liberalism claims to possess, is all the neutrality that there can be in this area. We do not pretend to have established this conclusion definitively; but if we have done enough to make it plausible, then, from the point of view of the fifth element of the communitarian critique, the fundamental question about anti-perfectionist liberalism would be the following. Given that such a view of politics is and must be grounded in a liberal conception of human well-being, just how substantial is the state neutrality that flows from that conception? We attempt to explore the answer to that question in chapter 9.

So much for one problem that the structure of our matrix might seem to generate. A second such problem, which is in fact related to the critical question we just formulated, can be dealt with a little more cursorily here. As we saw in chapter 7, Rawls's exclusion of comprehensive doctrines from political decision-making is importantly qualified; it applies only to decisions affecting constitutional essentials and matters of basic justice. The limits of these categories, and the justification for treating cases which fall outside them differently, are by no means obvious; but what *is* clear is that Rawls regards such questions as the funding of museums and the arts as exceptions to his exclusionary principle. It is thus perfectly possible for a Rawlsian state to act in accordance with judgements as to the relative merits of the different ways of life people might choose, and to support its cultural structure, in ways that are often taken to be characteristic of perfectionist polities. What matters, for Rawls, is that the state not do so on what he calls fundamental matters. When we term the Rawlsian state anti-perfectionist, then, we must be understood to be referring specifically to its role in matters relating to constitutional essentials and matters of basic justice; on non-fundamental matters, citizens may properly vote in accordance with their views about what kinds of life are most worth living and the state may act in accordance with those views.

We shall have to bear such definitional complexities in mind in the coming chapters – particularly since both Dworkin and Raz each offer their own, very different, justifications for state support of culture and the arts. The issue is especially pressing with respect to Dworkin, for obvious reasons. Since Raz is a perfectionist liberal, state policies of this kind are ones that he can justify by making explicit reference to judgements about the relative merits of the different ways of life espoused by citizens; but since Dworkin defends a state that is supposed to eschew such judgements, his defence of such policies raises important questions about the precise nature of the neutrality he requires of his state, and so about the clarity and stability of any line that we might attempt to draw between perfectionist and anti-perfectionist varieties of liberalism. Since, however, these difficulties in applying the organizing terms of our matrix reflect difficulties of real substance – both in grasping the nature of the various theories, and in illuminating an important set of political issues – we believe that struggling with them is not an unhappy consequence of choosing inappropriate classificatory principles, but a fruitful way of gaining a clear view of what is often obscure and treacherous terrain.

8
RORTY:
liberalism without foundations

In a paper entitled 'The Priority of Democracy to Philosophy' and a book entitled *Contingency, Irony and Solidarity* Rorty develops a form of anti-foundationalist liberalism, attributes it to the new Rawls and defends it against the communitarians. Attributing such anti-foundationalism to Rawls is, in our view, a complete misreading of the import of the latter's political liberalism. As we attempted to demonstrate in the second part of this book, Rawls's decision to restrict himself in his theorizing to the ideas and values that are latent in the shared public political culture of contemporary Western liberal democracies is motivated by a substantive commitment to the value of public justifiability; it manifests his recognition of the value of a society in which the state's use of coercive power over free and equal citizens is capable of being justified to each and every one of those citizens in terms of values they all accept. Rorty heartily agrees with Rawls's conclusion, but he is driven to it by fundamentally philosophical arguments against the possibility of pursuing any other strategy; for on his view, anyone who believes that the liberal values and ideas latent in our public political culture might require or could conceivably be furnished with independent support is guilty of certain philosophical confusions. In short, where Rawls's turn to the public political culture is a self-denying ordinance fuelled by a specifically liberal value commitment, Rorty's is the political manifestation of a general philosophical hostility to any attempt to provide rational foundations for systems of values and concepts.

However, the very fact that Rorty overestimates his kinship with the new Rawls means that (as we mentioned in our Introduction to this part of the book) he may be able to buttress Rawls's commitment to a purely political liberalism by providing a version of it that avoids the difficulties that we identified in chapter 7. Certainly, it would be imprudent to draw the conclusion that the general strategy of articulating a political theory that stays on the surface is doomed to failure before investigating the nature and viability of the most prominent and provocative contemporary representative of that school of thought. And regardless of the true nature of Rorty's relation to Rawls, his critique of the communitarians is very relevant to our purposes in this book; indeed, his distinctive and controversial reasons for restricting political theorizing to the realm of public culture are made manifest in that critique, so we shall devote most of our attention in this chapter to it.

In effect, Rorty attempts to justify his proposed restriction on political theorizing by attacking three commonly held reasons for thinking that it cannot or should not be observed. Those considerations are:

1 The belief that all political theories have philosophical or metaphysical foundations that raise issues and ideas not to be found in the public political culture.
2 The belief that justifying a political system merely by invoking the public values that grow up around it simply begs the question against those who reject both the system and its supporting culture.
3 The belief that proving the validity of certain values and ideas present in the public political culture involves determining whether or not they (as well any philosophical doctrines that they might presuppose) correspond to a reality external to that culture.

Rorty's view is that the communitarian critique of Rawls's theory of justice embodies a version of all three claims. This view seems initially plausible: for as we have seen, much of the communitarian attack has understood its focus to be not so much on Rawls's substantive theory but rather on the purportedly more value-neutral conception of the person upon which that theory is based, and so seems to take it for granted that political theories are and must be possessed of metaphysical foundations, and that they must accordingly be committed to defending this foundational conception as *the* correct or valid conception of personhood.

According to Rorty, however, no version of these three claims is coherent. Theories of the self are not value-neutral foundations for political theories but rather another way of articulating (in a different mode of discourse) the very same value commitments with which the political theory is imbued; accordingly, since their invocation can add nothing to the rational credentials or the plausibility of that political doctrine, we need not (*qua* political theorists) go beyond the confines of the public political culture in order to address the issues that such philosophical discourses might raise. Moreover, the notion that the values and conception of the person embodied in such a theory must be justifiable in terms that do not beg the question against those who do not share those values and conceptions is a philosophical confusion; and so is the notion that they must be justifiable in terms of their correspondence to a reality that is external to them. Not one of these three assumptions therefore provides any reason for liberals to think that, in order to justify their doctrine, system and culture, they must utilize resources that go beyond the values and conceptions that make it up. On the contrary: the resources latent in the public political culture of the liberal democracies seem to be all that is available, and so must be all that is required, to justify the liberal political system. As Rorty puts it: '. . . it is not evident that [liberal democratic institutions] are to be measured by anything more specific than the moral intuitions of the particular historical community that has created those institutions'.[1] In effect, then, liberals are free to ignore any critics of liberalism whose criticisms are so radical as to put in question the moral intuitions of Western liberal democracies; or, as Rorty prefers to phrase it, it is right that '. . . we heirs of the Enlightenment think of enemies of liberal democracy like Nietzsche or Loyola as, to use Rawls's word, "mad" '.[2]

In the remainder of this chapter, we will attempt to assess the cogency of this philosophically motivated turn to the public political culture by asking whether Rorty's arguments really do give him the licence to ignore Nietzschean, Loyolan (or communitarian) criticisms of liberalism.

Foundational theories of the person

Rorty's first claim is that theories of the person should not be viewed as indispensable and value-neutral foundations upon which any blueprint for society must be erected. In order to convince us of this, he offers the following characterization of Rawls's references to the nature of the person in his political theory:

> He does not *want* a 'complete deontological vision', one that would explain *why* we should give justice priority over our conception of the good. He is filling out the consequences of the claim that it is prior, not its presuppositions. Rawls is not interested in conditions for the identity of the self, but only in conditions for citizenship in a liberal society . . . Rawls is not attempting a transcendental deduction of American liberalism or supplying philosophical foundations for democratic institutions, but simply trying to systematize the principles and intuitions typical of American liberals.[3]

This claim seems very plausible. There is of course much talk about the nature of personhood in the context of moral and political arguments; but its focus and purpose seems very different from such talk in the context of philosophical metaphysics. In the latter case, we might for example want an account of the criteria we have for judging the identity of a person over time, an answer to the question 'What makes person A at time X the same person as person B at time Y?' In the former case, we want to know what it is about human beings that means that they should be treated in certain ways, for example, to know why their autonomy should be respected. To provide a political theory of the person is thus not a matter of straying into metaphysics; but neither is it a matter of providing a foundation for one's theory of society that was in any sense lacking hitherto. It is rather an attempt to articulate under a new aspect the specific vision of life and the concomitant set of values that must already be implicit in any blueprint for the basic structures of society. After all, given that such blueprints have to do with the organization of the communal life of human beings, it would be extremely surprising if they were not to embody a view of what matters about them as persons, and the same point holds in reverse; but there seems no obvious *a priori* order of priority between the two ways of articulating that underlying vision.

To this extent, Rorty's claim is compatible with that of communitarians such as Charles Taylor. However, whereas Taylor also argues that resort to such a theory is not dispensable, Rorty concludes that it is: since it adds nothing to the content or credentials of the original blueprint, that entire mode of discourse can if necessary be avoided without rational penalty; and since participating in it opens the liberal to complex and tortuous controversies, discretion would seem to be the better part of valour. (Rorty also happens to think that if the liberal *did* wish to advance a theory of the person, the most appropriate one would not be that which the communitarians attribute to Rawls but rather the one they offer as their own best account of the matter. But that further twist in Rorty's argument is fundamentally marginal to it, since – by his own lights – the liberal should eschew any such wish.)

But the conclusion that such theories are dispensable is not warranted. It may follow from what has been said that a defender of a given political theory might eschew *articulating* her vision of society in terms of a theory of the person; but it does not follow (as Rorty claims) that she is free to ignore criticisms of her political blueprint that are couched in terms relating to the nature of the people that blueprint would create.

Someone who responds to Rawls's blueprint by saying 'But this is not the way people ought to live!' or 'This society would cripple and distort its citizens!' may or may not be employing a vocabulary that Rawls himself might have wished to avoid; but since talk of the nature of the person is one alternative arena for articulating and arguing about a set of values that also underlies talk of the structure of one's ideal society, then an attack upon liberalism couched in terms of the person is *ipso facto* an attack upon liberal social blueprints. Such forms of critique are focused upon values that are central to the liberal position irrespective of the aspect under which it is presented; accordingly, they cannot simply be ignored by the defender of liberalism. In short, even if a liberal theory of the person is an optional adjunct to the Rawlsian project, insofar as that theory of the person does genuinely accord with or give expression to the values underlying liberalism, then anyone committed to the Rawlsian blueprint is thereby committed to the theory of the person. *Pace* Rorty, he is also thereby committed to the task of responding to criticisms of that theory of the person, and so of venturing beyond the terrain of the public political culture.

Alien vocabularies

Rorty continues his anti-foundationalist critique of the communitarians by attacking an assumption that he takes to be ubiquitous in political theorizing, namely that a given social blueprint can only be regarded as superior to its competitors if it is possible to produce justifications of it that any interlocutor must be able to acknowledge as valid regardless of his value commitments. Given this assumption, then invoking a philosophical or metaphysical theory of the person to justify one's political theory will appear to provide precisely the abstract, value-neutral terrain that the project of rational justification requires; such a move would, for example, allow the liberal and the anti-liberal to confront one another in terms that will make sense to, but that do not beg the question against, either vocabulary. But Rorty rejects the assumption that the liberal is obliged to make any such move:

> We have to insist that not every argument needs to be met in the terms in which it is presented. Accommodation and tolerance must stop short of a willingness to work within any vocabulary that one's interlocutor wishes to use, to take seriously any topic that he puts forward for discussion . . . there may not be enough overlap between two such networks to make possible agreement about political topics, or even profitable discussion of such topics.[4]

It is important to note at once that Rorty offers no reason to accept that this assumption of tolerance is what motivates the communitarian focus on philosophical theories of the person; even if cleaving to such an assumption would be *one* explanation of their turn to philosophy, there are many other equally plausible explanations, and Rorty gives us no grounds for excluding them. However, even if this particular speculative diagnosis of Rorty's *were* right, it remains very unclear whether that assumption of tolerance is incoherent in the way he suggests.

There is, of course, a kernel of truth in his remarks: for if the vocabularies of two political thinkers are incommensurable to a degree that hinders the articulation of their views in terms comprehensible to both, then a failure to reach agreement does not invalidate the position of either. Moreover, even if the two disputants comprehend one another and yet still fail to agree, this does not in itself condemn either party's view; indeed, the issue over which they are disputing may be so fundamental to the outlook of one that a failure to prevent the other party from acting upon her own views would constitute a failure of commitment: for example, as we saw when discussing Walzer in chapter 4, a failure to convince an Aztec society that human sacrifice was wrong does not in itself make intervention to prevent such sacrifice immoral or unjustifiable. In short, eliciting the agreement of all those we might encounter in political debate is not in itself a criterion for the correctness of our position in that debate.

However, this valid point does not entail that we might simply dismiss or ignore all anti-liberal critiques on the grounds that they are ineradicably alien; for it is the process of attempting to comprehend, evaluate and change the opinions of a given interlocutor that alone can determine whether her views make sense, her agreement constitutes something we should value and her criticism something we should heed. For an interlocutor to be an interlocutor, her remarks must indeed be intelligible to 'we' liberals; and liberals need not *necessarily* worry if their arguments fail to elicit agreement from all non-liberal interlocutors. It does not, however, follow that liberals need only justify themselves to liberals; for being alien in the relevant sense is not determined by whether the interlocutor is or is not a liberal. It is determined by the process of argument.

On occasion, Rorty seems to recognize this banal truth: 'We do not conclude that Nietzsche and Loyola are crazy because they hold unusual views on certain 'fundamental' topics; rather, we conclude this only after extensive attempts at an exchange of political views have made us realize that we are not going to get anywhere.'[5] Moreover, there are even points in his article when he hints at the routes he would take in such political exchanges: 'The liberal response . . . must be, therefore, that even if the typical character types of liberal democracies *are* bland, calculating, petty, and unheroic, the prevalence of such people may be a reasonable price to pay for political freedom.'[6] Such sketches of an argument may reap dividends if they were to be filled out in ways that the article simply leaves to our imagination; but it is clear that this is where Rorty's real work against the anti-liberals must be done. And if this *is* the true site of the conflict, then Rorty's suggestion that the criticisms of such anti-liberals must be beyond the bounds of intelligibility simply because they reject the constituent ideas of liberal political cultures is no more than wishful thinking. The fact that the notion of universal agreement is a chimera in political theory (as well as elsewhere in philosophy) gives Rorty no basis for ignoring or dismissing all anti-liberal critiques in advance, and so no basis for restricting political discourse to the resources of the dominant contemporary culture.

Concepts, truth and reality

So, if Rorty's rejection of the first two assumptions we listed earlier was the sole basis for his suggested revisions of methodology in political theory, then those revisions would have no real justification; rejecting those assumptions simply does not entail restricting political theorists to the materials that are latent in the public political culture. What remains is his attack on the third assumption on that list, namely the belief that we must go beyond the confines of the public political culture in order to justify the values it embodies, because such justification is a matter of establishing the degree to which they correspond to a reality that is somehow external to that culture. Why is this picture of justification as correspondence incoherent? And even if it is, does it follow that, in attempting to justify a given political system, we have no alternative but to restrict ourselves to the materials provided by that culture?

Although Rorty holds that this picture of justification is deeply embedded in the forms of political philosophy he opposes, he makes little attempt in his article on the communitarians to expound and clarify his reasons for regarding that assumption as flawed. To appreciate those reasons, we must turn to his book *Contingency, Irony and Solidarity*, from which it becomes clear that this assumption is a specific inflection of the general metaphysical tendency against which Rorty has set his face for more than a decade. In the first chapter of that book, he provides a critique of the idea that *anything* – mind or matter, self, society or any other entity in the world – has an intrinsic nature that a body of discourse might express or represent. If, as he argues, no sense can be made of the idea that any given vocabulary might stand in a relation of fitting or correspondence to the world or to any given part of it, then the incoherence of the idea that a given concept or theory of the person (or a given political vocabulary) must be assessed in terms of its correspondence to the reality of human nature will be an inevitable consequence. It is this general anti-foundational theme that is the crucial backbone of Rorty's enterprise, in the domain of political philosophy as well as elsewhere.

Rorty's view on this matter is clear:

> . . . great scientists invent descriptions of the world which are useful for purposes of predicting and controlling what happens, just as poets and political thinkers invent other descriptions of it for other purposes. But there is no sense in which *any* of these descriptions is an accurate representation of the way the world is in itself . . . the very idea of such a representation [is] pointless . . . [7]

According to Rorty, we have failed to see the pointlessness of this idea because we have failed to bear in mind the distinction between single sentences and vocabularies:

> For we often let the world decide the competition between alternative sentences (e.g., . . . between 'The butler did it' and 'The doctor did it'). In such cases, it is easy to run together the fact that the world contains the causes of our being justified in holding a belief with the claim that some non-linguistic state of the world is itself an example of truth, or that some such state 'makes a belief true' by 'corresponding' to it. But it is not so easy when we turn from individual sentences to vocabularies as wholes. When we consider examples of alternative language games – the vocabulary of ancient Athenian politics versus Jefferson's, the moral vocabulary of Saint Paul versus Freud's, the jargon of Newton versus that of Aristotle, the idiom of Blake versus that of Dryden – it is difficult to think of the world as making one of these better than the other, of the world as deciding between them. When the notion of 'description of the world' is moved from the level of criterion-governed sentences within language games to language games as wholes, games which we do not choose between by reference to criteria, the idea that the world decides which descriptions are true can no longer be given a clear sense. [8]

The sentence that contains the kernel of argument in the above passage is the following: 'When the notion of "description of the world" is moved from the level of criterion-governed sentences within language games to language games as wholes, games which we do not choose between by reference to criteria, the idea that the world decides which descriptions are true can no longer be given a clear sense.' The concentration of Wittgensteinian terminology suggests that this sentence should be read as a reference to the considerations that led Wittgenstein to characterize grammar as autonomous, an insight that rests upon emphasizing an essential difference between grammatical remarks and empirical propositions. Empirical propositions are capable of being true and of being false; they claim that something is true of the world, and their claim is evaluated by reference to the facts, to the way the world is. If, for example, someone claims that the sea is blue, we need only observe the colour of the body of water referred to in order to assess the truth of the claim. Obviously, such propositions could only be framed if their constituent terms have meaning, that is if there is a set of rules governing their use, a set of what Wittgenstein sometimes calls criteria. These function as standards which distinguish correct from incorrect applications of a given term; they mark the boundary between sense and nonsense, between meaningful uses of the term and unintelligible ones. For example, if someone defines water as H_2O, then anyone who applies the term 'water' (as part of a factual claim) to something that does not have that chemical composition has misused the term, and so failed to say anything meaningful. Propositions that elucidate criteria or meaning-rules are what Wittgenstein calls grammatical remarks.

The crucial point to follow from these reminders is that, unlike empirical propositions, grammatical remarks are incapable of being true or false; this is because they are rule formulations, not descriptions or factual claims. It makes no sense to talk of a rule being true or false; that, one could say, is an aspect of the grammar of the term 'rule' – and an aspect of the grammar of the terms 'true' and 'false'. (How, for example, might it be *false* to define 'water' as 'H_2O'? Even if the world lacked any substance with that particular chemical composition, this would show only that there was no water in the world, not that our definition of the term had failed to represent it accurately.) Of course, in the absence of a grammatical or conceptual framework, no meaningful empirical proposition could be constructed, and in this sense the possibility of a true (as well as of a false) empirical proposition is a function of the existence of a set of grammatical rules; but the actual truth or falsity of the propositions thus constructed neither validates nor falsifies that set of rules. The world may be such as to make one grammar more useful or more appropriate than another, but it could not make it more accurate or closer to the facts. Since, then, sentences that formulate rules are not in the business of describing the world, they can neither correspond nor fail to correspond with that world. To imagine that they can is akin to treating a set of grammatical rules as a series of descriptions or factual claims, as if the expression of a rule governing the use of a word were part of a theory about the world – as if a definition were a truth-value candidate. In short, for Rorty it simply makes no sense to characterize the grammatical or conceptual framework of any language game as a description of the world, for it is not a description at all.

Communitarianism and correspondence

Such, on our reading, is Rorty's argument for his general anti-foundationalist attack upon the picture of justification as correspondence.[9] It seems powerful; but even if we grant its cogency, a question remains as to its consequences for political theory. What would follow from rejecting the general picture of justification as correspondence in that specific domain? If it *is* a piece of metaphysics, how might this new knowledge alter our understanding of political morality and its rational underpinnings? Rorty identifies two consequences of such a rejection: first, that it would allow us to dismiss the communitarian critique of liberalism, since that critique is couched in terms that imply the coherence of this picture; and second, that it would reveal the very idea of an external standard against which to assess the political vocabulary of liberalism to be chimerical, and so allow us to remain content with the standards of justification that are internal to that vocabulary and its supporting culture. In the following section of this chapter we shall examine this second, more general claim; but in this section we shall evaluate Rorty's first, more specific anti-communitarian conclusion. Does the communitarian attack on the liberal conception of the person as flawed, inaccurate or just plain wrong entail that communitarians are committed to the incoherent assumption that concepts of the person are in the business of accurately describing the metaphysical Reality of human nature?

The answer to this question varies from communitarian to communitarian. In the case of Taylor, Rorty's attack seems entirely misplaced: for the assumption that there is a timeless essence of the self against which conceptions of the self must be measured would contradict his conception of human beings as self-interpreting animals, as beings whose identity is fixed by the terms in which they understand it and so is transformable by a shift in those understandings and their concomitant social matrices. In the case of MacIntyre, Rorty seems to be equally inaccurate: MacIntyre does indeed think that he can demonstrate that an emotivist conception of the self is flawed, but it is flawed because it fails to provide the resources needed to comprehend the concepts of personal identity and morality; it is not that liberals misrepresent the true nature of those phenomena, but rather that their conceptual framework cannot make adequate sense of them. With respect to Sandel, however, Rorty seems to be on firmer ground. Certainly, Sandel articulates his criticisms of Rawls in terms that imply that Rawls has misdescribed the nature of the human self – more specifically, that he has overlooked that self's capacity for constitutive attachments; and this is something that Sandel seems prone to think of as a metaphysical truth about distinctively human beings.

However, the most interesting question that Rorty raises is not that of measuring the degree to which the attacks made by the communitarians did or did not involve formulations and turns of phrase that might be read as entailing a commitment to the erroneous view Rorty has identified. The real issue is whether their criticisms can be articulated in ways that entirely dispense with such locutions, and yet maintain their original force. For, although this metaphysical confusion may be widespread in our culture, it seems entirely extrinsic to the content of any particular ethical system: it might be a part of the articulation of almost any ethic, and yet not be an indispensable part of any of them. When someone engaged in an ethical or political argument says 'This view of the self fails to capture the truth about human nature' or 'But my concept of human nature is the only right one!' or 'This is how all human beings ought to live, and anyone who doesn't is wrong!', no commitment to a metaphysical confusion need be inferred. It may simply be that these are manifestations of the sincerity with which someone cleaves to a vision of life, or an expression of her belief that the answer to such questions is not a matter of personal preference. As Rorty himself puts it in a slightly different context: 'Everybody is just insisting that the beliefs and desires they hold most dear should come first in the order of discussion. That is not arbitrariness but sincerity.'[10]

If we reread Sandel in such a light, then his attack on liberalism can easily be viewed as a passionate assault upon the values underlying the liberal social blueprint, which happens to be couched in terms of the conception of the person that he takes to be associated with that blueprint. And since, as we argued earlier, Rorty's view that the liberal need not articulate his values in those terms gives him no ground for believing that the liberal need not defend himself against criticisms that employ those terms, we find ourselves back where we started – with an obligation to understand, assess and respond to the specific content of the communitarian critique. In other words, Rorty's anti-foundationalist attack upon the picture of justification as correspondence does not provide us with any speedy way of dismissing the communitarians.

Metaphysics and politics

However, Rorty also makes a second claim about the consequences of rejecting the picture of justification as correspondence: the claim that this rejection entails that political argument and justification in general must be conducted within the confines of the prevailing public political culture. How does he reach this more sweeping conclusion?

> The realization that the world does not tell us what language games to play should not, however, lead us to say that a decision about which to play is arbitrary, nor to say that it is the expression of something deep within us. The moral is not that objective criteria for choice of vocabulary are to be replaced with subjective criteria, reason with will or feeling. It is rather that the notions of criteria and choice (including the idea of 'arbitrary' choice) are no longer in point when it comes to changes from one language game to another. Europe did not *decide* to accept the idiom of Romantic poetry, or of socialist politics, or of Galilean mechanics. That sort of shift was no more an act of will than it was a result of argument. Rather, Europe gradually lost the habit of using certain words and gradually acquired the habit of using others . . .[11]

The point upon which Rorty is fastening here is important: the concept of decision, as it is employed within the context of a given language game (for example, to decide between competing descriptions of a given state of affairs), has no obvious application at the level of language games as a whole. But he takes this to imply that cultural change is itself primarily a matter of shifts in vocabulary which are as little affected by human will and reason as is the weather. And what is true of culture *per se* must be true of political culture: in other words, for Rorty, liberalism is now simply a part of our cultural weather system. Just as Western Europe acquired Galilean vocabulary and dispensed with its Aristotelian predecessor, so our contemporary culture has got out of the habit of employing any political vocabulary other than that of liberalism. And since we cannot object to that vocabulary on the grounds that it misrepresents the Truth about the Reality of the self or of human nature (for the very idea of such an external measure or standard is incoherent), we should simply get on with the business of developing and refining the political vocabulary with which we find ourselves equipped, in accordance with the standards that are internal to that vocabulary and culture. In short, we should, as political theorists, restrict ourselves to the resources latent in our public political culture.

In this respect, the situation in politics is precisely analogous to the situation as Rorty describes it in contemporary philosophy:

> To say that we should drop the idea of truth as out there waiting to be discovered is not to say that we have discovered that, out there, there is no truth. It is to say that our purposes would be served best by ceasing to see truth as a deep matter, as a topic of philosophical interest, or 'true' as a term which repays analysis. 'The nature of truth' is an unprofitable topic, resembling in this respect 'the nature of man' and 'the nature of God', and differing from 'the nature of the positron', and 'the nature of Oedipal fixation'. But this claim about relative profitability, in turn, is just the recommendation that we in fact *say* little about these topics, and see how we get on.[12]

As his use of this analogy brings out, Rorty takes his discovery that vocabularies as a whole do not represent reality to show that the task of persuading someone to adopt a new vocabulary can amount to nothing more than simply ignoring their old vocabulary and elaborating the new one in a way that emphasizes its attractions. His advice is to 'try to ignore the apparently futile traditional questions by substituting the following new and possibly interesting questions'.[13] This is why he then goes on to expound the views of Davidson, Freud and Nietzsche (amongst others); and it is why he feels that he can safely ignore the doctrines of Loyola and Nietzsche (in his anti-liberal incarnation) – not to mention the communitarians. But does Rorty's argument actually support this sweeping reconception and restriction of political theory?

The difficulty with Rorty's strategy is not its positive side but its negative one. It seems eminently plausible that one way of persuading someone to adopt a new outlook on life would be to emphasize the scope, sophistication, flexibility etc. of the concepts that embody it; in fact, communitarians such as Taylor and MacIntyre would agree whole-heartedly that this is an essential aspect of practical reasoning. However, another equally important part of such reasoning must be that of engaging with the old vocabulary, for example by highlighting its unwieldiness, its failure to mark certain distinctions, its propensity to obscure or play down certain fundamental aspects of human behaviour and experience – and by responding to similar claims that its proponents make about the new vocabulary. Rorty assumes that this negative or combative part of the process can simply be dispensed with in the case of any fundamentally anti-liberal thinker; but his grounds for this assumption are inadequate. Critical engagements that employ terms of criticism of the sort mentioned above no more assume that concepts describe or represent reality than does the positive part of the process that Rorty endorses. So, his only reason for dispensing with them must be the implicit presumption that a cultural transformation in the West has already disposed of every serious opponent of liberalism.

To be sure, in the late twentieth century, it might be safe to assume that an Aristotelian or Samurai moral vocabulary is no longer a viable contender for the status of 'most favoured discourse'; in such cases, the idea of critically engaging with such a vocabulary seems to be one whose time has passed: they can, perhaps, be simply ignored or dismissed as irrelevant. But this does not allow us to ignore or dismiss *in advance* any attempts to reconstruct or reinterpret such moral codes in ways more adapted to the present time (an attempt that Alisdair MacIntyre, for example, has made on Aristotle's behalf). And it certainly does not permit us to ignore or dismiss in advance every non-liberal vocabulary in the sphere of ethics and politics; for in the case of a vast array of such frameworks it simply cannot seriously be claimed that the march of cultural history has left them entirely by the wayside.

One cannot respond *a priori* to every critique of liberalism with the suggestion that we simply ignore the questions it raises; for this is to assume in advance that our opponent has already lost, at the level of the culture as a whole, the 'argument' she wishes to have with us on a one-to-one basis. It is to assume the validity of a sociological conclusion without the provision of any sociological evidence, and then to utilize that conclusion in order to avoid engaging in personal, individual political argument. It may well be that the ethical and political vocabularies of Nietzsche and Loyola are losing their grip on Western culture as a whole; but any individual who regards this development as a good thing and wants to speed it up, must do so by revealing the poverty, ugliness and irrelevance of those vocabularies in argument, not by declaring that development to have been completed already. However devoutly to be wished this consummation may be, it will not be brought about by wishing alone – certainly not when the wishing takes the form of stipulation.

In conclusion, we can say that this examination of the three pillars of Rorty's philosophical anti-foundationalism has revealed them to be insufficient to justify either his specific attacks on the communitarians or his more general desire to restrict political theorizing to the resources latent in our public political culture. This form of political liberalism lacks foundations in a sense that even an anti-foundationalist cannot simply shrug off; so those liberals who wish to pursue the general methodological strategy of avoiding the use of comprehensive moral doctrines must look elsewhere for a tenable version of it.

Notes

1　Rorty, 'The Priority of Democracy to Philosophy', p. 190. All page references to this article refer to the collection Rorty, *Objectivity, Relativism and Truth*.
2　Ibid., p. 187.
3　Ibid., p. 189.
4　Ibid., p. 190.
5　Ibid., p. 190.
6　Ibid., p. 190.

7 Rorty, *Contingency, Irony and Solidarity*, p. 4.
8 Ibid., pp. 5–6.
9 For those interested in and familiar with the philosophical background to Rorty's work, it may be worth noting at this point that certain other aspects of Rorty's text suggest an alternative reading of his argument, one according to which he is indebted to Quine rather than Wittgenstein. On that reading, Rorty's reason for rejecting the picture of correspondence would not be that this picture mistakenly treats a grammatical system as if it were an empirical theory, but rather that any such vocabulary is a web of propositions whose complexity and capacity to accommodate a wide range of empirical phenomena is so great that it is almost impossible to refute it. Our reason for not pursuing this reading in the text, however, is that such an argument would not put paid to the correspondence picture; for if such a vocabulary *were* akin to an empirical theory, then it would to that degree be in the business of attempting to describe or characterize reality, and so could at least in principle be accused of failing to correspond to that reality.
10 Rorty, 'The Priority of Democracy to Philosophy', p. 193.
11 Rorty, *Contingency, Irony and Solidarity*, p. 6.
12 Ibid., p. 8.
13 Ibid., p. 9.

9
DWORKIN:
philosophical foundations for state neutrality

Ronald Dworkin is regarded by many as the clearest and most forthright advocate of liberal neutrality. In a well-known and oft-cited essay on 'Liberalism', first published in 1978, he argued that the constitutive morality of that doctrine is 'a theory of equality that requires official neutrality amongst theories of what is valuable in life'.[1] Central to liberalism, he maintained, is the idea that the government should treat its citizens as equals; since those citizens disagree in their conceptions of the good life, the government fails to satisfy this condition if it prefers one conception to another. Our introduction to this last part of the book, where we identified Dworkin as a comprehensive anti-perfectionist, should already have sensitized the reader to the variety of issues that this position raises, and it is notable that, in the more recent exposition of his liberalism that we focus on here, he admits to having abandoned his earlier claim that neutrality among theories of the good is essential to it. Rather than being an axiom, he says, such neutrality should rather be regarded as a theorem, something derivable from more basic propositions. In this chapter we will examine the kind of state neutrality that Dworkin continues to argue for, and the comprehensive philosophical doctrine from which that neutrality is now derived.

In explaining the precise nature of Dworkin's comprehensive anti-perfectionism, we shall focus most of our attention upon his 1988 Tanner Lecture – 'Foundations of Liberal Equality' (hereafter *FLE*) – and leave largely unexamined his influential series of articles 'What Is Equality? Parts 1–4', in which he presents his version of liberal equality and develops a liberal interpretation of liberty and democracy that complements it.[2] The justification for this imbalance is simple: we do not have the space to cover every significant aspect of Dworkin's wider project here, and the 'Equality' articles (as their title suggests) are primarily concerned with the distributional questions that we excluded from consideration in our Preface, whereas the Tanner Lecture explicitly confront the issues raised by the matrix that we presented in our introduction to this last part of the book. Nevertheless, certain parts of that series of articles – together with an article called 'Liberal Community' – make direct contact with the themes that are central to the communitarian critique of liberalism; so we will refer to them whenever that seems necessary to give the reader a full and fair picture of Dworkin's position.

Dworkin's philosophical foundations

The strategy of discontinuity

Dworkin begins his Tanner Lecture by outlining his reasons for not following Rawls in defending anti-perfectionist liberalism by purely political means. He calls such a mode of defence 'the strategy of discontinuity', because it involves disconnecting ethics and politics. Since an apparently central liberal political commitment is to toleration of and neutrality between competing ethical ideals, it seems both natural and advisable that liberals should defend that commitment in ways that do not themselves depend upon a particular ethical ideal. We thus appear to be forced into a stance of detachment in politics: we must set aside our most deeply-held convictions about human well-being when in the political arena, and support only those decisions that treat all members of the political community with equal concern. But such detachment and impartiality are entirely alien to the way we live our ordinary lives. As ethical agents, we are thoroughly committed to certain values and ideals, and prone to care a great deal more for some people (family, friends and fellow nationals) than others. Indeed, we value our capacity to do so; being committed, attached and partial is not just how we are, but how we think we ought to be. Since politics is part of living, it seems entirely natural to carry these views forward into political activity. If, for example, we are convinced that certain forms of life are miserable and unfulfilling, why not vote for legislation that will discourage them or make them impossible? A liberalism that disconnects ethics and politics asks us to put our most profound convictions to sleep.

> Liberalism therefore seems a politics of ethical and moral schizo-phrenia; it seems to ask us to become, in and for politics, people we cannot recognize as ourselves, special political creatures wholly different from ordinary people who decide for themselves, in their ordinary lives, what to be and what to praise and whom they love. (*FLE*, p. 202)

In Dworkin's view, this point is the true heart of the communitarian critique of liberalism; although this is often obscured by their invocations of the metaphysics of personal identity, the communitarians are best understood as putting their finger on the apparent conflict between the fundamental political claims of liberalism and our most compelling personal convictions about the character of a worthwhile life. In his view, no defence of liberalism can be adequate that does not in some way resolve this conflict, and thereby reconcile the two perspectives.

Proponents of a discontinuity strategy tackle this problem by arguing that the two perspectives are compatible because the political perspective is *artificial*. It is a social construction that is not founded on any single set of ethical convictions about politics, precisely so that as many people as possible (regardless of their personal perspective) can participate in it; and such general participation is worth securing because benefits not otherwise obtainable (the benefits of social cooperation) will then accrue to all involved. The political perspective of liberalism is thus discontinuous from the personal or ethical perspective in substance but not in motivation; each citizen has good personal reasons for subscribing to the joint project of constructing and occupying an artificial political viewpoint whose terms do not coincide with any particular personal viewpoint.

The difficulty lies in identifying the personal interests or convictions that might give people good reasons to subscribe to this artificial perspective. Two broad options seem available: to invoke self-interest (a citizen's preferences for money, pleasure and security, on the one hand, or her ethical beliefs about what it is for her to lead a good life on the other), or morality (a citizen's beliefs about how she should or must respond to the needs and interests of others). Hobbes, Locke and contemporary games theorists take the first option; Rawls, in Dworkin's view, takes the second. Those who invoke self-interest face the obvious and seemingly insurmountable difficulty of showing that liberal principles of political equality are in *everyone's* self-interest (including all those advantaged by wealth or talents, or convinced of the superiority of their form of life); so Dworkin concludes that the key question is whether all or most of us share convictions that recommend discontinuity on moral grounds.

Clearly, we cannot simply say that our settled moral convictions about fairness entail discontinuity. Ordinary morality distinguishes between legitimate special concerns for particular others and illegitimate discrimination or prejudice against others. We may act unfairly if we give money to white beggars and not to black ones; but we do not act unfairly if we make donations only to charities that support causes and ways of life that we feel are morally superior to others. In short, our idea of fairness reflects rather than excludes the attachments and ideals of the good life; as Dworkin puts it, 'ethics shapes justice' (*FLE*, p. 214); our sense of what morality requires draws on our sense of what a good life is, and most of us think that even after giving *full* effect to morality we are rightly guided, in day-to-day life, by passion and partiality. So how could the same moral principles have such different force in constructing a political perspective?

They could do so only if there is something special about the sphere of politics that might justify the application of special moral principles to it. Perhaps special demands are made on us in our political activities because politics is especially coercive, or involves spending taxes that are collected from everyone. Dworkin discusses two such ways of acknowledging the distinctiveness of the political sphere, ways that have been presented as generating a distinctively liberal vision of politics. The first asserts that every citizen has an obligation, when she acts in ways that seriously affect other people, to observe principles that they could not reasonably reject; the second asserts that every citizen has an obligation, when she acts in ways that seriously affect her fellow citizens, to observe principles that are latent in their shared public political culture and its history. Dworkin associates Rawls only with the second of these lines of argument; but, as we saw in Part II of this book, Rawls also invokes a conception of what a citizen can reasonably reject. In other words, he combines the lines of argument that Dworkin considers separately; so Dworkin's discussion of both is relevant to any assessment of Rawls's turn to the political.[3]

Dworkin's objection to the first line of argument is simple: 'my views about what other people would be unreasonable to reject reflect my convictions about what lives are good or bad just as much as my views about fairness do' (*FLE*, p. 215). If I think that abortion is wicked or that people's wealth should in justice reflect their talent, then I will almost certainly think that it is unreasonable to reject those principles. I may not think people blameworthy for not agreeing with me; but I can hardly think that they have good reason to disagree, that is, that their failure to agree is not unreasonable. The same holds for any parallel version of this line of argument. We might, for example, think that reasonableness involves some consideration of the distribution of burdens imposed by particular policies – perhaps judging that it is unreasonable for me to object to a particular proposed arrangement if any other would be worse for some other person than that proposed is for me. The problem with this kind of argument, according to Dworkin, is that our conception of what counts as a burden will reflect our convictions about what are good and fulfilling forms of human life; if we think that homosexuality is degrading, then we will regard the burdens imposed by laws forbidding its practice as slight in comparison with their benefits.

Dworkin's criticism of the second line of argument is equally fundamental. The idea that latent in the public political culture there is a set of principles that provide the best interpretation of the events that make up its history is something that appeals to him, since it parallels certain arguments he has put forward about how judges might establish and develop the best *legal* principles for a particular community.[4] But he is suspicious of the idea that the same argument can work in the domain of politics, because the history of any political community includes controversy as well as tradition, and so no single set of principles can fit all parts of any community's traditions and history to perfection. In particular, 'two very different political conceptions, which would justify very different controversial political decisions now, might each fit the record and rhetoric of a community's political history roughly equally well' (*FLE*, p. 219).

Of course, one of these two equally good interpretations may win majority support in the political arena; but simply asking which best interprets the political community's public culture will not help to determine the winner. And if we ask instead which offers the more politically attractive interpretation, our answer will not only be controversial, drawing upon ranges of settled conviction not shared by everyone in the community, but will also presuppose some basic sense of what it might be for one interpretation to be more politically attractive than another – a sense that could not therefore be derived from either of the available interpretations, on pain of question-begging circularity. As Dworkin puts it, 'we can only decide which principles are latent when we already have in hand some conception of justice whose categorical force we can defend in some *other* way, as not dependent on or derived from its congruence with the community's traditions' (*FLE*, p. 221).

In short, Dworkin sees insuperable difficulties in the way of any attempt to prosecute the strategy of discontinuity in defending liberal anti-perfectionism. And since he associates Rawls's recent turn to the political with this kind of strategy, he clearly regards political liberalism as vulnerable to his critique. It would obviously be a very complicated matter to judge whether this last conclusion is warranted. Our discussion of *Political Liberalism* suggests that Rawls's most recent position combines elements of both the lines of argument that Dworkin criticizes (rather than just the second, with which Dworkin explicitly associates Rawls); but it also suggests that Rawls's particular version of those lines of argument (in particular, his distinctive conception of the burdens of judgement and the limits of the reasonable) is not obviously vulnerable to Dworkin's critique. As we noted, however, Dworkin bases his interpretation of Rawls upon articles whose publication precedes that of *Political Liberalism*; and he may feel that this book presents a very different position from that advanced in those articles. Pursuing these issues in any detail here is not, therefore, likely to clarify the matters with which we are most concerned. What matters for our purposes is simply this: although it is not at all evident that he has done so, Dworkin believes that his arguments definitively undermine the best available versions of the discontinuity strategy.

The strategy of continuity

Dworkin's alternative defence of anti-perfectionist liberalism employs the strategy of continuity. This strategy aims to construct a liberal ethics – a body of instincts and convictions about the character and ends of human life with which anti-perfectionist intuitions about politics can be seen to be continuous – and then to show that these instincts and convictions already form the central part of how many of us imagine what it is to live well. Such a strategy offers a more integrated, less schizophrenic moral experience, presenting the political perspective as growing from people's more general intuitions about the good life rather than demanding that they be set aside. But if the liberalism it justifies must in some sense be neutral between different conceptions of the good, then this liberal ethics must be abstract. It cannot consist in some detailed description of the good life that is a matter of controversy in the political community; and yet – insofar as it is a *liberal* ethics, an ethical foundation for political anti-perfectionism – it must be sufficiently discriminating to ensure that anyone embracing it will also tend to embrace a liberal political perspective. The general form of Dworkin's solution to the problem is as follows:

> A liberal ethics must have a structural and philosophical rather than substantive character. It must consist in propositions . . . which do not rule out any substantive, detailed conception of a good life likely to be popular in our political community [but which are] sufficiently muscular to form a distinctive *liberal* ethics . . . (*FLE*, pp. 207–8)

Dworkin's comprehensive foundation to political anti-perfectionism is thus philosophical rather than substantive. He is drawing a distinction between two very different sorts of comprehensive doctrine that Rawls tends to run together – on the one hand, a substantive and detailed conception of the good life for human beings, and on the other, a philosophical or metaphysical account of ethical matters. The distinction he appears to have in mind is roughly that between a specific ethical doctrine about how one ought to live and a specific view about matters (such as value, well-being and practical reasoning) that are drawn upon in any ethical doctrine – between a blueprint for the good life and an account of what is presupposed or otherwise drawn upon in articulating such blueprints. By focusing on these foundational or metaphysical aspects of ethics Dworkin hopes to avoid endorsing any particular ethical blueprint; but because they are nonetheless aspects of *ethics* – having to do with such things as how one ought best to conceive the nature of ethical value – he also hopes that establishing certain conclusions in this area will nonetheless allow him to discriminate between certain types of ethical blueprint and certain others on the grounds of their philosophical adequacy. And it is no accident that he thinks of that adequacy as a 'structural' matter; for that metaphor makes plausible what might otherwise appear highly problematic – Dworkin's positing a level of analysis at which he can help himself simultaneously to the benefits of abstraction *and* of discrimination. For just as the structure of a building makes it suitable for a certain range of human activities but not for every such activity, so (the metaphor implies) the structure of ethical value does not uniquely determine an answer to the question of how one should live, but it does place limits on suitable answers to that question.

The Challenge Model of Ethical Value

The philosophical or structural question that Dworkin wants to address is: what *kind* of goodness does a good life have? He begins by distinguishing between volitional and critical well-being. Someone's volitional well-being is improved when she gets whatever she happens to want; her critical well-being is improved when she gets whatever she *should* want. If I happen to dislike dental work, my life goes better, in the volitional sense, when I succeed in avoiding it; but my life would not become a worse life – something to regret or be ashamed of – simply because I suffer occasionally in the dentist's chair or never even develop an interest in avoiding dentistry. My desire for close relationships with my family and friends, however, is very different; I believe not only that my life goes less well if I fail to satisfy that desire, but also that it would have gone less well if I had never even conceived of it. We can, therefore, be mistaken about our critical interests, but not about our volitional interests; it doesn't make much sense to ask someone who gets pleasure from eating vanilla ice-cream whether they really ought to like its taste so much.

Dworkin aims to show that those who care about their critical interests will naturally be led towards a liberal form of political community; and he does so by drawing upon what he calls the challenge model of critical ethical value. This holds that the critical value of a good life lies in the inherent value of a skilful performance of the tasks of living. Dworkin believes that the challenge model fits best with our ordinary intuitions about ethical value, and that a liberal ethics (and so a liberal view of politics) has a serious claim on us because it gives the challenge model appropriate prominence in its conception of what it is to live well.

The first stage of his philosophical or metaphysical argument is therefore to demonstrate that, unlike its rivals – in particular, the impact model, which holds that the value of a good life consists in its product, its consequences for the world – the challenge model can account for our central intuitions about value, has no serious counter-intuitive implications, and can resolve a number of fundamental problems or worries most people have about the nature of ethics. For example: where the impact model implies that our concern over matters that have little or no valuable con-sequences are merely silly or self-indulgent – our interest in having close relations with our children, or in mastering a certain field of learning with no thought of its consequences, for example – the challenge model can think of them as having the inherent value of a skilful performance of a challenging task. The challenge model is not blind to intuitions supportive of the alternative impact perspective: it can accommodate our admiration for the consequential work of great scientists and politicians insofar as we think of inventing a cure for disease or improving the lives of one's fellow citizens as one brilliant way of meeting the challenge life sets us. And because living a life constitutes the most comprehensive and important challenge we face as human beings, our critical interests should be seen as lying in the achievements and experiences that show that we have met that challenge well.

Many of the details of this demonstration, though clearly relevant to an assessment of Dworkin's position as a whole, are of no significance for our purposes. The ways that the challenge model resolves some of these puzzles, however, relate to our central questions of culture, social justice and autonomy and are thus worth more detailed attention.

Transcendence

Are ethical values transcendent or indexed? Are the components of a good life always and everywhere the same, or does what counts as a good life depend upon the context? The fact that critical interests are not simply a matter of what someone happens to want but of what she should want might seem to suggest that these components of a good life are everywhere the same; but it seems no less plausible to hold that ethical standards are in some way indexed to the cultural, biographical and personal circumstances of individuals, that the best life for someone in one situation and period of history may be entirely different from that for someone in very different circumstances.

The challenge model strongly implies that the challenge life poses (and so the value of the response a person makes to it) will vary with circumstances. A life of courtly virtue might be a skilful response to the challenge set by life in medieval France, but not to that set by life in contemporary Chicago. Indeed, part of any life's value will reside in successfully determining what it might be to live well in the particular circumstances one faces rather than simply applying a timeless blueprint to any and all circumstances. Nevertheless, it appears that Dworkin regards the challenge model itself as applicable regardless of context. The substance of a skilful response to the challenge set by life may depend upon the cultural and historical circumstances in which that challenge is faced; but what the challenge model requires of a person – the capacity for a skilful response to life's challenge, the capacity to determine what such a response might be in any given circumstances, and so on – will surely remain invariant, and so any general character traits, talents and abilities that might be required if one is to meet these invariant requirements must also (it seems) possess an importance and value regardless of context.

Justice

Is there any connection between personal well-being and morality? Can an unjust person nonetheless live a good life, or at least a life that has some value? Or is it impossible to flourish if one contravenes the rights of other people or benefits from their being contravened, so that just treatment of others is a necessary condition of well-being?

To answer these questions, Dworkin builds upon a distinction between those circumstances that act as limitations and those that serve as parameters: the former are those that either help or hinder a person in living well, the latter are those that help define what a good performance of living would be for that person. For some people, for example, their nationality is a parameter, being a Briton is part of what makes a particular life the right one for them – it is a condition of the good life for them; for others, it is just a fact, a limitation on their available choices that might be either enabling or disabling, depending upon how they define the challenge their life poses. If the previous argument is right, and ethical value is not transcendent, then some of a person's circumstances *must* be parameters. Otherwise, she would have no idea what the challenge of her life actually is; if all her circumstances were limitations, but she had no circumstance-independent ideal of what it is for her to live her life well, she could give no content to what it is that those limitations sometimes help and sometimes hinder her in doing. But *all* her circumstances could not be parameters, part of what any good life for her must incorporate; for that would mean that life posed no challenges at all – she could successfully face the challenge of living simply by continuing to live. In short, to treat life as a challenge presupposes treating one's circumstances as a combination of parameters and limitations.

Many of those parameters are normative: they specify not our actual situation but our situation as it should be. This means that our lives can go badly not just because we fail to respond properly to our actual circumstances, but because the circumstances that we face are the wrong ones. If the challenge they pose is not the one we should be facing, then no matter how successfully we cope with it, we do not have the same opportunity for success as we would if we had faced the right challenge. For example, we conceive of a human life as occupying a certain span of time (and thus offering the kinds of challenging internal complexity that come with ageing, having to relate to younger generations, and so on); so we think of someone who dies young as having been deprived of the chance of living a fully good life because she has been deprived of certain challenges that she ought to have faced. Parameters can also be hard or soft. Hard parameters state essential conditions: if they are violated, the performance is a total failure regardless of its success in other respects; for example, the formal structure of a sonnet imposes hard parameters on a poet. Violating soft parameters reduces the value of a performance, but does not necessarily annihilate it; an example would be that of dying young – Mozart's life was brilliantly successful despite its brevity.

But if some of our circumstances are normative parameters of living well, on Dworkin's view it is difficult not to regard justice as figuring among them. If so, a good life should neither contain unjust acts nor draw upon unjust shares of resources:

> Certainly resources must figure as parameters in some way, because we cannot describe the challenge of living well without making some assumptions about the resources a good life should have available to it. Resources cannot count only as limitations, because we can make no sense of the best possible life abstracting from its economic circumstances altogether. We must therefore find some suitable account of the way in which resources enter ethics as parameters of the good life, and we have, I think, no alternative but to bring justice into that story by stipulating that a good life is a life suitable to circumstances in which resources are justly distributed. (*FLE*, p. 259)

If we think that people should only have their fair share of resources, we cannot also think that the circumstances that are appropriate in deciding how to live well can be ones in which we have an unfair share. Here, the distinction between the moral (other-regarding) and the ethical (self-regarding) requirements of human well-being simply breaks down. If, in our conception of what the challenge that life sets us ought to be, we specified resource-parameters that either permitted or encouraged us to secure a level of resources that presupposed an unjust social distribution, we would in effect be saying that we ought to want resources that we can have only by acting as we think no one ought to act. If living well means responding in the right way to the right challenge, then a life goes worse when that challenge cannot be faced – and it goes worse ethically, not just morally. So if the resource parameters of a life well lived ought to conform to the requirements of justice, and we find ourselves in a society where resources are unjustly distributed, then those of us who receive an excessive share of those resources are not able to live as well as we could in a different, more justly organized, society. Our lives in those conditions will still go better than those who receive resources below the just level – the rich can can lead a more complex, exciting and challenging life than can the poor; but the injustice from which we benefit nonetheless limits the goodness of any life we lead.

According to Dworkin, Plato's views about justice are an extreme version of this challenge-based interpretation of well-being and justice. Plato's claim that nothing can redeem a life spoilt by the misfortune of living in an unjust state amounts to the view that justice is a hard parameter of ethics; no one can live a genuinely good life by using more resources than they are entitled to have, any more than a poet can produce a good sonnet by adding more lines. But Dworkin's own view is less stark; for him, justice is a soft parameter of ethics. Although no one supported by unjust wealth can fully succeed in living a good life, it is by no means thereby rendered altogether worthless, and it may be very good. This, perhaps, is just as well, since, as we will see shortly, Dworkin believes that we have yet to see a just society; combining Plato's claim about the relation between justice and well-being with Dworkin's view of what justice involves would lead to the unhappy conclusion that nobody had ever lived a life of any value. Indeed, Dworkin goes further, allowing the possibility that someone might live a better life under unjust circumstances than anyone could under just ones; perhaps a painting genius whose career depends upon unjustly wealthy patrons. Nevertheless, such cases seem extremely rare; for Dworkin, Plato was nearly right.

Endorsement

Are the components of a genuinely good life worth having if one fails to endorse them as good? Is someone better off by having the love of others even if she fails to recognize it or to regard it as important to her well-being – what Dworkin calls the additive view? Or is her endorsement of such love as valuable a necessary precondition for it to improve her well-being – the constitutive view? The difficulty is that, whilst we wish to say that a particular life cannot be good for me just because I think it good (that we can make mistakes about what is good), we also want to say that it could not be in anyone's interests to live a life she despises and thinks is degrading (how could such a life be good *for her*?).

For the challenge model, the connection between conviction and value is constitutive rather than additive: my life cannot be better for me in virtue of some feature or component I think has no value. We give no credit to a performer for features of her performance that she was struggling to avoid, or which she would not recognize (even in retrospect) as good; the right motive, intention or sense is necessary for something to be the right performance. And a successful performance cannot be achieved by overriding the autonomy of the performer; an artist has not succeeded in meeting the challenge of producing a great painting if another artist directs her brush-strokes or holds her back from actions that would ruin the painting. Thus, although a proponent of the challenge model may have very strong views about what sort of responses to the challenges posed by life are best, she will not think that a person's forced adoption of that response confers any value on her life. The challenge is directed *at her*, her life goes well if and only if *she* meets that challenge, and she cannot be thought to have met it at all if her responses are determined by the intentions and actions of others.

Dworkin presents this as a question of integrity, and its ethical priority. Part of the challenge with which life confronts us is that of determining precisely what sort of challenge our circumstances represent – which are limitations and which parameters; and it is a parameter of *that* challenge (something without which it would not be the challenge it ought to be) that we determine this for ourselves.

> Ethical integrity is the condition someone achieves who is able to live out of the conviction that his life, in its central features, is an appropriate one for him, that no other life he might live would be a plainly better response to the parameters of his ethical situation rightly judged . . . Giving priority to ethical integrity makes a merger of conviction and life a parameter of ethical success, and it stipulates that a life that never achieves that kind of integrity cannot be critically better for someone to lead than a life that does. (*FLE*, p. 267)

The task is not to live comfortably with whatever convictions one happens to have; living out of conviction requires precisely a commitment to reflection, coherence, self-criticism and openness to the examples of others. I must still live a good life, and not just a life I *think* to be good; but I cannot live a good life if I do not think that it *is* good. So, if a friend chooses a form of life I regard as valueless rather than one I think valuable, then – although I must believe that her living such a life in the full conviction of its rightness is less valuable than her living that other life with similar conviction – I must also believe that her living such a life with integrity is more valuable than her living that other life in the conviction that it is valueless. I can of course try to persuade my friend of her mistake, but the general implication is that we should not attempt to influence either the content or the context of another's ethical choices – except in short-term and non-invasive ways that experience shows are likely to be genuinely endorsed retrospectively. Even if we simply filtered out what we judged to be most damaging or least valuable from the list of possible ways of life that a person faces, in order to increase the chances of her making good choices such paternalism would not improve her chances of living well but seriously damage them; to think otherwise simply confuses parameters with limitations. It assumes that living well means living in whatever way is best, and so interprets the need to identify the best way to live as an obstacle to the main business of ethics; whereas facing the challenge of judging how we should live is in fact a parameter of what it is to live well.

From ethics to politics: the emergence of Dworkinian state neutrality

Of course, the fact that we have summarized the grounds Dworkin offers for accepting the challenge model of ethical value in as favourable a light as possible does not mean that we regard its superiority over its rivals as unquestionable. On the contrary; it should be clear that both its central elements and its overall shape are highly controversial. For example, his claim that justice is a soft parameter for living well embodies an extremely austere conception of human well-being. It means that a properly good life not only must not contain unjust acts, but also must not draw upon unjust shares of resources – no matter how far control over that last matter lies outside the power of the individual concerned, and regardless of the degree of satisfaction and genuine human achievement those resources make possible. More generally, the idea that living well is a matter of skilfully responding to the challenges life sets runs contrary to many highly influential modern conceptions of human well-being – conceptions that give a central role to maximizing utility or want-satisfaction, or that concentrate upon the (individual or social) consequences of human actions. It may be that this controversy serves only to highlight the many ambiguities and complexities hidden within the concept of 'well-being'; but this would only serve to intensify the difficulties involved in establishing the superiority of a single basic model in this area of philosophical endeavour.

Nevertheless, for our purposes we shall simply assume that Dworkin has provisionally established that the challenge model is superior to its rivals as a philosophical account of the nature of ethical value. His next task is to demonstrate that the species of liberalism in politics that he favours develops naturally from any ethical vision that explicitly incorporates, or is at least consistent with, that model. He does so by constructing a thought-experiment: he asks what principles for governing a political community would emerge from deliberations conducted by members of that community whose individual ethical positions differ widely from one another in content but are nonetheless all understood by them in terms of the challenge model. In other words, each deliberator is concerned to advance her own critical interests, her interests in living a life that responds in the right way to her circumstances as they ought to be.

This means that, although Dworkin's general strategy here is strongly reminiscent of that of Rawls, his deliberators are very different from the parties to the original position. First, there are no limitations on the information available to them: they know everything actual people know about their own interests, convictions and situation. And second, they have no *a priori* interest in gaining more rather than fewer of the resources for whose distribution they are seeking to determine principles (as Rawls stipulates with respect to his primary goods). They will of course hope that a just distribution will deliver a larger rather than a smaller share, since that would allow them to lead a more complex and challenging life; but since they accept justice as (at least) a soft normative parameter of well-being, they will only want such a larger share on the condition that it *is* just. Where Rawls derives justice from self-interest only by adding in negotiation and ignorance, Dworkin's understanding of well-being is such that the link between the two is much closer; indeed, justice is part of self-interest.

On Dworkin's view, citizens so conceived would converge upon the version of liberalism that he has elaborated in the series of articles to which we referred earlier. Without going into the details of this position, which its author calls 'liberal equality', we can sketch out its general shape. Liberal equality holds that a just resource distribution is achieved only when the resources different people control are equal in their opportunity costs – that is, the value they would have in the hands of other people. Dworkin utilizes various more or less artificial economic devices to establish what that opportunity cost is, and then requires a redistribution of social resources in accordance with the results. Inequalities in impersonal resources (parts of the environment such as land, raw materials and houses) are rectified by simple transfers, and inequalities in personal resources (non-transferable qualities of mind and body such as talents and health) by a compensatory taxation scheme whose levels are set by calculating the premiums that it would be rational for individuals to pay in order to insure themselves against being disadvantaged to varying extents. Since, however, the opportunity costs of resources depend upon their true value to others, and since that value is fixed by the contribution they would make to achieving those others' most deeply considered and endorsed life-plans, true opportunity costs can only be established insofar as people can develop and give expression to their authentic convictions; and for that, they require liberty. If, for example, certain ways of life were prohibited, any indications of the existence and intensity of citizens' commitments to those activities would be obliterated, and so would the true value of the resources those activities presuppose. Thus, for liberal equality, any invasion of liberty that is not designed to protect just distributions of resources (e.g. laws against theft) is an invasion of equality; the two values stand or fall together.

This version of liberalism in politics is clearly distinctive in several ways – ways that Dworkin sees as being particularly appealing to ethical liberals, wedded as they are to a challenge model of ethical value. We shall highlight those that bear most directly on our concerns.

Equality and partiality

For Dworkin, if those deliberating about the attractions of liberal equality are ethical liberals, the goal of an equal distribution of resources is bound to appeal; for it amounts to ensuring that all members of the political community face the same abstract challenge in this respect. The standard arguments for non-egalitarian distributions of resources would simply have no relevance for them. We could not, for example, argue that inequality would increase the community's overall prosperity, because for an ethical liberal there is no presumption that increased economic resources are in the critical interests of citizens. The same applies to any attempt to justify inequality by appealing to an inherent difference in the worth or value of different groups in the community, proposing a differential distribution of privilege based upon a differential distribution of social status, talent or skin colour. For ethical liberals, this would mean determining in advance for all individuals which of their circumstances and attributes are the core of their ethical status and identity; and this removes from them a central part of the challenge that life poses for individuals – namely, that of deciding just which of their circumstances and attributes they will treat as parameters for, and which as limitations upon, their ethical striving. Such non-egalitarian theories demean ethics by supposing that it is the business of politics, rather than people, to construct the parameters of ethical identity. Just as justice limits ethics, so too does ethics limit justice. 'A scheme of justice must fit our sense of the character and depth of the ethical challenge, and that supports equality as the best theory of justice' (*FLE*, p. 290).

Moreover, this emphasis upon equality does not conflict with our ordinary ethical beliefs in the rightness of discriminating between the virtuous and the vicious, or favouring one's family and friends; on the contrary, it licenses them. If justice is a soft normative parameter of well-being, then whenever its demands are not met, the goodness of our lives (and so the goodness of our ethical practices of partiality) is significantly reduced. But, once its demands have been met, we are morally entitled to use our resources partially if we so wish. No use of my own fair share of resources can make the share of resources received by others any less fair; so my non-political partialities cannot be condemned as even indirectly contributing to injustice. Our natural partiality is not in conflict with egalitarian politics; it is rather in conflict with any other kind.

Tolerance and partiality

Liberal equality specifies that government must not discriminate against any of its citizens on the basis of their ethical position or values. Such a principle of tolerance does not mean that the political liberal cannot be as strongly committed as anyone else in her private life to convictions about the relative superiority of certain forms of life over others; indeed, she can perfectly well continue that private campaign for what she sees as the good into the political arena. But she will not be able to do so by intolerant means, for example, by forbidding someone to lead the life they genuinely regard as good simply because she thinks that it is not good. For her account of justice invokes a conception of equality of resources and circumstances, and the law is clearly one such circumstance – helping to determine the opportunities and limitations to which individuals must respond in attempting to live well. To endorse a law forbidding some to lead the lives that they think best for them simply because others disagree would plainly make citizens' circumstances unequal, and would therefore amount to endorsing injustice rather than establishing it as a normative parameter for the lives of all in the political community. Even if that community homogenously endorsed the form of life she thinks best, it would only be best *for her* if such a circumstance were established and maintained by just means. And since another's life cannot be made better against their steady conviction about what is good for them, coercive political actions of the kind we have been contemplating cannot be thought to serve *others'* best interests either; their convictions are not limitations or handicaps. For the ethical liberal, therefore, the tolerance required by liberal equality does not impose any form of ethical schizophrenia.

Community

On Dworkin's view, although our intuitions strongly favour the idea that what really matters about ethics is that individual lives go well, they also suggest that individual well-being depends at least in part on the critical success of the life of the communities in which individuals live out their lives. On some occasions, he suggests, 'we sense that the most fundamental ethical unit is collective not individual, that the question of whether my life is going well is subordinate to the question whether, for some group of which I am a member, *our* life is going well' (*FLE*, p. 239). This is to consider a more radical fusion of individual and collective concerns than that involved merely in acknowledging that a good life cannot be a selfish life, or that our ethical beliefs are socially conditioned. It is to suppose that the value or goodness of a person's life is to some extent a function of the value of the life of the community in which she lives. Where some have taken this kind of argument in perfectionist directions – arguing that this licenses state action to ensure an ethically healthy rather than degenerate community – Dworkin's claim is that it is quite consistent with his own anti-perfectionist conception of liberal equality.

Dworkin accepts that political communities have a life with which the lives of its citizens are integrated, that the critical success of any of their lives is an aspect of, and so dependent upon, the goodness of the community as a whole, and so that citizens must be as concerned for the well-being of their community as they are for their own. This is because the political community can be what he calls a 'unit of agency' – an entity held responsible for actions, some of which importantly affect the well-being of its citizens; in particular, citizens can share in the ethical success or failure of community actions in which they have played no direct personal part. When a nation-state wages an unjust war, it is the political community that does so; and its moral failure is the failure of all its citizens – even those who actively oppose it. But this ethical integration is not based on a baroque metaphysics, in which communities are ontologically fundamental; rather, those communities are constituted by human social practices and attitudes. An orchestra has a collective life because its members recognize a personified unit of agency in which they figure as components; its life consists in the musical activities they treat as constituting its collective life. That collective life accordingly has limits: 'the communal life of a community includes only those acts treated as collective by the practices and attitudes that create the community as a collective agent'.[5]

The collective life of a political community is similarly limited. That life is manifest in its legislative, judicial and executive actions – actions widely identified as those of a distinct legal entity, performed by individuals deliberately acting in the name of that entity, and affecting the lives of all its citizens. It does not, for example, have a collective sexual life: our social practices do not recognize national sexual actions, individual sexual acts are not performed in its name, and citizenship criteria are not sexual;

moreover, no sub-group can create such a life simply by declaring it to exist. To be sure, there may be other communities that do have a collective sex life in the relevant sense. But the national political community is defined in terms only of its formal political life, and accepting the ethical priority of *this* can happily be combined with a liberal conception of the form its life should take: we simply specify that, for all the reasons outlined above, success at political decisions requires liberal tolerance and neutrality about the good life. We are right to care that our political collective life goes well, but there is nothing in this idea to threaten liberal values.

Dworkin and communitarianism

We are now in a position to offer a critical assessment of Dworkin's comprehensive anti-perfectionism, by relating it to our agenda of issues. We can, we trust, be brief, for many of the points have already emerged in our exegesis. By way of introduction, it is worth noting that Dworkin's approach does not allow him to respond to some communitarian criticisms of liberalism in the way available to Rawls – namely, by denying their relevance. This is implied by his recognition that the heart of the communitarian critique is its justified concern about the kind of schizophrenia that liberalism seems to involve, for it is this recognition that leads him to stress his own rejection of the liberal strategy of discontinuity. Whereas Rawls's belief that his liberalism is purely political allows him to deny that he is committed to any of the ethical, metaphysical and philosophical doctrines that communitarians have attributed to his theory of justice as fairness, Dworkin's strategy of continuity deprives him of any such room for manoeuvre. He must rather show that the specific comprehensive conception of ethical value upon which he founds his political liberalism does not embody or imply any of the views upon which the communitarians have concentrated their critical fire. Since, however, we showed in chapter 6 that many responses to communitarian objections were available to Rawls even before he shifted to his distinctively political brand of liberalism, we should not, in this context, overstate the differences between the two theorists; under various headings there need be no incompatibility between what Rawls and Dworkin could say to a communitarian critic, and in that sense some of the responses here may overlap with, or at least complement, those that we identified in our earlier chapter. The differences are most significant on the issues of universalism and, of course, neutrality.

Conception of the person

Since the decision procedure for political justice that Dworkin relies upon is importantly different from that of Rawls's original position, he cannot be accused of cleaving to the conception of the person that communitarians claim to find embedded in the original position. In particular, since he does not employ any version of a veil of ignorance, he cannot be accused of presupposing that individuals are antecedently individuated, or distinct from their social and personal particularity, or capable of detaching themselves from their conceptions of the good. On the contrary, Dworkin explicitly endorses several of the points utilized by communitarians to criticize the conception of the person that they attribute to Rawls. For example, he is happy to concur with Sandel's claim that people are constituted as individuals by attachments to particular communities, for some of those attachments must be parameters rather than limitations:

> My biological, social and national associations, those I was born with or fell into, not those I chose, seem obvious candidates to me, though they may not to others. The fact that I am a member of the American political community is not a limitation on my ability to lead a good life . . . It rather states a condition of a good life for me . . . (*FLE*, p. 255)

Nonetheless, for Dworkin it is up to the individual to decide which of her circumstances are parameter and which limitations:

> For ethical liberals, living well includes – begins in – trying to answer that question, and the question assumes that the challenge of living is more abstract than the challenge of living in any particular role. It obscures and demeans the stark challenge of ethics, the categorical force of the imperative to live well, to locate its source in anything more contingent than our being persons to live with. (*FLE*, pp. 289–90)

Dworkin would not accept, then, Sandel's view that our ends are discovered though neither is he willing to accept the stark alternative that they are voluntarily chosen:

> Liberal equality does not assume that people choose their beliefs about ethics any more than their beliefs about geography. It does suppose that they *reflect* on their ethical beliefs and that they choose how to behave on the basis of those reflections. (*FLE*, p. 295)

Even in the case of those decisions that we find we have made automatically, without reflection, we can force ourselves to think about whether we have made the right one, though we cannot review them all simultaneously, and Sandel is wrong to think that liberals think that we can.

Asocial individualism

Dworkinian liberalism not only does not endorse, but explicitly denies, asocial individualism in both of the forms we distinguished. First, the challenge model of ethical value conceives of the challenge faced by individuals as importantly determined by the particular array of social and cultural options with which their historical context presents them and, as we just noted, Dworkin is happy to regard some of those circumstances as parameters of individual well-being: recall Dworkin's observation that different kinds of life will count as skilful responses to the challenges of medieval France and contemporary Chicago. He can therefore happily accommodate the claim that the social matrix is an important source of an individual's conceptions of the good. He has, moreover, no problem in acknowledging the existence of communal goods, whether at the sub-political or political level. Indeed, since justice is a parameter of well-being, an essentially communal good is central to any proper liberal understanding of human flourishing. This is the significance of Dworkin's insistence on the point that his anti-perfectionist liberalism provides the proper way to achieve that integration of individual and community that communitarians have accused it of neglecting. The integrated liberal, for Dworkin, will not

> draw a sharp line between what justice requires of him and the critical success of his own life . . . he will count his own life as diminished – a

less good life than he might have had – if he lives in an unjust community, no matter how hard he has tried to make it just. That fusion of political morality and critical self-interest seems to me to be the true nerve of civic republicanism, the important way in which individual citizens should merge their interests and personality into community. It states a distinctly liberal ideal, one that flourishes only within a liberal society.[6]

Universalism

Dworkin's position on this issue is complex. On the one hand, the challenge model regards ethical value as essentially indexed to historical, cultural and social contexts, and so as varying across time and space – 'living well, judged as a performance, means . . . living in a way responsive and appropriate to one's culture and other circumstances' (*FLE*, p. 250). This goes along with his recognition of the priority of the social matrix. But, on the other, he does not appear to regard either the challenge model itself or the specific conception of politics that grows from it as being context-specific. Although the specific challenge life poses is historically and culturally variable, that human life should be conceived as posing one or another sort of challenge is not; it is rather the essential core of our best available philosophical account of the nature of human well-being and ethical value. Nor is there any hint in Dworkin's presentations of liberal equality that its political principles are historically limited in their application; understood as a vision of the ideal polity, they may be Utopian in the sense of being impossible to attain in their full perfection, but they do appear to function as a goal towards which all political communities should strive.

Subjectivism/objectivism

Dworkin explicitly distances himself from any taint of subjectivism about ethical value. The challenge model is committed to a constitutive view of value, and so to the idea that no one can live well unless they genuinely think that their form of life is good: 'no component may even so much as contribute to the value of a person's life without his endorsement' (*FLE*, p. 237). But it does *not* claim that someone's thinking that a given form of life is good is enough to make it good. Its notion of critical interests entails that what a person happens to want is not necessarily what she ought to want, that convictions should be the result of critical reflection rather than the simple endorsement of an existing schedule of preferences.

> How far and in what way does my having a good life depend on my thinking it good? We make no sense of ethical experience except on the supposition that these are objective: a particular life cannot be good for me just because I think it is, and I can make a mistake in thinking a particular life good. (*FLE*, pp. 262–3)

Anti-perfectionism and neutrality

Though it does not use the term, liberal equality is a species of what we are calling anti-perfectionism. It is committed to tolerance and an insistence that

> government must be neutral in ethics in the following sense. It must not forbid or reward any private activity on the ground that one substantive set of ethical values, one set of opinions about the best way to lead a life, is superior or inferior to others. (*FLE*, p. 228)

Although no longer regarding political neutrality as a methodological axiom, it still hopes to arrive at neutrality in the course of the argument. But, as we indicated in our Introduction to this last part of the book, the very fact that Dworkin relies upon a philosophical account of the nature of well-being suggests that there is a distinct kind of neutrality, political-theoretical rather than political, to which he need not and cannot lay claim. Unfortunately, as we will now explain, things are not that simple. In the first place, Dworkin does claim something like this second kind of neutrality for his theory, under the label of 'neutrality of appeal', although he does so in a rather half-hearted way. And, furthermore, there are grounds for suspecting that he does not altogether comply with his own understanding of the requirement that the state be 'neutral in operation' as between the conceptions of the good espoused by its citizens.

Let us begin with the second of these two concerns. There are, of course, clear limits on the kind of neutrality that Dworkin claims for his liberal state. In the standard disclaimer, he recognizes that liberal equality is not neutral in effect or consequences, for some forms of life – most obviously expensive ones – will be more difficult to lead in a society of liberal equality. Nor is it neutral with respect to ethical ideals that directly challenge its conception of justice; in particular, it is not neutral about what he calls third-person ethics, for it insists on the proposition, denied by some citizens, that another's life cannot be made to go well by coercive paternalism. But it does claim to be neutral in operation as between first-person ethics; to be neutral, that is, as between its citizens' views about what kinds of life are valuable for themselves (except in those cases where a person's conception of what is good for her involves her treating others unjustly).

It is when dealing with the issue of whether the state can support the arts that Dworkin seems to violate his own understanding of the sense in which the state should be neutral in operation. As we have seen, he argues that ethical liberalism, being committed to the value of individual integrity, cannot endorse any form of paternalism that involves filtering the choices available to people, for that bowdlerizes the challenge that life poses them by removing the specific challenge of making their own decision about which of their circumstances are limitations and which parameters. However, he immediately qualifies this in a footnote, claiming that

> That does not mean that the government has no responsibility for the cultural background against which people decide how to live. A sensible answer to the question of normative parameters might well insist that citizens should choose against a background that includes opportunities and examples that have been thought to be part of living well by reflective people in the past and that are part of a cultural heritage . . . It might also insist that, consistently with the requirements of justice, the right background requires collective decisions about which lives to promote or recommend as better, particularly when popular culture presses the other way and so provides too few examples of those lives . . . [N]othing in my argument here denies that a state that has fulfilled the requirements of justice can properly use public funds to support art that the market will allow to perish, on the substantive ground that art improves the value of lives available in the community. (*FLE*, p. 272 n. 44)

How might Dworkin reconcile this with his earlier insistence on neutrality in the passage cited above? There are, as he makes explicit, two distinct arguments here, and we will consider them in turn.

The first, involving the idea that the government is responsible for the culture within which people make their choices, is developed most fully in an earlier article – 'Can a Liberal State Support Art?'. In it, Dworkin distinguishes between two consequences culture has for citizens:

> It provides the particular paintings, performances and novels . . . that we value and take delight in; but it also provides the structural frame that makes aesthetic values of that sort possible . . . We should try . . . to define a rich cultural structure, one that multiplies distinct possibilities and opportunities of value, and count ourselves trustees for protecting the richness of our culture for those who will live their lives in it after us . . . We can . . . insist – how can we deny this? – that it is better for people to have complexity and depth in the forms of life open to them . . .[7]

For Dworkin, preserving the richness of our cultural structure is not an objectionable form of paternalism because it does not entail endorsing or condemning specific options within the structure, or forcing anyone to make particular choices within it; and it does not aim to create or forestall specific preferences that are identified in advance as good or bad. 'On the contrary, it allows a greater rather than a lesser choice, for that is exactly the respect in which we believe people are better off with a richer than a poorer [culture]'.[8] On this argument, the art-supporting state is not judging that a life involving art is better than one which does not, but rather that any life goes better when an individual's decisions about how to live are made against a rich and complex background of options rather than an impoverished one. No one committed to the challenge model of ethical value could easily deny this; how could maintaining or increasing the variety and sophistication of the choices available to people do other than enhance their ability skilfully to perform the task of living? And since all those choosing political principles in Dworkin's 'original position' are, by hypothesis, committed to the challenge model, a principle requiring state support of cultural structures is likely to receive unanimous endorsement.

This argument depends on interpreting the cultural 'richness' to which Dworkin refers in a value-neutral way; it assumes that we can distinguish between rich and impoverished cultures by means of criteria (such as complexity or multiplicity) which do not involve us in judging the relative worth of the specific options they embody. Even so, of course, it is not without its problems. There may, for example, be great practical difficulties involved in its implementation. Dworkin suggests that the culture-supporting state might avoid discriminating between particular artworks and art forms by offering tax exemptions for donations to any cultural institutions; but this will only ensure a rich and complex culture if the relevant donors choose to support diversity and innovation. In fact, however, it is far from clear that the value-neutral interpretation of cultural richness is what Dworkin has in mind. For his formulation of the argument explicitly suggests that the background culture should contain those opportunities and examples that have been thought to be 'part of living well' by reflective people in the past; and this implies that he cannot define what he means by a 'rich and diverse' culture without invoking past judgements about the worth of specific cultural products. If so, then he cannot even specify his avowed aim without implicitly endorsing evaluations of a kind concerning which he appears to claim neutrality. Such an implicit endorsement could not therefore be regarded as one more perfectly legitimate instance of liberal neutrality having non-neutral effects or consequences; for this implicit endorsement is not an effect or consequence of implementing Dworkin's avowed aim of supporting cultural richness and diversity – it is rather an essential component of it.

This last suspicion is that Dworkin cannot prevent judgements about the intrinsic value of different forms of life from entering into the decisions a state will make when acting so as to preserve the right kind of cultural structure. That such judgements can indeed play a role in politics is explicitly accepted by his second argument, which allows that a state may support art 'on the substantive ground that art improves the value of lives available in the community'. *Prima facie*, this looks to be in straightforward contradiction with Dworkin's commitment to neutrality. Even assuming that the demands of justice are met before this support is given, if the government's reason for supporting art with public funds is that its availability improves the lives of its citizens, it must surely be relying on a judgement about the relative value of lives that include art-related activities and those that do not.

The way to avoid this apparent contradiction is to note that Dworkin's objections to cultural paternalism are always formulated on the assumption that it involves *either* the narrowing of options, as if the point of such paternalism were to reduce the possibility of someone choosing a worthless form of life, *or* a coercive forcing of culture on people. Both of these are inconsistent with the challenge model: the former because a challenge cannot be more interesting or valuable when it has been narrowed in advance, the latter because nothing can improve the critical value of a life unless it is seen as an improvement by the person whose life it is. But there is nothing in these arguments that makes the *provision* of valuable ways of life incompatible with the challenge model of value. On this account, then, there is a crucial asymmetry between a state's filtering out ways of life because they are bad and its supporting them because they are good, and so there is a kind of 'cultural paternalism' that is perfectly consistent with his brand of liberal neutrality.

Dworkin expands on this point in the following passage.

> The challenge model does not rule out the possibility that the community should endorse and recommend ethical ideals not adequately supported by the culture. Nor does it rule out compulsory education and other forms of regulation which experience shows are likely to be endorsed in a genuine rather than manipulated way, when these are sufficiently short-term and non-invasive and not subject to other, independent objection. All this follows from the central, constitutive role the model of challenge assigns to reflective or intuitive judgement. (*FLE*, p. 273)

The difficulty here lies in seeing just how the role assigned to judgement by the challenge model justifies such endorsement of specific, ethically substantive, ideals and constraints. The challenge model tells us that a central part of living well is being free to decide on the basis of one's reflective judgement which way of life is right for us. But why can such judgement only be properly exercised in a cultural context which includes options and regulations that have been deemed valuable in the past (even if they are not adequately supported now), or that experience shows to be the likely object of genuine endorsement? Clearly, if people are to employ their judgement at all, there must be a range of options that is sufficiently wide to provide scope for its exercise; but this doesn't provide an argument for the state to ensure that this range includes specific options that have been, or are, deemed more valuable than others which might also die out in the absence of state support.

A further problem with this account of Dworkin's argument is that, although it certainly seems consistent with some of the formulations that he employs when defining the kind of neutrality that he requires of his liberal state, it sits far less happily with others. For example, when attempting to articulate worries that are very naturally raised by a liberal commitment to state neutrality of the kind that he endorses, Dworkin constructs a series of rhetorical questions:

> Why should a majority not be able to enforce its ethics through the criminal law, as it enforces its other convictions of policy? And if there are reasons why it should not use the criminal law in that way, why should it not enact legislation that would improve ethical consciousness in other, less coercive, ways? (*FLE*, p. 229)

If justified in the manner outlined above, it can be argued that state support for a society's cultural structure does not amount to a coercive imposition of culture on its citizens; but it is difficult to deny that it nevertheless constitutes a less coercive way of improving its citizens' ethical life and consciousness – a policy of just the kind against which Dworkin implicitly sets his face in this quotation. And this raises a fundamental worry, not just about Dworkinian state neutrality, but about liberal anti-perfectionism in general: if (as both Dworkin and Rawls appear to believe, although for very different reasons) it really is consistent with such policies as state support for culture, just how substantial a kind of neutrality does it embody?

We have been careful to make it clear that liberal anti-perfectionism need make no claims to certain kinds of neutrality – neutrality with respect to the realm of value in general, neutrality as between liberalism and other views of politics, neutrality of effect or outcome. If, however, the species of state neutrality to which it must lay claim – a neutrality of justification for state actions – is interpreted in such a way as to permit state support for background culture (and so to permit the state, implicitly and indirectly but

ineluctably, to endorse past and present judgements of the relative
value of various ways of life), then it becomes increasingly difficult
to detect a clear dividing line between anti-perfectionist and
perfectionist varieties of liberalism. Note that this is not a purely
semantic worry. It is not generated by our choice of terminology, or
by our choice of categories for constructing the matrix we
introduced earlier; it is a substantive worry about the clarity and
the rigour of a commonly made distinction between those (anti-
perfectionist) liberals who advocate a state which justifies its policies
in ways that are in some sense neutral between competing
conceptions of the good, and those (perfectionist) liberals who
reject any such neutrality. It is a worry to which we shall return in
chapter 10, when we examine Raz's perfectionist liberalism – in
which we shall see deployed a line of argument in favour of state
support for background culture that is remarkably similar to the one
we have hypothetically attributed to Dworkin.

So much for the suspicion that Dworkin's state is not as neutral in
operation – or as anti-perfectionist – as he sometimes suggests. What
of the other dimension of neutrality – what does Dworkin mean by
claiming that his theory has 'neutrality of appeal', can that claim be
sustained, and does it matter?

What he means in claiming neutrality of appeal is that all of its
principles can be accepted by people from a very great variety of
ethical traditions. For its political anti-perfectionism is based on a
comprehensive conception of ethical value (the challenge model)
that is suffcently formal and abstract to be widely acceptable, and
yet muscular enough to deliver liberal equality as the conception of
politics with which it is most deeply congruent. For Dworkin, the
challenge model is as much a philosophical as an ethical
commitment. It provides a meta-ethical conception of the nature of
ethical value, and so might in principle be compatible with a wide
variety of blueprints for the good life rather than simply embodying
one such blueprint; a religious believer and someone committed to a
life of unconventional sexual variety might both treat their
convictions as views about the most skilful performance of living.

However, as Dworkin explicitly admits, 'the challenge model
captures and organizes only some of the intuitions people have
about ethics, and . . . has implications that many people have
certainly not accepted' (*FLE*, pp. 298–9) – the idea that justice is a soft
parameter of well-being being one obvious example. The model

cannot therefore be thought of as something to which everyone (or almost everyone) is already committed. So Dworkin retreats to a weaker claim – that ethical liberalism could be generally accepted without people having to abandon what is most important to them.

> [T]he challenge model captures intuitions which almost everyone has about ethics. It captures them in a more satisfactory way than rival views about the nature of ethical value do, and it resolves puzzles and dilemmas in these intuitions that they cannot; the model should appeal to people for that reason. (*FLE*, p. 300)

In other words, Dworkin is arguing, not that everyone already cleaves to the challenge model, but that everyone should do so. He believes that his philosophical analysis of the foundations of ethics provides him with arguments sufficiently strong to give grounds for thinking that most people would, on reflection, come to accept that analysis. This is the reason for his optimistic assessment of the 'consensual promise' of the challenge model and hence liberalism in politics.

Even if we share his optimism, however, it is difficult to see how his assessment amounts to anything other than the claim that accepting ethical liberalism is eminently reasonable, and so that those who persist in rejecting it must eventually be regarded as unreasonable. But if so, it is no longer clear how Dworkin's defence of liberal equality differs from one variant of the liberal discontinuity strategy that he condemned so decisively at the outset – that which deploys a conception of 'the reasonable' in defending its vision of politics. Dworkin therefore appears vulnerable to his own earlier critique of that strategy – namely, that it invokes a conception of 'the reasonable' that is inevitably substantive rather than abstract or neutral in the manner required by anti-perfectionist liberalism.

Furthermore, he might then in turn be vulnerable to a broadly Rawlsian counter-charge against those who defend liberalism by comprehensive means. For if the challenge model is not universally held and cannot accommodate all of our intuitions about ethical value, then to aim for its universal adoption is to propel oneself into arguments about ineliminably controversial matters of ethical substance, and to establish political institutions that presuppose its truth in the absence of its universal adoption would amount to coercing those who refuse to accept it. From this critical viewpoint, it

might therefore be argued that Dworkinian anti-perfectionism could
end by violating one if its most fundamental principles – that one
cannot and should not try to improve another's life by forcing her to
go against her will and her convictions.

Notes

1 'Liberalism', p. 203.
2 Dworkin's Tanner Lecture is most readily available in the collection
   Equal Freedom, edited by Stephen Darwall. All page numbers refer to this
   collection.
3. It will be clear from the publication dates that the critique of Rawls by
    Dworkin that we are sketching here was formulated in response to the
    sequence of articles that preceded *Political Liberalism* rather than to the
    position presented in that book. It may be that Dworkin would regard
    Rawls's later statement as presenting a position different from that
    which is attacked here. The introduction to *Political Liberalism* acknow-
    ledges Rawls's debt to Dworkin for many conversations between 1987
    and 1991, most evocatively for 'a rare illuminating midnight conversa-
    tion in the deserted bar of the Santa Lucia Hotel in Napoli' (*PL*, p. xxxi).
4. Dworkin is as well-known for his work in legal theory as he is for his
    contributions to political philosophy. See *Law's Empire* for a full
    statement of his views in this area.
5 'Liberal Community', p. 212. Page reference is to version in Avineri and
   de-Shalit (eds).
6 'Liberal Community', p. 219.
7 'Can A Liberal State Support Art?', p. 229.
8 'Can A Liberal State Support Art?', p. 230.

10

RAZ:

the politics of perfection

Our chapters on Rawls's political liberalism indicated various senses in which his conception of justice as fairness might be regarded as communitarian; and our investigation of Dworkin's argument from an ethics of challenge to an anti-perfectionist liberal state revealed him also to have the means to accommodate or reject as misguided a number of communitarian objections. In this our final chapter we consider the political philosophy presented by another theorist, Joseph Raz, in his book *The Morality of Freedom* (hereafter *MF*) which will also be seen to combine, though in quite different ways, strands of liberal and communitarian thought.

Raz is a perfectionist liberal. Where Rawls thinks that there are good reasons why we should exclude from our consideration of fundamental political questions reasons emanating from those comprehensive doctrines that guide our private lives, and Dworkin holds that a correct understanding of the nature of ethical value implies that the state should be (largely) neutral between the first-person conceptions of the good espoused by its citizens, Raz argues that it is legitimate for the state to seek to promote the well-being of citizens in a way that involves it in the business of judging the value of particular ways of life. For Raz

it is the goal of all political action to enable individuals to pursue valid conceptions of the good and to discourage evil or empty ones. (*MF*, p. 133)

If not a political philosophy that seeks a neutral state, what makes Raz's perfectionism nonetheless *liberal* is his claim that, at least in modern societies, a good life must be an autonomous life: a person's well-being depends on her being the maker or author of her own life and on the availability to her of a multiplicity of valuable options. In attempting to sever the connection between liberalism and anti-perfectionism or neutrality whilst keeping autonomy and moral pluralism central, Raz effects a synthesis of his own that transcends the opposition between liberalism and communitarianism.

Raz can, then, be regarded as differing from Rawls over questions of neutrality in both of the ways distinguished in our introduction to this part of the book. Along the political-theoretical axis, he shares with Dworkin the feature of grounding his liberalism in what Rawls regards as a comprehensive ethical ideal. Indeed, Raz is deeply suspicious of the Rawlsian distinction between the political and the non-political and quite ready to defend his political philosophy by appeal to a thick and controversial conception of personal well-being. As he says, near the beginning of his book:

> Influential voices among political theorists argue for the existence of a relatively independent body of moral principles, addressed primarily to the government and constituting a (semi-) autonomous political morality. The critical evaluation of such views is one of the main tasks of this book. Their rejection means that the positive conclusions argued for in the book concerning the morality of political freedom are based on the considerations of individual morality to a greater degree than is common in many contemporary works of political philosophy. (*MF*, p. 4)

He differs further from Rawls, however, and differs also from Dworkin, along the substantively political dimension; his understanding of personal well-being is of such a kind that it permits the state to make, and to embody in its laws, perfectionist judgements, judgements about the relative value of different ways in which people might lead their lives. There is, for Raz, no reason why the state should exclude from consideration those reasons that lead people in their personal lives to judge some way of life better, and worse, than others. In a phrase, Raz's liberalism is perfectionist and not exclusionary.

This further feature of Raz's position makes him an excellent way to conclude our introduction to the debates between liberals and communitarians. Where Rawls's liberalism is communitarian precisely in being anti-perfectionist, fundamental political decisions having to exclude, for the sake of a community that is publicly justifiable, reasons arising from controversial understandings of how people should lead their non-political lives, Raz's perfectionist liberalism connects with the communitarian criticisms in rather different, but equally interesting, ways. It is partly because Raz recognizes the dependence of the individual's personal well-being on the social forms available to her in her society that Raz advocates his perfectionism, so discussion of his position brings out, more clearly than we have been able to so far, aspects of what is at stake in the debate between liberals and communitarians.

A brief disclaimer: *The Morality of Freedom* is a long and difficult book, and one that addresses, in a highly sophisticated manner, a wide range of issues in political philosophy. We do not, in this chapter, pretend to do justice to the variety and complexity of argument to be found in it. Our presentation of Raz's ideas will necessarily be selective and, at least when compared with his own meticulous articulation of them, somewhat superficial. Our selection will inevitably be informed by the reading of the background themes and debates which we have presented heretofore. Thus, for example, in seeking to identify only those strands of argument of most immediate relevance, we all but ignore his important and influential discussion of political authority. And even within the bounds set by our particular area of concern, we aim to do no more than indicate the bare outline of his position; for example, we gloss over his distinction between neutral political concern and anti-perfectionism, regarding, for our purposes, the two as equivalent. There is an unavoidable trade-off between clarity or accessibility on the one hand and precision or complexity on the other, and we are happy to acknowledge that, for the purposes of this book, we value the former qualities above the latter. If, by presenting Raz's ideas in a relatively introductory way, we can encourage the reader to take up his own more advanced exposition of them, we shall have achieved our aim.

Raz's perfectionist autonomy

At the heart of Raz's theory is a conception of autonomy; *prima facie,* this might suggest that he should advocate an anti-perfectionist state. After all, how can the decisions that individuals make about how they should live be genuinely autonomous if the state is using its coercive power to back up its own judgements as to the relative merits of the different choices they might make? For Raz, this argument misunderstands the nature of autonomy and what is valuable about it:

> the autonomy principle is a perfectionist principle. Autonomous life is valuable only if it is spent in the pursuit of acceptable and valuable projects and relationships. The autonomy principle permits and even requires governments to create morally valuable opportunities, and to eliminate repugnant ones. (p. 417)

This understanding of autonomy, and its implications for the legitimate role of the state, means, of course, that a great deal more is up for political grabs than would be the case on a strictly anti-perfectionist view. Where the latter can dismiss as irrelevant to politics judgements about which ways of life are better or worse than others – however depraved or ennobling particular conceptions of the good may be, the state has no business acting on such assessments – the perfectionist liberal has to get involved in substantive debate on precisely such matters. She has to argue, at least in certain circumstances, not only for the value of the individual's freedom to make her own choice but also for the value of the choice that she makes.

We shall begin to expand on these introductory remarks by identifying Raz's negative arguments against anti-perfectionism – his reasons for rejecting the view that we should exclude ideals from politics. Perfectionism, he maintains, does not have three worrying implications that it might appear to have. First, allowing controversial ideals into politics does not necessarily mean that the beliefs of some are being allowed to overrule the beliefs of other. Second, perfectionist politics do not necessarily involve the coercive imposition of styles of life by some groups upon others. Finally, permitting governments to act on reasons that arise from ideals does not necessarily imply a rigoristic moral outlook, in that it does not mean that all but one morally approved form of life will be suppressed. Presentation of these negative points will of course involve us in the articulation of Raz's more positive articulation of a perfectionist liberalism based on autonomy and pluralism.

Ideals *qua* valid not *qua* beliefs: perfectionism against scepticism

The anti-perfectionist liberal thinks that the validity of a moral ideal is not a reason for the state to act on it, that the state should exclude moral considerations arising out of perfectionist ideals, even where that ideal is valid. One way in which the motivation for such exclusion is sometimes put is that, since people disagree over the validity of such ideals, the state is failing to treat its citizens with respect if it takes them into account. Raz's response is quick:

> Is one treating another with respect if one treats him in accordance with sound moral principles, or does respect for persons require ignoring morality (or parts of it) in our relations with others. There can be little doubt that stated in this way the question admits of only one answer. One would be showing disrespect to another if one ignored moral considerations in treating him. (MF, p. 157)

Such a response might seem *too* quick. The anti-perfectionist intuition may be that people's beliefs about how they should live their lives are worthy of respect purely in virtue of being their beliefs, and it is this respect for the moral opinions of her fellow citizens that leads this kind of liberal to exclude even valid ideals from politics. Allowing controversial ideals into politics necessarily involves, it would appear, allowing the beliefs of some citizens about how people should lead their lives to overrule the beliefs of others. Since people have different beliefs about what makes a life valuable, it might seem that the only way to treat them with respect is to constrain the state to exclude such beliefs from its policies.

This way of formulating the anti-perfectionist case, that people's beliefs have moral status simply *qua* their beliefs, brings us to an aspect of Raz's liberalism that coincides with elements in the position put forward by Dworkin in the previous chapter. For Raz, a person's well-being does not depend upon her living the life that she believes to be of value, it depends upon her living a life that is valuable for reasons independent of her belief in its value. It is indeed the case that, as for Dworkin, for a life to be valuable it must be consciously endorsed by the person living it, and, as we shall see must, at least in modern conditions, be autonomous in the sense we shall discuss below; but it does not follow that any life that is consciously endorsed and autonomous is thereby endowed with value. On the contrary, for Raz 'a person's well-being depends on the value of his goals and pursuits' (*MF*, p. 298), and not, we may add, on her belief in their value. It is perfectly possible for a person's belief about the worth of her conception of the good to be mistaken, and, if it is, we do not respect her, nor promote her well-being, by ignoring the fact.

The fundamental point here is the reason-dependent character of goals and desires.

> A person who spends all his time gambling has, other things being equal, less successful a life, even if he is a successful gambler, than a live stock farmer busily minding his farm . . . The reason is that they engage in what they do because they believe it to be a valuable, worthwhile activity (perhaps but not necessarily because of its value to others). They care about what they do on that basis. To the extent that their valuation is mistaken it affects the success of their life. (*MF*, pp. 298–9)

People pursue goals for reasons, because they believe that they are valuable. If they are mistaken, if they are acting in accordance with beliefs that lack (good) reasons, then they are not living successful lives. 'Satisfaction of goals based on false reasons does not contribute to one's well-being' (*MF*, p. 301). And once we admit that some ideals are valid and some are not, that there are (good) reasons for pursuing some ideals and none for pursuing others, and acknowledge that a person derives no well-being from a life spent in pursuit of the latter, then it will look as if we have little reason to respect a person's mistaken belief in the validity of an invalid ideal.

Perfectionists do not have to argue that it is justifiable for the beliefs of some to overrule the beliefs of others, for perfectionist ideals may enter politics not because people believe in them but because they are valid; they are supported by true reasons, they correctly identify a valuable form of life. As Raz puts it:

> the fact that the state *considers* anything to be valuable or valueless is

no reason for anything. Only its being valuable or valueless is a reason. If it is likely that the government will not judge such matters correctly then it has no authority to judge them at all. (*MF*, p. 412)

This way of presenting the point brings out the extent to which Raz's perfectionist liberalism rejects any form of moral subjectivism or scepticism, and it is important therefore that we should make clear that perfectionist conclusions do not necessarily follow from this rejection. After all, as we have already seen, Dworkin too holds that 'a particular life cannot be good for me just because I think it is, and I can make a mistake in thinking a particular life good' (*FLE*, pp. 75–6), and Rawls likewise insists that his political liberalism does not imply scepticism about the truth (or falsity) of the various comprehensive doctrines the validity (or invalidity) of which it must not presuppose. The fact that both argue nonetheless for a state that is in certain important senses neutral as between the lives favoured by its citizens shows that other bits of theoretical baggage – Dworkin's challenge model or Rawls's liberal ideal of public justifiability – can reconcile an anti-perfectionist state with the rejection of scepticism. Nonetheless, we believe that scepticism of various kinds is sufficiently central to other, perhaps less theoretically self-conscious, kinds of anti-perfectionist thinking as to make this point worthy of elaboration.

It is clear, as we argued in our introduction, that the liberal cannot coherently regard all moral judgements as mere expressions of subjective opinion. She must at least regard as objectively valid the judgement that people should be free to make up their own minds about how they live their lives. What we are considering here is the thought that one reason for the objective judgement that people should be free to live the way of life that they choose is the claim that such choices themselves lack objective foundation. There is, then, for someone espousing this form of liberalism, a distinction between two kinds of moral judgement: judgements about the good life, which are subjective and should be kept out of politics, and judgements about the rights and duties that people have and that should govern their relations with one another, which are objective and are properly protected and enforced by the coercive apparatus of the liberal state. Raz is deeply suspicious of the idea that these two types of judgement are different in this way:

is there reason to think that one is more likely to be wrong about the character of the good life than about the sort of moral considerations which all agree should influence political action such as the right to life, to free expression, or free religious worship? I know of no such arguments. (*MF*, p. 160)

In fact, as we shall see later, Raz is suspicious of the whole distinction between what he calls 'morality in the narrow sense', which is meant to include 'only all those principles which restrict the individual's pursuit of his personal goals and his advancement of his self-interest' and 'the art of life', on the other, which consists of 'the precepts instructing people how to live and what makes for a successful, meaningful, and worthwhile life' (*MF*, p. 214). Our specific concern here is his claim that we should be no more sceptical with regard to judgements that concern the art of life than with regard to those that concern, for example, the rights of others. If Raz is right to think that we can be as sure that the life of a livestock farmer is better than that of a gambler as we can that people should be free to worship the religion of their choice, then he removes an important motivation for anti-perfectionism. Taken in combination, his rejection of scepticism in matters concerning the art of life and his claim that a person's well-being depends on the value of the goals she pursues lead strongly in the direction of the conclusion that the state should be allowed, and perhaps even required, to act on judgements as to what makes a life meaningful or valuable. Strongly, but as Rawls and Dworkin show, not decisively.

Sceptical doubts of a different kind may remain, however, and, because they form distinct motivations for anti-perfectionist politics that have played a significant role in the liberal tradition, they warrant attention here. Even if there is no reason in principle why judgements about the art of life are more likely to be wrong than judgements about people's rights and duties, might we not think that governments are not to be trusted to get them right? Perfectionist ideals should be kept out of politics, the role of government should be limited to that relating to morality in the narrow sense, not because we cannot not know which ideals are valid but because we cannot expect governments to act on those which are. Scepticism about how politics works might be more persuasive than philosophical scepticism.

Quite apart from the practical worry that governments may be corrupt, the theoretically important issue here is that those whose judgements as to the validity of ideals determine what the government does may, however well-intentioned, make mistakes. As Raz says:

> it is possible that the appeal of anti-perfectionism is at least in part indirect. There is no way of acting, politically or otherwise, in pursuit of ideals except by relying on the judgment of some people as to which ideals are valid and imposing it on others who disagree. Those whose views are imposed on the community do not regard the fact that they hold those views as a reason for their imposition on others who reject them. They maintain that their conception of the good is valid and that is the reason which justifies its imposition. But such an action is constitutionally justified on the ground that the rulers, the majority, etc. chose to act in that way, regardless of the truth or soundness of their views. (*MF*, p. 158)

Once we recognize that, whatever the philosophical justifiability of perfectionist politics, what actually happens is that the beliefs of some overrule the beliefs of others, and that such beliefs may be wrong, we may feel that Raz's arguments have somehow missed the point.

Raz's theory of authority, the essence of which (that it is only if the government is likely to make correct judgements that it has the authority to judge at all) we have already glimpsed in passing, may seem rather to beg than to answer the question. But one way of rendering Raz's position plausible is simply to note that exactly the same worries apply to those moral judgements that the anti-perfectionist does think are proper within the realm of politics. Those who decide what rights people have, whether they be democratic majorities or constitution-founding elites, may be wrong too, so the 'argument from the possibility of mistake' must apply there also. The tempting way to resist the implication that either states should act on all moral judgements or that they should act on none is to claim that some kinds of judgement are more likely to be right than others, but we have already seen that Raz rejects this view.

Raz recognizes the force of these worries. While holding that governments can play a more positive role in helping their citizens to achieve well-being than would be allowed by the anti-perfectionist liberalism, he cannot disguise the dangers inherent in the concentration of power in few hands, the dangers of corruption, of bureaucratic distortions and insensitivities, of fallibility of judgment, and uncertainty of purpose, and the . . . insufficiency and the distortion of information reaching the central organs of government. (*MF*, p. 427)

Taking considerations such as these into account, he acknowledges, may well mean that people should be freer from governmental action than is implied by the 'pure' theory he outlines. Our point, and the reason to emphasize this acknowledgement, is simply that such impure considerations have been influential in the motivation for anti-perfectionist liberalism.

The same is true of what Raz calls another 'regrettable source of political freedom', and it is with this that we shall conclude this part of our presentation of his argument. Although, as we saw, Rawls's anti-perfectionism does not value agreement on pragmatic grounds, as the only way to avoid social conflict between groups who disagree about conceptions of the good, this line of thought can indeed lead in the direction of anti-perfectionist conclusions. Raz sees this:

> The pursuit of full-blooded perfectionist policies, even of those which are entirely sound and justified, is likely, in many countries if not in all, to backfire by arousing popular resistance leading to civil strife. In such circumstances compromise is the order of the day . . . [which] will confine perfectionist measures to matters which command a large measure of social consensus . . . (*MF*, p. 429)

Given adverse circumstances, where the implementation of policies based on perfectionist ideals, however valid, would lead to civil strife, there are good reasons to exclude those ideals from politics. Here again we see that Raz acknowledges the force of considerations which have provided a great deal of the motivation for the view that the state should keep out of the business of judging how its citizens should lead their lives. Here the fear is neither that governments will be wicked nor mistaken, it is that their well-intentioned implementation of sound perfectionist policies may be counter-productive.

Not coercive imposition

The second thought supportive of anti-perfectionism that Raz rejects is that which sees it as necessary to prevent the coercive imposition of styles of life by some groups upon others. This neatly breaks down into two distinct components, the idea that perfectionist politics must be directed by some groups against others and the idea that it must be coercive. For Raz, both of these involve confusion.

With respect to the first, it simply need not be the case that perfectionist political action seeks to get one or more groups to conform to the ways of life of another.

> Perfectionist political action may be taken in support of social institutions which enjoy unanimous support in the community, in order to give them formal recognition, bring legal and administrative arrangements into line with them, facilitate their use by members of the community who wish to do so, and encourage the transmission of belief in their value to future generations. In many countries this is the significance of the legal recognition of monogamous marriage and prohibition of polygamy. (*MF*, p. 161)

It would seem to be crucial for this part of Raz's argument that the social institutions in question really do enjoy unanimous support. If any group of people in a political community practises polygamy rather than monogamy, for example, then legal recognition of the latter but not the former will indeed look like an attempt to get some to live the way of life favoured by others. While we have already seen that Raz has reasons why this may indeed be justified (if, that is, a monogamous life is indeed more valuable than a polygamous one – something which Raz himself does not assert), it is important to note that these are quite distinct from the point he is making here.

Raz's remarks about the possibility of unanimity take us back to the problem we identified in Rawls's position, which argues for anti-perfectionism via the desirability of a political community that is publicly justifiable. As we pointed out, and as Raz's example shows, these two aspects of his position can come apart. While it may be 'reasonable' for people to disagree about how they should live their sexual lives, there is no reason why such disagreement should be regarded as inevitable and permanent. In some societies, Raz claims, there is unanimity on the value of monogamy. If a particular non-political ideal, such as monogamous marriage, enjoys unanimous support in a society, then it looks as if it can be justified publicly, without appeal to any controversial doctrine and, in that case, Rawls would seem to have lost the reason to exclude this particular perfectionist consideration. Either Rawls's anti-perfectionism is circumstantial, applicable only if and to the extent that people disagree, in which case he can have no objection to the kind of perfectionism proposed by Raz here, or his commitment to the freedom of the individual to live the life of her choice without any kind of interference from the state is not in fact grounded in the desire for public justifiability.

The second anti-perfectionist confusion is the view that state 'interference' which the perfectionist is prepared to countenance must involve coercion. For Raz,

> not all perfectionist action is a coercive imposition of a style of life. Much of it could be encouraging and facilitating action of the desired kind, or discouraging undesired modes of behaviour. Conferring honours on creative and performing artists, giving grants or loans to people who start community centres, taxing one kind of leisure activity (e.g. hunting) more heavily than others are all cases in which political action in pursuit of conceptions of the good falls far short of the threatening popular image of imprisoning people who follow their religion, express their views in public, grow long hair, or consume harmless drugs. (*MF*, p. 161)

Indeed, the previous example of legal recognition of monogamous marriage can also be used to show that there can be perfectionism without coercion. After all, the state does not force people to get married, and it can support marriage in many ways without criminalizing polygamy.

Later in the chapter we shall see that Raz thinks that some reasons can justify coercive action by the state, and a fuller discussion of this issue will have to wait until then. Here it may be helpful just to make a couple of introductory observations on the simple point that he makes here. The essence of his argument, which is surely right, is that there is a big difference between locking a person up if they perform (or fail to perform) certain actions, and using taxation or subsidy to discourage (or encourage) their performance of those actions. The former involves coercion in a way that the latter does not, and, since Raz's central value is autonomy, which seems straightforwardly to require the absence of coercion, it is not hard to see why this difference is important to him. Granted that a distinction between these two kinds of state action can be made, however, it is worth pointing out the issues raised by any attempt to do so, if only because they allow us to see why an anti-perfectionist might object even to the apparently innocuous non-coercive action which Raz endorses.

In the first place, it is undeniable that taxation and subsidy involve the deliberate alteration of the costs and benefits attaching to particular actions, and this already suggests a couple of problems. To begin with, it would seem that the obvious way to think about the concept of coercion is in terms of the deliberate attaching of a sanction or penalty to a particular action: 'If you do not cut your hair, we will send you to prison' would seem to be a paradigm example of a coercive threat. What is the difference, the anti-perfectionist might ask, between this, which Raz acknowledges to be coercive, and the statement 'If you do not stop hunting, the state will tax you heavily', which he argues is not. Clearly, the penalty for non-compliance is greater in the first case than in the second, but it is not obvious that this is a difference of quality rather than of quantity, that it warrants calling one coercion and the other not. Raz discusses at length the question of what makes a threat coercive, and we do not mean to suggest that he has no answer; it is our purpose only to alert the reader to the fact that there is an interesting issue here.

In addition to this, however, even if we allow that we can distinguish between coercive and non-coercive sanctions, this will not save taxation and subsidy from conflicting with the anti-perfectionist intuition that *any* deliberate alteration of the costs and benefits attaching to particular actions invades autonomy. The easiest way to see this as a distinct point is to consider cases of subsidy rather than taxation, since it is hard to argue that *reducing* the costs of an activity can amount to coercion. The thought here is that the state's decision to subsidize the arts, for example, while clearly not coercive, nonetheless involves an interference with people's choices, the introduction of deliberate bias into the options from which people choose to make their lives, which contravenes respect for their autonomy. If a life with art is more valuable than one without, should not people make this judgement for themselves, without artificial incentives to live one rather than another? The suggestion is that, even if not coercive, subsidy and taxation involve manipulation. If they do, then Raz concedes that they would be autonomy-invading:

> Manipulation, unlike coercion, does not interfere with a person's options. Instead it perverts the way that person reaches decisions, forms preferences or adopts goals. It too is an invasion of autonomy ... (*MF*, pp. 377–8)

We have already seen why Raz thinks that respect for citizens cannot require that the state should ignore moral considerations in its dealings with them. But the idea that citizens are shown more respect, are better able to exercise their capacity for autonomy, if they are left to make up their own minds, without interference, about the value of different ways of life than if they make their choices in an environment biased by the state's judgements is not absurd.

In the second place, there is the crucial point that all state action involves taxation and taxation is compulsory. Even if we grant that perfectionist state action need not be *used* coercively, but merely to promote particular valuable ways of life, the fact is that the money used to do the promoting has been *raised* coercively. In the last resort, the penalty attaching to non-payment of taxation is imprisonment, so what happens when the state decides to tax some activities and subsidize others is that it is using its coercive power to enforce its judgements about the relative merits of different activities. We shall see later that Raz acknowledges this, and argues that taxation, since compulsory, is only justified where coercion is so. For now the point is simply to be clear that the state's encouragement of artistic pursuits does involve coercion, even though, of course, nobody is forced to go to the theatre.

Raz's claim that the state can encourage, facilitate or discourage particular ways of life without coercively imposing (or prohibiting) them, is a point that we saw also to be crucial to Dworkin's argument for why his liberal state can act to support the kind of cultural structure in which people face the right kind of challenge. Although we pointed to various difficulties of interpretation and substance in Dworkin's position, it is clear that, on any reading, it is only because such action need not involve coercion that it does not immediately subvert the idea of people choosing for themselves that lies at the heart of the challenge model. This implies that the objections we have been considering in this discussion of Raz – those concerning the coercive nature of taxation and the manipulative aspect of the state's altering the environment within which individuals make their choices – apply equally to Dworkin also. But it also indicates that Raz's point, which is regarded by him as revealing that a plausible objection to perfectionism does not in fact apply, can be turned around and used by those with anti-perfectionist leanings to justify certain kinds of state action that might otherwise seem unacceptable. The fact, if it is one, that state interference aimed at altering the context within which individuals make their choices does not involve coercion enables Raz to allay certain fears about perfectionism; but it also gives Dworkin what he needs to claim that state action to promote the right kind of cultural structure is consistent with the kind of neutrality to which he aspires.

Autonomy and value pluralism

The third and final notion that might lead one to endorse anti-perfectionism and that Raz rejects is the idea that perfectionism implies that the state will be permitted to give its approval to one, morally approved, style of life, and suppress all others. Perfectionism, it might seem, goes together with a rigoristic moral outlook that holds one particular set of ideals to be valid and requires government to promote that set alone, suppressing the ideals held by those who are not in power. For Raz, on the contrary, perfectionism is consistent with moral pluralism, which allows that 'there are many morally valuable forms of life which are incompatible with each other' (*MF*, p. 161). The anti-sceptical claim that some conceptions of the good are valid (and some are not) does not mean that only one set of ideals is so. We can know that the life of an artist is valuable and that of a foxhunter is not without knowing that the former is the only valuable form of life. If there are many valuable ways of life, then the state can be perfectionist and pluralist.

Here Raz's negative arguments against anti-perfectionism overlap with the more positive articulation of the concept of autonomy that lies at the heart of his liberalism. We have already seen his view that autonomy is only valuable if it is exercised in pursuit of the good, and we will see shortly that it requires only the availability of morally acceptable options. It is important now to see what this does not imply:

> This may sound a very rigoristic moral view, which it is not. A moral theory which recognises the value of autonomy inevitably upholds a pluralistic view. It admits the value of a large number of greatly differing pursuits among which individuals are free to choose. (*MF*, p. 381)

In contrast to the view that what matters is just that people choose for themselves how they live their lives and not what they choose, Raz's claim that autonomy is only valuable if exercised in pursuit of the good might seem to warrant state interference, even if not coercion, in support of a single set of options, a single conception of what makes life valuable. What rules out this implication is the relation between autonomy and pluralism.

Raz's discussion of value pluralism contains many different strands of argument, and our focus on its relation to autonomy picks out one of these in particular. It is important to acknowledge this because the strand on which we shall concentrate presents the case for pluralism in rather an unusual form. A more straightforward and direct line of argument would claim that there are many incompatible valuable forms of life, and that it follows from this that a state concerned to promote the valuable autonomy of its citizens has no reason to favour any particular one. While his chapter on the incommensurability of values does present an argument with this general shape, the particular train of thought we shall look at here seeks to establish a more distinctive position. The more usual argument allows him to reach his pluralistic conclusion but it regards the claim that a life is only valuable if it is in pursuit of a valid ideal that has been autonomously chosen, and the claim that there are many conflicting such ideals, as quite separate. The peculiar and particularly interesting feature of the argument we shall outline here is the way it seeks to establish an internal relation between these two claims. As he puts it:

> if autonomy is an ideal then we are committed to such a view of morality: valuing autonomy leads to the endorsement of moral pluralism. (*MF*, p. 399)

His conception of autonomy seems to presuppose the truth of moral pluralism, not merely to be compatible with it.

The crucial step in Raz's argument is the claim that a person's life can only be autonomous and valuable if the person living it has a variety of morally acceptable options to choose from. If this is right, then it follows that if valuable autonomy is to be possible then moral pluralism must be true. It is relatively unproblematic to see why a person cannot be autonomous unless they have choices to make. 'The ruling idea behind the ideal of personal autonomy is that people should make their own lives' (*MF*, p. 369) and it is hard to see how someone who has only one option available to her can be thought of as fitting this description. But it should be clear that the mere availability of options is not sufficient to establish Raz's claim, for this would be satisfied by a situation in which a person has a variety of options from which to choose but only one of them is a good one, which is exactly what the monist, the person who thinks that there is only one valuable way of life, asserts, and exactly what Raz is arguing against.

To understand why Raz thinks that autonomy requires a choice between *good* options we need only to see that he regards the choice between good and evil as no choice at all. Someone with the choice between becoming an electrician and having to murder someone is not choosing autonomously if he chooses to become an electrician, for his choice is forced. If he is to be moral, then he has no choice. Just as autonomy cannot be achieved by a person whose every thought and action is concerned with avoiding death, with the fight for physical survival, so it cannot be obtained by a person who is constantly fighting for what Raz calls 'moral survival' (*MF*, p. 380).

This argument is so simple that it resists any elucidation. What is happening here is that Raz is further enriching his ideal of autonomy, and further distinguishing it from any thin notion, of the kind we might associate with anti-perfectionism, such as the individual's mere capacity to choose for herself how she lives her life. Not only is autonomy only valuable in pursuit of the good, it is only autonomy if a plurality of valuable options are available, so that the agent is choosing between goods. The thickness of Raz's ideal autonomy ties in with our observation about the unusual structure of his case for pluralism, for the more controversial that ideal, the more surprising it is to find an argument for pluralism that takes its validity as a premise. Raz's argument says that if autonomy, thickly understood, is to be possible, then value must be plural. Just as the anti-perfectionist may reject the claim that autonomy is only valuable in pursuit of the good, so the monist may simply deny that autonomy in Raz's strong sense is possible. We do not at all mean to suggest that either would be right to do so, our point is just that a lot of work is being done by the notion of autonomy. Here, as we have seen, it is spelled out in a way that not only renders it compatible with value pluralism but presupposes that doctrine. That is why, first appearances to the contrary, Raz's perfectionism by no means warrants the state seeking to promote a particular way of life above all others.

Autonomy, social forms and state perfectionism

The arguments so far are negative in the sense that they are intended to show why perfectionism does not have some of the counter-intuitive implications that would tell against it. The general thrust of the previous section has been to argue that the state *can*, contrary intuitions notwithstanding, be justified in acting in pursuit of perfectionist ideals. This raises the question of why the state *should* act in such ways, and it is to this aspect of Raz's position that we must now turn our attention. It is here that the communitarian strands in that position come to the fore: in arguing that personal well-being depends to a large extent on social forms, Raz accommodates the communitarian insistence on the priority of the social matrix to the individual. It is by adding to this the claim that political action is needed to ensure that such forms are and remain available, that he turns it into an argument for state perfectionism. We shall also see, at the end of this section, that Raz's recognition of the importance of social forms leads him rather further in a communitarian direction than might have been expected: autonomy, he argues, is only of value to people living in certain kinds of society, those whose social forms are such that they are based on individual choice. In order to keep things as clear as possible, we shall not in this section attempt to point out in any detail the various ways in which Raz's liberalism relates to the communitarian critique. Rather we shall defer a full discussion of Raz's communitarian leanings until our final section, and concentrate here upon that aspect of his argument which links his recognition of the importance of the social matrix to the case for state perfectionism.

Well-being depends on social forms

The reasons for Raz's claim that

A person's well-being depends to a large extent on success in socially
defined and determined pursuits and activities (*MP*, p. 309)

can best be approached by dividing it into its two component sub-
claims. First, that well-being depends importantly upon success in
one's comprehensive goals, and second, that comprehensive goals
must be based on social forms of behaviour.

Comprehensive goals are, for Raz, the goals that people have the
ramifications of which pervade important dimensions of their lives,
those that provide the structure within which their lesser goals are
nested, that provide their life with overall shape and orientation. If
he is right to think, roughly speaking, that a person's well-being
consists in the successful pursuit of her (valuable) goals then it is
easy to see why success in her comprehensive goals (assuming they
are valuable) will be the major source of her well-being. It is hard to
characterize this conception of well-being, itself a notoriously
slippery concept, except by regarding it as occupying a kind of
middle ground between two diametrically opposed views, one of
which holds that a person's life can go well even if they are not
content in their situation, even if they do not willingly accept the
goals set for them, the other of which that holds that something is
only valuable for a person if it seems so to them. If we accept that
when we consider a person's well-being we are considering how
good or successful her life is from her point of view, then it would
seem clear that this is a question of how she is doing in relation to
the (valuable) goals that she has set herself. If I decide to devote my
life to becoming a concert pianist, in such a way that it becomes a
comprehensive goal for me, then it seems plausible to hold that my
well-being depends, at least in large part, on my success in the
venture.

It is the claim that

a person can have a comprehensive goal only if it is based on existing
social forms, i.e. on forms of behaviour which are in fact widely
practised in his society (*MF*, p. 308)

which most clearly brings Raz's position into contact with some of the communitarian strands of argument which we have looked at. He presents two kinds of reason in support of it. First, there is the point that the significance of individual behaviour depends on the existence of social forms. While this is most obvious in the case of activities which directly involve social institutions – 'one cannot pursue a legal career except in a society governed by law, one cannot practise medicine except in a society in which such a practice is recognized . . .' (*MF*, p. 310) – the idea that what my actions *mean* depends necessarily upon the social or cultural practices and conventions that surround them embraces less thoroughly institutionalized areas also. Although any sighted person in the vicinity of birds can watch them, this does not make him into a bird watcher. To be that he must live in a society that recognizes bird watching, or something like it, as a leisure activity, that which has certain attitudes to nature, and so on. What it means to be a bird watcher depends upon the inevitably social environment of significance that surrounds the activity of watching birds. Comprehensive goals, those that pervade important dimensions of a person's life, are inevitably going to be bound up with, perhaps straightforwardly to instantiate, social forms in this way.

Not only do the activities of individuals derive their meaning from society, but also, and this is Raz's second point, individuals can only acquire and maintain goals through continuous familiarity with social forms. We learn how to be parents, or friends, not through any process of explicit instruction, indeed the conventions governing appropriate behaviour in specific friendship contexts, for example, are too dense to be codified, but through an ongoing process of participation in and observation of the social form of friendship. Micro-sociologists who study the minutiae of personal interaction tell us, what we already know but leave unspoken, that the development of a relationship between two people depends upon the significance of thousands of tiny bits of body language. As Raz says:

> All these are derived from the common culture, from the shared social forms, and though they receive the individual stamp of each person, their foundation in shared social forms is continuing and lasting. Just as the eye continues to guide the hand all the way to its target, and is not limited to determining its original trajectory, so our continued

awareness of the common culture continuously nourishes and directs our behaviour in pursuit of our goals. (*MF*, p. 312)

Raz can hardly be accused of grounding his liberalism in an asocial individualism of the kind to which communitarians object.

It is important to see that there are two things which Raz is not claiming. First, he is very clear that his argument for the dependence of personal well-being on social forms is 'not a conventionalist thesis. It does not claim that whatever is practised with social approval is for that reason valuable' (*MF*, p. 310). We should have expected him to take this position: just as a person can be wrong about what is good for her, and her belief in the value of a goal does not make it valuable, so the same is true of societies. Second, the fact that a person's comprehensive goals will necessarily be derived from social forms does not mean that there is no place for deviation from, or even transcendence of, existing conventions. His thesis that comprehensive goals are inevitably based on socially existing forms is meant to be consistent with experimentation and with variations on a common theme, and sometimes these may be so extensive as to constitute real innovation.

It is not that a person cannot, through the development of his own variations and combinations, transcend the social form. People can, and sometimes do, do this, but inevitably in such cases the distance they have travelled away from the shared forms is, in these cases, the most significant aspect of their situation. It more than anything else then determines the significance of their situation and its possibilities for those people. (*MF*, pp. 312–13)

Deviations from social forms always derive their meaning from the matrix of meanings in which they are embedded, a matrix that is itself necessarily social. Although the individual is not bound by existing practices, nor can she only live a valuable life if she goes along with them, she cannot escape the social web of significance.

Since, as we saw above, autonomy requires the availability of a variety of valuable options, and since, as we have just seen, valuable options depend in large part on social forms, it follows that autonomy requires the existence of a variety of social forms. If Raz is right, then the liberal ideal of individual autonomy is nothing like as individualistic as it seems:

autonomy is only possible if various collective goods are available. The opportunity to form a family of one kind or another, to forge friendships, to pursue many of the skills, professions and occupations, to enjoy fiction, poetry, and the arts, to engage in many of the common leisure activities: these and others require an appropriate common culture to make them possible and valuable. (*MF*, p. 247)

We can, without getting into the details of Raz's understanding of what makes a good 'collective' and his more general rejection of what he calls 'moral individualism', see the general thrust of his position. Since 'the provision of many collective goods is constitutive of the very possibility of autonomy' (*MF*, p. 207), we are a long way indeed from any form of liberalism that builds upon the abstract individual and neglects the role of the community in providing the conditions necessary if individuals are to live valuable lives.

Even things as apparently individualistic as rights are given a communitarian defence. First Raz rejects the idea that people have a right to autonomy:

> A right to autonomy can be had only if the interest of the right-holder justifies holding members of the society at large to be duty-bound to him to provide him with the social environment necessary to give him a chance to have an autonomous life. Assuming that the interests of one person cannot justify holding so many to be subject to potentially burdensome duties . . . it follows that there is no right to personal autonomy. (*MF*, p. 247)

For Raz, as we have just seen, collective goods are constitutive of the very possibility of autonomy, yet no individual can have a right to collective goods, for that would imply implausibly onerous duties. It follows that no individual can have the right to autonomy.

Rather than being tied to an individualistic picture of the relation between the individual and society, however, rights should be conceived and defended in terms that relate to their contribution to the public culture. Raz argues

> that the liberal tradition is not unequivocally individualistic, and that some of the typically liberal rights depend for their value on the existence of a certain public culture, which their protection serves to defend and promote . . . [T]heir role is not in articulating fundamental moral or political principles, nor in the protection of individualistic

personal interests of absolute weight. It is to maintain and protect the fundamental moral and political culture of a community through specific institutional arrangements or political conventions. (*MF*, p. 245)

In contrast to the asocially individualistic liberal scheme, which would see rights such as freedom of expression, association and assembly, of the press and of religion, as grounded ultimately in the freedom of the pre-social individual, Raz holds that these rights are really justified as helping to promote goods that are inherently social, such as the good of an open society. For him, 'The importance of liberal rights is in their service to the public good' (*MF*, p. 256).

Social forms require perfectionist political action

Granted that personal autonomy requires the availability of an adequate range of acceptable options and that such options depend necessarily upon social forms, how does this justify state perfectionism? Raz's answer is that the state must do what it can to ensure that its citizens live autonomous lives and that perfectionist political action is needed to sustain those social forms necessary for autonomy. It is the duty of the state to promote the well-being of its citizens, and without state action there will not be the social preconditions of such well-being. Here, then, we have in effect two quite distinct claims, one a normative argument concerning the proper role of the state, what the state is permitted to do for its citizens, and one an empirical claim concerning the necessity of its doing it.

On the first, the point about political action is that it involves coercion, and Raz is quite prepared to acknowledge this. Although, as we saw, Raz is keen to point out that perfectionist goals need not be pursued by the use of coercion, that the government can encourage activities by non-coercive means such as subsidy and advertisement, he at the same time recognizes the point that we made earlier:

It is no objection to point out that the funds necessary for all these policies are raised by compulsory taxation. I assume that tax is raised to provide adequate opportunities, and is justified by the principle of

autonomy in a way consistent with the harm principle . . . The
government has an obligation to create an environment providing
individuals with an adequate range of options and the opportunities
to use them. The duty arises out of people's interest in having a
valuable autonomous life . . . A tax which cannot be justified by the
argument outlined here should not be raised. (*MF*, pp. 417–18)

For Raz, coercion is justified as long as it is used to enforce the duty
to provide people with the conditions of autonomy, for then it will
be consistent with the harm principle. We shall now see what he
means by this.

According to Raz, we all have autonomy-based duties, duties to
provide one another with the conditions of autonomy, and the state
is justified in using coercion to enforce these duties, for, and here we
again glimpse his theory of authority, it is then only discharging on
our behalf obligations which we have in any case. There are three
kinds of condition of autonomy and correspondingly three kinds of
duty. It is relatively straightforward to see that in order to be
autonomous people need to be independent, to be free from coercion
and manipulation, and this leads to the standard liberal duty to
refrain from coercing and manipulating others and the standard
justification of state action to ensure that we do so. To this Raz adds
two further conditions and duties. First, there are those conditions
which he describes as 'mental abilities'. We all have duties to

help in creating the inner capacities required for the conduct of an
autonomous life. Some of these concern cognitive capacities, such as
the power to absorb, remember and use information, reasoning
abilities, and the like. Others concern one's emotional and imaginative
make-up. Still others concern health, and physical abilities and skills.
Finally, there are character traits essential or helpful for a life of
autonomy. They include stability, loyalty and the ability to form
personal attachments and to maintain intimate relationships. (*MF*, p.
408)

The second additional condition of autonomy we have already
touched on in our discussion of the relation between autonomy and
pluralism: for Raz a person cannot be autonomous unless she has
available to her an adequate range of valuable options. This gives
rise to an autonomy-based duty to create for all people an adequate
range of valuable options from which to choose.

There are, then, three kinds of condition of autonomy, three kinds of autonomy-based duty, and three kinds of reason why the state might be justified in using coercion. For Raz, and contrary to appearances, these do not contravene the traditional liberal view, famously formulated by Mill and usually referred to as the 'harm principle', which asserts that the only justification for coercively interfering with a person is to prevent harm to others. Once we see that one can harm another by denying her what is due to her, that someone who fails to fulfil his autonomy-based obligations towards another is harming her, even if the obligations are designed to promote her autonomy rather than to prevent its deterioration, then:

> It follows that a government whose responsibility is to promote the autonomy of its citizens is entitled to redistribute resources, to provide public goods and to engage in the provision of other services on a compulsory basis, provided its laws merely reflect and make concrete autonomy-based duties of its citizens. If the law reflects autonomy-based duties then failure to comply harms others and the harm principle is satisfied. (*MF*, p. 417)

The state can coercively enforce people's autonomy-based duties to provide one another with the conditions of autonomy and this is consistent with the harm principle properly understood.

It may be helpful to point out a possible difference between the first two kinds of condition (or duty) and the third: the former can be argued to be consistent with anti-perfectionism, as not involving the state in judgements about the relative merits of different ways of life, in a way that the latter cannot. This is obvious in the case of the duty to refrain from coercion or manipulation, but applies also to the provision of the mental capacities necessary for autonomy. The advocate of autonomy who rejects Raz's view that it is appropriate for the state to act on judgements as to the relative merits of different forms of life might nonetheless think it proper for the state to provide people with whatever they need to make their own choices. One does not have to be a perfectionist to support taxation for health care and education, one need only hold that physical and mental health, and the capacity to acquire, process and rationally reflect upon information, are conditions of an agent's being able to make genuinely autonomous choices. Similarly, it is quite usual for the anti-perfectionist to advocate redistributive taxation on the grounds that autonomy requires a certain level of control over material resources. In principle, there is no reason why she should not recognize that autonomy requires other abilities also: perhaps, for example, one can only make an autonomous choice between two courses of action if one has the capacity to imagine what it would be like to choose each course. What is crucial about all these cases, however, is that here the state is using coercion to provide people with the conditions of autonomy without making any judgements as to the value of particular options which people might choose.

Of course, Raz's particular list of the inner capacities necessary for autonomy might well be disputed by the anti-perfectionist. It might be argued that, by including, for example, particular character traits such as loyalty, he so enriches or thickens the concept of autonomy as to obscure the distinction between the conditions of choosing and proper objects of choice. For Raz of course, since there is no reason to make that distinction, this is not a problem, and we may well feel that the very recognition that not just any choice can count as an autonomous one already sets the anti-perfectionist on a slippery slope which leads unavoidably to a rejection of the distinction with which she started. While the anti-perfectionist might seek to argue that the state can support the arts purely on the grounds that they promote the capacities necessary for people to make autonomous choice and without making the perfectionist judgement that people choosing to go to art galleries or theatres are making better choices than those frequenting casinos, that the arts come in, along with education, solely as providing people with what they need to make their own autonomous choices in a neutral framework, we might have doubts about whether such a position can be sustained. Since there is clearly here the judgement that a life with the arts is better than one without, what reason do we have to deny that theatre-going is more valuable than gambling?

Whatever one's conclusions on such matters, it is the third condition and coercively-enforceable duty which is most clearly distinctive of Raz's approach, and it is here that we can begin to think about our second question, that which concerns whether it is necessary for the state to act if people are to have the conditions of autonomy. While the anti-perfectionist need perhaps have no problem with the idea of taxation for health, education, and even straightforward redistribution of resources, and can acknowledge that the state must tax for these reasons if its citizens are to be autonomous, it looks as if she is committed to resisting the idea that the state can use its coercive power to provide people with an adequate range of valuable options, for that necessarily involves the state in the business of acting on judgements as to which options are valuable. We saw in our discussion of his views on the support for the cultural structure that a sophisticated advocate of a qualified brand of state neutrality like Dworkin might seek to justify such a role for the state, so we should not perhaps be too ready to assume such a commitment; though we also stressed that it was not altogether obvious either what Dworkin's argument was or how it could ultimately be rendered consistent with other aspects of his position. But it is clear in any case that Raz has in mind perfectionist action different in kind from, and argued for rather more directly than, that envisaged by Dworkin. Raz's empirical claim is thus crucial:

> Supporting valuable forms of life is a social rather than an individual matter. Monogamy, assuming that it is the only morally valuable form of marriage, cannot be practiced by an individual. It requires a culture which recognises it, and which supports it through the public's attitude and through its formal institutions . . . [P]erfectionist ideals require public action for their viability. Anti-perfectionism in practice would lead not merely to a political stand-off from support for valuable conceptions of the good. It would undermine the chances of survival of many cherished aspects of our culture. (*MF*, p. 162)

If Raz is right to think that valuable options require perfectionist political action, then it would seem that the anti-perfectionist faces a real problem. If the cost of anti-perfectionism is indeed the withering away of cherished aspects of our culture, then the anti-perfectionist may feel the need to rethink her position; perhaps even to rethink it in ways more radical than Dworkin.

But is he right? We can grant the point that valuable ways of life require social and cultural recognition, support, and even institutionalization, without conceding that political action is necessary for their survival. Consider all those associations and organizations that exist below or above the level of the state and of which the anti-perfectionist Rawls was so keen to remind us, such as churches or scientific associations. Surely these promote and sustain valuable forms of life within a neutral framework and without requiring state support. Raz's own example of bird watching is clearly an example of a valuable social form that can survive without state action. Is Raz too quick in jumping from his recognition of the dependence of valuable ways of life, and hence of autonomy, on *social* forms to the claim that this warrants perfectionist political action by the *state*? It is true that some valuable social forms may derive part of their significance from the very fact that they are endorsed or recognized by the state. It is arguable that part of what makes marriage the institution that it is in our culture is precisely the fact that it is the form of sexual union that enjoys official state support and encouragement. Social forms of this kind, what we might call inherently political forms, would indeed lose or change their meaning in an anti-perfectionist state, but it is hard to see that this point is very wide in its application.

The thought that perfectionist action may not be necessary after all gains strength when we remember that even if some valuable forms of life would indeed fail to survive without state support, this is not enough for Raz's argument to justify coercive action on their behalf. For people to be autonomous they need only to have available an adequate range of options, and this means that there is no justification for the state's using coercive action to support valuable options if there would be an adequate range even without such action. The anti-perfectionist may acknowledge that it would be a problem for her position if the society she advocates was likely to fail to provide people with a range of valuable ways of life to live but respond that simply that it is unlikely; that even if some ways of life would disappear, Raz's own argument would not justify state action on their behalf. Such action would only be justified if society, in the absence of state action, failed to sustain an adequate range of valuable options.

Clearly it might matter a great deal what counts as 'adequate', and it is true that Raz has rather a wide notion of adequacy.

> To be autonomous and to have an autonomous life, a person must have options which enable him to sustain throughout his life activities which, taken together, exercise all the capacities human beings have an innate drive to exercise, as well as to decline to develop any of them. (*MF*, p. 375)

But even on this definition, and even granting that these 'innate drives' include the drive to engage our imagination and to occupy our mind, it is not clear that Raz has any reason to worry about the loss of that perhaps rather limited set of valuable options whose continued survival depends upon state action on their behalf. Even if it were the case that opera, for example, would not survive without state subsidy, and even if opera is one of the most valuable and cherished forms currently available to people, it would be hard to argue that a society without opera fails to provide its members with an adequate range of valuable options from which to choose.

Two aspects of this point are worth emphasizing. First, we assume that when Raz talks about the duty to provide one another with the conditions of autonomy, he has in mind some sort of threshold notion; that there is a range of options, hard to define but in principle definable, which is sufficient for someone to be autonomous even if there is another set of options which would enable them to live more valuable lives. The point here is that one does not have to deny that a life with opera is more valuable than one without in order to deny that, on Raz's own account, the state is justified in coercing people to provide one another with opera. The alternative would be the view that we have a coercively enforceable duty to provide one another with as valuable a life as is possible, which is surely too strong. Second, it may well be that our focus on the issue of the survival of valuable forms, although encouraged by Raz himself, misses the real impact of his position. Even if an adequate range of valuable forms would survive without state support, it might be argued, they would do so in such a way that they are available only to a wealthy elite. If some forms of art must be available to people for them to be autonomous, they must really be available, not just present somewhere in the society at prohibitive cost. Political action, according to this line of argument, is needed not so much to secure the survival of a valuable range of options as to give people the opportunities to use them. But this raises again the question of why such action must be perfectionist in the sense identified as specific to the third condition of autonomy, why this must involve judgements as to the relative value of different options. If we grant that valuable forms will survive without state support, and argue that such support is needed only to give people effective opportunities to choose them, then it looks as if this could be done simply by the kind of egalitarian redistribution of resources which is consistent with anti-perfectionism. This is the beginning rather than the end of argument, and we do not mean to suggest that Raz has no response. Perhaps, the kind of egalitarian redistribution envisaged would itself lead to the withering away of valuable forms, that their survival depends on the same unequal distribution of resources which puts them beyond the reach of most people. In that case the anti-perfectionist's move to avoid the unpalatable consequences of her position may be unavailable to her: if all people are to have genuine access to valuable art forms, then state action to subsidize those forms specifically, involving judgements as to their value, may be necessary after all. There are complex and difficult issues here which we cannot address here. Our aim is only to point out their existence.

We have seen, then, that Raz thinks that the state is justified in using its coercive power of taxation to support valuable social forms because the availability of an adequate range of such forms is a condition of autonomy and because the very fact that they are social means that they will not survive without such support. Having raised some questions about this aspect of his argument, we can now turn to what we can think of as the other side of the coin. If the state can use coercion to encourage some ways of life, can it do so to discourage others? We saw early on in the chapter his claim that the autonomy principle permits and even requires governments to eliminate repugnant opportunities, and it is now time to see what he means by this. Should the state tolerate repugnant options?

We have already seen that Raz thinks that autonomy is only valuable in pursuit of the good. In fact, he argues the stronger claim that autonomously doing wrong is worse than doing it non-autonomously:

> Has autonomy any value qua autonomy when it is abused? Is the autonomous wrongdoer a morally better person than the non-autonomous wrongdoer? Our intuitions rebel against such a view. It is surely the other way round. The wrongdoing casts a deeper shadow on its perpetrator if it is autonomously done by him. A murderer who was led to his deed by the foreseen inner logic of his autonomously chosen career is morally worse than one who murders because he momentarily succumbs to the prospect of an easy gain. (*MF*, p. 380)

It would seem to follow that the state would be promoting the well-being of its citizens if it banned bad options. If, as Raz thinks, there are some options that one is better off not having, if autonomously choosing the bad makes one's life worse than is a comparable non-autonomous life, then there would seem to be no reason to desist from using coercion to prevent people making such choices.

In fact, Raz resists such a conclusion. Even though one cannot defend pursuit of the morally repugnant from coercive interference on the ground that being an autonomous choice endows it with value, nonetheless such interference violates the autonomy of its victim, and in two ways.

> First, it violates the condition of independence and expresses a relation of domination and an attitude of disrespect for the coerced individual. Second, coercion by criminal penalties is a global and indiscriminate invasion of autonomy. . . . there is no practical way of ensuring that the coercion will restrict the victims' choice of repugnant options but will not interfere with their other choices. (*MF*, pp. 418–19)

This is surprising. The second consideration, the idea that it is impossible to stop choosing bad options without interfering with her choice of others, seems to depend on contingencies, but it at least makes sense in the context of Raz's overall argument. The first, on the other hand, seems to go against the whole thrust of his position. If people derive no well-being from bad choices, what is it about autonomy that means we should respect the individual's autonomous but bad choice? What happened to the idea that respect for people cannot require us to ignore moral considerations in our dealings with them?

Although it looks as if Raz is here endorsing, willy-nilly, that understanding of autonomy which means that there is value in the very fact of the individual choosing for herself, all is not what it seems. As the following passage makes clear, it is only because the state is likely to make mistakes in its judgements as to which options are immoral that coercive action based on such judgements violates the independence of agents who might choose them. *Both* the first and the second points depend on contingent facts; namely

> the non-existence at the present time of means of coercion which do not infringe autonomy, and the fact that conditions justify suspecting governments of lacking respect for individuals. What if it became possible to coerce people to avoid immoral but harmless conduct without restricting them in any other way; suppose we had institutions which could be relied on to do so only to stop

immoralities, and would not mistake what is worth while for what is evil nor would they abuse their power? They would be free from suspicion that they do not respect their subjects. In such a case both the conditions of adequacy of options and of independence would be satisfied. (*MF*, p. 419)

This scepticism about the government's ability to make the right judgements about which ways of life are immoral, which is one of his two reasons for rejecting coercive action to prevent people choosing repugnant options, sits oddly alongside his rejection of such scepticism about its ability correctly to identify valuable forms of life. While he rather backs away from his early claim that the state may be permitted and even required to eliminate repugnant opportunities, at least if we assume that 'elimination' involves coercion, Raz's reasons for doing so are in both cases oddly, though avowedly, contingent and in one case apparently contrary to the anti-scepticism on which his perfectionism depends.

Autonomy only conditionally valuable

One further, and at first sight surprising, aspect of Raz's position, relevant to our general theme here, can be presented very quickly. Given the apparently wholehearted endorsement of the ideal of personal autonomy that pervades Raz's argument, it comes as rather a shock to be told, initially in a footnote, that 'not everyone has an interest in autonomy. It is a cultural value, i.e. of value to people living in certain societies only' (*MF*, p. 189 n. 1). The reason, however, lies in the very claim presented above, and the implications of which we have just been discussing; namely, that personal well-being is dependent on social forms. It is because our social forms are autonomy-presupposing that autonomy is necessary for our well-being.

This aspect of Raz's position can give his formulations an air of resignation rather than exaltation, as if autonomy were something we have to put up with, something demanded of us by the society in which we live, rather than, as it might seem to liberals of a more universalistic kind, the realization of our essential nature. As he puts it:

For those who live in an autonomy-supporting environment there is no choice but to be autonomous, there is no other way to prosper in such a society . . . The value of personal autonomy is a fact of life. Since we live in a society whose social forms are to a considerable extent based on individual choice, and since our options are limited by what is available in our society, we can prosper in it only if we can be successfully autonomous. (*MF*, pp. 391, 394)

Our institution of marriage, to take our by now familiar example, has built into its very nature the idea that people have chosen their partners for themselves; one cannot prosper in that institution if one's marriage has been arranged.

In other kinds of society, however, where social forms do not presuppose or depend upon the value of autonomy, one can live a successful and valuable non-autonomous life.

Autonomy is, to be sure, inconsistent with various alternative forms of valuable lives. It cannot be obtained within societies which support social forms which do not leave enough room for individual choice. (*MF*, p. 395)

While, as we have already seen, Raz denies the conventionalist thesis that 'whatever is practised with social approval is for that reason valuable', and while he thinks that a non-autonomous but morally worthy sub-culture can in particular cases nonetheless be judged inferior to the dominant liberal culture in the midst of which its members may live, he is clearly sensitive to the relation between personal well-being and social or cultural context.

Raz and communitarianism

We have, in passing, made various observations about the extent to which Raz's liberalism recognizes and endorses aspects of the communitarian critique. In this last section we seek rather more systematically, and summarily, to identify the points of connection; once again, and for the last time, we shall organize our discussion around the five themes that have guided us from the beginning.

Conception of the person

Although he does not use the term, much of Raz's argument can readily be seen to be relevant to this first theme, and it is clear that his understanding of autonomy does not commit him to anything like the views identified as endemic to liberalism by its communitarian critics. That his self is not emotivist in MacIntyre's sense will be seen under the heading of objectivism and subjectivism; that he recognizes Sandel's insistence on the extent to which it is our community that provides the social matrix which contributes to the constitution of our self-understandings will be dealt with in our observations on asocial individualism. Here we point out simply that Raz's autonomy not only does not rule out the possibility of attachments and commitments, but in fact requires them.

We already touched on this point when we presented his account of the inner abilities that are among the conditions of autonomy, for the reader will recall that these included character traits such as stability, loyalty and the ability to form personal attachments and to maintain intimate relationships. Another passage indicates clearly how far Raz's autonomy is from the idea that the person is necessarily and always detached from her goals and projects:

> (Significantly) autonomous persons are those who can shape their life and determine its course. They are not merely rational agents who can choose between options after evaluating relevant information, but agents who can in addition adopt personal projects, develop relationships, and accept commitments to causes, through which their personal integrity and sense of dignity and self-respect are made concrete. Persons who are part creators of their own moral world have a commitment to projects, relationships, and causes which affect the kind of life that is for them worth living. (*MF*, p. 155)

Indeed, Raz goes so far as to say that, in extreme cases, an autonomous person may be so committed to a particular cause or project that certain actions, betraying or compromising that commitment, would render their life 'worthless or even impossible (in a moral sense)' (*MF*, p. 155). Clearly there is room here for Sandel's point that there are certain commitments which we cannot imagine ourselves not having, which we regard as constitutive of our identity.

He is similarly alert to MacIntyre's related emphasis on the importance of narrative unity to a person's life. Far from autonomy involving the notion of discrete moments of existential, arbitrary and radical choice, the fact that our life comprises the pursuit of goals means that it is sensitive to our past; the very fact that one has embraced certain commitments gives one new ways of succeeding and failing. Although one can be autonomous without imposing any particular unity on one's life, in that an autonomous life may consist of diverse and heterogeneous pursuits, one cannot be so without the capacity to form commitments and attachments which change one's subsequent reasons for action. It is partly because one has these reasons that Raz's account is immune from Sandel's charge that the liberal must regard the choice of how to live ones' life as the mere expression of preference or non-rational desire.

> Saying 'I want to . . .' can be a way of indicating that one is committed to a project, that one has embraced a certain pursuit, cares about a relationship. It is . . . part of a valid reason for action, once the initial commitment has been made. In this usage it does not signify the existence of a particular mental state, a desire. It signifies a commitment, deep or shallow, to a pursuit, which may be limited or lasting or comprehensive. (*MF*, p. 389)

The understanding of the way a person relates to her ends implied by Raz's notion of autonomy is a long way from that criticized as implicit in the liberal commitment to individual freedom of choice.

Asocial individualism

It will already be clear that Raz's liberalism is not susceptible to the first communitarian charge that we identified under this heading. His claim that comprehensive goals, and hence personal well-being, depend on social forms clearly involves recognition of the idea that society is prior to the individual in the sense that it provides her with the matrix of significance within which she can come to acquire the goals and the identities that make her moral life possible. We can perhaps identify two distinct points here, for not only is it the case that we need society in order to pursue particular comprehensive goals but, as we saw at the end of our discussion, the very value of autonomy itself, that which requires as its condition an adequate range of valuable options is, so to speak, secreted by the social forms within which we live our lives. There is no incompatibility here either with Taylor's or MacIntyre's arguments for the importance of the social matrix.

The second, substantive, issue, it will be recalled, concerns liberalism's purported failure to attend to the importance of social ties that are more than those of association between individuals, and its blindness to, or at least downgrading of, the value of goods that are strongly communal in content, whether these goods be political or non-political. Here, although he says little explicitly on this point, it is clear that Raz does not think that the only good way to live one's life is as a family man, or as a member of a community of religious believers, or as a citizen participating in the common life of one's political community. So much is implied by his understanding of personal autonomy and its relation to value pluralism; if the communitarian claim is that there is one, strongly communal, valuable way of life, then Raz rejects it. If, on the other hand, the claim is just that there are valuable ways of life which are of this kind, then it would seem that Raz's perfectionism enables him not only to leave room for them as consistent with the liberal political framework, which is roughly Rawls's position, but also, unlike Rawls, to envisage political action on their behalf. If family life, for example, is indeed valuable, then it may be perfectly legitimate for the state to use social policies to support and promote it. A way of life whose content is essentially communal and which is indeed valuable (and of course its value would need to be established in the particular case) would be more likely to survive in Raz's perfectionist state than in Rawls's anti-perfectionist one, though Raz would have no place for anything which conflicted with his central commitments to autonomy and pluralism.

More generally, Raz is suspicious of the whole idea that there is an essential tension between society and the interests of the individual. For him,

> individuals inevitably derive their goals by which they constitute their lives from the stock of social forms available to them, and the feasible variations on it. If those forms are morally valid, if they enshrine sound moral conceptions, then it is easy for people generally to find themselves with, and to choose for themselves, goals which lead to a

rough coincidence in their own lives of moral and personal concerns. In their careers, personal relations and other interests, they will be engaged in activities which serve themselves and others at the same time. By being teachers, production workers, drivers, public servants, loyal friends and family people, loyal to their communities, nature loving, and so on, they will be pursuing their own goals, enhancing their own well-being, and also serving their communities, and generally living in a morally worthy way. (*MF*, p. 319)

While the first sentence claims that it is the social matrix that is the source of the individual's aims and purposes (which is our first strand), his insistence on the point that individual interests will tend to coincide, rather than conflict, with those of others in their community can be read as a variation on the idea (which constitutes our second strand) that valuable ways of life will be communal in content. By pointing out the extent to which the goals we have as individuals, the attainment of which constitutes our individual well-being, are connected to the service of others and of our community, so that even individual goods are in this sense communal in content, Raz calls into question the whole opposition between individual and community in a way that seems to transcend the terms of debate between liberal and communitarian.

Universality

The issue of whether Raz's liberalism is universal in its application, is applicable cross-culturally, is complicated. On the one hand, as we have seen, his recognition of the dependence of well-being on social forms leads him to hold that autonomy is only conditionally valuable, valuable only in societies whose forms are based on the value of individual choice, and that a person, in a different kind of society, can live a valuable life that is non-autonomous. As he puts it elsewhere:

I think that there were, and there can be, non-repressive societies, and ones which enable people to spend their lives in worthwhile pursuits, even though their pursuits and the options open to them are not subject to individual choice. Careers may be determined by custom, marriages arranged by parents, child-bearing and child-rearing controlled only by sexual passion and traditions, past-time activities few and traditional, and engagement in them required rather than optional . . . I do not see that the absence of choice diminishes the value of human relations or the display of excellence in technical skills, physical ability, spirit and enterprise, leadership, scholarship, creativity, or imaginativeness, which can all be encompassed in such lives.[1]

On the other hand, he thinks that even a non-autonomy-supporting culture that is morally worthy, one that provides its members with social conditions that enable them to live valuable and successful lives, can in particular cases be judged inferior to the autonomy-supporting liberal culture within which it may find itself. While it does not follow from that judgement that we would be justified in coercively wrenching people out of their non-autonomy-supporting communities, for those brought up in such communities will not have acquired the capacities necessary to live a successful autonomous life, Raz does think that a liberal culture can act gradually to assimilate such people, even at the cost of letting their illiberal culture die.

Objectivism/subjectivism

That Raz's liberalism is not based in any subjectivist or sceptical meta-ethical position should be clear enough and requires only cursory restatement here; his perfectionism follows in part from his view that some ways of life are objectively better than others and we can know which are which. Not only is the value of autonomy substantively endorsed, but his rejection of the view that judgements concerning the 'art of life', those pertaining to the goals and ends which constitute people's conceptions of the good, are any more doubtful than those concerning the requirements of justice or 'morality in its narrow sense', is what drives his perfectionist conclusions. Since we can know some ways of life to be valuable and others not, and since people derive well-being only from those which are valuable, we have no reason to ignore such knowledge even in our political dealings with others. While MacIntyre's characterization of contemporary liberal culture as essentially emotivist may be justified, Raz's brand of liberalism is firmly grounded in the repudiation of such a view.

Anti-perfectionism/neutrality

Raz appeals not only to a comprehensive doctrine but also to one that justifies perfectionist state action. His theory is thus neutral in neither of the two senses that we have distinguished. The claims that the state has a duty to promote the well-being of its citizens, that well-being consists in the autonomous pursuit of valuable ways of life, and that valuable ways of life are necessarily social in form, combine to yield the conclusion that governments can be justified in acting on judgements about the relative merits of the conceptions of the good espoused by their citizens. Rather than regarding the proper role of that state as that of guaranteeing a neutral framework within which citizens should be left to make their own choices without interference and bias, Raz holds that the state can be justified in acting to encourage particular ways of life and discourage others. While direct coercion in the name of particular ideals would be self-defeating given the centrality of autonomy to well-being, it is permitted and even required that the state should use compulsory taxation to provide its citizens with the conditions of autonomy. Since such conditions include not only freedom from coercion and manipulation, and certain mental capacities necessary for a choice to be regarded as genuinely autonomous, but also the availability of an adequate range of valuable options, it is clear that, at least in certain situations, perfectionist political action will be justified. Where Rawls thinks that a community that is publicly justifiable to its citizens is of such value that it can give those citizens reason to ignore, when it comes to politics, reasons arising from their comprehensive conceptions of the good, Raz holds that what matters is that people live valuable lives, and that it is appropriate that we should use politics to help them do so.

Notes

1   'Facing Up: A Reply', p. 1227.

Conclusion

We will bring our investigation to a close by attempting to specify what the widening of focus introduced in the last part of the book has added to our understanding of the debate between liberalism and its communitarian critics.

What has emerged most forcefully from our exploration is the fact that matters arising under the fifth heading on our agenda of the communitarian critique – those relating to liberalism's claims to neutrality – appear to raise a host of significant and complex problems of interpretation and evaluation. Since Raz is, in the terms of our organizing matrix, a comprehensive perfectionist liberal, and so is committed neither to neutrality at the level of political substance nor to neutrality at the level of theoretical foundations, this issue is not one that is directly relevant to an assessment of his claims upon our attention; but it has turned out to be at the heart of any serious assessment of the merits of the varieties of liberalism advocated by Rawls, Rorty and Dworkin. All three count as anti-perfectionist liberals, since they advocate that the state should not act upon judgements as to the relative worth of the ways of life espoused by its citizens; and all are therefore, at least in principle, likely to be targeted by communitarians who hold that the claim to neutrality that is embodied or implied in such a view of politics is either untenable or significantly less substantial than it is often taken to be (and presented as being).

We have repeatedly stressed that the claim to neutrality that is essential to anti-perfectionist liberalism is compatible with non-neutrality of effect or consequences; and we have also suggested that, since no vision of politics can be articulated or justified except by making reference to some conception of human well-being, it might be thought that the anti-perfectionist's claim to neutrality cannot be undermined simply by pointing out that it draws upon a distinctively liberal conception of what is important to human flourishing (whether it be autonomy, or the freedom to respond skilfully to the challenge life poses, or some other such value). The critical importance of Rawls's recent work in political theory, culminating in his articulation of political liberalism, is that – paradoxically – it serves to undermine this defence of anti-perfectionist liberalism. For by introducing his distinction between comprehensive and purely political doctrines, he opens up the possibility of a doubly neutral anti-perfectionism – one which advocates state neutrality by drawing upon purely political values that are neutral between competing comprehensive doctrines in society. Measured against such a possibility, comprehensive anti-perfectionist liberalism – whether it depends upon a Dworkinian challenge model of human flourishing, or a conception of the importance of autonomy that appears (as in the presentation of justice as fairness in *A Theory of Justice*) to be part of a comprehensive conception of well-being – can be accused of failing to achieve a sufficiently radical or thoroughgoing neutrality, a political-theoretical as well as a political neutrality. In this respect, purely political liberalism might function as a stick with which the communitarians might beat comprehensive anti-perfectionists such as Dworkin and the early Rawls.

It cannot, however, be so used if political liberalism's claims to have achieved such a double neutrality cannot be properly defended. In chapter 7, we argued that Rawls's two attempts to justify political liberalism resulted in a vicious circularity, and appeared to require that he draw upon a comprehensive doctrine of human well-being; and in chapter 8, we argued that Rorty's alternative defence of a purely political anti-perfectionist liberal also failed. These arguments support the conclusion that the possibility of a doubly neutral liberalism is in fact an illusion, and so that the substantive or political neutrality to which comprehensive anti-perfectionism has always laid claim is the only kind of neutrality to be had in the sphere of politics.

It does not, however, follow that the communitarian critique of anti-perfectionist liberalism's claims to neutrality can simply be dismissed out of hand. In the first place, it has not always been as clear as it might have been, either to political theorists or to the citizens of Western liberal democracies, that the kind of neutrality to which anti-perfectionist liberal regimes might lay claim is restricted to the kind of justificatory neutrality we have attempted to define in these pages. Insofar as this is compatible not only with non-neutrality of effect or outcome, but also with its having a theoretical grounding in a distinctively liberal conception of human well-being, it may well be thought that a correspondingly modest tone would be appropriate when the advocates of justificatory neutrality contrast their claims to tolerance with those whose comprehensive conception of human well-being dictates support for state policies which *are* predicated upon judgements about the relative worth of the ways of life that citizens espouse.

Moreover, our detailed discussion of the kind of state neutrality advocated by comprehensive anti-perfectionists like Dworkin raises important questions about its precise nature. For as we saw in chapter 9, the theoretical foundations of Dworkin's anti-perfectionism permit (and in fact require) him, in his view, to advocate policies of state support for culture that aim to avoid coercing people into making particular choices of life-style but which nevertheless appear ineluctably to involve state endorsement of past and present reflective judgements about the worth of particular ways of life. As we also saw, establishing Dworkin's precise position on this matter, and the precise line of reasoning that leads him to it, is no easy matter; but the general question it raises is clear – and it is a question that also emerges when we take seriously Rawls's restriction of the state neutrality that he defends to matters affecting constitutional essentials and basic justice. If state neutrality of the sort that mainstream anti-perfectionists endorse is in fact compatible with policies of the above kind, if – in order to provide it with adequate theoretical foundations – it must be understood as subject to a variety of qualifications, modifications and restrictions, then we might be justified in regarding it as a great deal less substantial than it has often appeared to be.

We might even wish to question the tenability of the distinction by means of which anti-perfectionists standardly defend their claim to be advocating a state that is in any sense neutral – the distinction between abstract conceptions of human well-being and concrete ways of life. Suppose, for example, that we take Charles Taylor's work on the nature of moral judgement seriously, and accept that the proper significance of an individual's choice between ways of life is revealed only by their articulation of the grounds for that choice, and that any such articulation must draw upon a more or less broad conception of human well-being. If so, then every choice of a concrete way of life is also a commitment to the general conception of human flourishing from which that choice grows; the former and the latter are, in this sense, internally related – neither is properly comprehensible in the absence of the other. If this is so, the distinction between concrete ways of life and general conceptions of human well-being begins to look highly artificial; and the anti-perfectionist's claim to be neutral with respect to the former but not with respect to the latter begins to look highly misleading. For how, then, can a state that is avowedly non-neutral as between general conceptions of human well-being nevertheless be neutral as between the choices of concrete life-style which grow from and so are always rooted in such conceptions? A state may, for example, eschew policies explicitly based on a judgement of the worth of a specific religious faith, whose adherents are committed to an avowedly non-liberal conception of human well-being; but if its policies draw on a very different general conception of human flourishing, can they really treat life-style choices which are, and those which are not, grounded in a liberal conception of human flourishing with equal respect? Can such a state really be said to have preserved justificatory neutrality? We may rather conclude that the very distinction between anti-perfectionist and perfectionist liberalism threatens to break down.

If we take these questions about anti-perfectionism seriously, a species of liberalism such as that defended by Raz – a comprehensive perfectionist liberalism – will appear to be far less distant or exotic when compared with its anti-perfectionist competitors, and so to that degree more worthy of consideration. As we saw in chapter 10, Raz also deploys powerful arguments that attempt both to refute the standard criticisms, and to demonstrate the independent attractions, of perfectionist strategies in politics. As we also saw, however, various aspects of Raz's position are subject to a number of criticisms; so there are clearly important questions that must be answered before any conclusions about the relative merits of perfectionist and anti-perfectionist varieties of liberalism can be drawn.

The same words of warning apply to any attempt to draw conclusions about the outcome of the communitarian critique of liberalism. For if any liberal claim to political-theoretical neutrality stands or falls by the tenability of Rawlsian (or Rortyan) purely political liberalism, then the reasons we gave for suggesting its untenability imply that the new Rawls's (or Rorty's) main defensive strategy against the communitarian critique – that of claiming not to take up controversial comprehensive moral, philosophical or metaphysical positions of the kind that the communitarians claim to detect in liberal thinking – cannot work. In other words, insofar as any viable forms of perfectionist or anti-perfectionist liberalism must draw upon elements of comprehensive doctrines, they must in principle be vulnerable to attacks on those elements, and so must defend themselves on exactly this kind of complex and controversial terrain.

This is not, of course, an obligation that Dworkin or Raz would shirk; it is precisely the kind of argumentative work that their wide-ranging and ambitious theoretical labours are designed to accomplish. And even if Rawls did have to abandon his avoidance strategy, it does not follow that he would have no means of defending his own brand of liberal thought; after all, as we attempted to show in chapter 6, by no means all of the responses that he might make to communitarian criticisms presuppose the distinction between comprehensive and political doctrines upon which his political liberalism is founded. Indeed, our discussions of all four theorists have in large part been aimed at showing in some detail how each of them might be seen either as endorsing or at least as being able to accommodate many of the emphases that are central to the work of the various communitarian thinkers we have examined. Rawls (both old and new), Rorty, Dworkin and Raz each, in their different ways and to different degrees, appear to show a genuine awareness of the social origin of individual conceptions of the good, of the real value of constitutive attachments to communities and their values, and of the culture-relativity of many (if not most) human goods. We have also suggested that, where they fail to accommodate elements of the communitarian critique, it is often not a result of oversight but a consequence of their belief that those elements ought to be rejected.

Nevertheless, we cannot simply conclude either that there is no fundamental incompatibility between liberal and communitarian thought, or that, where there is, the former is liable to win out. For, even though some of the defensive liberal moves that we have outlined might appear very strong, none can be regarded as immune to criticism. It may well be that some of the communitarian critiques as originally formulated appear to miss their target, or to overlook an important element of the positions under attack; but nothing prevents their proponents from reformulating those points in more accurate and well-informed ways, or from pointing out that the defensive moves made by their liberal opponents are themselves open to question. In fact, we sketched out some of the ways in which these second-generation criticisms might be formulated in our critique of Rawls's political liberalism, and in the questions we raised about the coherence and substance of Dworkin's claims to neutrality and Raz's defence of political perfectionism. What we should therefore expect as this debate continues to develop is a renewed communitarian onslaught on the moral, metaphysical or ontological presuppositions of the original position, or the challenge model of value, or the doctrine of value pluralism; and what we can predict with some confidence is that no avoidance strategy will be sufficent to deal with them.

Bibliography

Ackerman, B., *Social Justice and the Liberal State* (New Haven: Yale University Press, 1980).

Arblaster, A., *The Rise and Decline of Western Liberalism* (Oxford: Blackwell, 1984).

Avineri, S. and de-Shalit, A. (eds), *Communitarianism and Individualism* (Oxford: Oxford University Press, 1992).

Bakhurst, D. and Sypnowich, C. (eds), *The Social Self* (London: Sage, 1995).

Bell, D., *Communitarianism and its Critics* (Oxford: Clarendon Press, 1993).

Berlin, I., 'Two Concepts of Liberty', in *Four Essays on Liberty* (Oxford: Oxford University Press, 1969).

Buchanan, A., *Marx and Justice* (London: Methuen, 1982).

Caney, S., 'Liberalism and Communitarianism: A Misconceived Debate', *Political Studies*, 40, 2 (1992), pp. 273–90.

Darwell, S. (ed.), *Equal Freedom: Selected Tanner Lectures on Human Values* (Ann Arbor: University of Michigan Press, 1995).

Dworkin, R., 'What is Equality? Part 1: Equality of Welfare', *Philosophy and Public Affairs*, 10, 3 (1981), pp. 185–246.

—— 'What is Equality? Part 2: Equality of Resources', *Philosophy and Public Affairs*, 10, 4 (1981), pp. 283–345.

—— 'Rights as Trumps', in *Theories of Rights*, ed. J. Waldron (Oxford: Oxford University Press, 1984).

—— *A Matter Of Principle* (Oxford: Oxford University Press, 1985).

—— 'Bakke's Case: Are Quotas Unfair?', in *A Matter of Principle*, (Oxford: Oxford University Press, 1985).

—— 'What Justice Isn't', in *A Matter of Principle* (Oxford: Oxford University Press, 1985).

—— 'Liberalism', in *A Matter of Principle* (Oxford: Oxford University Press, 1985).

—— 'Can A Liberal State Support Art?', in *A Matter of Principle* (Oxford: Oxford University Press, 1985).

—— *Law's Empire* (London: Fontana Press, 1986)

—— 'What is Equality? Part 4: Political Equality', *University of San Francisco Law Review*, 22, 1 (1987), pp. 1–30.

—— 'What is Equality? Part 3: The Place of Liberty', *Iowa Law Review*, 73, 1 (1988), pp. 1–54.

—— 'Liberal Community', *California Law Review*, 77, 3 (1989), pp. 479–520, and in Avineri and de-Shalit (eds), *Communitarianism and Individualism*.

—— 'The Foundations of Liberal Equality', in G. Petersen (ed.), *The Tanner Lectures on Human Values*; and in Darwall (ed.) *Equal Freedom*.

Etzioni, A., *The Spirit of Community: Rights, Responsibilities and the Communitarian Agenda* (New York: Crown Publishers Inc., 1993).

Frazer, E. and Lacey, N., *The Politics of Community: A Feminist Critique of the Liberal–Communitarian Debate* (London: Harvester Wheatsheaf, 1993).

Gramsci, A., *Selections from the Prison Notebooks*, ed. and trans. Q. Hoare and G. Nowell Smith (New York: International Publishers, 1971).

Gray, J., *Liberalism* (Milton Keynes: Open University Press, 1986).

Habermas, J., *Legitimation Crisis*, trans. Thomas McCarthy (Boston: Beacon Press, 1975).

Holmes, S., *The Anatomy of Antiliberalism* (Cambridge, Mass.: Harvard University Press, 1993).

Horton, J. and Mendus, S. (eds), *After MacIntyre* (Cambridge: Polity Press, 1994).

Jaggar, A., *Feminist Politics and Human Nature* (Brighton: Harvester, 1983).

Kukathas, C. and Pettit, P., *Rawls: A Theory of Justice and its Critics* (Cambridge: Polity, 1990).

Kymlicka, W., *Liberalism, Community and Culture* (Oxford: Oxford University Press, 1989).

MacIntyre, A., *After Virtue* (London: Duckworth, 1981).

—— *Whose Justice? Which Rationality?* (London: Duckworth, 1988).

—— *Three Rival Versions of Moral Enquiry* (London: Duckworth, 1990).

—— 'A Partial Response to my Critics', in Horton and Mendus (eds), *After MacIntyre*.

Malachowski, A. (ed.), *Reading Rorty* (Oxford: Blackwell, 1990).

Marx, K., *The German Ideology*, ed. C. J. Arthur (London: Lawrence and Wishart, 1970).

Miller, D. and Walzer, M. (eds), *Pluralism, Justice, and Equality* (Oxford: Oxford University Press, 1995).

Mulhall, S. and Swift, A., 'Liberalisms and Communitarianisms: Whose Misconceptions?', *Political Studies*, 41, 4 (1993), pp. 650–6.

—— 'The Social Self in Political Theory: The Communitarian Critique of the Liberal Subject', in Bakhurst and Sypnowich (eds), *The Social Self*.

Nozick, R., *Anarchy, State and Utopia* (Oxford: Blackwell, 1974).

Petersen, G. (ed.), *The Tanner Lectures on Human Values*, vol. 11 (Salt Lake City: University of Utah Press, 1990).

Peterson, M. D. and Vaughan, R. C. (eds), *The Virginia Statute on Religious Freedom* (Cambridge: Cambridge University Press, 1988).

Rawls, J., *A Theory of Justice* (Cambridge, Mass.: Harvard University Press, 1971).

—— 'Fairness to Goodness', *Philosophical Review*, 84 (1975), pp. 536–54.

—— 'The Basic Structure as Subject', *American Philosophical Quarterly*, 14, 2 (1977), pp. 159–65.

—— 'Kantian Constructivism in Moral Theory' (The Dewey Lectures), *Journal of Philosophy*, 77, 9 (1980), pp. 515–72.

—— 'Social Unity and Primary Goods', in *Utilitarianism and Beyond*, eds A. K. Sen and B. Williams (Cambridge: Cambridge University Press, 1982).

—— 'Justice as Fairness: Political not Metaphysical', *Philosophy and Public Affairs*, 14, 3 (1985), pp. 223–51.

—— 'The Idea of an Overlapping Consensus', *Oxford Journal of Legal Studies*, 7, 1 (1987), pp. 1–25.

—— 'The Priority of Right and Ideas of the Good', *Philosophy and Public Affairs*, 17, 4 (1988), pp. 251–76.

—— 'The Domain of the Political and Overlapping Consensus', *New York University Law Review*, 64, 2 (1989), pp. 233–55.

—— 'The Law of Peoples', in Shute and Hurley (eds), *On Human Rights: The Oxford Amnesty Lectures 1993*.

—— *Political Liberalism* (New York: Columbia University Press, 1993).

Raz, J., *The Morality of Freedom* (Oxford: Oxford University Press, 1986).

—— 'Facing Up: A Reply', *Southern California Law Review*, 62, 3–4 (1989), pp. 1153–235.

Rorty, R., 'The Priority of Democracy to Philosophy', in *The Virginia Statute on Religious Freedom*, eds M. D. Peterson and R. C. Vaughan (Cambridge: Cambridge University Press, 1988); and in *Reading Rorty*, ed. A. Malachowski (Oxford: Blackwell, 1990).

—— *Contingency, Irony and Solidarity* (Cambridge: Cambridge University Press, 1989).

—— *Philosophical Papers*, vol. 1: *Objectivity, Relativism and Truth* (Cambridge: Cambridge University Press, 1991).

Rosenblum, N. (ed.), *Liberalism and The Moral Life* (Cambridge: Harvard University Press, 1989).

Sandel, M., *Liberalism and the Limits of Justice* (Cambridge: Cambridge University Press, 1982).

Scruton, R., *The Meaning of Conservatism*, 2nd edn (London: Macmillan, 1984).

Sen, A. K. and Williams, B. (eds), *Utilitarianism and Beyond* (Cambridge: Cambridge University Press, 1982).

Shute, S. and Hurley, S. L. (eds), *On Human Rights: The Oxford Amnesty Lectures 1993* (New York: Basic Books, 1993).

Swift, A., 'The Sociology of Complex Equality', in Miller and Walzer (eds), *Justice, Pluralism and Equality* (Oxford: Oxford University Press, 1995), pp. 253–80.

Taylor, C., 'Interpretation and the Sciences of Man', *The Review of Metaphysics*, 25, 1 (1971), pp. 3–51, and in *Philosophical Papers*, vol. 2, (Cambridge: Cambridge University Press, 1985).

—— *Philosophical Papers*, vol. 1: *Human Agency and Language*; vol. 2: *Philosophy and the Human Sciences* (Cambridge: Cambridge University Press, 1985).

—— *Sources of the Self* (Cambridge: Cambridge University Press, 1990).

——'Cross-Purposes: The Liberal–Communitarian Debate', in *Liberalism and the Moral Life*, ed. N. Rosenblum (Cambridge, Mass.: Harvard University Press, 1989) and in *Philosophical Arguments* (Cambridge, Mass.: Harvard University Press, 1995).

—— *Philosophical Arguments* (Cambridge, Mass.: Harvard University Press, 1995).

Waldron, J. (ed.), *Theories of Rights* (Oxford: Oxford University Press, 1984).

Walzer, M., 'Philosophy and Democracy', *Political Theory* 9, 3 (1981), pp. 379–99.

—— *Spheres of Justice* (New York: Basic Books, 1983).

—— 'Liberalism and the Art of Separation', *Political Theory*, 12, 3 (1984), pp. 315–30.

—— *Interpretation and Social Criticism* (Cambridge, Mass.: Harvard University Press, 1987).

—— *The Company of Critics* (London: Peter Halban, 1989).

—— *Thick and Thin: Moral Argument at Home and Abroad* (Notre Dame: University of Notre Dame Press, 1994).

Wittgenstein, L., *Zettel*, 2nd edn (Oxford: Blackwell, 1981).

INDEX

DATE DUE

NOV 1 5 1999		
MAY 2 0 2007		
3608469		
JAN 4 2010		